NFL CENTURY

NFL CENTURY

THE ONE-HUNDRED-YEAR RISE OF AMERICA'S GREATEST SPORTS LEAGUE

JOE HORRIGAN

CROWN

NEW YORK

Published in the United States by Crown, an imprint of Random House,
a division of Penguin Random House LLC, New York.
crownpublishing.com

Crown and the Crown colophon are registered trademarks of
Penguin Random House LLC.

Case photographs: Robert Riger/Getty Images (Johnny Unitas, #19); Vic Stein/
Getty Images (Sid Luckman, #42); Al Bello/Getty Images (Odell Beckham catch);
Lambert/Getty Images (team huddle); Robert Riger/Getty Images (Jim Brown,
#32); Tom Hauck/Getty Images (Kevin Dyson, #87); Robert Riger/Getty Images
(Jim Taylor, #31); Roberto Schmidt/Getty Images (Lombardi Trophy); Focus On
Sport/Getty Images (John Elway, #7); Focus On Sport/Getty Images (Jerry Rice,
#80); Nate Fine/Getty Images (Bob Waterfield, #7).

Insert photographs: Courtesy of the Pro Football Hall of Fame, except page 6,
bottom, and page 7, top, which are from the Pro Football Hall of Fame/Tagliabue
Collection.

Library of Congress Cataloging-in-Publication Data
    Names: Horrigan, Joe, author.
    Title: NFL century : the one-hundred-year rise of America's greatest sports
        league / Joe Horrigan.
    Other titles: National Football League century
    Description: First Edition. | New York : Crown, [2019] | Includes index. |
    Identifiers: LCCN 2018057907 (print) | LCCN 2019001882 (ebook)
        ISBN 9781635653601 (ebook) | ISBN 9781635653595 (hardcover) |
        ISBN 9781984825278 (trade paperback)
    Subjects: LCSH: National Football League—History. | National Football
        League—History—20th century. | Football—United States—History.
    Classification: LCC GV954 (ebook) | LCC GV954 .H66 2019 (print) | DDC
        796.332/64—dc23
    LC record available at https://lccn.loc.gov/2018057907

ISBN 978-1-63565-359-5
Ebook ISBN 978-1-63565-360-1

Printed in the United States of America

Book design by Lauren Dong

10 9 8 7 6 5 4 3 2 1

First Edition

*This book is dedicated to the "home team"—
my wife, Mary Ann, and our sons, Daniel and Shaun.
I love you more than words can ever express.
And to my parents, Liz and Jack Horrigan,
and my brothers and sisters,
Jeremiah, Karen, Pat, Jack, Margaret, Mary, Liz, and Kathleen.
Thank you all for your love, support, and "tolerance."*

Contents

Introduction

THE NATIONAL FOOTBALL LEAGUE IS THE MOST popular and successful sports league in America. From television ratings to brand recognition and fan favorability, it dominates the competition. From its humble beginnings in small-town America in the 1920s to its present-day status as a multibillion-dollar industry, the NFL is an important and influential part of the multihued fabric of our society. Its rags-to-riches story and unrivaled popularity border on the unbelievable.

Reflecting its immense popularity, a multitude of books have been written on the NFL, ranging from stories on the game's greatest players, successful coaches, dynasty teams, and milestone games, and on every Super Bowl played. Biographies, motivational memoirs, stories of perseverance and achievement, and even a few "kiss and tell" tales can be found on bookstore shelves and online shopping sites. And, inspired by the NFL's one-hundredth season and centennial celebration, more historical reviews—including this one—will be added.

When I decided to write this book, my goal was to chronicle the NFL's storied past without sounding like an encyclopedic regurgitation of what has already been written. Sure, there are certain stories and characters that must be included in any retrospective look at the league's history. But I wanted this version to be different. I wanted to identify the important but not always visible recurring themes that emerge throughout the league's history, link decisions to decision makers, identify the circumstances of play that influenced the league's development, and, when possible, explain the resulting impact. I wanted to separate fiction from fact, offer a slightly different look at some familiar topics, and share some lesser-known stories that also helped shape the league's colorful history.

As someone who has studied the history of pro football and the NFL for more than four decades, I should have anticipated my first challenge. How on earth can I possibly do justice to the NFL's amazing story in just one volume? The fact is, there either have been or easily could be books written on each topic I wanted to address. There are simply too many tales to be told. I had to make some tough decisions. Suddenly, I began to appreciate how a coach must feel when he's faced with having to make roster cuts. Some really great stories didn't make my roster; I put a few first-round choices on the waiver wire.

An example of a great story that didn't make my final cut is how, in 1946, four African American pioneers—Marion Motley, Bill Willis, Woody Strode, and Kenny Washington—broke pro football's "color barrier," one year before Jackie Robinson did the same in Major League Baseball. Strode and Washington signed contracts to play for the NFL's Los Angeles Rams while Motley and Willis signed with the Cleveland Browns in the upstart rival All-America Football Conference. While it's an important pro football milestone, I chose to forgo telling this oft-told tale in favor of sharing the story of James "Shack" Harris. A rookie quarterback from Grambling State University, Harris was named the starting quarterback in the 1969 season opener for the Buffalo Bills. That may not sound all that unusual today, but when Shack took his first snap on that opening day in Buffalo, he became the first African American in pro football history to open a season as a team's starting quarterback. Back then, a black man simply did not play quarterback, let alone start.

While the collective signing of pro football contracts by Motley, Willis, Strode, and Washington was a seminal moment in pro football history, it did not mark the end of racial bias. There was still much to achieve, as demonstrated twenty-three years later by Harris. By the way, the quarterbacks Harris started ahead of on that day were veterans Jack Kemp and Tom Flores. Kemp went on to become a congressman and Republican nominee for vice president of the United States. Flores, the NFL's first Hispanic quarterback, is one of only two people in NFL history to win a Super Bowl as a player, an assistant coach, and a head coach. The other is Hall of Fame tight end Mike Ditka.

As for important recurring themes during the NFL's first century, my favorite thread began at the NFL's founding meeting. As I detail in chapter two, fifteen men representing ten teams gathered in Canton, Ohio, on September 17, 1920, in Ralph Hay's Hupmobile showroom and organized what would become the National Football League. Newspaper accounts of that meeting indicate that the league was organized for three principal reasons: to control players' high salary demands; to prevent players from jumping from one team to another; and to protect against the violation of college eligibility rules. One hundred years later, how are we doing? Those three founding tenets sure do sound a lot like today's salary cap, free agency, and the NFL college football draft issues. The more things change . . .

More than forty franchises failed during the league's first two decades. Gone were teams from such dubious locations as Muncie, Indiana; Evanston, Illinois; Tonawanda, New York; and LaRue, Ohio. Only two charter-member teams, the Chicago Bears (aka the Decatur Staleys) and the Chicago Cardinals, now the Arizona Cardinals, are still among the NFL's active franchises. Even entries from cities that would later become NFL mainstays, like New York, Detroit, Cincinnati, Buffalo, and Washington, DC, went belly-up during the league's early years.

While the NFL has obviously made tremendous strides since, it didn't happen without substantial growing pains and serious challenges. The league, to its well-deserved credit, survived the Great Depression, continued to operate during the unparalleled manpower shortage caused by the demands of World War II, met the challenges of rival leagues, and overcame controversies and scandals that tested the character and integrity of the men who dedicated their lives to the creation and development of the "postgraduate" brand of football.

My life's work has been and continues to be—pardon the cliché—a labor of love. My greatest reward for this lifelong addiction is the recognition I've received from others as one of the game's foremost historians. In a note, NFL commissioner Roger Goodell referred to me as "the finest historian I know." While I'm flattered and slightly embarrassed by his complimentary remark, it is that kind of unsolicited recognition that fuels my desire to share the amazingly underappreciated story of the strongest, most successful, and by far most interesting sports league in the world, the National Football League.

NFL CENTURY

CHAPTER 1

LEAGUE TALK

PROFESSIONAL FOOTBALL AS WE KNOW IT BEGAN in the fall of 1892 when one William "Pudge" Heffelfinger, an All-American tackle from Yale, accepted a $500 cash payment to play for the Allegheny Athletic Association. The AAA played out of what today is the North Shore of Pittsburgh.

If $500 sounds like a cheap deal, consider this: $500 back then had the buying power of roughly $13,000 today.

And this: Heffelfinger's payment from the AAA was for a single game, against their crosstown rival, the hated Pittsburgh Athletic Club (PAC). The AAA won the game 4–0 (touchdowns were worth four points from 1892 to 1898, five points from 1898 to 1911, and six points starting in 1912) and Heffelfinger earned his pay scoring the game's only touchdown on a 35-yard fumble recovery.

Evidence of Heffelfinger's role in the creation of professional football can be found today in the Pro Football Hall of Fame, preserved on a slightly yellowed page of the AAA's expense accounting ledger for November 12, 1892.

Ironically, what would have been considered damning evidence of unethical professionalism back then is now proudly displayed at the Hall of Fame as pro football's "birth certificate."

While the indelible-ink entry is proof positive of Heffelfinger's pay, it's unlikely that the recompense was truly the first time the purity of the sport's amateur code had been violated. In fact, under-the-table payments to "ringers" were becoming more and more commonplace. It's just that in Heffelfinger's case, the AAA put it in writing.

Eventually the practice of paying players became so routine that some amateur clubs, including the AAA, simply decided to be open about it.

While the result was better football, the high cost of bidding for the services of the best players created an unanticipated financial strain on some of the athletic clubs, so much so that one by one they began to drop football altogether.

Also, ringers were never fully embraced by team loyalists. One week player X was a welcomed member of the "home team" and the next he was an unwelcomed opponent. As a result, fan acceptance of the pro version of football, particularly in the "amateur athletic clubs" of Pennsylvania and New York, began to wilt.

However, in nearby Ohio, the opposite seemed to be happening. Amateur competition in cities like Akron, Canton, Dayton, Massillon, Shelby, and Youngstown became so competitive that teams began to openly recruit play-for-pay athletes.

In 1903, the Massillon Tigers became the first Ohio team to blatantly lure players with cash. Others followed, including Massillon's fiercest rival and Stark County neighbor, Canton. Prior to the start of the 1905 season, the Canton Athletic Club (CAC) announced that their football team would be a "professional organization," complete with a "professional coach." The mission of the rechristened Canton Bulldogs was simple: beat Massillon.

Suddenly, Ohio was the hotbed of professional football. A small group of pro teams, mostly from the northeastern part of the state, became known as the "Ohio League."

The Ohio League was an unstable entity whose makeup changed from year to year as teams folded and new ones emerged. The informal "league" usually included three to five teams and, depending on their fortunes, one or two from other Ohio cities like Columbus, Cincinnati, or Dayton. An imaginary title was claimed by the team faring the best against the other entries.

Although semipro or pro teams could be found in many small midwestern cities and towns by the early 1900s, the Ohio League teams were clearly the best. They recruited the best, paid the most, and drew the largest crowds.

But make no mistake—the game was far from being a serious challenge to college football, major-league baseball, boxing, or even horse racing. Critics claimed it lacked organization, stability, credibility, and integrity, and to a large extent, they were right.

Adding fuel to that fire was a controversy in which a Bulldogs player, Charles "Blondy" Wallace, allegedly attempted to fix an important late-season game in 1906, between Canton and Massillon. Although no real evidence to support the charges was presented, the well-publicized allegations helped to validate critics' claims that pro teams were nothing more than disorganized bunches of vagabond tramp athletes willing to play for the highest bidder.

The resulting lack of public confidence, compounded by the ever-increasing cost of securing well-known players, caused Canton to fold following the 1906 season. Though Massillon continued to operate, they did so as a second-tier team with a substantially smaller payroll. Gone after two seasons was Ohio's first pro football rivalry. And without its two best-known teams, the other Ohio League teams suffered as well.

Then, in 1912, a twenty-one-year-old "sports enthusiast" named Jack Cusack offered his unpaid services as treasurer and secretary to a newly organized Canton Professionals football team. Within weeks the aggressive rookie promoter found himself in total control of the born-again football club.

Cusack set out to restore Canton to its earlier prominence. To that end, in 1915 he lured Olympic champion Jim Thorpe, the biggest name in sports, to Canton. Anxious to resurrect the rivalry between Canton and Massillon, Cusack rechristened his Canton team the "Bulldogs" and scheduled two games—home and away—with the newly reorganized Massillon Tigers.

In Thorpe, pro football had its first bona fide star and a major gate attraction. Some fans could hardly believe it when word leaked that Cusack was paying him $250 per game.

"Even the most loyal Cantonites thought Cusack had lost his mind and would soon lose his shirt," wrote pro football historian Bob Carroll. But when 6,000 paying customers showed up for the first Canton-Massillon game and 8,000 for the second, the doubters were silenced. The Thorpe-led team went on to capture Ohio League championships in both 1916 and 1917.

While Thorpe's presence certainly bolstered attendance and revenues for Canton, things weren't as rosy for the other Ohio League teams. For them, except for games against Canton, attendance and revenues were down. A good part of the downturn, however, had nothing to do with the game.

On April 6, 1917, the United States officially entered World War I. Almost immediately teams felt its effect as players either enlisted or were drafted.

Compounding the problem, a deadly influenza pandemic swept the country in early 1918. To limit the spread of the outbreak, ordinances were passed restricting large gatherings, including sporting events. The manpower shortage and the fear of contagion caused most pro teams, including Canton and Massillon, to fold during the 1918 season.

While Cusack and other team managers proclaimed the interruption would be a one-year pause, no one could be certain pro football would survive.

Relief came with the war's end in 1919 and the simultaneous decline of the pandemic. Anxious to pick up where they had left off, the four "Ohio League" teams ended their hiatus. But some serious challenges remained.

To begin with, during the wartime layoff, Cusack sold the Bulldogs to Ralph E. Hay, a twenty-seven-year-old Canton entrepreneur and owner of the Ralph E. Hay Motor Company.

Over in Massillon, while Tigers owners Jack Donahue and Jack Whalen proclaimed their readiness to once again field a team, their constant complaints about how much money they'd lost in 1917 cast a question mark over the new season.

To the north, Akron Indians owner Vernon "Mac" McGinnis indicated he was ready to give it another go. And even though Youngstown Patricians manager Mickey Stambaugh was drowning in red ink and angry about having his roster poached in 1917, he said he was willing to forgive and forget and start anew.

Despite these challenges, a sense of optimism seemed to take root among these strange bedfellows. Hay emerged as the group's main cheerleader. Whether it was his naïveté as a rookie manager, previous entrepreneurial successes, having Thorpe under contract, or a combination of all three fortuitous circumstances, his passionate confidence was the dose of "recovery medicine" needed by a sport already on life support.

The same problems that faced the pro game ever since Heffelfinger's big payday continued to plague the Ohio League in 1919: players jumping from one team to another for a few dollars more, high salary demands and bidding wars for "big name" players, and the signing of amateur collegians. Sound familiar? In many ways, they're the same problems still facing the game today.

The Ohio League managers decided it was in their own best interest to at least discuss the issues. However, just getting together proved to be difficult. Three meetings in three different cities were needed to address the important matters before them.

Hay hosted the first meeting on July 14 in Canton. Massillon and Akron showed up. Youngstown didn't. Manager Stambaugh was reportedly "on vacation." Likely a hunting trip for additional investors.

Nevertheless, the three teams present reached several "agreements," including a "tacit understanding" that there would be no stealing of players by one team from another. Although a good first step, there was no punishment for a violation, other than to proclaim "team managers would fall into disgrace" if they got caught.

More surprising than that halfhearted agreement was a failed attempt to limit player salaries. It went down in flames. More surprising yet was that the loudest objection to the early-day salary cap came from Massillon's penny-pinching Donahue and Whalen, who incessantly whined of their $4,700 loss in 1917. "If a team manager wants to pay $10,000 for a player, that is his business," Donahue declared.

Due to Youngstown's absence, the all-important scheduling portion of the meeting had to be postponed until midsummer in Akron. Even though all four teams managed to attend the Akron summit, the gathering still concluded without a schedule.

This time it was a suddenly cautious Hay who put the brakes on finalizing the schedule. The Canton manager informed his colleagues that he hadn't spoken with Thorpe regarding the potential dates and asked for a third meeting in Pittsburgh in ten days. Hay promised that Thorpe, who'd be there playing baseball for the Boston Braves, would attend. The other managers understood and appreciated Thorpe's importance, so they agreed to meet again.

Hay's desire to have Thorpe attend the meeting may have been more than a polite gesture. Unbeknownst to his fellow managers, Hay had received a telegram from Thorpe, informing him that he'd arranged two open dates to play a team in New York's Polo Grounds. A big payday opportunity in New York City was big news. Hay's reluctance to share the good news immediately was likely to make sure that he had all the details and that the better of the two dates was secured for his Bulldogs. But, whether by leak or intent, a detailed account of Thorpe's arrangement quickly found its way to the press.

Apparently Thorpe had secured the Polo Grounds through his friend John McGraw, manager of New York's National League baseball club.

McGraw wanted Thorpe to organize and run a pro football team to play in the famed baseball stadium. But when McGraw learned Thorpe was under contract with Canton and had a financial interest in the team, he made an alternative offer: bring the Bulldogs to New York and play McGraw's soon-to-be-organized team. It seemed like a win-win arrangement.

Ten days later, Canton, Massillon, and Akron showed up for the Pittsburgh meeting. Once again Youngstown was absent. Frustrated, Hay did his best to reassure the others that Youngstown was still on board and "would be on hand when the bell rang."

In the meantime, the managers met with representatives from New York and Cleveland. Neither city had a team, but both indicated they'd have teams ready to play in the upcoming season.

Suddenly, the Ohio League's "Big Four" had big-city suitors. Was this good news or bad? Certainly, road games in major markets with large baseball stadiums would help the bottom line of the visiting small-city teams. But wouldn't it also exacerbate the problem of players jumping from small-market teams to the more lucrative opportunities in larger cities?

Market size and larger playing facilities were to become the Achilles' heel of small-city pro football. Sustainable markets and suitable stadiums were about to join the growing list of recurring challenges for pro football.

All that aside, it didn't take Hay long to accept McGraw's overture. The Canton manager formally announced his team would travel to the Gotham City in early November to play McGraw's team-in-the-making. Massillon, with less fanfare, claimed the second date.

Willingness by the two Ohio teams to play McGraw's New York team was largely influenced by the prospect of a big payday, rather than any visionary's notion of pro football's potential in New York City. Oddly, Hay's excitement at the possibility of playing in New York didn't extend to the league's other big-city suitor, Cleveland. Hay told the *Canton Evening Repository* that should Cleveland "put a worthy challenger on the field, he might find time to knock the Sixth City's championship aspirations for a goal." He also somewhat condescendingly reminded manager Jimmy O'Donnell that Akron, Canton, Massillon, and Youngstown were "the Big Four" of pro football and it was unlikely he'd risk bookings with the other three in favor of the upstart team from the north.

Shortly after announcing that the Bulldogs would play in New York, Hay was contacted by Paul Parduhn, manager of the Hammond, Indiana, Bobcats, a team that had claimed pro football's Midwest championship, an assertion built more on bravado than reality.

Parduhn had secured Chicago's Cubs Park as his home field and publicly proclaimed that he had an astonishing player payroll of $20,000. The Hammond promoter understood that a game in Chicago against the famous Thorpe-led Bulldogs would be lucrative.

Playing to Hay's competitive nature, Parduhn challenged him to bring his Bulldogs to Chicago to play Parduhn's Bobcats. He warned that failure to accept would result in Hammond's claiming "the true world's championship."

With the prospect of a big payday, Hay accepted. However, to insert Hammond into his suddenly-in-demand schedule, Hay had to back out of his agreement with McGraw. Realizing that an assured game in Chicago was better than a game in the Polo Grounds against a yet-to-be-organized squad, Hay unceremoniously canceled the New York game. And as bad as that news must have been for McGraw, things suddenly got worse for the baseball owner.

For many years, so-called blue laws, also known as Sunday laws, were enforced in New York City. One of the most notorious laws restricted playing baseball on the Sabbath.

McGraw thought he'd gotten a much-needed break in the spring of 1919 when the New York State legislature voted to lift the sports ban. McGraw believed the legislation applied to all sports. But he was wrong. It applied only to baseball.

And so it was on October 6, one day after McGraw's football team, "Brickley's Giants"—named after team captain and former All-American Charley Brickley—conducted their first practice, that he was informed of his error. There was to be no football on Sundays. With Saturday dates at the Polo Grounds committed to college football, a disappointed and somewhat embarrassed McGraw had little choice but to fold his football team before ever playing a down.

Meanwhile, with no blue laws in their cities to interfere, the four Ohio League teams launched their schedules. Although just resuming play after the one-year wartime layoff had to be considered something of a victory, little else that weekend indicated a very promising future for the reorganized Ohio League teams.

Surprisingly, the mighty Bulldogs struggled mightily, just to get past a vastly inferior Pitcairn, Pennsylvania, Quakers team, 13–7. In the only game pitting two Ohio League teams against each other, Massillon devoured Youngstown 27–0. The one-sided loss was enough to convince the on-again, off-again Patricians management to give up the ghost and fold their team for good.

The Akron Indians were perhaps the only Ohio League team to go relatively unscathed in the opening weekend. They coasted to an expected lopsided win over a weak Toledo AC, 47–0.

Things improved as the season progressed. Although Youngstown was gone, Jimmy O'Donnell's previously shunned Cleveland Tigers team stepped in to fill the void. Also in the plus column, Canton twice traveled to Chicago to play Parduhn's "$20,000 beauties," as the Bobcats became known, winning one and playing to a scoreless tie in the other. More important, both games drew crowds of more than 10,000 fans.

Also on a positive note, both Canton and Massillon managed to schedule games in Detroit against that city's pro team, the Heralds. The Detroit games somewhat offset the loss of their big-city pay-days in New York.

Later in the season, Massillon, attempting to capitalize on the Armistice Day holiday, played O'Donnell's Tigers on a Tuesday afternoon. But it wasn't the odd midweek game or even Cleveland's lackluster 3–0 win that captured headlines in the Cleveland *Plain Dealer*. It was the surprising announcement by Cleveland's financial backers that plans were under way "to form a grid league for the 1920 season."

"Organization is the next step," they confidently related. "A real, sure-enough league not entirely unlike the big baseball leagues."

The suddenly energized Cleveland investors went on to espouse much of what had been offered by the Ohio League in the past.

"Teams will enter agreements not to flirt with players on other teams and get them to jump." And, they added, teams would attempt to protect themselves "from the avaricious player who plays both ends against the middle, seeking offers from every club and boosting the ante from time to time."

While their proclamation of a possible pro league was encouraging, the fact that it was emanating from Cleveland, not Canton, was significant. While Hay was quick to endorse the idea, he left no doubt that he had not relinquished Canton's position as the epicenter of the pro football world or his position as its spokesman. "We will be on the ground when a meeting for the formation of a league is called," he sternly avowed.

As the 1919 season neared completion, Canton was again at the center of the pro football world. Ohio League championship bragging rights had come down to a season-ending game between the Thorpe-led Bulldogs and the roster-raiding Massillon Tigers. Massillon fell short, losing 3–0 to the Bulldogs, who were declared world champions of 1919.

But the Bulldogs' victory was also the league's swan song. The Youngstown Patricians folded early, and at season's end Massillon's Donahue and Whalen declared themselves done with pro football. Even the mighty Bulldogs, with smaller-than-expected home game attendance, felt the financial pinch. But their "big-city" road games to Detroit and Chicago provided just enough hope and cash for Hay to stay the course. In Akron, Art Ranney and partner Frank Nied vowed to return for another run in 1920. And Cleveland's outsider-turned-insider, Jimmy O'Donnell, pledged to return as well.

But Hay, Nied, Ranney, and O'Donnell knew they had to set their sights on bigger and better things in 1920. Changes had to be made and teams needed to be added. It was time to organize and create "a real, sure-enough league."

CHAPTER 2

A REAL SURE-ENOUGH LEAGUE

O N AUGUST 21, 1920, THE CANTON EVENING RE-
pository heralded that pro football "moguls" had formed a
"national body" to be known as the "American Professional
Football Conference." According to the paper, the meeting was
conducted in the business office of Ralph Hay's Hupmobile automobile dealership, and Hay was named temporary chairman of the
new body.

While the story sounded real enough, the APFC was more a
work in progress than a finished product. To borrow a football
phrase of the future—"after further review"—the announcement
was not only premature but a bit exaggerated.

Three former Ohio League teams—the Canton Bulldogs, the
Akron Professionals (formerly the Indians), and the Cleveland
Indians—along with another Ohio team, the Dayton Triangles,
gathered in Hay's office. And as they'd done in previous years, the
team representatives formulated their schedules and expressed their
never-ending concern about players jumping from one team to another, the players' high salary demands, and college eligibility issues.

But this time, something had changed. Perhaps buoyed by the
postwar surge in the game's popularity in cities like New York,
Cleveland, Detroit, and Chicago, the Ohioans seemed not only
ready but anxious to open the doors to other pro teams. Particularly to those from larger markets.

To give the appearance of being "national in scope," Hay announced that teams from Buffalo and Rochester, New York, and
Hammond, Indiana, had joined the organization. Further, he

suggested that the new organization would likely add a team from Rock Island, Illinois. While Hay's announcement was dutifully noted in the press, the official—and succinct—meeting minutes provide a more modest picture of what occurred that August evening:

> *Professional Football Representatives from Canton, Cleveland, Dayton and Akron held a meeting August 20, at which time schedules were drawn and plans formulated for the organizing of an association. Mr. Hay was appointed temporary Chairman. . . .*
>
> *A mutual agreement was reached that no club should sign or make terms with any player still attending college, nor should a Club do business with any man attached at the time to one of the above Clubs. Should two Clubs be dealing with the same man, terms should be agreed upon.*

The meeting was adjourned. Next meeting to be held at Canton, September 17.

Though brief, the minutes are specific—"plans were formulated," not finalized. A "temporary chairman" was appointed—not elected. Both actions suggest a developing organization but not a finished one.

Additionally, the "agreement" to protect college eligibility rules and refrain from raiding one another's rosters was nothing new. Every year the Ohio League teams professed their commitment to antiraiding and respect for college eligibility requirements, and every year team managers seemed to suffer from a form of collective amnesia, as they routinely raided rosters and broke eligibility rules.

Also, the minutes contained no mention of any other team joining the organization. There wasn't even mention of an official name for the group.

Significantly, newspapers reported, and the minutes confirmed, plans for a September 17 meeting. Newspapers also reported that a president would be elected then, information probably shared by "temporary chairman" Hay.

Clearly, it appears the four Ohio teams were taking steps to formally organize. But it's also apparent that they had more work to do before good intentions could become a reality. Until solid commitments were made, and permanent officers installed, talk of a "real league" was just that—talk.

Hay's announcement of a national organization was probably intended to generate interest and enthusiasm while encouraging other team managers to attend the September 17 meeting. And that's pretty much what happened.

A larger-than-expected turnout of would-be football moguls showed up at Hay's tiny automobile dealership for the meeting. According to news accounts, fifteen men representing ten teams gathered that evening to discuss the future of play-for-pay football.

The crowd was big enough and the office small enough that they had to move to the showroom floor, where those without a chair sat on the fenders or running boards of the dealership's four showroom cars. Legend has it that while chairs were scarce, refreshments weren't—Hay saw to it that there were plenty of buckets of beer for his guests to enjoy, even though Prohibition had been in effect since January.

The evening's cast of characters included the Bulldogs' Hay, Jim Thorpe, and team treasurer Lester Higgins. From the Cleveland Tigers came Jimmy O'Donnell and Stan Cofall. Carl Storck, who hung up his playing cleats in 1918, represented the Dayton Triangles, and Frank Nied and Art Ranney attended on behalf of the Akron Pros.

Traveling by train from Rochester, New York, was Leo Lyons, the do-everything player, coach, and owner of the Jeffersons. Walter Flanigan, another pro player turned owner, represented the Rock Island Independents. Earl Ball, the founder of the Muncie Flyers and owner of the Ball mason jar company, represented his team. Chris O'Brien, a painting and decorating contractor from Chicago, was there on behalf of the Racine Cardinals, and Dr. Alvin A. "Doc" Young presented himself as the Hammond Pros' front man.

Two individuals among this eclectic group were there on behalf of the Decatur Staleys, a team owned by A. E. Staley, owner of the A. E. Staley Manufacturing Company. If the name of Morgan P. O'Brien doesn't ring a bell, perhaps the other man who attended the meeting with him is more recognizable—George Halas.

A well-known three-sport star at the University of Illinois, Halas played professional football for the Hammond Pros and baseball for the New York Yankees in 1919. Staley hired him in 1920 to manage the company's sports and athletic department. He was also expected to play on and manage the newly organized football team.

"Morgan O'Brien, a Staley engineer and a football fan who was being very helpful in administrative matters, and I went to Canton on the train," Halas recalled in his autobiography, *Halas by Halas*. "The showroom, big enough for four cars—Hupmobiles and Jordans—occupied the ground floor of the three-story brick Odd Fellows Building. Chairs were few. I sat on a running board."

While the meeting minutes list the Massillon Tigers as represented, it was left to Hay to explain their absence. The Canton manager announced the team's withdrawal from participating in the 1920 season, while leaving the possibility of their return in 1921. On the surface, Hay's report concerning the Tigers seemed innocent enough, but in hindsight there's evidence of some skullduggery from the Canton and Akron interests.

Why announce a team that had withdrawn from professional football when, for example, no mention was made of Youngstown's similar decision to not field a team that year?

As it turned out, Hay and Akron's Nied and Ranney appeared to be holding on to the hope that another Massillon interest might emerge to save the day. Unfortunately, the only person expressing interest in the Tigers was Ranney's former partner "Mac" McGinnis, who wanted to buy the Massillon players and form a traveling unit. Neither man wanted McGinnis back in the picture. Announcing Massillon's withdrawal for the 1920 season while giving the impression of a possible return in 1921 essentially accomplished the duo's goal of blocking McGinnis's attempt to join the league.

Beyond the block-McGinnis maneuver, the September meeting went off without a hitch. Capitalizing on his celebrity, Thorpe was elected president of the organization now officially named the American Professional Football Association. Cofall, a former Notre Dame All-American, was elected vice president and Ranney was chosen as secretary-treasurer.

"Ten well-organized outfits" was how the Canton newspapers described the league's membership. Dutifully sharing the puffery provided by Hay, the papers suggested that Thorpe's prestige as a player and executive, coupled with the association's financial backing, made the APFA the equal of organized baseball.

Both assertions were wild exaggerations. While Thorpe was a brilliant athlete, he was hardly known for his business acumen. And the idea that there was strong financial support behind the APFA was just plain ludicrous. The upstart league's finances were nonexistent.

"We announced membership in the league would cost $100 per team," Halas remembered. "I can testify no money changed hands. I doubt if there was a hundred bucks in the whole room. We just wanted to give our new organization a façade of financial stability."

Illustrating just how unfamiliar some of the team managers were with one another, the Racine Cardinals are listed on the meeting minutes as being from Wisconsin. Apparently, Secretary Ranney didn't realize "Racine" was the Chicago street where the Cardinals' playing field was located, not its city of origin.

Besides being broke and unfamiliar with one another, much was still discussed and agreed upon.

A committee headed by the Hammond Pros' "Doc" Young was created to draft a constitution, bylaws, and rules for the association. Additionally, clubs agreed to provide by the first of every year a list of their rosters so each team would have first choice of services for their players the following season. It was the first formal agreement designed to prevent players from team jumping and to end the bidding for players already under contract.

With those important organizational steps taken, pro football did indeed seem to have its first "real, sure-enough league." A league that two years later would rename itself the National Football League.

And while a sense of accomplishment must have filled the air after that now-historic meeting, it's doubtful that even the most wide-eyed optimist—including Hay—could have imagined the successes, or more immediately, the enormous challenges that lay ahead. For an association whose modest stated purpose was simply to "promote good football and elevate the professional game," things quickly became complicated.

Although the APFA claimed ten charter members, news accounts made it clear that other pro teams were very welcome. The association announced that it would "provide for membership for every big city in the country which caters to patrons of the sport." Four teams—the Buffalo All-Americans, the Chicago Tigers, the Columbus Panhandles, and the Detroit Heralds—were the first beneficiaries of this open-door policy.

Although Buffalo had reportedly indicated in August its intent to join the new league, no representative attended either the August or September meetings and therefore it wasn't counted among the charter members. Presumably Buffalo, as well as Chicago, Detroit, and Columbus, eventually worked out the necessary details as they were considered members of the association before the start of the league's inaugural season.

The APFA acknowledged that it couldn't create a schedule for every club in time for the 1920 season. So teams could play games against nonleague teams. A more formal schedule was promised for 1921.

The first games between two APFA member clubs occurred on October 3. On that day, the Dayton Triangles shut out the Columbus Panhandles 14–0 before an encouraging crowd of 4,000. And in Rock Island, the Independents crushed the Muncie Flyers 45–0 before a crowd of 3,110.

The inaugural APFA season didn't look much different in 1920 than in 1919. The lack of a league-sanctioned schedule and no observable league leadership did little to separate member teams from nonmember teams and even less to project an image of anything close to "a real, sure-enough league."

The official standings for the APFA's first season ended with wildly divergent results. Due in large part to the outstanding play of their star halfback Fritz Pollard—one of only two African American players in the league—the Akron Pros finished the season with an undefeated record of 8-0-3, while the association's marquee team, the Canton Bulldogs, finished with a disappointing 7-4-2 record. Four of the team's wins and a tie came at the expense of unaffiliated second-tier teams. The Halas-led Decatur Staleys finished with an impressive 10-1-2 record that also included four nonleague games.

The confusing mix of league and nonleague games resulted in a season-ending squabble as to who had won the title, Akron, Decatur, or the 9-1-1 Buffalo All-Americans. All laid claim to the first league title. The controversy was tabled until the association's planned January meeting.

Despite the chaos, and the doubts of some, the league's founding fathers felt like they were beginning to realize their dreams. The question was, could this ragtag group turn their vision into a legitimate professional league? Serious questions remained. Who won the title? What were the league's plans for the coming season? Who was running the league? All good questions. All lacked answers.

It wasn't as though the league hadn't made any progress. It had. Attendance at some games exceeded 10,000 and favorable press coverage continued to grow.

Even as some managers expressed concern, most remained believers. Chief among them was Panhandles manager Joe Carr, who eagerly hoped the league's planned January meeting would refocus and rekindle the passion and optimism of his fellow managers. But when the scheduled winter meeting failed to materialize, even confident Carr likely questioned the league's viability.

Finally, on April 30, 1921, after languishing in a world of uncertainty, managers of nine of the fourteen APFA teams—Akron, the Chicago Cardinals, Hammond, Columbus, Decatur, Dayton, Rochester, Buffalo, and Canton—came together at the Portage Hotel in Akron. And make no mistake: they weren't there to celebrate the past season, lick their wounds, and move on. No, by then they had realized the seriousness of their situation.

While the APFA's inaugural season was in some ways a success—particularly in the bigger cities—it was already apparent that the long-term sustainability for the smaller league markets would be a challenge. Equally obvious was the league's need for an effective governing body and a true leader, someone with vision and know-how. Lacking both, it was clear to the league's founding fathers that the best way forward was to reorganize and try again.

But when the team managers gathered in Akron, both league president Thorpe and vice president Cofall were missing. The only league officer present was secretary-treasurer Ranney.

The absence of Thorpe and Cofall wasn't surprising. Remember, it was their notoriety as athletes, not their administrative skills, that prompted the league's founders to elect them in the first place. Frankly, had either shown up at the meeting, it's doubtful they would have been offered another term. In fact, almost from the start, Cofall demonstrated a lack of commitment to one of the league's core tenets: the prohibition of players jumping from one team to another.

Taking advantage of the Pennsylvania blue laws, Cofall would play on Saturdays as a member of the nonleague Union AA team of Phoenixville, then hop a train back to Cleveland and play for his Cleveland Tigers on Sunday. And as it turned out, several members of the Buffalo All-Americans squad did the same. They'd play a Saturday game as members of the Union AA team, then play the next day in Buffalo as members of the All-Americans.

At the April meeting, Ranney stepped down from his post in the spirit of a new beginning in favor of Dayton Triangles manager Carl Storck. He was assigned the role of "temporary secretary."

The first order of business for the club managers—albeit nearly six months after the fact—was to declare the undefeated Akron Pros the 1920 APFA champions. After they thanked the Brunswick-Balke-Collender Company for providing the championship trophy, the APFA's inaugural season was officially in the books.

The real reason for the meeting wasn't to award a trophy but rather to reorganize the league. To that end, Carr was elected president, the Decatur Staleys' Morgan P. O'Brien vice president, and Storck the secretary-treasurer by unanimous consent.

Although Carr would later claim he was elected "much against my will while I was out of the room," he assumed the position with energetic, if not prearranged, readiness.

In Carr, the league had the experienced leader it desperately needed. His sports resume was long and impressive.

In 1900, at the tender age of twenty, he organized and managed a successful semipro baseball team known as the "Famous (Columbus) Panhandle White Sox." Around the same time, he worked as the assistant sports editor of the *Ohio State Journal,* covering major boxing events and local sports. His football pedigree began in 1907, when he took over the dormant Columbus Panhandles football team that had operated from 1901 to 1904.

Carr's football team, like his baseball team, was built exclusively around employees of the Panhandle Division of the Pennsylvania Railroad, where he also worked as a machinist. The nucleus of the Panhandles was pro football's most notable family—the Nesser brothers. Of the eleven starting positions on the 1907 Panhandles squad, five were Nessers. In 1910 the brothers—Fred, Frank, Phil, John, and Ted—were joined by a sixth brother, Al. In 1921, a year after the Panhandles joined the APFA, Ted's son Charles joined his father for a game, making them the only father-son combo to appear in an APFA (NFL) lineup together.

While the Panhandles' overall record was only mediocre, Carr's promotional skills made them one of the best-known early-day teams in the country. A feature story on the unusual squad was even carried in *The Times* of London.

It was Carr's organizational skills, strong sports background, and conviction that pro football needed a league that set him apart from other candidates for the job.

"He had what the rest of us lacked, and that was real business sense," Halas said of Carr. "All we were interested in was winning games. He was a born organizer. It was Joe who said our real concern should be the future of the sport."

From his first day on the job, the bespectacled, unassuming Carr focused on creating that future. He immediately called for the implementation of the measures approved at the 1920 organizational meeting, especially the submission of each team's roster from the previous year for his review. He sternly reminded his fellow managers that no player under contract could be approached by another team until he was first—as with baseball's then–reserve clause—declared a free agent.

Next on his agenda, Carr prohibited players from playing on two different clubs in the same week. He argued that back-to-back games "damaged the integrity of the league," as players were often game-weary or sometimes injured. That, he said, "was not in the best interest of the fans."

Carr's final edict was to appoint a committee of three to draft a constitution and bylaws for the association, something that had been toyed with during the league's first season.

Carr's much-needed take-charge attitude was just the beginning of a whirlwind of change for the league and its founders. Carr had clearly been contemplating the "future of the sport" well before he was officially put in charge.

Consider, for instance, that by early September, just four and a half months after taking office, Carr announced the addition of eleven new franchises to the then-thirteen-team league. While three of them—Toledo, Ohio; Fort Wayne, Indiana; and New Haven, Connecticut—withdrew prior to the start of the season, eight others—Louisville, Kentucky (Brecks); Cincinnati (Celts); Minneapolis (Marines); Evansville, Indiana (Crimson Giants); Tonawanda, New York (Kardex); Brickley's New York Giants; Washington, DC (Senators); and a team from Green Bay, Wisconsin, known as the Packers—fielded teams for the 1921 season.

Some have suggested that Carr's rapid expansion was done haphazardly and without purposeful direction. But nothing could be further from the truth.

"It will be noted that no cities along the Atlantic seaboard are represented in the circuit," the Harrisburg *Evening News* reported on August 20, 1921. Although several cities had reportedly asked for franchises, the APFA was said to have decided to "stay out of the eastern district beyond Rochester."

The APFA's plan, according to the *Evening News*, was to have two separate leagues operating in 1922. There would be a new "eastern circuit" that would compete against teams "in the middle west," ending with "a sort of world's series" between the "championship teams of the east and west."

Carr's two-league plan with a championship playoff game has been underappreciated by historians and is nearly absent from the NFL's historical narrative. His visionary design should be recognized as one of his major accomplishments, even though it took longer than he expected for it to happen. When the NFL, more than a decade later, established two divisions and an annual championship game, there was no shortage of "visionaries" ready and willing to lay claim to the concept. The unassuming Carr was not among them.

While it was Carr's stated objective to have two separate leagues, it's hard to believe that even he envisioned it could happen by 1922. It does appear, however, that in the interim and using his baseball background as guidance, Carr planned for the creation of "major" and "minor" divisions starting in 1921. The September 11 edition of the *Detroit Free Press* confirmed as much:

> *In the major division of the American Professional Football Association, there are 12 clubs including the Detroit Tigers. . . . [O]ther teams in the division are the Decatur Staleys, and Racine Cardinals which play in Chicago, Hammond, Columbus Panhandles and Canton Bulldogs, Akron, Dayton Triangles, Cleveland Tigers, Buffalo All-Americans, and Rochester Jeffersons.*

The APFA's "minor division" was identified by the newspaper as the eight new franchises Carr brought into the fold, plus the Muncie Flyers, who, after their 0-1-0 record in 1920, were demoted to second-tier status. Suddenly Carr's rapid expansion made a lot more sense.

Although all twenty-one franchises are recognized as full-fledged members of the NFL, the "minor division" teams were for all intents and purposes there to fill out the schedules of the "major division" teams. Most of their games were played against one another.

Of the minor division teams, the Packers played the most games—four—against major division competition. Minneapolis and Washington played three, while Cincinnati and Brickley's New York Giants played two. Three teams—Tonawanda, Evansville, and Louisville—each played just one major division team. And the struggling Muncie Flyers failed to play any games against a major division team.

While Carr was focused on the sustainability of the major teams, he never lost sight of the need to continue to grow the league's credibility. But that credibility was constantly being challenged by pro football detractors, especially college coaches and administrators. It seemed that the more success the pro game realized, the more dogged the opposition became.

Critics of the professional model—most notably the National Collegiate Athletic Association (NCAA)—portrayed and fostered the idea that the pro game was an affront to the amateur version played on college campuses. So deeply opposed to pro football was the NCAA that at its 1920 winter meeting the organization declared former collegiate players "should under no circumstance participate in post-graduate football." The Western Conference went even further, adopting a rule that any football letter winner who played pro football would have his letter "annulled."

Carr, while acknowledging the sins of the past by pro teams, frequently shared his conviction that the NFL was doing just fine policing itself and was absolutely no threat to the amateur game.

He was also quick to differentiate between the objectionable practice of luring college-eligible players to the pro ranks from the signing of those players whose college eligibility had already expired: "It long has been the thought there should be a real outlet for college stars after their school days are over," he said. It was a shame, he said, that "as it used to be that boys are developed into wonderful gridiron athletes and then, just as they were in their football prime, they were graduated and had to lay aside their regalia for all time."

College football's failure to understand that pro football planned to operate like Major League Baseball and presented no threat to college football frustrated Carr.

He also understood that pro football's future was in major metropolitan areas, and that major-league baseball would welcome its presence. "Within two years," he predicted, "the big baseball leagues will be putting football teams into the field."

Chicago White Sox owner Charles Comiskey once suggested that if pro football could be made profitable, it would be "the answer to a problem that has confronted baseball owners since the game started." The problem, as he and other baseball owners could attest, was that their stadiums were used just three months a year and left idle the remainder of the year. Comiskey made it clear that baseball owners welcomed pro football teams as tenants.

Despite Carr's repeated intent to operate like organized baseball, most college football officials remained unconvinced and suspicious. And, as committed as Carr was to the league's no-tampering policy, it's unlikely he thought that simply banning such behavior would forever end the practice. It's also unlikely he anticipated the firestorm that would erupt at the end of his first season, a result of just one such violation.

CHAPTER 3

GROWING PAINS AND A NAME CHANGE

T WAS A CHILLY DAY, JANUARY 28, 1922, WHEN APFA owners and a few other wannabes gathered for the league's winter meeting in Canton's Courtland Hotel. It may have been cold outside, but inside the hotel's smoke-filled meeting room, an agenda of red-hot issues awaited. Some were sure to raise the room temperature even further.

There was the sudden and surprising matter of the contested ownership of the Decatur/Chicago Staleys franchise. The league title was also being contested by two clubs. But the real front-burner issue was the Green Bay Packers' admitted violation of the league's ban on the use of college-eligible players.

The contested ownership of the Decatur franchise stemmed from the planned transfer of the team from A. E. Staley to George Halas and his partner Edward "Dutch" Sternaman. As Halas tells the story in his 1979 autobiography, shortly after the 1921 season began, Staley called him to his office and informed him that he was getting out of the football business. But before Halas could even express his dismay, Staley shocked his player-coach-manager by offering him ownership of the franchise.

"I'll give you $5,000 seed money to pay costs until the gate receipts start coming in," he told Halas. The seed money, he explained, would come in the form of $3,000 for promoting the team and $2,000 to be paid toward player salaries, at the rate of $25 a week per player up to the total of nineteen players. The only stipulation was that the team operate for one season in Chicago as the

Staley Football Club. "Professional teams need a big-city base," Staley prophetically told Halas.

For Halas, it was a dream come true. "I could not believe such good fortune had come upon me," he wrote. "I was elated."

Halas immediately shared the news with the players and all but one agreed to join him in Chicago, where rooms at the Blackwood Apartment Hotel had been secured at two dollars a week per man. To help run his new enterprise, Halas enlisted Sternaman, his teammate and co-coach, to be his fifty-fifty partner.

Following the completion of the one-year commitment to play as the Chicago Staleys, Halas made his formal application to transfer ownership of the Decatur franchise to himself and Sternaman. But things got sticky when a Chicago promoter named Bill Harley laid claim to the franchise.

Halas explained in his autobiography that he had engaged Harley to secure the playing services of three Ohio State star players: Charles "Chick" Harley (the promoter's brother), Pete Stinchcomb, and John "Tarzan" Taylor. In exchange, Halas agreed that Harley would receive a share of the gate. Obviously, Halas insisted, that was all it meant and in no way did Harley have any claim on the franchise.

While Halas's recollection of the facts over the years went pretty much unchallenged, there are a few details he conveniently left out of his memoir:

According to a signed agreement dated July 21, 1921—a document still in possession of the Sternaman family—"Charles W. Harley, Edw. G. Sternaman, William Harley, and Geo. S. Halas" entered into an agreement "to manage the Decatur Staley Football team and to share equally in the profits and losses of said team." The brief handwritten agreement further states that the "above named will present to Geo. E. Chamberlain (a Staley Company executive) periodically during the football season of 1921 a sum of money to be designated therein." In other words, prior to the start of the 1921 season, Halas, Sternaman, and the Harley brothers were equal partners in managing the affairs of the team.

Harley's argument was that he and his brother were 50 percent partners. Halas's argument, and the one with the greater merit, was that he, not wanting to lose the services of the three players Harley had recruited, agreed to the management contract as written for the 1921 season only. After that, the agreement ended.

According to Halas, a long and heated debate continued into the evening. Apparently even a telephone call to Staley, who confirmed Halas's side of the story, failed to convince everyone of the legitimacy of Halas's claim. But when a vote was finally called, Halas and Sternaman were awarded the franchise by a vote of eight to two.

Then, as if that daylong debate weren't enough for the new Chicago owners, they found themselves at the center of the next fiery deliberation: Who had won the 1921 league title, Chicago or Buffalo?

The Staleys claimed their 9-1-1 record was better than the All-Americans' 9-1-2. The All-Americans questioned which games counted and which didn't, accusing the Staleys of including exhibition games in their record. But in the end, Halas and Sternaman once again prevailed; the Staleys were declared league champions.

But the most consequential issue of the winter meeting was what to do about the Packers. Team owner J. Emmitt Claire admitted to playing three University of Notre Dame players under assumed names against the Racine Legion in early December. The *South Bend Tribune* featured a front-page story naming the three Notre Dame men—Hartley "Hunk" Anderson, Arthur Garvey, and Fred Larson—and announcing they'd been banned from the team and their collegiate letters revoked.

Considering how hard Carr and others had worked to ensure that such behavior was a thing of the past, the charges against Green Bay weren't going to be taken lightly. And any leniency Claire may have thought possible was completely erased the morning of the league meeting, when newspapers reported nine University of Illinois players had been disqualified for accepting money to play for a semipro football team from Taylorville, Illinois, earlier that year. The papers also reported that as many as ten Notre Dame players would face a similar fate for having also played in the game as members of Taylorville's opponent, a team from neighboring Carlinville.

Reportedly, the two rival towns had wagered a whopping $100,000 between them and both thought it wise to bolster their chances of winning by recruiting collegians. While neither Taylorville nor Carlinville was a member of the APFA, the uproar over "professionalism" was immediate and loud. University of Chicago coach Amos Alonzo Stagg reiterated his belief that "professional football is a menace to college football." Several other prominent coaches and sportswriters piled on.

This devastating news left Carr and the league owners with no real option other than to come down hard—Claire and his Green Bay franchise were expelled from the league. Recognizing that even that might not be enough to satisfy the critics, Carr announced the unanimous adoption of a policy providing for a $1,000 deposit by each club that would also automatically be forfeited if a team hired college-eligible players.

While it was important for the APFA to act quickly and forcefully, Carr and the team managers took umbrage at what they considered unfair "guilt by association" charges leveled by the college coaches.

"Stagg is wrong if he attempts to put the blame on the professional football association for this recent trouble," declared Akron's Art Ranney. "It's not professional football that is a menace to college football. It's unorganized semiprofessional teams that are to blame, as the trouble at Taylorville shows."

Ranney pointed out that the league had no more jurisdiction over the Taylorville-Carlinville game than did the aggrieved colleges.

"So why blame us for the Taylorville incident? At our meeting Saturday, we expelled one club owner when it was proven that he had used college men in his games. Does that look as though we are bucking the colleges?"

Rochester Jeffersons manager Leo Lyons took it a step further. "It is a harsh thing to say, but there are few colleges in the country that can hold their hand in the air and boast of real 100 percent amateurism."

Carr insightfully preferred to push the message that the league was now even more resolute in its commitment to protect the status of amateurs. Recognizing that most newspapers were more in step with the college game than the pros, he wisely credited the *Chicago Tribune*'s investigation into the Green Bay matter as the impetus behind the league's quick punitive measures.

The *Tribune* took his bait and proudly bragged that Carr had personally sent a message to the newspaper stating, "the action of the American Professional Football Association was the direct result of an exposé by the *Tribune* of the conditions prevailing on the Green Bay team." Carr understood that flattery makes friends.

Amid the hubbub, even the name of the team came into question. It was a myth that the team was owned by the Acme Packing Company of Green Bay. The true owners were brothers J. Emmett and John Claire. The connection with the Acme Packing Company was merely that they provided the team's original uniforms, which included the company's name on the front of each jersey.

Although the Green Bay franchise had been revoked, a group headed by the team's star quarterback and future Hall of Famer Curly Lambeau applied for and was granted a *new* Green Bay franchise a few months later. To disassociate the new franchise from its recent past, the Lambeau group attempted to change the team name to the "Green Bay Blues," reflective of the uniforms' primary color. But Green Bay fans and most of the media ignored the change. For them the team was still the Packers.

While the Packers' name change failed, two other historically significant name changes did successfully transpire that year.

Immediately following the league's approval of the Chicago ownership shift to Halas and Sternaman, the two men announced their team would henceforth be known as the "Chicago Bears." At that same meeting, the owners decided to rename the American Professional Football Association the "National Football League."

For some reason, *The Official NFL Record and Fact Book— Chronology of Professional Football* incorrectly asserts the two historic name changes occurred five months later, at the league's June summer meeting.

Regardless of the actual date, Halas proudly remembered putting forth the motion to change the league's name. "I lacked enthusiasm for our name, the American Professional Football Association," he said. "In baseball, 'association' was applied to second-class teams. We were first-class."

CHAPTER 4

RED GRANGE TURNS PRO

THE DECADE OF THE 1920S HAS BEEN CALLED THE "Golden Era of Sports." Baseball, tennis, golf, swimming, boxing, and college football all flourished during that decade and each sport had its superstar. Baseball had Babe Ruth. Tennis could claim "Big Bill" Tilden, golf enthusiasts celebrated Bobby Jones, swimming had Johnny Weissmuller, boxing boasted Jack Dempsey, and college football had University of Illinois halfback Harold "Red" Grange.

While NFL teams had signed a substantial number of All-Americans, the pro league still lacked that headline-grabbing player who, just by stepping onto a playing field, could enhance the image of the entire league. In the pre-NFL era and the early 1920s, Jim Thorpe was that guy. But at thirty-seven, his playing days were behind him. A new headliner was needed.

In 1925, Grange was a sports legend, his fame so widespread that even people who knew little about football followed his exploits.

Not surprisingly, with his notoriety came speculation and rumors. Even before the start of his final season at Illinois, reports circulated that the "Galloping Ghost" had rejected lucrative offers from pro teams. Others suggested he'd already secretly signed a deal. So, on November 21, 1925, when Grange announced he'd signed with the Chicago Bears, it wasn't a complete surprise. Just the same, it was headline news across the country and a major coup for the pro game.

Joining Grange at his signing announcement were Bears co-owners Halas and Sternaman, and Charles C. Pyle, a man identified as Grange's manager. While all parties involved insisted that Grange hadn't signed any agreement prior to his final game at Illinois, the deal had clearly been in the works for weeks, if not months.

Pyle, better known as C.C. or "Cash and Carry," was an opportunistic promoter. Among his other interests, Pyle owned a movie theater in Champaign, Illinois, that was frequented by Illinois players. It was there that Pyle first connected with Grange.

As the story goes, Pyle spotted Grange in his theater and invited the Illinois star to join him in his office after the film. Assuming it was just another well-wisher wanting to make his acquaintance, Grange respectfully reported. Pyle quickly laid out a plan that he said could earn Grange $100,000 or more in just one winter.

Pyle proposed that Grange turn pro immediately after the college football season was over. He would join the Chicago Bears for the remainder of their season and then embark on a barnstorming tour that would begin in Florida.

Overwhelmed by Pyle's ambitious plan and the prospect of such a big payday, Grange agreed to allow the fast-talking promoter to proceed on his behalf. Not wanting to jeopardize his football eligibility, the two agreed there would be no contract or money exchanged between them until after the Illinois football season was over. Grange would then sign a contract making Pyle his manager. Or at least that's how the story goes.

Halas recalled in his autobiography that his first contact with Pyle was through an intermediary.

"One day late in October of 1925, a Chicago man named Frank Zambrino approached me. He was manager of a movie house and distributed films. He told me about a friend in Champaign named C. C. Pyle, who had been in vaudeville and now ran a movie theater in the college town. Pyle was thinking of becoming Red's manager. Zambrino said Pyle wanted to know if, were he successful, I would be interested in having Red play with the Bears and, perhaps, make a big tour after our season. I told him I liked the idea. Zambrino carried messages back and forth."

While Halas's reminiscence has always been accepted as gospel, documents from the Dutch Sternaman Collection, housed in the Pro Football Hall of Fame's archives, offer a different story.

Pyle's first contact with the Bears came much earlier than Halas recalled, in the form of a letter to Sternaman dated August 9, 1925. In the letter Pyle requests a meeting to discuss "a tour that I am interested in arranging for Red Grange this winter or as soon as his season with Illinois is over." While the letter establishes Pyle's first contact with the Bears—which came even before the start of Grange's final season at Illinois—it doesn't specifically say that Pyle had yet approached Grange with his scheme. Most likely he had not. In any case, Sternaman and Halas responded positively to Pyle's inquiry and communicated with him until a final agreement was reached.

As far as Pyle was concerned, the Bears were the perfect team for Grange. The University of Illinois had a large following in the Chicago area and both Halas and Sternaman were well-known former Illinois players. For the two stars, having Grange on their roster was an answer to a prayer.

While Grange, Halas, Sternaman, and Pyle all stuck to their line that Grange had not signed any agreement until after his final Illinois game, newspaper accounts cast serious doubt over their story.

An Associated Press report dated November 17, three days before Illinois's finale against Ohio State, claimed that C. P. Albertson, a former "publicity agent" of Pyle's, had signed a statement that he had seen a contract signed by Grange that made Pyle his manager for three years.

The AP also reported that Pyle was negotiating with Miami promoters for a Christmas Day game with Grange as the headliner. The wire service also related that Tampa sportswriters were similarly shown a contract bearing Grange's signature, assigning to Pyle "all proposals the Illinois star might receive for post-season pro football games, and otherwise act in the capacity of manager."

Grange denied having signed any contract with Pyle or anyone else, and despite the AP reports, neither Illinois nor Ohio State showed any taste for an investigation with their "big Grange game" just three days away.

The day after the AP report, Grange said, "It would be a violation of the university's rules and until next Saturday's game is over, I'm going to be loyal to my school and give it everything I have." Perhaps tipping his hand a bit, Grange added, "After that game, I'll be ready to talk business." In a November 18 *Chicago Tribune* story, Grange vented: "Folks have said I got money for playing football at Illinois. That's all the bunk. The only money I got I earned working on an ice wagon in the summer and the rest my father has given me. . . . The whole situation is this: I'm going back to Illinois tomorrow and practice for the Ohio game. I'm going to play Saturday and play my best for the school. After that game I'm going to listen to these offers. Maybe I'll accept one of them."

Halas later acknowledged that Grange had "earlier" agreed to the concept of playing for the Bears, but insisted he hadn't signed a contract until the day after the big game and that he did so in his presence:

"In the morning, he [Grange] met with Pyle, Dutch and me in my room at the Morrison Hotel," Halas wrote. "Red signed a contract making Pyle his manager."

That much we know is true. However, the signing, conveniently attended by press photographers, was a staged event, created to provide worldwide attention and publicity for the launch of Grange's pro career.

Interestingly, Halas made no reference to Grange signing a contract with the Bears. That's because he didn't. The Bears deal was with Pyle, not Grange. So, one could argue that the Bears didn't violate the league pledge not to sign individuals still enrolled in college—Pyle did. In the end, it was just a matter of semantics. Grange was finally a pro. It was a big day for Grange, the Bears, and pro football.

As might be expected, not everyone was pleased with Grange's decision. Illinois coach Bob Zuppke publicly criticized his former player. But more surprising were the public remarks made by Grange's father. Lyle Grange told the *Chicago Herald and*

Examiner that he attempted to dissuade his son from turning pro right up until an hour before the announcement.

"I'd rather that my boy had agreed to something that would have enabled him to stay in school if that were possible," the elder Grange said. But that wasn't all he had to say. "I want to say here and now, though, that I want my boy to have nothing to do with that Pyle, and you can go as strong as you like about that."

Just five days after he bid adieu to intercollegiate football, Grange made his pro debut with the Bears, his manager in tow. It was Thanksgiving Day. A sellout crowd of 36,000 fans at Cubs Park, the largest gathering for a pro football game to date, saw the Chicago Cardinals hold Grange to just 36 yards rushing. However, a respectable 56 yards on punt returns and an interception near the Bears' goal line that stopped the Cardinals' most serious scoring threat were enough to please most in attendance. And while the game ended in a scoreless tie, Grange, Pyle, Halas, and Sternaman scored a touchdown at the box office.

The game contract, rewritten after Grange joined the squad, provided that the first $14,000 net after deduction of war tax and park rental was to be divided equally between the Bears and Cardinals. After that, Pyle and Grange took 35 percent of the net balance. The remaining 65 percent was then again divided between the Cardinals and Bears. Grange and Pyle netted a hefty $9,007.43, which they divided 60/40—Grange scoring the larger share. Not too shabby, considering the average annual income in the United States in 1925 was $1,236.

Three days after his pro debut, 28,000 fans returned to a snow-covered Cubs Park to watch Grange and the Bears defeat the Columbus Tigers 14–13. It should be noted that a good pre-Grange attendance for the Bears at home would have been in the 6,000–8,000 range.

Five games remained on the Bears' 1925 schedule. On December 5 they traveled to Philadelphia to play the Frankford Yellow Jackets. One day later it was the Giants in New York, and on December 9 they played the Providence Steam Roller in Boston. There was a final road game in Detroit on December 12 against the

Panthers, followed by a season-ending rematch with the Giants in Chicago.

Somehow over the years, this final leg of the Bears' regular season, in which all except the season finale were on the road, has been misconstrued as a hastily scheduled exhibition "barnstorming tour." The fact is, the final five league games were scheduled by the Bears before Grange joined the team.

What has confused historians is that before Grange "officially" joined the team, Pyle, Halas, and Sternaman went back to each of the Bears' remaining opponents, tipping them off as to what was in the works, and insisted on changes to their existing contracts. Not only did the Bears and Pyle receive a larger share of the gate, but two teams, the Yellow Jackets and the Steam Roller, were told to abandon their small-capacity playing fields and relocate to larger venues.

Anxious to reap the rewards of a "Grange game," all happily complied with the revenue and venue changes. The Yellow Jackets relocated from Frankford's wooden bleacher Legion Stadium to Philadelphia's Shibe Park, while the Steam Roller moved from the Cycledrome, a bicycle racing stadium, to Braves Field in Boston.

An interesting footnote regarding the Yellow Jackets is that the team was run by the Frankford Athletic Association, a community-based nonprofit organization of residents and businesses. All team profits were donated to local charities that included the Frankford Hospital, the Frankford Day Nursery, the local Boy Scouts, and the local American Legion Post 211.

Charity, however, was not a part of Pyle's plan. Looking to maximize his earning potential, he arranged to play three additional exhibition games against nonleague "All-Star" aggregations, in between their already scheduled league games. The Grange-led Bears played exhibition games in St. Louis on December 2, Washington, DC, on December 8, and Pittsburgh on December 10. The result was a grueling eight games in twelve days, with varying results.

The exhibition game in St. Louis drew just 5,000 fans on a bitterly cold day. But three days later, a sellout crowd of 33,500 came to Shibe Park and saw Grange score both of Chicago's touchdowns in their 14–7 win over Frankford. The relocation to Shibe proved lucrative for all parties. Yellow Jackets manager Shep Royle claimed there "were four demands for each seat."

For his work that day Grange earned another $17,835 for himself and his manager, while both the Bears and the Yellow Jackets management walked away with more than $23,000 each. But it was the next day, December 6, that Grange and the Chicago Bears really made out, not only for themselves but for the Giants and pro football in general.

In 1925, the other big NFL story was that the league had finally placed a team in New York City. Local bookmaker (a legal profession at the time) Tim Mara agreed to try his luck at running an NFL team in the Gotham City, even though he'd never even attended a pro game.

Mara's inaugural NFL season had been a struggle. While the team was drawing decent crowds, his franchise was awash in red ink. But then along came the Bears and "Red" Grange.

Although the Giants lost 19–7, it was a great day for Mara. The gate receipts for the record crowd, reported to be 70,000, not only turned his red ink black, it was enough to convince him that there was a future in the sport and that he should stay the course.

"There gathered at the Polo Grounds in Harlem yesterday afternoon," wrote famed writer Damon Runyon in the *New York American,* "the largest crowd that ever witnessed a football game on the Island of Manhattan, drawn by the publicity that has been given one individual—Red Grange, late of the University of Illinois."

Another newspaper reported that Grange "drew almost one hundred reporters from papers from as far West as St. Louis, to the Polo Grounds to cover his playing and send out the news to millions." Never had an NFL team or player received such attention. "Red Grange had done what nothing else—World Series or Army Navy games—had ever accomplished," claimed an astonished Tom Tierney, a Polo Grounds Association executive. "He bought out 75,000." The *San Francisco Examiner* added that the game "lifted the promoters of the professional pastime in that city out of a deep financial hole."

Tim Mara was fond of saying, "I founded the Giants on brute strength and great ignorance—my players' strength and my ignorance." As for the Grange game's impact, he was considerably more serious. "I was about ready to toss in my hand until Grange turned pro. He proved that pro football didn't have to be a losing proposition. That, more than anything else, kept me in football."

While the Grange game may have saved Mara's Giants and provided unprecedented positive exposure for the NFL, it came at a price for Grange. The Giants, like all the opponents Grange faced, were pumped up by the extra attention and were hell-bent on stopping the famous halfback. Grange later recalled that matchup as one of his "most bruising battles." While it sounds almost minor, a kick to the forearm caused some serious damage. And although he played in the next three games, the pain eventually became too much for Grange to bear. According to Halas, Grange's arm "grew to twice its normal size." Exhausted and battered, the Illinois star spent the final two games of the season on the bench with his injured arm in a splint.

The December 13 season finale, a 9–3 loss to the Giants in Chicago, concluded Grange's ten-game commitment to the Bears. For the Bears squad, it was the end of a marathon twenty-game season. But the fun wasn't over yet.

After a two-week rest-and-recovery period, Grange and the Bears were back on the road as the stars of Pyle's "barnstorming tour." The crafty promoter's original plan was to form his own "All-Star" team with Grange as his headliner. But clearly, having a ready-made team in the Bears made much more sense.

Since the tour games would be exhibitions and didn't require NFL opponents, Pyle, Halas, and Sternaman agreed to a single contract to simplify their relationship. The Bears' co-owners maintained their role as managers of the team and would receive 10 percent of the first $300,000 of net profits after expenses and 7.5 percent of anything over $300,000. The players, except for Grange, would receive their usual NFL game salaries.

While the deal certainly favored Pyle and Grange, it did put all the expenses, including player salaries, travel, and accommodations, in Pyle's column. The nine-game, five-week tour had the potential of earning the Bears' co-owners $30,000-plus and called for far less risk on their part. Just show up and play.

As speculated back when Grange was denying his arrangement with Pyle, the tour began on Christmas Day in Coral Gables, Florida, where the construction of a 30,000-seat wooden stadium was completed just two days before the game. Only 5,000 seats were needed. The Coral Gables disappointment was followed by games in Tampa and Jacksonville. A stop in New Orleans was followed by three games in California—Los Angeles, San Diego, and San Francisco—and a final two in Portland, Oregon, and Seattle, Washington.

Although most of the games drew less than expected, the Los Angeles game drew 75,000; Grange and the Bears defeated a team billed as the Los Angeles Tigers 17–7.

Two weeks later in San Francisco, 23,000 disappointed fans saw Grange carry the ball just seven times for 43 yards. Following the game, rumors surfaced that Pyle was behind on his payments to the players and that tensions were growing between the Bears and Pyle. One San Francisco newspaper suggested that Grange's lack of carries and how he was used was the Bears' way of expressing their frustration with Pyle and perhaps a little "Grange fatigue."

"Grange, as everyone knows, receives the lion's share of gate receipts, while the Chicago Bears receive a pittance for the effort," the newspaper reported. "The Chicago Bears, it seems, do not warm up to the idea of playing second ukulele, and a dispute is said to have arisen between its chiefs and 'Cash and Carry' Pyle, manager of Grange."

Whether there was friction or not, the tour ended in Oregon with two lopsided wins for the Bears. In both games, Grange's star shone brightly. It was a fitting end to a very long and personally trying season for the Illinois legend. "I'm glad I turned pro," he said, "but I'll be glad to quit."

For the Bears players, Grange turning "pro" provided each with an extra twelve paychecks. The team of Sternaman and Halas made out okay as well, each earning $45,000 in "salary and bo-nuses" while the team recorded a $14,675 profit.

In the end, "Cash and Carry" Pyle delivered on his promise to Red Grange. Even his father and Coach Zupke agreed on that point. "Twice during the tour Pyle gave Red a check for $50,000," reported Halas. "When the final accounting was made of receipts and royalties, Red received another $100,000. Red came to the Bears famous. Ten weeks later he was rich." One of the first things Grange did with his newfound wealth was purchase a house for his father.

CHAPTER 5

FEBRUARY FALLOUT

WHEN JOE CARR STOOD BEFORE THE NFL CLUB owners gathered for their winter meeting at the Hotel Statler in Detroit on February 6, 1926, he knew he was facing a tough crowd. The NFL's sixth season had been a roller-coaster ride and the owners wanted some answers.

Carr began with the good news, which could be summarized in two words: "Red Grange."

His arrival had been controversial, Carr said, but "I am firmly convinced the net result has been in favor of our organization. Thousands upon thousands of people were attracted to their first game of professional football through a curiosity to see Grange in action, and many became profound advocates."

But there was some equally bad news to report:

"Just when it seemed our organization had gone fairly well toward its goal last season," Carr said, "two events happened that threatened the very foundation from under our league."

The first event—of which the owners were aware—involved a game in which the Milwaukee Badgers allowed four high school boys to play a game against the Chicago Cardinals.

The second problem, he said, was that, despite his direct orders, the Pottsville, Pennsylvania, Maroons had "invaded" another club's territory and played a non-NFL team.

To fully appreciate the gravity of Carr's pronouncements, it is important to understand why and how they occurred. While the events are in one respect unrelated, in another they are inexorably intertwined. It's a latter-day Tale of Two Cities that began on December 6 of the previous year.

The Pottsville Maroons were a first-year NFL team, sporting an impressive 9-2-0 record when they traveled to Chicago on that December day to play Chris O'Brien's 9-1-1 Cardinals. Intoxicated by their team's success, Maroons fans were already calling their team the best in the land. But O'Brien wasn't intimidated by the Maroons or their assertive fans. The veteran Cardinals manager knew he too had a good team, perhaps his best, led by triple-threat back Paddy Driscoll, a future Hall of Famer.

In addition to faith in his team, something else reinforced O'Brien's confidence—the Maroons' schedule. The Cardinals' manager believed Pottsville's winning record was inflated by home-game wins over travel-weary opponents in not exactly tip-top shape.

It was an accurate assessment. Eight of the Maroons' nine wins were home games, six of which were against teams that had one day earlier played the Frankford (Philadelphia) Yellow Jackets. A seventh home-game win came against a weak, travel-weary Rochester Jeffersons team that had played the Giants in New York four days earlier. And an eighth was against the similarly exhausted Packers, who had been manhandled by the Bears 21–0 four days earlier in Chicago.

In addition to playing beat-up teams, Pottsville played only two games on the road, a 34–0 win over the Providence Steam Roller and a 20–0 loss to the Frankford Yellow Jackets.

This competitive advantage was for the most part the unintended but fortunate—at least for Pottsville—result of blue laws that prohibited teams from playing on Sundays in Frankford. After playing the tough Yellow Jackets on Saturdays, worn-down teams, motivated by a second payday in as many days, would travel the hundred or so miles to Pottsville, where there were no blue laws, and play the Maroons.

O'Brien was sure his Cardinals would beat a team he considered false contenders and thereby finish atop the league standings, increasing his team's appeal for a season-ending game with the Chicago Bears and Red Grange. Unfortunately for the overconfident Cardinals manager, the Maroons were as good as advertised. They defeated O'Brien's team 21–7.

Suddenly the 10-2-0 Maroons were ahead of the 9-2-1 Cardinals in the standings and had become a potentially more appealing opponent for that lucrative season-ender with the Grange-led Bears.

What followed was a series of events that illustrate the allure of scheduling a game with the headline-grabbing, gate-receipt-growing Grange.

On December 8, two days after his team's loss to Pottsville, O'Brien sensed his window of opportunity closing. He sent a telegram to Bears owners George Halas and Dutch Sternaman, challenging them to a December 20 season-ending game. The *Chicago Tribune,* likely alerted by O'Brien, reported that the Cardinals boss had already scheduled a Saturday game against the Hammond Pros, "and believes his team will win, thereby getting on even terms with the Pottsville outfit and making it desirable that the Bears meet the southsiders for the title."

Now, the title decision referred to by the *Tribune* was not between the Cardinals and the Bears, but between the Cardinals and the Maroons. The Bears were merely the "kingmakers." If the Bears won, the Maroons were champs, but if the Cardinals won, they would reign.

The next day, O'Brien pulled out all the stops, upping the ante by scheduling an additional Thursday game against the Milwaukee Badgers.

But no sooner had he announced his second game than O'Brien received a telegram from the Bears management confirming his worst fear:

"Have opportunity to play Pottsville at Cubs Park, Dec. twenty," the Western Union notice read. "On what basis will you play us in Cubs Park on that date. Wire Hotel Schenley Pittsburgh tonight." Hoping the window wasn't completely shut, O'Brien responded immediately:

"Am playing Milwaukee Thursday and Hammond Saturday," he wired. "If we win both games will lead league race."

Obviously trying everything he could to secure the season-ending game, he threw in this nugget: "Would toss coin to settle place to play—terms would be three-way split of net—saw Pyle today told him same. He was in favor of Sox Park."

O'Brien's last best-shot effort suggested that Grange's manager, who got an equal share of the Bears' gate, favored the game and believed the Chicago-versus-Chicago affair would require the larger White Sox Park.

It was a good plan. Officially the league schedule ran until December 20. The final two weeks were intended to be a period when teams still in contention—such as the Cardinals and the Maroons—would schedule games to settle the championship race. Teams no longer in contention usually packed it in before the two-week scramble got under way—unless they were lucky enough to be an opponent. It was a flawed system, no question. But it was league law.

It was during this season-ending scramble that the story broke of the Milwaukee Badgers' use of four high school boys. It seems Milwaukee manager Ambrose McGurk was unable to assemble enough of his recently disbanded squad to play in the hastily scheduled game. Rather than withdraw and lose his guarantee, McGurk, with an assist from a Cardinals player named Art Folz, secured the four high school boys as last-minute additions.

The high school player scandal broke almost immediately after the game. O'Brien insisted he'd only learned of the four boys just before kickoff and hoped they'd go unnoticed. But within days, the four Englewood High School students were banished from further athletic competition.

A week later, a remorseful O'Brien offered an apology in the *Chicago Tribune* as well as his explanation of why and what transpired.

"No one is as sorry over what happened to these four Englewood High School boys as I am," O'Brien said. The Cardinals manager also admitted "selfishness" on his part, offering that he hadn't experienced a very good year and had hoped that another game with the Bears and Grange might reverse his fortunes.

O'Brien acknowledged that he expected to beat Pottsville in their December 6 game, but was quick to cite the league rules regarding end-of-season scheduling.

"According to our rules," he explained, "any team can schedule games up until December 20 and they count in the standing. I was only half a game behind. The Bears were scheduling lots of extra games. I thought of McGurk, the manager of the Milwaukee team. He lived in Chicago and I hunted him up. I suggested a Thursday game and he was willing."

O'Brien wondered out loud if McGurk would "come through with a team all right." He said that one of his players, Folz, said that "he could pick up some extra players if some were needed."

"I paid no more attention to it," O'Brien said, claiming he believed McGurk would "put a legitimate team on the field."

O'Brien acknowledged that shortly before the game, Folz arrived with four players. Although he admitted that he may have been introduced to them before the game, he said he was not made aware of their high school status.

"Just before the game I learned there were high school amateurs on the Milwaukee team," O'Brien said. "Now I know the mistake I made was not cancelling the game right then." Citing the fact that there were several hundred fans in attendance and that "things were moving fast," O'Brien said he just didn't take time to think it out carefully. "Anyway," he said, "I didn't stop it."

O'Brien closed his apology to the fans by offering a final measure of repentance.

"Naturally, I wish to do anything about it I can to square those schoolboys," he said. "I have always tried to give the public square football. I am willing to do anything to save those schoolboys and put professional football in the right light."

Folz also offered his explanation of the events to the *Tribune* and attempted to take the lion's share of responsibility. "Those boys were blameless in the affair," he wrote. "So was Chris O'Brien. I made the big mistake."

O'Brien never said he wanted to win the NFL championship. His primary motivation for the late games was to make his team the most desirable opponent for a lucrative season-ending game against the Grange-led Bears.

As things turned out, all of O'Brien's maneuverings were for naught. An arm injury suffered earlier by Grange worsened and his season was over, and so too was O'Brien's hope for a big payday.

As for Pottsville, their violation was also rooted in the desire for a big end-of-season payday. Riding high on their league-leading status, Pottsville manager Dr. J. G. Striegel agreed to play an exhibition game on December 12 in Philadelphia's Shibe Park. His Maroons would play a team of former Notre Dame All-Stars that included the famous "Four Horsemen."

The Pottsville–Notre Dame All-Stars game had the potential to be almost as financially rewarding as one against Grange and the Bears. But there was a problem. Shibe Park was within the protected territory of the Frankford Yellow Jackets. The ink had hardly dried on the contract between Striegel and the game promoter before Yellow Jackets manager Shep Royle filed a protest with league president Carr.

Frankford's objection, though legitimate, had a "spoil sport" aspect to it as well. When the contract to bring the Notre Damers to Shibe Park was signed by the game's promoter, the Yellow Jackets fully expected to be the host team. Instead the Maroons, with their newfound fame as the leading contender for the NFL title, were offered the game. In a move partly designed to further substantiate his invasion claim, Royle scheduled a game in his home venue, the neighboring Frankford Stadium, for the same day against the 1924 NFL champion Cleveland Bulldogs. It was something he had every right to do, and under normal circumstances he would have likely drawn a very good crowd.

No one understood the importance of a protected home territory better than Carr. It was one of the main reasons a team would purchase a franchise in the NFL. Alarmed by Pottsville's actions, Carr acted swiftly, warning Striegel on three occasions not to play, "under all penalties that the league could inflict." Striegel ignored

Carr's warnings, citing concerns of potential legal liabilities if the Maroons didn't play in the heavily promoted game.

While Pottsville defeated the All-Stars, 9–7, only 8,000 fans attended. The game was a financial flop. Across town, at Frankford Stadium, the Bulldogs defeated the Yellow Jackets, 3–0, before another disappointing crowd of 8,000—about half of what the popular team normally drew at home.

Nearly three weeks later, after a thorough investigation, Carr announced that he had "dealt out the limits" of punitive actions allowed by the league's bylaws.

For using the high school boys, the Milwaukee Club was fined $500 and sent McGurk packing. Carr gave him ninety days from January 1 "to dispose of his assets at Milwaukee after which he must retire from the League."

As for the Cardinals, Carr said he could find no clear evidence that O'Brien had "guilty knowledge" of the presence of the boys until it was too late. Nonetheless, he fined O'Brien $1,000 and placed the team on probation for one year. Also, the Milwaukee game was stricken from the records, although for some inexplicable reason it's still included in *The Official NFL Record & Fact Book*.

That same day, Doc Striegel received his bad-news telegram from Carr. Striegel was fined $500, the team was suspended from all rights and privileges, and his franchise was forfeited to the league.

Even though he was forewarned, the Maroons' Striegel was taken aback by the severity of his punishment. Insisting he hadn't been given a fair hearing, he and his brother traveled to Carr's office in Columbus and pleaded with him to reconsider.

While Carr declared that he wouldn't back down from his decision, he relented to the degree that he would submit the matter to the owners for their review at the league's February 6 winter meeting.

True to his word, following his end-of-year report, Carr left open the opportunity for the owners to reconsider his actions. But not before he made one brief remark.

"While the penalties that were imposed on those who violated our rules seemed severe, nevertheless I felt that in many cases in our league, immense sums of money have been invested and still greater will be expended," he said. "The only protection this money has is the protection that your officers give it through the enforcement of the rules, and if the clubs feel that the rules may be broken with impunity and are permitted to do it, then, the history of the National Football League is already written."

Carr looked to his audience for a reaction. No further discussion was needed. The uncharacteristically quiet owners moved to accept the President's Report; his decisions were unanimously upheld.

As stirring as Carr's closing remarks were, there was still more drama to play out at the winter meeting. For one thing, the league championship had to be awarded.

A motion was made to award the championship to the Chicago Cardinals, who, even without the disallowed Milwaukee game, had the best record. However, O'Brien, still stinging from the Milwaukee fiasco and humbled by his one-year probation, indicated he wouldn't accept the honor.

The owners were caught off guard by O'Brien's response. After discussion and debate, they considered an amendment that "there be no championship awarded in the league and that the money be spent on the next championship." After more discussion, both the motion to award the title to the Cardinals and the amendment that there be no champion were withdrawn.

Who won the title was a matter only the owners could collectively decide. And since no other club stepped forward to stake its claim for the title, the Cardinals were awarded the 1925 title—whether O'Brien accepted it or not.

The owners also had to contend with the maneuverings of Grange's manager, C. C. Pyle, who wanted to claim a franchise for New York City. Another contentious issue.

Emboldened by the success of the "Grange Tour," Pyle demanded that Halas and Sternaman agree to change their ownership agreement. Pyle would get a one-third ownership share and a five-figure salary for Grange. When the Bears' owners balked, Pyle countered by signing a lease to play in Yankee Stadium. Then, just days before the NFL's February meeting, Pyle announced that he and Grange had applied for a New York franchise of their own. Naturally, Giants owner Tim Mara took issue with the plan.

"I have control of Greater New York and all territory within five miles of the outer city limits," Mara told reporters. "If Grange comes in here it will be as an outlaw. The league is solidly behind me." Again, as was the case with Pottsville playing in Frankford's protected territory, Mara was completely within his right to block the application.

Pyle was both surprised and disappointed. The blustery promoter then claimed that while the rest of the league supported his application, Mara had single-handedly blocked it.

"The story that nineteen clubs voted in favor of the admission of his team and I was alone in opposing Grange is false," Mara responded. "The matter never came before the league for a vote. No franchise can come up for a vote unless it is sanctioned by the club who already holds that territory. In Grange's case I applied my sanction and explained my reasons. They didn't need explaining. Everybody knew I was right."

While some owners were truly anxious to capitalize on Grange's popularity, they realized a team's "territorial rights" were more important than a fast buck. Territorial rights, a critical provision of the league's bylaws, now had been defended and affirmed twice at the same meeting. It was a major victory for Carr and the NFL.

Apparently, when Pyle was given the bad news, things between him and Mara got heated. According to one observer, "Pyle's chin narrowly missed a massaging."

Infuriated by his rejection, but with his chin still in place, Pyle took a new approach. If you can't join 'em, beat 'em. Within days of his rejection, "Cash and Carry" announced the formation of his own league, which he named the American Football League.

Pyle's hastily formed AFL included his New York franchise and franchises in Philadelphia, Cleveland, Chicago, Boston, Brooklyn, Newark, and a traveling team based out of Chicago, called the Los Angeles Wild Cats or Wilson's Wildcats, in recognition of the team's popular All-American captain from the University of Washington, George "Wild Cat" Wilson.

In a surprise move, the NFL's Rock Island Independents jumped to the new league. Apparently no one on the NFL side was too upset. "He [Pyle] took over the loquacious gentleman from Rock Island, which was good riddance of bad rubbish," wrote former Giants secretary Harry March in his 1934 book, *Pro Football: Its Ups and Downs.*

Pyle also tried to convince O'Brien to bring his Cardinals into the fold. When O'Brien passed, Pyle offered Bears quarterback Joey Sternaman—Dutch's kid brother—an opportunity to become owner, coach, and quarterback of the AFL's Chicago Bulls franchise. It was an offer too good to refuse, and Sternaman jumped leagues.

While the younger Sternaman's defection hurt the Bears, when he secured the rights to Comiskey Park, it almost destroyed the Cardinals. O'Brien was left to play in Normal Park, a run-down high school stadium. Already in debt, the Cardinals' owner was forced to sell his star player, Paddy Driscoll, to the Bears for $3,000 just to keep his franchise solvent. Though Driscoll was a more than adequate replacement for Sternaman, the price Halas paid for his services was no doubt inflated to help his friend O'Brien during his time of need.

Even in the face of financial ruin, O'Brien was unflappable. "We have most of the high-class stars under contract and a war chest on which to draw," he said of the NFL. "If the newcomers think they can break in without a fight, they are welcome to try it."

"Chris O'Brien stuck to the old league when every possible financial inducement was made to have him desert to the new outlaws," wrote March. "His loyalty and stability under the stress, in my opinion, have never been thoroughly appreciated by the team owners or the public."

The controversy had its various victims. Furious at Joey Sternaman's exodus from the Bears, Halas openly accused his partner, Dutch Sternaman, of plotting to join his brother as a co-owner of the Bulls. Although the elder Sternaman denied any such intention,

Halas was convinced his partner's loyalties were with his younger brother, not the Bears. Accusations and denials flew and the bond that once existed between the two began to irreparably deteriorate.

While the AFL initially looked to be serious competition in some NFL cities, the league's wartime strategy was to fight the football neophytes head-on. Whether coincidental or intentional, at that same February meeting, the league owners voted to expand roster sizes from sixteen to eighteen and to increase league membership from twenty teams to twenty-two, including a team in Brooklyn that had been blessed by Mara. The NFL's Brooklyn team scored an early victory by securing a contract for Ebbets Field while the AFL's entry played in a dilapidated fenced lot "way out at the loose end of some otherwise unexplored subway line," according to the *Chicago Tribune*.

By the end of October, three AFL teams—Newark, Cleveland, and Brooklyn—had folded. And by season's end, only New York, Philadelphia, Chicago, and the traveling Los Angeles teams were still standing. Pyle was underwriting three of them.

In a last-ditch effort to salvage something from the disastrous season, the AFL champion Philadelphia Quakers challenged the NFL's champion Frankford Yellow Jackets to a world championship game. The Yellow Jackets saw no reason to reward its neighboring rival and immediately declined the invitation. But, in a surprising move, Mara agreed to allow his seventh-place Giants team to meet the Quakers at the Polo Grounds.

Not surprisingly, the mediocre Giants clobbered the Quakers 31–0, and in so doing, delivered a knockout punch to the AFL and Pyle's competitive chin. Although Mara was later slapped on the wrist for playing the game, most of his fellow owners offered him a wink of the eye and an approving slap on the back.

CHAPTER 6

REDUCED, UNDER LIGHTS, AND INDOORS

AFTER SEVEN SEASONS OF A SEEMINGLY OPEN-door policy for new franchises, managers of the "ruling clubs" of the NFL realized that the time had come to end their laissez-faire system. It was also time to consider cutting loose the league's financially struggling second-tier teams.

The NFL tables had turned. No longer were the league's marquee teams located in smaller cities like Akron or Canton. Pro football and its star players were transitioning to the big cities. Larger-market teams, like Chicago, New York, and Philadelphia, were reluctant to schedule the struggling clubs, since they were no longer much of an attendance draw. And they weren't going to travel to cities and towns with small venues that couldn't equal the gate receipts of the stronger clubs.

Aaron Hertzman, former owner of the Louisville Brecks, summarized the shift in a 1961 letter to his old friend Leo Lyons, the former owner of the Rochester Jeffersons.

> *The majority of present owners know nothing of the hardships Joe Carr went through in finding new clubs each year, most of which lasted only one season, but they did contribute dues and assessments, which were essential to the continuance of the league until it finally got on its own feet. The three or four or five games they filled in the schedules of the ruling clubs enabled the league to keep going.*

Hertzman's assessment was spot-on. As major-market teams developed their own fan base, signed collegiate stars, and developed rivalries with other major-market teams, the weaker small-market teams simply couldn't compete.

At the league's 1927 winter meeting, Carr appointed a committee to develop a plan to reorganize the unwieldy twenty-two-team league. Their initial recommendation: create "Class A" and "Class B" leagues. It resembled Carr's earlier idea of major and minor leagues.

However, the "Class B" teams—Akron, Canton, Columbus, Dayton, Hammond, Hartford, Louisville, Racine, Rochester, and Minneapolis—said they'd accept the recommendation only if the league bought back their $2,500 application fees.

Unwilling to pay, and unable to find an acceptable alternative, the committee turned to Carr for a solution.

It was an arduous task. After all, he'd recruited or championed most of the now-struggling teams, including his own Columbus Panhandles. Worse, several of the managers were longtime friends. At a special meeting in late April, he unveiled his tough-love plan.

Franchise holders could either withdraw from the league with a prorated share of "any money in the League Treasury," or suspend operations for the upcoming season without payment of membership dues.

A "suspended" club could sell any player's contract up until the start of the season, providing the team then disbanded. Also, no new franchises that year would be added unless all those suspended franchises had been sold or canceled. And—to protect the interests of the remaining clubs—a suspended club could sell its franchise only to someone "voted on favorably by the League."

Carr's proposal was accepted and the managers agreed to meet again in July, at which time each club would declare their intent. At that meeting, eleven clubs—Buffalo, Cleveland, Chicago Bears, Chicago Cardinals, Dayton, Duluth, Frankford (Philadelphia), Green Bay, New York, Pottsville, and Providence—deposited the necessary fee. The others withdrew.

Pottsville, it should be noted, had been conditionally reinstated prior to the start of the 1926 season. It was a move to keep the team from joining the rival AFL. In 1929 the team moved to Boston, where it played one season as the "Bulldogs" before folding for good.

A surprise addition was made following the July reorganizational meeting. A twelfth franchise was added, but as per the agreement, it was not a new franchise. Tim Mara agreed to transfer the Brooklyn franchise, which he held in lieu of debt from the previous owner, to none other than C. C. Pyle. While Mara agreed to sell the franchise to his old nemesis, Pyle agreed his New York Yankees team would operate primarily as a road team.

Still, the NFL's franchise version of "musical chairs" wasn't over. As the Roaring Twenties gave way to the Great Depression, league membership dropped in 1929 to ten franchises, and then to a record low of eight in 1932.

One of the Depression casualties was the Providence Steam Roller. Although Providence won the 1928 NFL championship—the last team not currently in the NFL to win a title—the economic downturn was too much for the team's ownership, so following the 1931 season the team ceased operations.

While only a league member for seven seasons, the Steam Roller will be remembered as a major part of a significant NFL "first." On November 6, 1929, Providence hosted the Chicago Cardinals in the NFL's first night game.

The historic game was originally scheduled to be played five days after the October 29 stock market crash. But Providence was suddenly forced to cancel. It wasn't the crash that caused the cancellation, it was a heavy rainstorm that made the Steam Roller's home field unplayable. Providence played at the Cycledrome, a 10,000-seat bicycle-racing stadium. With neither team wanting to miss a payday, the teams agreed to play three days later, on Wednesday night, at Kinsley Park Stadium, a minor-league baseball facility in nearby Pawtucket.

To make the game possible, additional stadium lights were needed. The *Providence Journal* described the new lighting system as "33 giant projectors on poles 53 feet high, and nine poles on top of the grandstand." Electricians reportedly worked through the day of the game, "stringing wires and hanging additional lights."

"Nobody thought we could pull it off," Pearce Johnson, the team's longtime manager, said in an interview many years later. And although "the end zones were dark and there was a long dark stripe down the middle of the field," he said he was satisfied with the results.

The ball was painted white to help make it more visible. One newspaper compared it to an egg and joked that there was a "panicky feeling that the player who made the catch would be splattered with yellow yolk."

While the field was lit, it was Cardinals fullback Ernie Nevers who lit up the scoreboard. The future Hall of Famer accounted for all his team's points in their 16–0 shutout win over the Steam Roller. Nevers threw a 45-yard touchdown pass, kicked a 23-yard field goal, and ran for another touchdown. He also added one point after touchdown.

But as impressive as his scoring frenzy was, it wouldn't be the only time that season Nevers scored all his team's points. Three weeks later, the versatile fullback scored 19 points—three touchdowns and an extra point—in a 19–0 win over the Dayton Triangles. Then, just four days later, on Thanksgiving Day, he set the longest-standing all-time individual NFL record when he scored 40 points—six rushing touchdowns and four extra points—in a 40–6 victory over the Bears.

Even though Nevers stole the show, the NFL's first night game was, according to Johnson, "a huge success." Six thousand fans, 1,500 more than the average, were witness to history. "We went ahead and had permanent lights installed," Johnson bragged.

While the night game may not have had an immediate impact on pro football, it did have an impact on the Steam Roller players. Beginning in 1930 they were paid $125 "for all league daylight games and sixty percent of that sum for all league floodlight games."

Johnson explained that the pay reduction was "to help pay the installation costs of the floodlights." Hard to imagine players agreeing to such a provision today.

+ + +

WHILE RAIN was the spark that led to the NFL's first night game, it was snow and freezing temperatures in Chicago that precipitated another game shift and three important rules changes.

On a frigid afternoon on December 11, the Bears defeated the Packers 9–0 in their season finale. The game ended the Packers' three-year reign as NFL champions. But, more important, it meant that the Bears at 6-1-6 were tied with the 6-1-4 Portsmouth Spartans for league honors. (Tied games weren't factored in when considering a team's winning percentage.) While ending the season tied for first place was good news for Halas, the poorly attended game presented a problem.

"Lee, I'm out of chalk," he told Green Bay president Lee Joannes when it came time to pay the $2,500 game guarantee. Fortunately, Joannes was a friend and sympathetic to Halas's cash flow dilemma.

"It had snowed heavily in Chicago," Joannes recalled. "The result was very slim attendance. Halas gave me $1,000 and a note for $1,500."

The next year when the Bears traveled to Green Bay, Halas instructed Joannes to take the $1,500 out of the Bears' game guarantee. Instead Joannes simply marked the note "paid in full."

"Halas did much more than pay me back," Joannes said later of his old friend.

Relieved by Joannes's patience, Halas huddled up with Carr and Spartans president Harry Snyder to resolve the season-ending tie between the two teams. They decided the teams would play an extra game to determine the league champion. It would not be a postseason game, but an additional regular-season game, and would count in the standings. The winner would be declared NFL champion.

Carr, wanting to make certain that a victor emerged, declared that should the game end in a tie, a ten-minute overtime period would be played. It was the NFL's first overtime provision. Now all that was left to decide was where to play the game.

The city of Portsmouth had been hit hard by the Depression and the projected attendance for an extra game was, to say the least, worrisome. Discussions of a neutral site didn't pan out, either. Playing another game in the Windy City in mid-December was equally concerning. The solution? Move the game to Chicago Stadium, an indoor civic arena designed for large events. Built in 1929, it had already served as the site for both the Democratic and Republican national conventions in 1932 and was the home of the National Hockey League's Chicago Blackhawks.

Novel as the solution sounds today, it wasn't the first time the Bears had played there. Two years earlier they'd played the Chicago Cardinals in an exhibition charity game.

Having already played a game in Chicago Stadium made it easier for both teams to agree that the indoor venue was the right decision. The *Chicago Tribune* concurred:

"The decision to bring the Bears and Spartans indoors from the snowy wastes of Wrigley Field was more in the interest of the spectators than the players," the *Tribune* said. The newspaper acknowledged the financial wisdom of the move, too. "After all, professional football is a business," it said.

As Halas was aware, the arena was not quite large enough for a full-sized football field. Modifications had to be made. The football field was reduced to 80 yards long and 145 feet wide, with shallow half-moon-shaped end zones.

A temporary playing surface—a combination of tanbark mulch and dirt—was trucked in. A popular after-dinner yarn had it that a circus performed in the arena a few days earlier and that the tanbark and dirt combination included animal manure. Although a guaranteed laugh-getter, the truth was that the circus performed one week later.

Rules modifications for the game included the assessment of a 20-yard setback for both teams to be enforced sometime before reaching midfield to "make possible a regulation drive for a touchdown." Kickoffs were made from the 10-yard line and touchbacks were returned to the 10-yard line. Additionally, the ball was moved in fifteen yards from the sidelines following an out-of-bounds play (normally, it was brought in only one yard), but the agreed-upon move would also come with a loss of down. The inbounds move was made necessary by the wooden hockey dasher boards that encircled the field.

Although punting was allowed, no attempts to score from the field by placekicks or dropkicks were permitted. Only one set of goalposts was used, and it was placed on the goal line, not at the end line.

Interestingly, the kicking ban wasn't the result of ceiling height or any other physical limitation. It was a pickup of a restriction put in place for the 1930 indoor game.

"The scoring weapon," it was reported in the *Chicago Tribune*, "has been ruled out due to the lack of wind and weather conditions which make field goals difficult to accomplish in outdoor football."

One reporter sarcastically suggested, however, that punting should have been restricted. "Players standing on their own goal lines punted into the other team's end zone all evening," he wrote. "Punts from the middle of the field landed in the mezzanine, balcony and adjacent territory. One kick knocked the 'Bl' out of the Black Hawks' hockey sign."

Another scribe compared his sideline seat experience to attending a boxing match. "It was the difference between sitting ringside at a heavyweight fight or in the last row of the upper deck; all the awful sounds of human beings smashing other human beings were right there and very real."

A big part of the pregame hype, besides the unusual venue, was that the game would feature a matchup between the Bears' Red Grange and the Spartans' triple-threat quarterback Dutch Clark.

Unfortunately for the Spartans, Clark was summoned at the last minute back to Colorado College to resume his job as head basketball coach.

Despite losing their star player, the Spartans contained the Bears for three quarters. In fact, neither team scored until the game's final quarter. Then Chicago halfback Dick Nesbitt intercepted a pass from Spartan fullback Ace Gutowsky and returned it ten yards before being knocked out of bounds at Portsmouth's seven-yard line.

As the new rule provided, the ball was moved in ten yards but at the cost of a down. So, on second down, Bears fullback Bronko

Nagurski plowed six yards to the Spartans' one. But on the next play he was dropped for a one-yard loss. Facing a fourth and two, it was Nagurski again. This time he faked his patented straight-ahead line plunge and instead backed up a few steps, then fired a pass to Red Grange in the end zone for a Bears touchdown.

Or was it?

"I lined up as usual four yards back," recalled Nagurski. "Red went in motion. The ball came to me. I took a step or two forward as though to begin the plunge everyone expected. The defenders converged, doubling up on the line to stop me. There was no way through. I stopped. I moved back a couple steps. Grange had gone around the end and was in the end zone all by himself. I threw him a short pass."

Grange remembered his touchdown grab with a little more flavor than Nagurski's matter-of-fact account:

"Actually, I was on my back," he recalled. "Someone had knocked me down. But I got the ball and hung on to it."

The rule book back then stipulated that a forward pass could be thrown only from five or more yards behind the line of scrimmage. Immediately after Grange nestled the pigskin into his chest, Spartans coach Potsy Clark accosted the game official, screaming that Nagurski wasn't the required distance behind the line. The official politely disagreed. The touchdown stood. The Bears kicked the extra point for a 7–0 lead. In the final minute of play the Bears added a safety, giving them a 9–0 victory and their first title since 1921.

"It wasn't like the Super Bowl is today," recalled Spartans half-back Glenn Presnell. "It counted in the standings and we got our regular per-game salary. I got $175 and was happy to get it during the Depression."

The indoor game inspired three important rules changes: 1) the ball was to be moved in ten yards from the sidelines after going out of bounds, but without costing the team a loss of down; 2) the goalposts were moved from the end line to the goal line to increase scoring from the field; 3) and most important, the forward pass was allowed from anywhere behind the line of scrimmage.

The chairman of the committee that crafted the rules changes was Halas, then a veteran of two indoor games.

At that same meeting, George Preston Marshall, who joined the NFL that year as owner of the Boston Braves (now Washington Redskins), cited the "playoff atmosphere" of the indoor game, urging his fellow owners to reorganize into Eastern and Western divisions to include a postseason championship game. Carr, who'd worked toward that end for more than a decade, just smiled. The tireless visionary didn't seek credit and would have deflected it had it been offered. Besides, he was already working on his next big dream.

While attending a minor-league baseball meeting in Minneapolis earlier that winter, Carr learned of plans for a new municipal fieldhouse. He offered his advice to the attending newspapermen. "If they only knew how near our football league is to moving indoors, and what a smashing success we are going to make of the pro game under cover, they would not hesitate for a moment to spend the additional money needed to size the building up to the requirements of that game."

In 2016, the Minnesota Vikings opened their second stadium, designed for the "pro game under cover."

CHAPTER 7

TELEVISION DEBUTS

W HEN THE 1939 NFL SCHEDULE WAS FINALIZED, the Brooklyn Dodgers' October 22 game against the Philadelphia Eagles looked pretty much like any other game on the schedule. But in hindsight, it was more than that—it was a Hollywood movie in the making.

The setting was Brooklyn's Ebbets Field, a stadium best known as the home of baseball's Dodgers. The popular baseball cathedral was located roughly thirty minutes by public transport from Flushing Meadows Park in Queens, where atop a former coal ash dump site sat the newly constructed 1939 New York World's Fair. What's that got to do with this all-but-forgotten Dodgers-Eagles football game? As it turns out, everything.

Billed as the "Dawn of a New Day," the New York World's Fair was the brainchild of a group of prominent businessmen, bankers, and politicians looking for a way to help lift their city and maybe even the country out of the Great Depression. Even though several other countries participated, the futuristic fair was largely a showcase for new products and emerging technologies of American industry, rather than serious presentation of science inquiry.

One of the exposition's many "space-age" eye-openers was "Electro," a seven-foot-tall, walking, talking, cigarette-smoking robot that mesmerized attentive audiences at the Westinghouse Pavilion.

But even more amazing was another "scientific marvel" at the nearby RCA Pavilion—a marvel that would make history.

RCA president David Sarnoff chose the World's Fair to formally introduce his company's "future is now" product: television. Most people found it astonishing. But to a minority, it appeared to be a hoax, something comparable to a popular movie of the day.

You'll remember how Dorothy and her friends first reacted to the floating image of the "great and powerful Oz" in the classic 1939 film *The Wizard of Oz*. And who could forget how Dorothy's dog, Toto, shattered their sense of wonderment when he pulled back the curtain and exposed the unimpressive little man behind it.

So, to protect against such skepticism, RCA's "Wizard" let his audience "look behind the curtain." One of the several television sets in the pavilion had a translucent case so all the internal components could be seen. Sarnoff also positioned a camera to capture live images of the astonished visitors as they gazed at the TV sets. Visitors were given a card certifying that they had been "Televised at the RCA Building." No wizardry here, just science.

RCA and broadcasting partner NBC also used the World's Fair to announce a pro football first—live broadcasts of NFL games in Ebbets Field.

All Brooklyn Dodgers home games, beginning with their game against the Philadelphia Eagles on October 22, would be "televised" by NBC's experimental station W2XBS, broadcast back to the RCA Pavilion and then to the two hundred or so TV sets scattered throughout the New York metropolitan area.

You might expect this to have been big news. But that wasn't the case. Although NBC issued a brief press release confirming the time and date of the game, it got little attention from the press and even less from the teams involved.

The big story that week was the heartwarming news that two thousand children from eleven New York–area orphanages would attend the game as guests of Dodgers owner Dan Topping. But even with all those very special and undoubtedly appreciative guests, only 13,051 fans showed up at Ebbets Field that day. Few if any knew they were a part of pro football and television history.

As for the game, the *Brooklyn Daily Eagle* described it as having some "spectacular stuff."

Dodgers quarterback and future Hall of Famer Ace Parker hit on 8 of his 19 passing attempts, including one that traveled "close to 50 yards in the air" before landing in the arms of end Perry Schwartz for a touchdown. Halfback-kicker Ralph Kercheval added to the excitement by turning in a career performance booting three long field goals, including a then-record 44-yarder.

Eagles halfback Fran Murray scored on a short sweep while end Bill Hewitt, who famously played without a helmet, caught a touchdown pass from the diminutive but dangerous five-foot-seven Davey O'Brien.

But in the end, the day belonged to the home team Dodgers as they plastered the Eagles 23–14.

But even in the celebratory notes of New York sports scribes, there was no mention of the game having been "televised." And apparently none of the players were aware of their role in pro football history, either.

"I didn't know about it," Parker told pro football historian Jim Campbell in a 1975 interview. Teammate Bruiser Kinard, a future Hall of Fame tackle, agreed. "I certainly wasn't aware of it. That sure is interesting."

The broadcast was plagued with problems. Allen Walz, a former New York City Golden Gloves champion and New York University football star, was the announcer for the little-watched affair.

"It was late in October on a cloudy day and when the sun crept behind the stadium there wasn't enough light for the cameras," he told Campbell. "The picture would get darker and darker and eventually it would be completely blank and we'd revert to a radio broadcast."

Conditions were primitive to say the least:

"We used two iconoscope cameras. I'd sit with my chin on the rail in the mezzanine and the camera would be over my shoulder. I did my own spotting and when the play moved up and down the field, on punts and kickoffs, I'd point to tell the cameraman what I'd be talking about and we used hand signals to communicate. The other camera was on the field, at the 50-yard line, but it couldn't move so we didn't use it much."

Despite those conditions, Walz had an inkling of how radically different TV broadcasting would be:

"We decided right away that the way to do television was to comment on the game, not tell what was happening like we did on radio. We wanted to describe the plays, the line-ups (Brooklyn used a single wing, I don't remember what Philadelphia used), the way the tailback cut because of the blocking or whatever. And, we had to be accurate. We were selling television at the time and people had to believe in television."

Belief was hard to come by, given the medium's limitations.

In a letter dated November 30, 1939, Alfred Morton, NBC's vice president in charge of television, offered his apologies to President Franklin Roosevelt for being unable to connect the president's Hyde Park, New York, home to a subsequent New York Giants game played in the Polo Grounds.

"Living in or near New York often gives us the feeling of living in an enlightened age of progress," Morton wrote to the president. "But alas—such has not been the case in our efforts to televise the professional football games from the Polo Grounds on November 26th and December 3rd."

And the difficulty was not broadcast technology. The network's dilemma was that the owner of the only property adjacent to the stadium wouldn't allow them to park their production trucks on his property.

"We offered to reimburse him for any damage to his property," Morton wrote. "Sad but true, he told us as far as our television trucks were concerned, he just didn't want any hifalutin' contraptions around. We tried every argument we could think of to get the game for you but in vain."

Morton apologized and offered that instead of professional football on Sunday, the president could watch a series of fencing matches by members of "New York's exclusive Fencer's Club."

"Who knows?" he wrote. "Thrust and riposte, lunge and parry, may prove more exciting than a forward pass or an end run. The time is still the same—2:30 PM—and we hope you like it."

It's unknown whether FDR tuned in to watch.

CHAPTER 8

THE T-FORMATION AND THE MAN-IN-MOTION

ON DECEMBER 8, 1940, A LITTLE MORE THAN A year after the NFL's first televised game, the Mutual Broadcasting System transmitted the first nationwide radio broadcast of an NFL championship game, a lopsided 73–0 win by the Chicago Bears against the Washington Redskins.

But as historic as this game was, there was another element that made it even more memorable: this was the game in which George Halas unleashed the Bears' game-changing "T-formation with a man-in-motion."

Halas's new wrinkle on an old formation was transformative. It changed the game from being a slow, sluggish, power-running game to a more open, exciting, and less predictable game.

The traditional T-formation is as old as the game itself. It features three running backs lined up in a straight line about five yards behind the quarterback, giving the appearance of the letter *T*.

"I had grown up with the T," Halas related in his autobiography. "I had played it at Illinois, with the Navy, with Hammond [Pros]. I had used it with the [Decatur] Staleys. I kept it all through the twenties with the Bears."

If the T-formation was second nature to Halas, its development and refinement was a long time coming.

For one thing, the relationship between Halas and Dutch Sternaman, his co-owner and co-coach, had so unraveled that the two men could barely work together during the late 1920s. Eventually their strained relationship impacted their ability to work together as coaches.

"The consequence was that I would tell the team to do this and Sternaman would tell them to do that," Halas said. "The time had come for Dutch and me to stop coaching, or more accurately, miscoaching."

So, in 1929, following a disappointing 4-8-2 season, the clashing co-coaches agreed to relinquish their responsibilities in favor of a single coach. Ralph Jones, a former assistant football coach at Illinois, and more recently the athletic director of a small secondary school in Chicago, was the surprise choice.

Though they were 50/50 partners, Sternaman was admittedly less interested in the Bears' day-to-day business operations than was Halas. Since his interest was primarily in coaching, Sternaman decided in 1931 to sell his 50 percent ownership stake to Halas.

While the two owners devised the terms of their separation, Jones focused on the Bears' playbook. One of his first alterations was to increase the space between offensive linemen from one foot to one yard. "The change," Halas joked later, "gave the defense new opportunities to enter our backfield."

To combat that likelihood, Jones made other adjustments. Backfield men were coached to hit the larger gaps more quickly, while offensive linemen were taught to deflect their defensive counterparts, just enough to allow the runner to slide through the hole. "The idea was not to flatten the defender but to knock him out of the way," Halas explained.

To speed up the offense and create more options, Jones exploited a little-used rule that allowed one man to move as soon as offensive signals began. That one-man movement did not require the compulsory one-second halt that was mandated for line shifts. This became the "man-in-motion."

The man-in-motion changed the traditional T-formation from a power-run package to a more versatile run-pass formation. It not only made possible a quick-to-the-hole running attack; it also allowed the halfback to shift toward the line of scrimmage, making himself a target for a lateral or forward pass. The formation could serve up misdirection plays, counterplays, and even an early version of the three-wide-receiver set.

In 1933 the Bears' T caught the eye of the newly hired University of Chicago coach Clark Shaughnessy. Wanting to learn more, he sought out Halas, who had resumed his role as head coach. Impressed by Shaughnessy's football knowledge, Halas eventually offered him a $2,500 part-time position to assist him in analyzing upcoming opponents.

"I did a good bit of inventing," Shaughnessy said of his role with the Bears. "But George did the selecting and correcting. I'd come along with something and say, 'You know football; you pick this to pieces and take what you like.' That's the way it was done, gradually, experimentally."

Shaughnessy always credited Halas with his success.

"Football is a science to me," Shaughnessy wrote in 1942. "So, when George Halas didn't laugh at my theories, I naturally warmed up to him. He didn't make fun of me and was willing to listen. . . . As I propounded some of these pet theories of mine, he'd take them, try them out. Some results were apparent."

As revolutionary as the man-in-motion T-formation was, it took nearly a decade to perfect. Most coaches considered the formation with all its variables a "gadget" offense.

While Shaughnessy and Halas remained undaunted by doubters, they knew something was missing. Then, in 1939, they realized what—or rather who—that missing element was.

His name was Sid Luckman, an outstanding quarterback from Columbia University. When the Bears signed him, the two Chicago coaches realized that what their T required was a smart ball handler who could make quick, intelligent decisions. With Luckman that's exactly what they got—plus a damn good passer. He was the perfect T-formation quarterback.

Although a quick learner, Luckman initially struggled making the transition from a single-wing halfback to a T-formation quarterback. But midway through the 1939 season, it became apparent he was the ideal man to lead the Bears' offense.

"In all my years in football," Halas said following that season, "I've never seen a player who worked as hard as Luckman. When everybody else left the practice field, he stayed on. He practiced pivoting and ball handling by the hour. He became a great player simply because he devoted about four hundred percent more effort to it than most athletes are willing to do."

Then, in 1940, just as the Bears' offensive strategy was beginning to blossom, the University of Chicago dropped its football program and Shaughnessy left to become the head coach at Stanford University. He continued his development of the T while other major college coaches continued to scoff. But after Shaughnessy took Stanford from a 1-7-1 record to 9-0 and a Rose Bowl win, his competitors' attitudes changed dramatically.

Meanwhile, the 1940 Bears were off to a promising 6-2 start before they met George Preston Marshall's Washington Redskins. That hard-fought game ended on a controversial play and a 7–3 loss for the Bears.

As time ran out, Luckman tossed a pass to running back Bill Osmanski in the end zone. But Osmanski, as he immediately and forcefully informed the game official, couldn't catch the perfectly thrown pass because his arms were pinned to his sides by Redskins defensive back Bob Titchenal. Halas and the Bears' bench loudly echoed Osmanski's objection, but to no avail. The game was over, and the Redskins won.

Marshall later told reporters that Halas and the Bears were nothing short of "front-runners, quitters and crybabies."

Using Marshall's insults as inspiration, Halas pushed the motivation pedal to the metal. The Bears and their T-formation in hyperdrive scored 78 points in their final two games. They finished atop the Western Division with an 8-3 record. A championship game showdown was scheduled in Washington with Marshall's division-leading 9-2 Redskins.

On the Thursday before the big game, Shuaghnessy, fresh off his Rose Bowl win, rejoined his friend and mentor Halas for a marathon film study.

"We discussed for hours which of our plays might be most effective against the Washington defense," Halas recalled. "We stayed up all night to again review the game movies. We chose about twenty plays. We selected other plays to fit every conceivable pertinent defense Washington might adopt."

Leaving no motivational stone unturned, Halas distributed copies of Marshall's critical comments in the locker room.

"Gentlemen, this is what George Preston Marshall thinks of you," he said. "I think you're a great football team, the greatest ever assembled. Go out on the field and prove it."

It didn't take long for the team to respond. Fifty-five seconds into the game, Osmanski rumbled 68 yards to the same end zone where he'd earlier been denied a touchdown.

And that was just for starters.

On their second possession, the Bears gained 80 yards in 17 plays, ending with Luckman scoring on a quarterback sneak. By halftime, with Chicago ahead 28–0, Halas had Luckman take a seat.

"This is the story of a man who this afternoon directed the greatest team that professional football has ever produced," the *Chicago Tribune*'s Wilfred Smith wrote in his game summary. "Luckman's generalship unquestionably was the factor which smashed Washington's defenses and maintained a steady and irresistible attack which eventually turned this championship battle into a rout."

The Bears' offense, featuring their man-in-motion, scored eight touchdowns, one by air and seven on the ground. The defense was also brilliant, scoring touchdowns on three of their eight interceptions, and holding the Redskins to just 31 yards rushing.

Halas relished the win, telling reporters after the game that the turning point was "the second play after the opening kickoff."

Pouring salt on the wound, ten different players scored touchdowns and six players attempted extra-point conversions. Following the ninth touchdown and having lost eight footballs to lucky fans in the bleachers, referee Red Friesell asked the Bears to forgo kicking the extra point in favor of running or passing.

"It was the most humiliating thing I ever went through on the football field," Redskins quarterback Sammy Baugh said after the game.

Marshall, along with much of the disappointed home crowd, didn't wait for the final gun to sound before leaving. However, the owner's attempt to escape early didn't go unnoticed. When a taunting fan yelled, "Take your Redskins back to Boston, you lug," Marshall, who had moved the team to DC in 1937, erupted and charged the grandstand where the fan was seated. Fortunately for both, the local police intervened before any damage was done.

When United Press reporter George Kirksey confronted Marshall as he walked out, Marshall again suggested there were "quitters" on the field. This time, though, it was his own Redskins he was insulting. "Those guys out there quit," he grumbled.

A better summary of the one-sided affair was offered by *New York Times* sportswriter Arthur Daley: "The weather was perfect. So were the Bears."

CHAPTER 9

THE NFL'S FIRST COMMISSIONER

T HE NFL SURVIVED MORE THAN ITS FAIR SHARE OF challenges during its first two decades. It endured the Great Depression, overcame competition from rival leagues, and weathered internal disputes that tested the loyalty of the sometimes-divided band of football brothers.

At times, its business strategy seemed more trial and error than a deliberate, thought-out plan. More than forty franchises came and went during the league's first twenty years. Gone were teams from such unlikely places as Muncie, Indiana; Evanston, Illinois; Tonawanda, New York; and LaRue, Ohio.

Only two teams from the NFL's inaugural season, the Chicago Bears (aka the Decatur Staleys) and the Chicago Cardinals, were still active as the NFL closed out its second decade.

In retrospect, it's easier to appreciate how the league's transition from small cities to major-league municipalities was not only critical but intentional. That—as well as many of the league's other early successes—was very much a part of NFL president Joe Carr's vision.

Every year under Carr's leadership the NFL grew in popularity and credibility. In fact, during each of his final three seasons at the helm, the league registered record attendance, and in 1939 it recorded its first million-spectator milestone. It was something Carr confidently anticipated, but didn't live to see. The man who had overseen and helped create the NFL succumbed to a heart attack on May 20, 1939.

A few months before he died, Carr described the reason for the league's success: "We who have given a good deal of time to developing postgraduate football have steadfastly maintained that the American public would respond enthusiastically to this great sport so long as it was cleanly handled, and kept above reproach."

George Halas gave Carr full credit for the league's success. Its remarkable growth and popularity were due entirely to Carr's "fair and impartial administration of its affairs and his steadfast belief in the game." Halas described Carr's untimely death as "irreparable."

Other owners offered similar tributes. Cardinals owner Charley Bidwill called Carr "pro football's balance wheel" and said he believed finding his successor would be impossible.

While the high praise was sincere and deserved, the club owners also understood that they had to find that successor. Some, like Redskins owner George Preston Marshall, felt the next leader should be a high-profile executive, a "czar" like baseball's Kenesaw Mountain Landis. The always-outspoken Marshall let his feelings be known even while Carr was still in office. He publicly recommended that James A. Farley, the US postmaster general, be named commissioner. He even suggested a $75,000 annual salary to secure Farley's services.

That suggestion brought an immediate and angry reaction from G. A. Richards, owner of the Detroit Lions. In an interview with Henry McLemore, a provocative columnist for the Hearst chain of newspapers, Richards, who was in Palm Springs, California, recuperating from a heart ailment he blamed on "having to deal with the numbskulls who run the National Professional Football League," said that the hiring of Farley was "nothing more than a wild and silly dream."

When pressed about his objection, Richards exploded.

"Why? Did you read the salary figure? Just $75,000, that's all. Where's that coming from? . . . Not three years ago, my fellow owners pooh-poohed a suggestion of mine that we hire a nationally known man to head the league because I thought we would have to pay $25,000 to get him . . . they said they couldn't afford it."

Seven days after McLemore's interview hit the newsstands, league owners, sans the ailing Richards, gathered in Chicago for their annual winter meeting. There, in a show of support for Carr and an outright rejection of Marshall's unsolicited plan, the owners surprised Carr with a new and unprecedented ten-year contract for $10,000 per year.

Three months later the most important man in the NFL's first two decades was dead.

Finding a replacement became a contentious issue among the owners.

Initially, they turned to Carl Storck, the league vice president and treasurer and former Dayton Triangles manager, to serve as interim president. It was at best a stopgap measure.

Years later, Pittsburgh Steelers chairman Dan Rooney recalled how his father, Steelers founder Art Rooney, once said "the only contribution Storck brought to the NFL was the big boxes of candy he brought to every league meeting."

At the league's 1939 summer meeting—their first after Carr's death—the owners wanted to know if Storck wanted the job.

He said he would, but on one condition: he didn't feel he could do the job part time. Storck reminded the owners that his full-time job was as an employee of General Motors, and that they'd been "very accommodating to his hobby, this league, for the past eighteen years."

Storck's description of his NFL role as a part-time hobby wasn't what the owners wanted to hear.

For some, like Marshall, Richards, and Halas, it was an easy decision. And they were already hunting for that "high-profile executive" to replace Carr. Others, like Rooney and Green Bay's Curly Lambeau, agreed that the league needed a prominent national figure.

Two early candidates emerged. The first was Arch Ward, the influential sports editor of the *Chicago Tribune,* and the promotional genius behind baseball's all-star game and football's college all-star game. The other was FBI director J. Edgar Hoover.

Both men declined.

So, with no serious candidate to put forth at the next meeting, the owners extended Storck's interim status for another year. It was a stall, not a vote of confidence.

Convinced that Storck was a lame duck, Halas, with the support of other owners, made a second appeal to Ward in December 1940. They upped the ante from $20,000 per year to $25,000 and he accepted. Then, ten days later, on Christmas Eve, Ward backed out of the deal. The *Tribune* had offered him a lucrative new contract that he said he couldn't refuse.

The owners went back to Ward a third time in early 1941. This time, however, they merely sought his advice.

"The owners picked three men, including Elmer Layden, then athletic director and head coach at Notre Dame," wrote Walter Byers in *Liberty* magazine. John Kelly, Democratic leader of Philadelphia, and Frank McCormick, Minnesota's director of athletics, were the other contenders.

While Ward claimed he didn't suggest Layden, the owners later said he went all out in pushing him.

Halas officially offered Layden the job on February 2, 1941, and he accepted.

While the Halas-led recruitment of Layden earned much public praise, it also drew the ire of a few of his fellow owners, including Brooklyn Dodgers owner Dan Topping and Philadelphia Eagles owner Alexis Thompson.

Their objection wasn't so much about who or how much but rather how the hiring occurred.

Thompson accused Halas of ignoring Kelly and McCormick and not consulting Bell, whom the owners had also assigned to interview the prospective candidates. Moreover, Thompson complained, any offer was to be "unofficial" until the other owners voted. Bell, he contended, "wasn't even in on the signing of Layden."

While Bell said he had no objection to Layden, he also believed that the owners were entitled to vote on the selection.

Halas contended he had the approval of the owners, including some who were now complaining.

"We talked to them by telephone the same as the other owners," he said. "A majority of the club owners voted for Layden and a majority is all the league constitution demands on any matter of business.

"There always is some opposition to any new venture, but there is nothing Thompson and Topping can do about it. Layden's pay will start March 1, and he's in as commissioner for the next five years."

Several other owners expressed their support for Layden.

"Layden is the finest available man in the United States for commissioner of football," Rooney said. Marshall, whose Redskins had been embarrassed 73–0 by Halas's Bears just a few months earlier, said, "The league owes a debt of gratitude to George Halas for signing Elmer Layden. It's another victory for the T-formation."

In the end, all sides came together and at the April 5 league meeting Layden was officially approved as NFL commissioner, though not before a little grandstanding by John O'Keefe, one of Thompson's front-office executives.

O'Keefe made a motion that Layden's deal should officially begin on April 5, not March 1, as Halas had indicated. But, the Eagles exec slyly added, Layden should be compensated from March 1, when Halas hired him. O'Keefe's generosity was intended to be at the expense of Halas, who'd already paid Layden's March salary.

Marshall, reading through O'Keefe's less-than-subtle suggestion, jumped in and added to the motion that "the league should be obligated to reimburse those who paid money to Mr. Layden for the month of March."

The motion carried unanimously, and peace was restored.

Although the plan was to retain Storck as NFL president under the direction of the new commissioner, he chose instead to resign.

While Storck may not have been the ideal choice for commissioner in 1941, history should not forget his pioneering role. Not only was he a charter member of the league; he served very capably as the league's vice president and treasurer from 1921 until 1939—even if it was a "part-time" job.

News of Layden's hiring was well received. Newswires, sports columnists, and beat reporters sang his praises.

The *Los Angeles Times'* Dick Hyland wrote that "the pros have borrowed Notre Dame's past to bolster their future."

And, true to his Notre Dame experience and tradition, one of

Layden's first moves as commissioner was to summon the league's publicity men to his Chicago office for a "publicity clinic." The new commissioner cautioned them against what he called promotional provincialism. Publicity outside the teams' immediate region, Layden preached, was "as important and imperative to the life of the game and the welfare of the league as the exploitation individual clubs carry on in their own neighborhoods."

To that end, Layden instructed every club in the league to send complete sets of photographs and regular releases throughout the season to all the newspapers in league cities and all major wire services. The image-conscious commissioner also urged team spokesmen to be "more reporter than propagandist" and be on the constant lookout for human-interest anecdotes that could be used in feature stories and column briefs.

The straitlaced Layden reminded the publicists that in keeping their efforts on a "high, dignified plane," they should help "prevent coaches and players from endorsing or lending their name to advertisements for liquor, cigarettes, and laxatives."

While Layden singled out liquor, cigarettes, and personal purgative products, he apparently saw no harm in personally pitching men's underwear.

"One of the best aids to keeping fit I know is Jockey Longs," the commissioner was quoted as saying in sales ads.

But, except for that one brief (pun intended) episode, Layden was widely seen as the poster child of all that was good in college football and the perfect choice as the pro league's first "czar."

With Layden's hiring, the NFL had its first commissioner. Nineteen forty-one was also the fifth consecutive season with the same ten cities as members, a first in NFL history.

More important, the men behind the teams were solid football men. Eight of them—Halas, Mara, Rooney, Bell, Marshall, Bidwill, Lambeau, and Cleveland Rams owner Dan Reeves—would eventually be elected to the Pro Football Hall of Fame.

The next few years would demonstrate how critical strong leadership can be.

CHAPTER 10

A WORLD AT WAR

I N THE LATE 1930S THERE WAS A STRONG UNDER-current of worry that the United States might get dragged into war. All that changed just before 1 p.m. Eastern time on Sunday, December 7, 1941, when Japanese fighter planes attacked the American naval base at Pearl Harbor near Honolulu, Hawaii. The following day America officially entered World War II.

Three NFL games were under way when Pearl Harbor was attacked. The New York Giants were playing the Brooklyn Dodgers at the Polo Grounds, where Giants fans were celebrating "Tuffy Leemans' Day," a tribute for the team's star running back. The game was interrupted by a public-address announcement alerting William J. Donovan, the wartime head of the Office of Strategic Services, to call Operator 19 in Washington immediately.

Giants owner Wellington Mara was told the electrifying news by the team's chaplain at halftime, even as the rest of the world was learning of the attack through radio reports.

Mel Hein, the Hall of Fame center of the Giants, remembered the day well:

"We knew something was going on because every few minutes during the game the PA announcer would call for some military person to report to his post," said Hein. "Then after the game the word came that the Japanese had bombed Pearl Harbor."

At Griffith Stadium in Washington, the Redskins were hosting the Philadelphia Eagles. There, uneasiness filled the air as government officials and high-ranking military officers were summoned by the public-address announcer to "report to their offices immediately." Newspaper bureau chiefs, editors, and reporters were also paged.

And in Chicago's Comiskey Park, where the Bears and the Chicago Cardinals were playing, the scene was much the same.

"We were in a strange frame of mind because we had to beat the Cardinals that day in order to tie for the conference title," Hall of Fame halfback George McAfee told Tony Barnhart of the *Atlanta Journal-Constitution*.

McAfee's most vivid memory of the day was spending the rest of the afternoon and that night in an opponent's apartment listening to news accounts on the radio.

The unthinkable had happened. The country was at war.

World War II forced an abrupt change in the American way of life. Citizens were asked to ration food, gas, and clothing. Community drives for scrap metal, aluminum, and rubber to help the war effort became commonplace. Women joined the workforce as electricians, welders, and riveters in defense plants. And, while sporting events were viewed by most as brief respites from the worries of war, some questioned how exactly sports could contribute to the effort.

It was a question Commissioner Layden deferred answering until March, four months after Pearl Harbor.

Layden called the March meeting "the most important meeting since a band of hardy visionaries gathered in a Canton, Ohio, automobile agency 22 years ago to organize the National League."

In the days leading up to the meeting, Layden attempted to set the stage for what to expect from the owners.

"Until federal authorities decide greater benefits will accrue from some other policy, professional football's wartime effort will center about normal operations with emphasis on participation in civilian emergency activities," he said.

The commissioner also chose to promote the idea of a need for normalcy during the days ahead, invoking the name of a man few football players or fans were likely familiar with:

"From Aristotle's time on down, we have been told, and it has been demonstrated, that sports and entertainment are necessary for the relaxation of the people in times of stress and worry," he said. The league "would strive to help meet this need with the men the government has not yet called for combat service, either because of dependents, disabilities, or luck of the draw in the Army draft."

Layden recruited other league dignitaries to offer their support. Packers coach Curly Lambeau's statement would have made future Green Bay coach Vince Lombardi—a man who knew a thing or two about inspiration—proud:

"For professional sports, the easiest method would be to call the whole thing off," he said. "But what kind of example would that be for the youngster who looks to the stars for guidance and inspiration? Only one course is open to sports, that is—carry on without regard to the sacrifice. This is no time for sports to look for a profit!"

While intended to reassure the public, Lambeau's remarks were also directed at undecided owners who hadn't yet come to that conclusion on their own.

Jimmy Conzelman, the fiery coach of the Chicago Cardinals and a well-known orator, was the subject of a "One Minute Interview" in a May 7, 1942, NFL press release exclusive to radio. He forcefully defended the game and the league:

"Football coaches have always been apologists for their profession," he said. "For years we've been on the defensive against attacks from reformers who regard us as muscle-bound mentalities exploiting kids for an easy living. Football has been under fire because it involves body contact and it teaches violence. It was considered useless, even dangerous. But that's all over now.

"The bleeding hearts haven't the courtesy to apologize to us," he grumbled. "But they're coming around and asking our help in the national emergency. Why? Because the college commencement classes this month find the customary challenges of life a pale prelude to the demands of a world at war. Instead of job seekers, or home makers, the graduates suddenly have become defenders of a familiar way of life, of an ideology, a religion and of a nation. They have been taught to build. Now they must learn to destroy.

". . . The young man must be toughened not only physically, but mentally. He must become accustomed to violence. Football is the number one medium for attuning a man to body-contact and violent physical shock. It teaches that after all, there isn't anything so terrifying about a punch in the puss."

Three days later, Conzelman repeated those sentiments and much more as the commencement speaker at the University of Dayton. His presentation, "The Young Man's Mental and Physical Approach to War," became required reading at the United States Military Academy at West Point.

Collectively, Layden, Lambeau, and Conzelman pretty much summarized the NFL's wartime strategy and its public position.

While Layden attempted to downplay the war's impact on the game, a severe shortage of players quickly became apparent. More than one thousand players, coaches, and owners interrupted or postponed their pro football careers to serve their country.

When the Brooklyn Dodgers opened their 1943 training camp, only seven players from the 1942 squad were available. League rosters were supplemented by recently retired or deferred players, who under normal circumstances wouldn't have been signed to a contract.

Notable retired players answering their teams' SOS included three future Hall of Famers. Bronko Nagurski, the Bears' famous bulldozing fullback who'd retired in 1937, returned to his team in 1943 to play tackle. Green Bay quarterback Arnie Herber, who had last played in 1940, signed on with the 1944 Giants, as did half-back Ken Strong, who'd retired from the team five years earlier.

Although there was talk of suspending operations, the NFL owners unanimously voted to play on. Some, however, simply could not.

Just eighteen players reported to the Cleveland Rams' training camp in 1943. And with co-owners Dan Reeves and Fred Levy Jr. due to report to active military duty, the team was granted a one-year suspension of play.

To avoid a similar fate, Pittsburgh Steelers owner Art Rooney and Philadelphia Eagles owner Alexis Thompson announced that their roster-ravaged teams would merge for the 1943 season. The "Steagles" as they were nicknamed, split home games between the two cities.

As Al Wistert, a two-way player who began his nine-year pro career with the Steagles, later said, the NFL had "combined two bad teams and made them worse."

Fortunately, in 1944, the Rams resumed play and the Steelers and Eagles dissolved their merger. But, still suffering from a shortage of able-bodied players, Pittsburgh found it necessary to again merge with another team. This time they joined forces with the Cardinals. Officially known as the Card-Pitt Combine, the combined squad went 0-10 and was so bad that the press referred to them as the "Carpets." Following the 1944 season, both teams returned to full operation.

But the manpower shortage was still far from over. Two more teams, the Boston Yanks and the Brooklyn Tigers, joined forces and played the 1945 season as the "Yanks," with no city designation. They played four home games in Boston and one in New York.

Even though just surviving was a struggle for some teams, the league looked for additional ways to make a difference during the war.

One particularly successful league-wide initiative, selling war bonds, resulted in sales of $4 million in 1942. Three Packers—Lambeau, quarterback Cecil Isbell, and end Don Hutson—were credited with selling pledges worth $2.1 million in a single night at a rally in Milwaukee.

Additionally, revenues from fifteen exhibition games amounting to $680,384 were donated to service charities.

As difficult as it was to fill wartime-ravaged rosters, the same wasn't true when it came to filling stadium seats. In 1942 the NFL drew a then-record 1,115,154 fans. By 1944 the league drew 1,234,750. Apparently, as Layden proclaimed, sports and entertainment did play an important role during "times of stress and worry."

While doing its best to help on the home front, the NFL was

not immune to the worst ravages of war. Twenty-two NFL men—twenty active or former players, an ex–head coach, and a team executive—lost their lives while serving their country. It was the highest casualty rate of any professional sports organization.

The best-known player fatality was New York Giants tackle Al Blozis. Just six weeks after playing in the 1944 championship game, the six-six, 256-pound all-league tackle was killed while searching for two missing members of his platoon in the snowy Vosges Mountains of France.

Blozis insisted on joining the Army, even though he'd already been exempted because of his size.

One of the most remarkable stories of survival was that of former Cardinals fullback Mario "Motts" Tonelli.

Tonelli was taken prisoner after US and Filipino troops surrendered to the Japanese on the island of Luzon in 1942. Thousands of troops were forced to march in what's since become known as the Bataan Death March.

During the first day of the forced march, a Japanese guard confiscating valuables from prisoners threatened to kill Tonelli if he didn't relinquish his Notre Dame class ring. Reluctantly, and only after a fellow prisoner implored him not to resist, Tonelli turned it over. A few minutes later, a Japanese officer who spoke perfect English approached him.

"I was educated in America, at the University of Southern California," Tonelli later recalled the officer saying. "I know a little about the famous Notre Dame football team. In fact, I watched you beat USC in 1937. I know how much this ring means to you, so I wanted to get it back to you."

The strange exchange stunned Tonelli. But whatever brief hope the unexpected gesture provided him was almost immediately dashed. It was just the beginning of Tonelli's three-and-a-half-year nightmare.

In 1944, Tonelli was shipped from a Manila prison camp to Japan aboard one of the infamous "hell boats," a horrific journey in an unmarked merchant ship that became a floating graveyard for many GIs.

When his boat landed in Japan, Tonelli was assigned a number—58—the same number he wore while playing at Notre Dame. "It cheered me up," he said. "It gave me a feeling that I was going to make it."

And make it he did. After almost three and a half years as a POW, a frail and sick Tonelli could hardly believe his eyes when a US dive bomber dropped packages of cigarettes into what would be his final prison compound. Attached were handkerchiefs bearing the message "Hostilities have ceased. Will see you soon." Though he weighed less than a hundred pounds, Tonelli attributed his survival to the rigorous workouts and toughness developed playing football.

Tonelli returned to the gridiron in 1945 as a member of the Cardinals. Although Tonelli was far from fully recovered, and was still a hospital outpatient, Cardinals owner Charley Bidwill insisted he sign a contract and rejoin the team. It was a gesture Tonelli would never forget.

"I was stupid enough to think that I could come back and get healthy and play again," he said. "It was my desire to play." Even though he managed to gain weight and appear briefly in one game, the reality was that his time as a POW had taken too big a toll. But that didn't matter to Bidwill.

"I'm very grateful for Charley Bidwill," Tonelli recollected years later. "He really started my life again."

Bidwill's signing of Tonelli did more than lift his former player's spirits. It had a huge impact on the war hero's later life. By signing a contract, Tonelli's years of military service, sandwiched between his two NFL seasons of 1940 and 1945, qualified him for a pension plan created by the NFL owners and NFL Players Association in 1987.

+ + +

OTHER NFL men distinguished themselves during World War II.

Philadelphia Eagles center-linebacker Chuck Bednarik flew thirty long-range bombing missions over Germany as an Army Air

Corps waist gunner in a B-24 Liberator. The tough-as-nails player nicknamed "Concrete Charlie" often spoke of how fortunate he was to have survived.

"There was antiaircraft fire all around. You just waited for your turn to get hit, but, thankfully, ours never came," he recalled.

As a nineteen-year-old, Tom Landry, the future head coach of the Dallas Cowboys, flew thirty missions as a B-17 co-pilot, surviving a crash in Belgium after a bombing run over Czechoslovakia.

Three servicemen with pro football ties—Morris Britt, Joe Foss, and Jack Lummus—were awarded the country's highest military honor, the Congressional Medal of Honor.

Britt, who played end for the Detroit Lions in 1941, was severely injured during a fierce battle in Mignano, Italy, in 1943. He was recognized for his "gallantry and intrepidity at the risk of his life above and beyond the call of duty."

Foss went on to become the governor of South Dakota and the first commissioner of the American Football League in 1960. A Marine Corps major and leader of a squadron known as the "Joe Foss Flying Circus," he was recognized for his courageous air combat during the struggle to hold Guadalcanal.

Lummus, an end with the 1941 New York Giants, made the ultimate sacrifice for his country during the Battle of Iwo Jima. After weeks of intense fighting, the promising two-way end was mortally wounded after stepping on a land mine.

In a letter to Lummus's mother, his commanding officer wrote, "Jack suffered very little for he didn't live long. I saw Jack soon after he was hit. With calmness, serenity and complacency, Jack said, 'The New York Giants lost a good man.' We all lost a good man."

In addition to the hundreds of players and coaches who served during the war, several NFL club owners and future owners also answered the call. Among them were Dan Topping of the Brooklyn Dodgers; Dan Reeves and Fred Levy Jr. of the Rams; brothers Jack and Wellington Mara, co-owners of the Giants; and Eagles owner Alexis Thompson.

For George Halas, World War II was his second enlistment, since he also enlisted during World War I.

Future NFL owners who served include Houston Oilers/ Tennessee Titans founder-owner Bud Adams; New Orleans Saints owner Tom Benson; Detroit Lions owner William Clay Ford; Cleveland Browns owner Art Modell; and San Diego Chargers owner Alex Spanos. Ed McCaskey, a former chairman of the board of the Chicago Bears, also served, as did Buffalo Bills founder-owner Ralph Wilson Jr.

While in the war, Lieutenant Wilson served in some of the most dangerous duty of all—working aboard a minesweeper. He was the commander of Yard Mine Sweeper No. 29, a small wooden ship just 136 feet in length. The YMS No. 29 was active both at Anzio beachhead and on D-Day. It was at Anzio that another YMS that had worked alongside No. 29 for a year struck a mine.

"It was horrible," Wilson said. "These men in my crew had fought a lot more war than most people ever will. But that night took the starch out of them."

Wilson saw action in both the Atlantic and Pacific theaters and was an early witness to the devastation at Pearl Harbor.

"Ships were lying on their sides in the water," he recalled in a 2012 interview. "It was a terrible scene."

Wilson's ship entered Tokyo Bay following the bombing of Hiroshima. From there he was assigned a smaller ship to travel to a nearby location.

"I was the first American to see Hiroshima," he said. "It was a complete wasteland."

Wilson was still in Tokyo Bay on September 2, 1945, when the Japanese formally signed their surrender on the USS *Missouri*.

Cheers of celebration filled the air.

The war was finally over, the boys were coming home, and the NFL was ready to resume its role as a great American pastime.

CHAPTER 11

THE NFL'S FOUR-YEAR WAR

W HILE THE US INVOLVEMENT IN WORLD WAR II triggered several league-wide challenges, it didn't discourage some entrepreneurs from speculating on the NFL's promising postwar future.

Don Ameche, a popular radio voice and film star, was one such person.

In early 1942 Ameche called on his friend Arch Ward to help him buy an NFL franchise. A few weeks later, the *Chicago Tribune* sports editor presented the league with Ameche's application together with a certified check for $25,000—half the price of a franchise.

Ward told the owners that Ameche preferred his franchise to be in Los Angeles, but if that wasn't feasible he'd consider Buffalo.

What Ward hadn't considered was the possibility that his NFL friends might not respond favorably to Ameche's application. And that's exactly what happened. Citing the uncertainties of the war, they tabled Ameche's request and returned his check.

Not accustomed to being rejected, Ward—the same guy the owners had twice earlier asked to be their commissioner—left the meeting swearing "heads would roll."

So it was on June 4, 1944, that Ward and six others—some of whom had also been spurned by the NFL—secretly met in St. Louis to lay the foundation for a new league.

Following a second meeting, on September 2, Ward publicly introduced his new venture.

The All-America Football Conference would begin operations

in 1945, he said in his *Chicago Tribune* column. He promised teams would play in eight or possibly ten major cities.

Ward identified seven owners and franchise cities. Prominent among them was Ameche, who was introduced as a co-owner of the new league's Los Angeles franchise.

The league's other franchise cities were Baltimore, Buffalo, Chicago, New York, San Francisco, and Cleveland. Miami would join three months later.

"I organized the All-America conference because I think the growth of a second conference during the postwar era is inevitable," Ward said. "I have a desire to help in the organization of the right kind of a league that has the best chance to make good."

Although he was the voice of the new league, Ward made it clear he had no desire to be the AAFC commissioner. That job was assigned to Jim Crowley, who, like NFL commissioner Layden, was one of Notre Dame's famous "Four Horsemen." A point that wasn't lost on anyone.

A masterful promoter, Ward was focused on the opportunities of postwar football rather than the uncertainties postwar America might provide.

The AAFC immediately began signing NFL players and college stars while they were still on active military duty.

For example, Northwestern quarterback Otto Graham signed what was called an "All-America Football Conference War-Time Players Agreement" with the unnamed Cleveland franchise in March 1945. He was the first player signed by Cleveland's general manager and head coach Paul Brown.

In addition to a $7,500 yearly salary, the two-year agreement also paid Graham $250 per month while he served in the armed forces. A pretty good deal, considering Uncle Sam paid between $50 and $138 per month (depending on rank) for enlistees with one to three years of service. Graham also got a $1,000 signing bonus.

"Old Navy men say I rooted for the war to last forever," Graham told *Los Angeles Times* reporter Bob Oates in a 1985 interview.

Even though the new league was successful at signing players, other challenges, like the sudden withdrawal of the Baltimore franchise, made it apparent that the AAFC wouldn't field teams until 1946.

The delay, however, didn't slow down Ward's persistent and effective public promotion in the *Tribune*. As one critic put it, "Anyone could become a great promoter with a million people buying his releases every day."

From the beginning, Ward insisted his goal was to coexist with the NFL. In fact, in May 1945, he assigned three league executives—Christy Walsh, co-owner of the Los Angeles franchise; John Keeshin, owner of the Chicago franchise; and Brown—to seek a meeting with Layden.

Their message was simple: the AAFC was ready to form a major-league alliance with the NFL, much like baseball's American and National Leagues.

But Layden was having none of it.

"All I know of new leagues is what I read in the newspapers," he said. "There is nothing for the National Football League to talk about as far as new leagues are concerned until someone gets a football and plays a game."

A shortened, paraphrased version, "Tell them to get a football first," was cited in newspapers across the country.

Layden's statement provided the AAFC with a battle cry, and, as Walter Byers wrote in *Liberty*, "the basis for a successful publicity campaign."

Unfortunately for Layden, his remarks were misrepresented as arrogant or dismissive. In fact, his words were a failed attempt at humor directed at Chicago owner John Keeshin.

A few days earlier, Keeshin had presented his new head coach, Dick Hanley, to the press. Staffers were caught clumsily looking for a football to have their coach hold as a prop. None was found. It was an awkward moment that wasn't lost on the attending press corps.

"The Chicago front office couldn't beg, borrow, buy or steal a football to lend a gridiron atmosphere to the shots," *Brooklyn Daily Eagle* columnist Tommy Holmes reported.

While Layden's misconstrued remark would draw the ire of some NFL owners, it was nothing compared to the uproar caused by Brooklyn Tigers owner Dan Topping when he announced he was bolting from the NFL.

For months, Topping—who was also part owner of the baseball Yankees—had been battling Giants owner Tim Mara for permission to relocate his Tigers from Brooklyn's Ebbets Field to Yankee Stadium. But, before Mara would waive his territorial rights, he insisted on a slew of conditions, including choice of playing dates and a significant rights fee. Topping decided he'd had enough and signed on with the AAFC.

Capitalizing on his baseball team's popularity, he renamed his AAFC team the New York Yankees.

In addition to Topping's baseball fame, his social status as the grandson of the wealthy and well-known industrialist Daniel Reid further enhanced the AAFC's image.

"It seems to me, that the chances of success for the All-America Conference today are about five times greater than they were a week ago, when Topping was fighting a gallant but losing battle with the National Football League," the *Brooklyn Eagle*'s Holmes wrote.

While some were surprised by Topping's decision, Mara calmly insisted that he wasn't shocked by the news:

"We have been doing business here at the Polo Grounds for at least twenty-one years while teams in the Yankee Stadium have come and gone.

"We wish them luck," he told the *Brooklyn Eagle*. But, in a parting shot, he added, "They'll need it if they have the same management that ruined the Brooklyn franchise."

Topping fired back, saying he'd run Mara and his Giants "right out of this town."

Having a franchise in Yankee Stadium was a major coup for the AAFC. But it didn't come cheaply. Topping was paid $75,000 by the AAFC owners, plus a promise of another $25,000 from gate receipts. He was also promised "player help" from each of the clubs.

Layden also paid a heavy price for the move. A month after Topping's defection, the NFL abruptly dismissed its commissioner.

"The vagueness and apparent ineptitude of Mr. Layden in coping with the threat of the new All-America Conference caused us to make this move," Boston Yanks executive William Shea said.

Redskins owner George Preston Marshall echoed Shea's harsh assessment.

"We have been trying to imitate the Ivy League too long. Now we'll show them the kind of aggressive action they [the AAFC] have been asking for," he said.

Some newspapers, like the Davenport *Daily Times,* suggested a change at the top had been in the works for some time:

"It was known that some club owners objected to Layden's attitude toward the All-America, notably his advice to the new loop to 'go out and get a football first,' when the All-America outfit wanted to meet with the National several months ago."

Other papers, including the *Pittsburgh Post-Gazette,* supported Layden:

"As the commissioner, he steered the league, insofar as the public was concerned, along a successful highway. His was the old story of an inability to satisfy a group of employers, some of whom from time to time, had conflicting desires. . . ."

Even Ward came to Layden's defense:

"The greatest damage to National League prestige was the removal of Elmer Layden as commissioner," he said.

"When a square shooting, even-tempered man like Layden can't get along with a group operating the National League, it's plain they don't want a leader. To the man on the street on whom pro football must depend for support, Layden stands for the finest qualities and traditions of sportsmanship."

Wasting no time, the NFL announced that Bert Bell, founder and former owner-coach of the Philadelphia Eagles, co-owner of the Pittsburgh Steelers, and the architect of the NFL draft, had been appointed commissioner.

Bell's appointment showed that the NFL was ready, willing, and able to take on the young AAFC.

Bell made a series of rapid-fire decisions designed to put the AAFC on alert. First, the league reversed itself and gave the 1945

NFL champion Cleveland Rams permission to relocate to Los Angeles, a move Rams owner Dan Reeves had long wanted, but one his fellow owners rejected. Now they had a reason. Stop the AAFC.

In a further demonstration of their newfound resolve, the NFL owners made two changes to their constitution and bylaws: first was to cap NFL membership at ten teams, and then to prohibit "more than one franchise in any city in the future."

"By doing this, we are fixing it so that no outside team can get into our league just by making an application," an unnamed league official said.

The owners also provided that any change to the new provisions would require a unanimous consent, rather than the customary four-fifths majority vote.

By early 1946, the AAFC had signed more than 100 former NFL stars coming out of the military, as well as 40 of the 66 members of the 1946 College All-Star team.

The AAFC—the Brooklyn Dodgers, Buffalo Bisons, Chicago Rockets, Cleveland Browns, Los Angeles Dons, Miami Seahawks, New York Yankees, and the San Francisco 49ers—had finally gotten a football and they were ready to play.

WITH ALL the veteran players signed by the AAFC, the quality of play was almost immediately at a level comparable to that of the NFL. But quality football was more evident in some teams than others.

The 3-11 Miami Seahawks failed both on and off the field. After one miserable season, the team folded and was replaced by a new Baltimore team called the "Colts."

The new league's biggest success story was the 1946 Browns. The team that replaced the NFL champion Rams in Cleveland posted an impressive 12-2 record and was well received by fans across the northeast Ohio region. They were also the only team that year—thanks to owner Mickey McBride's commitment to his team's success—to make a profit.

"We intend to spare neither money nor effort to give Cleveland the best pro football club in the country," he told the Associated Press in 1945.

Also, Topping's 1946 Yankees finished with a strong 10-3-1 record, and the league's two West Coast teams, the 49ers and Dons, both had winning records.

The Dons, with their celebrity ownership group that not only included Ameche but minority owners Bing Crosby, Bob Hope, George Raft, Pat O'Brien, and moviemaker Louis B. Mayer, drew a lot of attention and fan support on the West Coast.

But the real force behind the Dons was Ben Lindheimer, a Chicago horse racing multimillionaire. Lindheimer would eventually emerge as the team's principal owner and a league power broker.

There were some surprises in the league's inaugural season. Keeshin's Chicago Rockets, expected to be one of the league's better teams, struggled.

When Ward convinced Keeshin to join the AAFC, he suggested that the NFL's Cardinals were "underfinanced" and he could eventually run them out of town. Keeshin, in a quest to capture the Windy City, even tried to sign star players away from the mighty Bears, including quarterback Sid Luckman.

While Keeshin owned the Chicago franchise, it was rumored that Ward—not wanting to see failure in his home city—was also "keeping a watchful eye on the team."

But those who played for the team weren't so sure that he did.

In 1986, *Los Angeles Times* reporter Bob Oates wrote of one instance of the Rockets' neglect: "One night in New York, when the Rockets showed up at the airport after a game with the Brooklyn Dodgers at Ebbets Field, they were told that their plane wouldn't start." Eventually the players were informed by the club management that the mechanical problem might delay their flight indefinitely. Blankets and pillows were distributed for their comfort.

"Indefinitely" became an all-night sleepover on the charter plane.

"We learned later that our plane was scheduled for a seven a.m.

departure all along," the team's former equipment manager Bill Granholm told Oates. "The club kept us aboard all night just to get out of a hotel bill."

While competing against two established NFL franchises in Chicago was tough enough, a mediocre 5-6-3 finish in 1946 only made it tougher for the Rockets.

Hoping to turn the franchise around, AAFC commissioner Crowley resigned and joined the team as part owner, vice president, general manager, and head coach. It didn't help. They finished 1-13 in 1947. Meanwhile, the "underfinanced" Cardinals won the NFL championship.

Jonas Ingram, the highly respected former commander of the US Navy's Atlantic Fleet, replaced Crowley as AAFC commissioner. In a move meant to be a statement, Ingram relocated the AAFC offices from Chicago to the Empire State Building in New York City.

Adding polish to the league's image, Topping's baseball Yankees co-owners—Larry MacPhail and Del Webb—joined his football ownership group.

Also, the 49ers and the renamed Buffalo Bills both made key signings in 1947. San Francisco signed Illinois University star running back Buddy Young and the Bills penned Notre Dame quarterback George Ratterman.

But, even as some clubs prospered, others struggled, so much so that before the start of the 1948 season, Ingram took the extraordinary step of ordering the league's leading teams to make players available to the weaker teams. His directive was basically ignored—only the Yankees made any meaningful contributions.

In addition to competitive imbalance, three teams—the Colts, Dodgers, and Rockets—were restructured. Robert Embry headed a group that assumed control of the Baltimore franchise; Branch Rickey, the president of the baseball Dodgers, took over the football Dodgers; and Edward Garn headed up a community group that hoped to refuel the Rockets.

Through all the turmoil, the Browns remained the best.

The 1948 squad—featuring future Hall of Famers Otto Graham,

fullback Marion Motley, and end Dante Lavelli—became the first pro football team to go undefeated and untied in both the regular and postseason. The Browns posted a perfect 15-0 record twenty-four years before the Miami Dolphins posted their 17-0 perfect season in 1972.

Near the end of the AAFC's third season, reports began to circulate that peace between the two leagues might be near.

Contributing to the suspicion, Ingram told the Associated Press, "I have explored every avenue leading to peace. I believe it is necessary for the welfare of pro football, the National League as well as ours."

Three days later, representatives of five AAFC teams—led by Lindheimer, chairman of the executive committee—met in Philadelphia with representatives of the ten NFL clubs.

While it was widely reported that the NFL's position was that they'd "absorb" Cleveland and San Francisco, and expand in 1949 from 10 to 12 teams, the AAFC's position wasn't quite so cut-and-dried.

Lindheimer's group pushed for a two-division league that included four AAFC teams.

All parties agreed Cleveland and San Francisco would be a part of any new configuration, but the group couldn't agree on much else.

A frustrated Lindheimer said it was Baltimore's unyielding insistence on being one of the teams to move to the NFL that caused the stalemate.

The lack of a united front from Lindheimer and the AAFC led Redskins owner George Marshall to quip, "Maybe we ought to let them go back and try another year and they'd get tired and give up altogether."

After it became apparent that no solution was in sight, Bell and Lindheimer issued a joint statement that a deal had not been reached.

The statement seemed to leave the door open for further negotiations, saying some formula for a "common understanding" might yet develop.

Ingram, who had suggested he might resign if peace was not achieved, did just that. He was replaced by his assistant, O. O. Kessing.

While formally the meetings were off, informal conversations between the leagues continued. In late January 1949, rumors of an agreement surfaced again.

Although initially denied, secret talks had taken place, but to no avail.

This time the finger-pointing was aimed at Marshall, who remained adamantly opposed to Baltimore being admitted.

The costly war continued, and things got tougher, particularly for the financially hurting franchises in both leagues.

The NFL's Packers, Steelers, and Lions were reportedly in dire financial straits. In the AAFC, the Dodgers and Yankees merged. Six former Dodgers were assigned to the combined team and the rest were added to the Chicago franchise, which was then sold and renamed the Hornets.

With just seven teams, the AAFC abandoned the two-division structure and operated as a one-division league.

Money was so short in Chicago that in the home finale, players from the Hornets and the visiting Browns had to double as grounds crew and clear snow from the field before the game.

Then, on December 7, Bell and J. Arthur Friedlund, the AAFC's legal counsel, met secretly in Philadelphia and restarted the stalled merger talks.

On December 10, after a marathon meeting, the two sides reached an agreement. The NFL would be split into two divisions, the National and American, with the winners of each to meet annually in a "world football championship."

The new league, renamed the National-American Football League, would consist of the ten existing NFL teams plus three AAFC teams—Cleveland, San Francisco, and Baltimore.

Marshall was a surprise supporter of the new league.

"Look at it from this standpoint," he said. "Baltimore is only an hour away by train. The crowds could be tremendous."

The AAFC's Yankees were, in a sense, returning to the NFL.

Ted Collins, the owner of the NFL's New York Bulldogs, purchased Topping's combined Yankees/Dodgers team. As a part of that deal, six Yankees/Dodgers players were allotted to the Giants as restitution. The Bulldogs also purchased Topping's Yankee Stadium lease.

"The merger will get the club owners out of the headlines and the players back in," said Wellington Mara, Tim's son and the Giants' vice president.

The Hornets and the Dons were the only AAFC teams to be completely disbanded.

In a "player-for-stock" deal, Bills owner James Breuil received a one-fourth interest in the Browns in exchange for the rights to three Bills players—halfback Rex Bumgardner, tackle John Kissel, and guard Abe Gibron.

Lindheimer was offered a similar opportunity to "cast his lot" with the Rams. But due to a health condition described as a serious heart ailment, he decided to follow his doctor's orders, which were to "get out of football."

Although the Buffalo and Los Angeles agreements were widely reported as a part of the merger, they were actually "side deals" negotiated by Bell:

"These deals are the results of off-the-record talks last December at which time I promised to do something about making Breuil a part owner of the Cleveland team," Bell said.

The remaining AAFC players whose teams did not wholly merge with the NFL were distributed to the thirteen teams of the new National-American Football League through a special player draft.

While the merger may not have been as inclusive as some of the AAFC franchisees desired, it had a positive impact on the NFL. Pushed by competition, the NFL developed into a truly coast-to-coast league. The AAFC firmly established pro football in cities like Cleveland and Buffalo, where NFL franchises had failed before but would later succeed. And, as the *Chicago Tribune* pointed out in its review of the AAFC's contributions, "It forced the old league to seek new horizons."

One final merger-related change was announced about four months after the agreement was signed: the restructured league would drop its new name and revert to being the NFL.

The league would consist of two "conferences," the National and American—the latter being the only tribute to the AAFC.

While the AAFC did "get a football," in the end it was pretty much deflated.

CHAPTER 12

THE CLEVELAND BROWNS' NFL DEBUT

T HE EAGLES MAY CHASE US OFF THE GRIDIRON," Cleveland Browns coach Paul Brown said. "But we'll be on hand for the game with no alibis."

It was classic Paul Brown. A master at keeping things in perspective.

Part coach, part teacher, and part psychologist, Brown knew how to manage expectations while getting the most out of his players.

The game Brown promised to "be on hand for" was the 1950 NFL season opener between the Browns and the Philadelphia Eagles. This game was different. It wasn't just the beginning of a new season: this was the first game between an NFL team and a team from the defunct All-America Football Conference.

For four seasons the AAFC competed with the NFL for players and fans. But all that ended when the two leagues signed a peace accord and became one entity. The AAFC Browns, San Francisco 49ers, and Baltimore Colts were now full-fledged members of the NFL.

Adding to the game's significance was that the Eagles were the reigning two-time NFL champs (1948 and 1949) while the Browns were the only champions the AAFC had during its four-year existence (1946–49). It was a game that many had hoped would be played at the end of the previous season—before the leagues officially "merged."

Most NFL loyalists were certain their league's best would easily handle the AAFC's best. But there were others—especially those who'd followed the Browns—who thought otherwise.

Ironically, Cleveland's obvious superiority may have hurt the AAFC. Simply said, the Browns might have been "too good." Fans began to believe that a game against Cleveland was a foregone conclusion.

"When I was with the [Chicago] Rockets and we played Cleveland," Hall of Fame halfback and end Elroy "Crazylegs" Hirsch recalled, "it was not whether we would win or lose, but just how bad they were going to beat us that day."

Although the costly four-year war was officially over, pride and pent-up bitterness among AAFC players and coaches, including Paul Brown, remained.

"We never said we could beat the Eagles," he said before the season opener. "We never even claimed we could beat a low-ranking NFL team. All we asked for was the chance."

While a game between champions was attractive, some quietly wondered if it was a trap. Did Bell, who founded the Eagles back in 1933, want his former team and reigning NFL champions to close the book on the Browns and the AAFC? Brown suspected as much.

Publicly, Bell tried to appear unbiased. When asked why he scheduled the best from both leagues as the season opener, he responded bluntly: "Money."

The matchup had special prominence—it was the only NFL game scheduled for Saturday night, September 16. The rest of the league's teams would begin their season the next day. This night was reserved for the champions.

Bell predicted the game would be decided on which team got the breaks.

"I can't see any other difference between the Browns and the two-time winners in the National League," he said.

Well, maybe. Notice how Bell referred to the Eagles as the "two-time winners in the National League" and Cleveland simply as "the Browns."

Although the rival leagues never shared game films, Brown somehow managed to secure several films of recent Eagles games. "Not everyone hated the Browns," he said, suggesting a possible insider assist.

By the time the Browns broke training camp, the Cleveland coaching staff had charted every Eagles play and every offensive and defensive tendency. The coaches and players were ready.

"Brown put teaching into coaching," recalled Hall of Fame coach Don Shula, who played for Brown in the early 1950s. "He brought the classroom into pro football. You'd learn by listening, reading, writing, and reviewing, and then practice on the practice field in order to be ready to utilize your skills."

On the other side, Eagles coach Earl "Greasy" Neale hadn't scouted the Browns and had little access to relevant game films.

"We watched old films," Eagles defensive tackle Bucko Kilroy said. "But they weren't even the same team, really. We wound up playing an AAFC all-star team."

Kilroy correctly pointed out that the Browns added six players to their roster from the other dissolved AAFC teams. Three were awarded as part of a player-for-stock deal worked out between Buffalo owner James Breuil and the Browns. The other three were awarded through a distribution draft of the AAFC players from teams not absorbed into the NFL—Buffalo, Los Angeles, and Chicago. Each of the thirteen NFL teams—including the Eagles—selected three players from the AAFC talent pool.

But for the Eagles, it was the loss of star halfback and future Hall of Famer Steve Van Buren to a foot injury that had the greatest impact on their roster.

Both teams had plenty of quality players. The Browns' offense included Graham, fullback Marion Motley, ends Dante "Glue Fingers" Lavelli and Mac Speedie, and middle guard Bill Willis on defense.

The Eagles were loaded, too. They had quarterback Tommy Thompson, ends Pete Pihos and Jack Ferrante, and center and linebacker Chuck Bednarik.

With an air of excitement usually reserved for a championship game, a largely partisan crowd of 71,237 came to Philadelphia's Municipal Stadium to witness the much-ballyhooed season opener.

The Eagles were confident. But the Browns were prepared.

"If we play the game we're capable of, we'll win," Neale said.

"We know they don't like us," Brown told his team before the game. "It may get rough out there. But remember, the worst thing you can do to an opponent is defeat him. Nothing hurts as bad as losing."

But, in the end, the Eagles played right into the ever-so-ready hands of Brown. Neale's run-stuffing 5-4 "Eagle defense" was relentlessly exploited by Brown's overloaded offense.

Although the Eagles scored first on a 15-yard field goal, the game's momentum quickly shifted to Cleveland.

The Browns' film study paid off. Brown and his staff identified a key weakness in Neale's defense. They put halfback Rex Bumgardner in motion, forcing a defensive back to follow. That put a linebacker on halfback-flanker Dub Jones, who was once described as being "only slightly faster than sound."

"No one can cover our guys one-on-one," Graham recalled. "When we saw that, we knew we had them."

After running the same simple square-out route a few times, Jones let Graham know it was time to strike. The speedy receiver lined up as if to run the same pattern, but this time, after a pump-fake from Graham, Jones cut back behind the defender and turned on the afterburners. Graham dropped a perfectly thrown pass into his open arms. Jones cruised the final 25 yards of the 59-yard touchdown play.

It was the beginning of an all-out aerial assault.

The Browns' passing attack came as no surprise to Neale, who once mockingly joked that Brown was more suited to be a basketball coach, "because all he does is put the ball in the air."

Brown didn't laugh then, and on this day, he and Graham got their revenge. Leading 7–3, with just a minute remaining in the first quarter, Graham hit Lavelli for 26 yards and another score. In the third quarter, he flipped the last of seven pass completions for a 13-yard touchdown to Speedie, making the score 21–3.

Cleveland's "basketball coach" called just three running plays in the first quarter, five in the second, and two in the third. And still Neale stuck with his 5-4 defense.

The Eagles did have one third-quarter drive that provided

Philly fans a measure of hope—for a moment. With a first down at the Browns' six-yard line, Brown—in a surprise move—inserted fullback Motley as a linebacker. Motley provided four consecutive run-stopping tackles. The score remained 21–3.

Then, in the fourth quarter, clearly making a statement, Brown turned almost exclusively to the run. Early in the quarter, with his team at the Eagles' 28-yard line, Brown called seven consecutive, in-your-face running plays, leaving the last one—a one-yard touchdown plunge—for his quarterback. Later, halfback Bumgardner ran two yards for the fifth and final score, and a 35–10 rout.

"I think Paul wanted to make a point," said Graham, who completed 21 of 28 attempts for 346 yards. "I also remember that the next time we played the Eagles after that, we beat them 13-7, and we didn't throw a pass all game."

Brown was his usual stoic self after the game. "We're happy," he said. "But we are not going to gloat when we win a ball game. There's too many others still ahead."

Brown had already cautioned his players not to be bad winners. He famously told his players to "act like you've been here before."

Taking a page from his coach's playbook, Graham restrained himself when asked if the Eagles were "stiffer opposition" than the teams from the AAFC.

"When you play football, you play to win and even the weaker are cocked up to beat us," he said. "There's been a lot written about the two leagues, but any football team is tough to beat."

While Graham was named the game MVP, he made certain to share the glory. "I've been playing with those guys [Lavelli, Speedie, and Jones] since I've been a pro. I know just what they're going to do and no matter what you say, they're the greatest receivers I know of."

In the Eagles' locker room, the mood was understandably somber. Still, Neale and his players congratulated their rivals.

Calling the Browns a great team, Neale praised Graham and said the Browns deserved to win. And in a remark that was half praise and half excuse, he added, "I never saw a team with so many guns."

"Graham," Kilroy added, "may be the best quarterback that ever played the game."

Kilroy's early praise of the four-year pro was well deserved. One can only imagine how he felt when Graham retired following the 1955 season. During his ten-year career Graham led the Browns to ten division or league crowns and was voted all-league in every season but one.

+ + +

SO, WAS the game's lopsided victory enough to win over NFL skeptics? Bell sure sounded convinced:

"What a team," he said. "It's the greatest outfit I ever saw. They're terrific. Really terrific. I could watch them every day."

Then, remembering his role as league commissioner, he tempered his remarks.

"Mind you, I'm not partisan. I'm for a strong NFL. I don't care who wins, as long as the clubs make money, but just the same you can't escape the fact that the Cleveland team looked great—they were great against the Eagles. Even rabid Eagles fans will admit that."

Then, as if suddenly remembering Paul Brown's pregame remarks, Bell said: "And they aren't alibiing their loss."

Later, in a rare emotional display, Brown smiled and confessed that his humility was partly an act.

"I lived in fear all week that we'd blow too soon," he said. "It hardly seemed possible we could hold out another day. I think today we were the best football team I've ever seen. And I've seen a lot."

Then he confessed the secret for his success:

"Four years of ridicule helped us get ready," he said. "Four years of being called a minor-league team. That game meant a great deal to us."

CHAPTER 13

THE NFL'S FINAL FAILED FRANCHISES

THE 1950S ARE FREQUENTLY REFERRED TO AS THE "Golden Age" of the NFL. It was an era of peace and prosperity. It was a decade that began with the addition of three new franchises, as well as the end of a costly war with a rival league.

It featured exciting offenses as typified by the Los Angeles Rams, and bruising defenses as embodied by the New York Giants. It was a decade during which pro football and its television courtship blossomed into a rewarding marriage. And it was an era in which an unforgettable "sudden-death" championship game catapulted the NFL to being America's most popular sport.

However, had it not been for some masterful maneuvering by Bert Bell, the decade might have been remembered very differently.

For all its successes, the NFL faced major challenges during the early part of the 1950s. Three franchises—the 1950 Baltimore Colts, the 1951 New York Yanks, and the 1952 Dallas Texans—all went belly-up.

But Bell managed to take the three separate fiascoes and turn them into one of the biggest sports success stories of the decade: the 1958 NFL championship game.

The Colts, originally a replacement team for the AAFC's Miami Seahawks, were—along with the Cleveland Browns and the San Francisco 49ers—one of the three All-America Football Conference teams absorbed into the NFL as part of the 1950 NFL-AAFC merger. While the admission of Cleveland and San Francisco was unquestioned, the inclusion of the Colts surprised many. Not only had the team won only five games in their three seasons in the

AAFC, but they were located within the protected territory of the Washington Redskins.

Initially, Redskins owner George Preston Marshall vetoed Baltimore. But when the league agreed to require a $150,000 "territorial rights fee" over a three-year period, Marshall changed his tune. (That fee is roughly equal to $1.6 million today.)

How the famously underfinanced Colts would meet this requirement remained a mystery, especially after the Colts had told the NFL immediately after the merger that it would not sink any more money into the franchise. The board's answer was to turn the team over to club president Abe Watner in the hope that he could somehow right the ship.

But Watner, the likable owner of a Baltimore cemetery, couldn't do much to resurrect the floundering team.

After a 1-11 record in 1950, and a personal loss of $106,000, for which his board refused to reimburse him, Watner threw in the towel, but not before the league agreed to pay him $50,000 for the team's 65 player contracts.

Angered by Watner's decision to fold the team, and the payment he received for the contracts, a small group of the team's investors claimed they'd been sold down the river and so petitioned Bell to reinstate their failed franchise.

The commissioner told the unhappy investors he would do that if they cleared some debts and paid Marshall $150,000—his territorial rights fee—and an additional $50,000 for the player contracts. Otherwise, Bell ruled, the franchise would be forfeited to the league.

Unwilling—and likely unable—to accept Bell's terms, the group instead filed a lawsuit seeking an injunction and damages for the "fraudulent surrender" of the franchise.

As the Colts' investors attempted to litigate their way back into the NFL, Ted Collins, owner of the struggling New York Yanks franchise, was fighting to remain a league member.

Collins's Yanks originally called Boston their home. But in 1949, after five unsuccessful seasons there, he made a deal with the

NFL to cancel his Boston franchise and grant him a new franchise for New York.

But Collins first had to make some tough concessions to play in the protected territory of Tim Mara's New York Giants and in the same Polo Grounds stadium.

First, there was to be an annual territorial rights fee of $25,000. Then Collins had to agree that the Giants would have first choice of all home game dates.

That provision left Collins few opportunities to book attractive games. Twice, Collins's team, which he named "Bulldogs," played on a Friday night and once on an even less appealing Thursday night. Other than a game against the stadium-sharing Giants that drew 17,704 fans, the Bulldogs averaged only 6,060 fans at home games.

The truth is, the NFL never really intended for Collins's team to play in the Polo Grounds in 1949. They placed them there simply because the league was convinced the AAFC was going to fold or come to some merger agreement that would allow the Bulldogs to shift over to Yankee Stadium.

Then, right on cue, as a part of the NFL-AAFC merger agreement, Collins purchased the assets of Dan Topping's combined AAFC Yankees-Dodgers team, which included an eight-year lease on Yankee Stadium.

While Collins's team—which he renamed the "Yanks"—would no longer share the Polo Grounds, the Giants still retained the first-choice rights of home game dates.

And, as an additional concession to Mara—who was victimized by competition from the AAFC—the Giants were awarded contract rights to six players of Mara's choosing from the Yankees-Dodgers roster.

But even without the six players Mara gobbled up, Collins's Yanks were much improved. Quarterback George Ratterman, who came over to the Yanks from the AAFC's Buffalo Bills, led the squad to a respectable 7-5 record in 1950.

The next year things went south—or rather north. Ratterman

jumped to the Canadian Football League and the Yanks plummeted to a 1-9-2 record.

Making matters worse, two of the Yanks' home games had to be played on the road because the World Series was being played in Yankee Stadium. The Yanks' average attendance for four home games was just over 9,000.

Rumors began to circulate that after eight years of red ink and losing teams, Collins was looking to sell his franchise. But if selling was his plan, he sure didn't sound like it at the NFL's 1952 winter meeting.

On the first day of the three-day gathering, Collins told his fellow owners he was there to insist on "equality with every other member club in the league." That meant he wanted to schedule six home games on Sundays at Yankee Stadium after the baseball season had ended, regardless of the Giants' schedule.

Having reportedly lost $1,500,000, most owners were convinced Collins wanted out. To that end, Bell was already quietly in talks with at least one suitor.

While working on that prospect, the commissioner learned that the Colts' investors who were suing the league planned to make a pitch to Collins to relocate his team to Baltimore.

Bell was not pleased.

"Baltimore interests expressed a desire to reenter the league last year," he told reporters. "We gave them the opportunity to meet all requirements by October 1, 1951. When they didn't do so, we forgot about it."

Bell then strategically shared his news that a thirty-one-year-old textile millionaire named Giles Miller had offered to buy the Yanks. Three days later, Bell announced that Miller's $300,000 offer had been accepted and the Yanks were moving to Dallas. Collins would be paid $100,000 for his franchise and $200,000 would be paid to settle the remaining seven years of the Yankee Stadium lease.

As a part of the deal, Mara also agreed to forgive the $175,000 owed him for the remaining seven years of his territorial-rights arrangement with Collins.

"The Giants now will be the only football team in New York—
and that's forever," Mara proclaimed.

While some questioned the NFL's judgment of placing a team
in Dallas—a city where college football was king—others questioned Miller's sanity for attempting to do so with the Yanks'
castoff players. More generous critics called Miller's move
"courageous."

Whether crazy or courageous, Miller expressed complete confidence in the move. "We have everything in Texas to make our
venture a huge success—football interest, a big stadium, a source
of tremendous native material, and an enthusiastic group of owners
who love the game and are willing to go along if they never make a
dollar of it," he said.

Miller's first order of business was to assure the good folks of
Texas that he would change the team's unholy nickname. The
team was first called the Texas Rangers, but Miller later changed
it to the Dallas Texans, reflecting his belief that a team's nickname
should include the name of the city that supported it.

Asked if he felt Texans would support pro football, Miller said,
"There is room enough in Texas for all kinds of football."

Jinx Tucker, a columnist for the *Waco Tribune-Herald*, didn't
share Miller's optimism. The day before the Texans' home opener
against the Giants, Tucker wrote:

> *The Texans have not demonstrated that they have a team
> capable of getting into contention, and while the opener may
> draw well, prospects are not bright for pro football to be a fi-
> nancial success in Dallas. The big drawing card in Dallas
> is very apt to continue to be SMU. Few cities in the land will
> support a pro team and a major college team.*

Tucker was right. The Texans wouldn't be a contender. Their
opening day roster included twelve former Yanks players, sixteen
rookies, and a mishmash of mostly discarded players from other
teams.

And even though there was "room enough" for pro football in

Dallas's 75,000-seat Cotton Bowl, it wasn't needed. Only 17,499 curious spectators showed up for the team's debut.

Though the turnout was disappointing, the game began on an optimistic note when the Texans scored first.

Just minutes into the contest, a New York defensive back fumbled a punt that was recovered by the Texans on the Giants' 22-yard-line. Two plays later Dallas halfback George Taliaferro threw a two-yard touchdown pass to halfback Buddy Young. The extra-point attempt failed, something the Texans would do six more times during the season.

Photos of the first NFL touchdown in Dallas show the nearest defender to Young was the same Giants player who fumbled the punt—Tom Landry, the future Dallas Cowboys Hall of Fame coach.

Also—although you won't find this note in any pro football history book—the Taliaferro-to-Young touchdown pass was the first pass completion for a touchdown between two African American players in NFL history.

Still, the Texans fell to the Giants 24–6 that day. And things only got worse from there. Dallas continued to lose and crowds continued to shrink.

Amazingly, as bad as the team played, the roster did include two future Hall of Fame players: end Gino Marchetti and tackle Art Donovan. And there was the explosive backfield of Young and Taliaferro. But potentially more explosive than the Young-Taliaferro backfield was the Cotton Bowl's policy of segregated seating. It was an issue Miller attempted to address before the start of the season.

"In Texas, Negroes and Whites get along very well," he said. "They sit in their own sections, but we are reserving just as good seats for our Negro fans as we do for the whites."

One Dallas newspaper noted, "Anticipating heavy demand for tickets from Negro fans, the Texans have set aside reserved seats and general admission sections for them."

Whether as a result of public pressure or more likely an overall lack of ticket requests, a minor blow for social justice seemed to have been struck when segregated seating appeared not to materialize.

"The Texans knocked out Jim Crow," Young suggested some years later. But Taliaferro remembered it differently.

In a 2017 interview the ninety-one-year-old halfback told the *Dayton Daily News* that his wife was not permitted to sit with the other wives at home games; she was instead relegated to the distant "colored section."

Since the Texans' four home games in the cavernous 75,000-seat Cotton Bowl averaged only 13,500 attendees, it's hard to say for sure whether the segregated seating law was enforced. In the end, whether it was a "colored section" or a "whites-only section," most sections looked identical—because they were empty.

After just seven money-losing games, Miller was forced to turn his franchise back over to the league.

Bell minced no words in accepting ownership of the team. Flanked by two league attorneys and standing before a small group of reporters, Bell telephoned Miller to officially inform him that his franchise was forfeited and that the players' contracts were taken over by the league.

For the final five games of the season, the Texans were wards of the league and operated as a road team out of Hershey, Pennsylvania. Their two remaining home games were relocated. One, against the Lions, was shifted from Dallas to Detroit, and the other, against the Bears, was played at Akron, Ohio.

The Akron game was booked as the second part of a Thanksgiving Day football doubleheader. The first game, played between two local high school teams, outdrew the Texans-Bears game.

There were so few people in the stands that Texans coach Jimmy Phelan was said to have suggested that rather than being introduced on the field, his team should "go into the stands and shake hands with each fan."

Phelan hadn't lost his sense of humor and his team hadn't lost its will to win. The Texans stunned the overconfident Bears 27–23 that day.

"We had a good time in spite of everything," said Donovan, "mostly because of Phelan."

Phelan was popular with the team. His disdain for practice was particularly appealing to his players.

"Once, we ran a couple of plays without fouling up," Donovan recalled. "Jimmy stopped practice, loaded everybody on a bus, and took us to the racetrack. Jimmy loved the races."

Another popular Phelan story is how he cut quarterback Don Klosterman after missing a field goal in the Texans' opener. Klosterman, who'd led the nation's passers at Loyola the previous year, was understandably irate.

"Hell, I was a quarterback, not a kicking specialist," he said. "The ball hit the upright and bounced back. And the next day I got cut."

Later, while he was reviewing the game film with the team, Klosterman's kick came up on the screen. Phelan, sensing some players were still upset with his decision, stopped the film and ran it back a second time. "There!" he shouted. "Who says I didn't give him a second chance?"

The Texans' failure was a combination of bad timing, bad management, and bad luck. As Phelan put it, "We got all the breaks and they were all bad."

As bad as the Texans were, there was a silver lining. The need for a replacement team to balance the resulting eleven-team league had the potential for ending the Baltimore lawsuit.

Bell recognized that a new Baltimore franchise would not only fill the void created by Dallas's forfeiture, but it might also end the ongoing lawsuit.

Careful not to overplay his hand, Bell portrayed the restarted talks with Baltimore as having no connection to the Dallas situation.

"I have been talking with the group in Baltimore for the last year and a half about a league franchise," he told reporters, "and I'm still talking with them, but no agreement has been reached whatsoever."

Attempting to further distance his negotiations from the failed Dallas franchise, Bell emphasized that any group entering the league would be granted a new franchise, not a "reconditioned franchise from some other city."

If Baltimore were the league's choice, "the team would not be operated by the old Colt organization." On this point he was explicit. Any Baltimore franchise would be a new franchise, not a continuation of the Dallas franchise, nor a rebirth of the canceled Baltimore franchise.

Though the stars seemed to be aligning in Baltimore's favor, and Bell truly wanted a franchise in that city, he was still skeptical about the city's ability to support a team. His solution was to conditionally grant a franchise with the stipulation that 15,000 season tickets had to be sold before the league's next meeting, which was just seven weeks away.

It was a daunting task that was enthusiastically accepted by community leaders. Motivated by the prospect of pro football's return, Bell's ticket sales challenge was met with more than two weeks to spare.

Within days, a five-man syndicate headed by Carroll Rosenbloom—a textile manufacturer and acquaintance of Bell—was introduced as the owners of the new Baltimore franchise. Initially, Rosenbloom indicated he wasn't interested, but Bell convinced him otherwise.

Joining Rosenbloom as a minority investor was Bruce Livie, an automobile dealer and thoroughbred breeder. In an apparent compromise, three former Colts investors were included as minority investors.

Would Baltimore have been granted a new franchise had Dallas not purchased the Yanks and then gone "belly-up"? Who knows?

What is certain is that the Baltimore franchise was not, as some contend, a continuation of either the New York Yanks–Dallas Texans franchise, or the earlier Baltimore Colts franchise. The 1953 Baltimore team was a new, unencumbered franchise, plain and simple.

And it was that franchise that went on to close out the Golden Age of the NFL with back-to-back championships, including their first, the 1958 NFL championship game, remembered by many as "the greatest game ever played."

To paraphrase Jimmy Phelan, "Who says the NFL didn't give the Colts a second chance?"

CHAPTER 14

THE GREATEST GAME EVER PLAYED AND THE LEGEND OF JOHNNY UNITAS

THE 1958 NFL CHAMPIONSHIP GAME BETWEEN THE New York Giants and the Baltimore Colts had a little bit of everything: dramatic drives, a big second-half comeback, eight momentum-changing turnovers, a controversial forward-progress call, a blocked field goal, a clutch field goal, a timely interruption of play, and a one-yard game-winning run.

It was classic David versus Goliath—a young blue-collar Colts team facing the establishment Giants, whose roots went back to the league's leather-helmet days of the 1920s. It included a contrast in quarterbacks—the Giants' popular-but-aging Charlie Conerly against the Colts' youthful, up-and-coming Johnny Unitas.

The game also featured some of the league's greatest players.

Only two seasons removed from an NFL crown, the Giants' star-studded roster included halfback Frank Gifford, tackle Roosevelt Brown, linebacker Sam Huff, end Don Maynard, safety Emlen Tunnell, and defensive end Andy Robustelli. Every one of them is in the Hall of Fame. Their head coach, an ex-Marine named Jim Lee Howell, had two assistants, both future Hall of Famers: Tom Landry on defense and Vince Lombardi on offense.

As for the Colts, their Canton-bound contingent included tackles Art Donovan and Jim Parker, defensive end Gino Marchetti, running back–flanker Lenny Moore, end Raymond Berry, quarterback Unitas, and coach Weeb Ewbank.

When you include Giants owner Tim Mara and his son, team vice president and owner-to-be Wellington Mara, there were seventeen future Hall of Fame players, coaches, and administrators involved in the game.

And if that's not enough, it ended in sudden-death overtime, a first in NFL championship play.

Forty-five million fans tuned in to NBC-TV for the nationally broadcast game. Chris Schenkel, the Giants' regular announcer, and Chuck Thompson, the voice of the Colts, shared the play-by-play duties.

Astonishingly, the game didn't sell out and was blacked out in the New York City market. Some blame the ticket-sales slump on a nineteen-day citywide newspaper strike that ended the day after the game. And there's a good chance they were right, considering that much of the pregame hype and ticket promotion was lost due to the missing news dailies.

Some 20,000 Colts fans didn't need the New York papers to remind them where and when the championship game would be played.

Still, 6,000 fewer fans were at the title game than had attended the two teams' earlier regular-season matchup. The Giants won that one, 24–21, after which thirty-seven-year-old Conerly remarked, "We out-gutted them."

While Conerly's remark was meant as a salute to his teammates for winning a "tough one," that wasn't how it was interpreted by Colts fans and players alike. They took it as a shot at Unitas, who had been sidelined by an injury sustained the week before.

In that game, against the Green Bay Packers, Unitas took a hard hit from linebacker John Symank. The next morning he paid a visit to his doctor, who found he had three broken ribs and a collapsed lung.

It appeared Unitas's season was over. And for a mere mortal, it probably would have been. But after sitting out the next two games, Unitas—fitted with a nine-pound sponge-and-rubber-lined aluminum corset—returned to action. The tough-as-nails kid from Pittsburgh managed to split the Colts' remaining four games. Baltimore finished with a Western Conference best 9-3 record.

Over in the Eastern Conference, Conerly's Giants posted an identical record. It would be a rematch—this time for the title.

Like every coach does before the big game, Ewbank looked for just the right message to deliver to his squad before their first championship battle.

In a stroke of genius, the mild-mannered coach decided to remind his squad that many of them had been discarded or cast off by other teams.

"Nobody wanted you guys," he told his team, reminding them that fourteen of their numbers had been cut or traded from other teams.

Gino Marchetti remembered it well.

"In fourteen years, I heard them all. Win one for Mother. Win one for Father. Don't disappoint all these people watching on television," he said. "He didn't miss anybody—Ameche, Green Bay didn't want you; Lipscomb, you were released; Berry, people said you'd never be a pro; Donovan, they got rid of you—too fat and slow."

And, as Ewbank continued, one player after another, he eventually got to Unitas. Everyone wanted to hear what he'd say about their quarterback's arduous journey to the big leagues.

Unitas was born in Pittsburgh on May 7, 1933, the third of four children. When he was five years old, his father died.

With little in his life to inspire him, Unitas developed a love of football. He would later say that all he ever wanted was to be a football player.

He got his first chance at St. Justin's, a small Catholic high school just across the Ohio River from Pittsburgh's North Side. Only about 250 boys attended St. Justin's, compared to the 1,300 or so who attended Pittsburgh's Central Catholic or the 1,000-plus attending North Catholic.

Dan Rooney, the son of Pittsburgh Steelers owner Art Rooney, attended North Catholic and was the football team's starting quarterback.

"The kids at North Catholic considered St. Justin's a 'B-league team,'" Rooney wrote in his autobiography. But, as the future head

Professional football was born on November 12, 1892, when William "Pudge" Heffelfinger, an All-American guard at Yale, accepted $500 to play for the Allegheny Athletic Association in a game against the Pittsburgh Athletic Club, the first known instance of a player being paid.

This expense accounting sheet of the Allegheny Athletic Association documents Pudge Heffelfinger's acceptance of $500 to play one game of football.

The National Football League—originally known as the American Professional Football Association—was founded in Canton, Ohio, on September 17, 1920, in Canton Bulldogs owner Ralph Hay's Hupmobile automobile dealership located in the Odd Fellows Building.

Joe Carr, who served as NFL president from 1921 until his death in 1939, was one of the NFL's most significant pioneers. Carr was also the founder of one of pro football's most notable early-day teams, the Columbus Panhandles.

The Washington Senators were members of the NFL for just one season (1921). Although they played a full schedule, only three games were against league members and two of those were against the Canton Bulldogs. This rare program is from the Senators' inaugural NFL game on November 27, 1921, against the Bulldogs.

One of pro football's most unusual teams was the Oorang Indians. A member of the NFL for the 1922 and 1923 seasons, the team was composed entirely of Native Americans and featured player-coach Jim Thorpe.

The decade of the 1920s is often referred to as the Golden Age of American Sports. Seemingly every major sport had its own superstar. In college football, the star was Harold "Red" Grange. When he turned pro and joined the NFL's Chicago Bears in 1925, it was headline news.

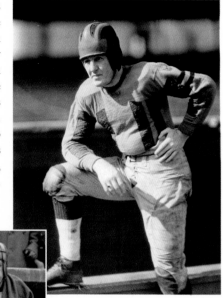

Even while sitting on the bench nursing an injury, Red Grange was "newsworthy," as this wire service photo suggests.

It wasn't unusual in the NFL's early years for the season to end with more than one team claiming the league title, a matter that would ultimately be resolved by vote at the next owners' meeting. No debate was more contentious, however, than the one over the 1925 title, which was eventually awarded to the Chicago Cardinals.

The first NFL game played under lights was on Wednesday, November 6, 1929, after a heavy rainstorm caused the Providence Steam Roller to cancel their scheduled Sunday home game against the Chicago Cardinals. The game was rescheduled in Kinsley Park, a minor-league baseball stadium in nearby Pawtucket. It was considered a success, and other night games—like this exhibition game between the Bears and the non-league Milwaukee Badgers in 1930—soon followed.

In 1932, the Chicago Bears and the Portsmouth Spartans played an extra game to break a tie in the standings and determine the league champion. Due to frigid conditions, the game was moved indoors to Chicago Stadium and played on an 80-yard field. The game's lone touchdown came on a pass play from Bronko Nagurski to Red Grange. The Bears won 9–0.

PITTSBURGH PIRATES PROFESSIONAL FOOTBALL SQUAD, 1933

FRONT ROW--LANTZ-CLARK-JANACEK-KATTIER-DECARBO-LETZINGER-WHELAN.
MIDDLE ROW--ARTHUR J. ROONEY, (PRESIDENT)-VAUGHAN-ROBINSON-DAILEY-
SWARTZ-SORTET-SHAFFER-COOPER-CRITICHFIELD-KELSCH-HOGAN (TRAINER)
BACK ROW--HOLM-TANQUAY-OEHLER-WOSS-TESSER-ARTMAN-RHOADES-KEMP-
MOORE-BROVELLI-DOUDS (COACH)

The NFL added three franchises in 1933: the Cincinnati Reds, the Pittsburgh Pirates, and the Philadelphia Eagles. While the Reds and the Pirates borrowed the names of their baseball counterparts, the Eagles, founded by Bert Bell, took their name and logo from the 1933 National Industrial Recovery Act. The Reds folded after the first eight games of the 1934 season. In 1940, the Pirates, founded by Art Rooney, were renamed the Steelers.

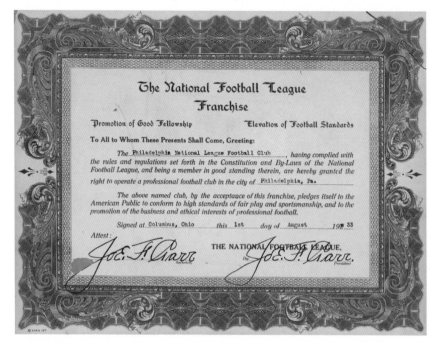

In 1932, George Preston Marshall was granted an NFL franchise for Boston. The team was originally named the Braves, but Marshall changed the name to Redskins in 1933. Following the 1936 season and after winning the NFL Championship, Marshall relocated his franchise to Washington, DC.

The National Broadcasting Company (NBC) made television and pro football history on October 22, 1939, by becoming the first network to televise an NFL game. Two cameras were used—one on the field and one shooting over the shoulder of play-by-play announcer Allen Walz.

In the 1940 NFL Championship Game, the Chicago Bears' offense, featuring their T-formation with the man-in-motion, scored eight touchdowns—one by air and seven on the ground. They also scored three touchdowns on interceptions. Bears halfback George McAfee (ball carrier) provided one of the game's eleven touchdowns, on a 35-yard interception return.

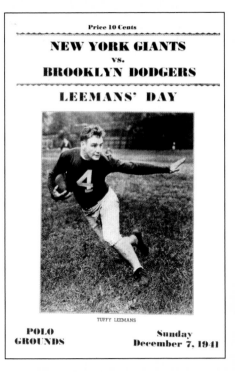

NEW YORK GIANTS
vs.
BROOKLYN DODGERS

LEEMANS' DAY

TUFFY LEEMANS

POLO GROUNDS

Sunday December 7, 1941

Three NFL games were under way when Japan attacked Pearl Harbor on December 7, 1941. In New York's Polo Grounds, where the Giants were playing the Brooklyn Dodgers and fans were celebrating "Tuffy Leemans' Day," the public-address announcer interrupted his commentary to tell all servicemen to report to their units. Similar announcements were made at Chicago's Comiskey Park and at Washington's Griffith Stadium.

In 1943, due to the shortage of NFL players caused by World War II military service, the Philadelphia Eagles merged for one season with the Pittsburgh Steelers. The team was frequently referred to as Phil-Pitt or the "Steagles."

OFFICIAL PROGRAM

EAGLES-STEELERS vs **GIANTS**
OCTOBER 9, 1943
PHILADELPHIA, PA.

This Program Sponsored by Navy League Service

OFFICIAL PROGRAM 25c

BROWNS
vs.
MIAMI
SEAHAWKS
SEPTEMBER 6th, 1946

CLEVELAND STADIUM

The Cleveland Browns played their first game as members of the new All-America Football Conference on September 6, 1946, against the Miami Seahawks. More than 60,000 fans were on hand to witness the league's first game. The Browns defeated the Seahawks 44–0 and went on to capture the AAFC title in each of the league's four years of existence.

Bert Bell, the founder/owner of the Philadelphia Eagles (1933) and creator of the NFL Draft (1936), was named NFL commissioner in 1946. Bell built the NFL's image to unprecedented heights and led the league through the four-year war with the rival All-America Football Conference.

There are seven Cleveland Browns from the original 1946 AAFC team who are members of the Pro Football Hall of Fame. Six of them are shown here (left to right): end Dante Lavelli, fullback Marion Motley, tackle/kicker Lou Groza, coach Paul Brown, quarterback Otto Graham, and center Frank Gatski. Absent is guard Bill Willis.

Pro football was reintegrated in 1946 when the AAFC's Cleveland Browns signed fullback Marion Motley (left) and guard Bill Willis (right), and the NFL's Los Angeles Rams signed halfback Kenny Washington and end Woody Strode.

of the Steelers organization pointed out, "that didn't keep them from taking note of Unitas."

Rooney often recounted how after the 1949–50 high school football season, he expected to be named first-team quarterback on the city's All-Catholic team. He was shocked when he fell to second team behind that "B-team" quarterback from St. Justin's.

Looking back on it, Rooney had to admit there was no shame in being second to the great Unitas.

Despite his All-Catholic recognition, Unitas received no college football scholarship offers. Notre Dame, the University of Indiana, and the University of Pittsburgh each gave him a quick look, but just as quickly sent him home.

It was one setback after another, but Unitas wouldn't give up on his dream. His determination was what inspired his high school coach, Max Carey, to keep looking for a place for his quarterback to play. Carey eventually reached out to the University of Louisville, whose team's backfield coach paid Unitas a visit—he quickly realized Unitas had more potential than the two quarterbacks already on the Louisville roster.

Louisville turned out to be a perfect fit. After a 1-3 start in 1951, coach Frank Camp decided to roll the dice and insert his long-shot quarterback into the starting lineup. Neither ever looked back.

The next season, Louisville "deemphasized" its football program, reducing the number of scholarships and the size of its roster. Still, Unitas, who was also playing defense, continued to turn heads.

One of those heads was Rooney's.

"When the 1955 NFL Draft took place in January, Unitas wasn't on anybody's—not the coaches' or sportswriters'—radar," Rooney recalled.

When the ninth round rolled around and Unitas hadn't been selected, Dan told a staff member, "We gotta get this guy now, 'cause we don't want him playing against us."

The Steelers already had three quarterbacks on their roster and Coach Walt Kiesling thought young Rooney's pick was "nuts." Maybe for that reason Kiesling took an instant disliking to Unitas.

Although the coach kept him throughout the preseason, he never put him in for a single play in a single game.

"It might have been better to have Kies cut Johnny at the beginning of camp rather than stringing him along through the final preseason game before letting him go," Rooney said. "Now he didn't have a chance to sign on with another team, at least for that year. Johnny never forgave him."

It's probably safe to say that given similar circumstances, most folks would have given up hope. But Unitas wasn't most folks. While working a construction job during the day to support his family, Unitas played sandlot football for six dollars a game with the Bloomfield, Pennsylvania, Rams.

At the end of the season, Bloomfield coach Chuck Rogers sent Colts general manager Don Kellett a letter recommending a Rams offensive lineman. The young Colts were so bad, they had open tryouts on Saturdays. Kellett wrote back that he was "looking for this guy named Unitas." Apparently someone had written a letter about the sandlot quarterback.

Rogers immediately told Unitas he'd been invited for a tryout in Baltimore.

Unitas thought it sounded a little too informal and almost didn't go. But he did. Then, after waiting more than a month for word back from the Colts, Kellett called. He told Unitas to come back and work out for Ewbank. If the coach was impressed, he'd be invited to training camp. If after that he made the final roster, he'd be paid $7,000.

Over the years, the story of the letter and Unitas's contract signing became a mainstay of Ewbank's repertoire. "We received a letter from a fan telling us there was a player in Bloomfield deserving a chance," Ewbank would recount. "I always accused Johnny of writing it."

Unitas's first game was hardly a thing of beauty. It was so forgettable, he remembered it incorrectly. For years Unitas told the story of how he made his debut in the fourth game of his rookie season against the Chicago Bears.

In his typically self-deprecating way, he'd tell how his first play resulted in an interception returned for a touchdown and how two of his fumbles were converted into touchdowns by the Bears.

Three plays, three turnovers, three touchdowns, and a 58–27 loss. An unremarkable debut, to say the least. But what was lost in his recollection of this oft-told tale was that his debut occurred two weeks earlier, in a Saturday night game against the Detroit Lions.

Down 31–14, Ewbank put his rookie quarterback in during the waning moments of the game to mop up as time ran out. Officially, Unitas began his pro football career with an incomplete pass, followed by a scramble for 23 yards, and then, as time ran out, he threw an interception.

So, if you add the last three plays of the Detroit game to the first three of the next game he played, Unitas began his career with an incomplete pass, two interceptions (one of which was returned for a touchdown), two fumbles (both of which resulted in touchdowns), and a 23-yard gain on a single rushing attempt. By any measure, it was a pitiful start.

But things got better fast. Within weeks the nervous rookie was performing like a seasoned veteran, winning four of the Colts' remaining eight games.

In his rookie-season finale, Unitas threw a 53-yard game-winning bomb with just twelve seconds remaining to defeat the Washington Redskins, 19–17. It was an exclamation point on a day that began with him being named the Colts' Rookie of the Year.

So, two years later, when Ewbank gathered his troops in that Yankee Stadium locker room, he could have carried on and on about Unitas's long and challenging road. Instead, though, he kept it simple. Ewbank reminded Unitas that, like all the others, he too had been overlooked and discarded.

But now Unitas and the rest of his team of castoffs were right where they deserved to be. They weren't fighting for a roster spot, they were fighting for the NFL championship. "So," Ewbank said with dramatic emphasis, "you should win this game for yourselves."

THE GAME

The Giants won the coin toss and elected to receive. Quarterback Don Heinrich, not Conerly, started the game. Starting Heinrich was a favorite ploy of offensive coordinator Lombardi. Heinrich would start, share what he saw with his coach, then, after a series or two, give way to Conerly.

The Giants also had some unusual strategic help from Wellington Mara, who took Polaroid photos of the Colts' alignments from atop the stadium press box. The near-real-time images were then placed in a weighted sock attached to a cable and launched to the sideline below and delivered to the coaches for review.

While Heinrich's opening series usually consisted of a few conservative running plays to get a sense of the defense, this day he came out throwing. Each of his unexpected aerials, however, fell harmlessly to the Yankee Stadium turf. The Giants ended their first series with a punt.

The Colts began their first drive on their own 30. Two running plays failed, so on third-and-six, Unitas dropped back to pass. A blitzing Sam Huff read the play beautifully. Busting through the line, he smashed into Unitas's chest, knocking the air out of his lungs and the ball out of his hand. The Giants recovered on the Colts' 37.

Looking like the G-men might score first, the Colts' defense toughened. Marchetti flattened Heinrich and recovered the loose ball. But the momentum switch was short-lived. On third-and-five, Unitas was intercepted. Three series and three turnovers. Both teams seemed to be suffering a major case of the jitters.

Following another good punt by the Giants, the Colts started their next drive from their own 15. Unitas caught the Giants' defense guessing run. They were wrong.

Unitas launched a perfectly thrown pass deep to a racing Lenny Moore, who pulled it in at the Giants' 25. But the big play had little impact. After gaining just one yard in the next three attempts, Ewbank called for kicker Steve Myhra to attempt a field goal. It went wide. But the Giants were offsides and Myhra got another chance, and five yards closer. Huff busted up the middle and blocked Myhra's kick.

Finally, late in the first quarter, the Giants put the game's first points on the board, a 36-yard field goal from Pat Summerall.

On the first play of the second quarter, Gifford, the Giants' reliable halfback, fumbled and the Colts recovered on the New York 20. Five plays later Alan Ameche scored on a two-yard run, giving the Colts a 7–3 lead.

The Keystone Cops routine of miscues by both teams continued. First the Colts fumbled a punt, turning the ball over on their own 10-yard line. Then, Gifford returned the favor and coughed the ball up again, this time at the Colts' 14. Fifteen plays later, Unitas connected with Berry on a 15-yard touchdown, giving the Colts a 14–3 halftime lead.

"I told the squad at intermission to assume we were two touchdowns behind and go out and get at least two to tie," Ewbank said. Over in the home team locker room, Jim Lee Howell didn't have to make believe.

But in the third quarter it looked as if it were the Giants who'd listened to Ewbank's pep talk. Down two scores, they came roaring back.

The comeback began with yet another fumble. On a third-and-two from their own 13, Conerly tossed a short pass to Kyle Rote, who ran to the Colts' 25. There the Colts' Andy Nelson stripped him of the ball. But Giants halfback Alex Hawkins, acting as if it were part of a designed play, grabbed the loose ball on its first bounce. He rumbled to the one-yard line. Two plays later, Giants fullback Mel Triplett scored.

On the Giants' first drive of the fourth quarter, Gifford, who'd already fumbled twice, redeemed himself with a 15-yard touchdown reception. Suddenly the Giants' two-score deficit was gone and the Colts were trailing, 17–14.

Twice the Colts threatened the Giants' lead, and twice they failed. As the clock ran down, the Giants looked for safe plays that would move the ball and kill the clock. A couple of first downs and they would be NFL champions.

"It was third down, right?" Donovan remembered. "They need four yards. And they give the ball to Gifford and it looks like he's gonna make the first down. If he does we're in deep trouble."

Gifford followed his blockers, but someone missed Marchetti, who grabbed the elusive halfback and pulled him down. Almost immediately the Colts' Don Shinnick and Gene "Big Daddy" Lipscomb piled on.

"Big Daddy fell on Gino," Donovan said. "His leg snapped and it sounded like a gunshot."

Confusion ensued. The referee called for time-out and the head linesman called for a stretcher. With all the commotion, several Giants players began to question if the referee had spotted Gifford's forward progress correctly.

"I made that first down," Gifford insisted after the game. "I know I did. But the officials ruled it otherwise, so what can you do."

"A lot of players wanted to go for it on fourth down," Howell later said. "But we had a great punter in Don Chandler and the best defense in the league. And there wasn't but a few minutes left. I thought the only way we were in trouble was if they blocked the punt."

Chandler did his part, forcing the Colts' return man, Carl Taseff, to make a fair catch at the Baltimore 14. Just 1:56 remained in regulation play.

In the huddle, Unitas told his players, "We need this one." Forgetting all the miscues and missed opportunities, Unitas then calmly went to work.

Throughout the game, the Giants' defense was faced with a tough choice. Should they double-team Moore or Berry? For much of the game it was Moore.

Colts ends coach Bob Shaw didn't think the Giants could get away with that for long.

"We were running what we call the 'I'-pattern, where Berry goes down the sidelines and either buttonhooks in or angles towards the center. When Johnny Unitas and Berry are hitting, it's tough to stop, and they were hitting."

As legendary *New York Times* sportswriter Art Daley saw it, "The real dramatics came when the Colts were seemingly beaten, 17–14, with only a little more than a minute from the end. That's when Unitas, the best pitcher Baltimore has seen since Iron Man

McGinnity, delivered three clutch plays. Berry clutched the ball on three passes that whisked 62 yards and set up the tying field goal."

Since there had never been an overtime game in regular- or postseason play, the fans in the stadium, the television audience, and even many of the players were uncertain what to expect of the tie. Would a tie mean co-champions? Would there be a tiebreaking game, or would it go into overtime?

Those questions not only added to the game's drama, they kept the eyes of the massive national TV audience glued to their screens.

Fortunately, the sudden-death overtime provision had been added—with little fanfare—to the NFL Rules Book in 1955.

The crowd roared with approval when the Giants won the coin toss to start the overtime period.

But whatever optimism they felt didn't last long. They couldn't convert on third down and were forced to end their first possession with a punt.

"We had the game locked up in the third period and almost blew it," said Unitas. "We were disgusted with ourselves and we struck back at the Giants with sort of a blind fury."

That fury began with Unitas's final drive in regulation and continued with his first drive in overtime.

From his own 20, he moved his team to the 41. But the Giants' defense hadn't given up, either. Unitas was dropped for a 15-yard loss. Then, facing a third-and-15, Unitas found Berry for a 21-yard completion to the New York 43.

In the huddle, Unitas calmly called for the same play. But when he got under center, he saw Huff falling back from his linebacker spot to help the secondary. The ever-aware Unitas audibled. Instead of a pass, he sent Ameche up the middle for 23 yards. Suddenly it was first-and-ten from the Giants' 20. A quick handoff to running back L. G. Dupree was stopped for no gain, followed by a 12-yard pass completion to Berry.

Then, as if the game hadn't had enough twists and turns, an official suddenly called time-out. What appeared to be an overly excited or drunk fan had run onto the field. Only later was it learned that it was a member of the NBC sideline crew.

The TV technician was frantically trying to alert field judge Chuck Sweeney that the game had somehow gone off the air. Anxious Colts fans attempting to make their way to the field had knocked loose a cable to the NBC equipment room.

The TV audience never saw Berry's 12-yard catch. Instead they saw a message that read "PLEASE STAND BY PICTURE TRANSMISSION HAS BEEN TEMPORARILY DISRUPTED."

Sensing the urgency of the moment, Sweeney called his own clutch play.

"I gave the guy an extra minute beyond the usual ninety seconds for a commercial time-out," he said. "He was holding a walkie-talkie to his head. Finally, I told him, 'That was it. We had to resume play.' But he was already smiling, and I knew we were back on."

With the television audience again looking on, Unitas handed off to Ameche for a one-yard gain to the Giants' seven-yard line. Then, well within field goal range, Unitas surprised everyone. Forgoing a safe running play, he threw a pass to Jim Mutscheller along the right sideline. Mutscheller pulled it in and was tackled at the one.

"There was no risk of interception," Unitas said after the game. "If Mutscheller didn't get it, nobody would."

With a third-and-one, everyone in Yankee Stadium, including the Giants' defense, anticipated a handoff to Ameche. However, instead of running behind the lead block of the Colts' all-world left tackle Jim Parker, Unitas called "16 Power," a play designed for Ameche to run between right guard Alex Sandusky and right tackle George Preas.

The exhausted but adrenaline-driven linemen delivered. Even Ameche seemed surprised by the size of the opening. He dove untouched into the end zone for the game-winning score.

"We just had to win because this was the better ball club out there," said Ewbank. "And," he added, remembering his pregame speech, "we never give up, that's us."

"We out-gutted them!" shouted Art Spinney in the winner's locker room, referencing Conerly's earlier but not-forgotten remark.

Howell was gracious in defeat.

"We were only a few feet and seconds away from taking it all, but they are great and we have nothing to be ashamed of. When you let a club go all the way twice like that then you know that they are great. We have a great defense and they went right through it."

Ewbank, who had been hired five years before, was overjoyed and lighthearted in the locker room. "I miscalculated," he told Colts owner Carroll Rosenbloom. "I predicted it would take five years to build a champion. It took me an extra quarter."

Gene Ward of the New York *Daily News* summarized the game this way: "In the years to come, when our children's children are listening to stories about football they'll be told about the greatest game ever played—the one between the Giants and Colts for the 1958 NFL championship. I never expect to see a better thriller."

As for Gifford's claim that he made the first down on the Giants' all-important last drive, Howell reviewed the film the following day. "We thought he made it," he said, "but it sure doesn't show on film. And the play happened right in front of our bench."

The ever-popular Marchetti, who watched the end of regulation play lying on a stretcher on the sidelines, missed the overtime period. Game officials, fearing he'd be trampled by onrushing fans, ordered him to the locker room.

"The worst part about being hurt," he told *Baltimore Sun* reporter Cameron Snyder, "was missing the last two minutes. I wanted to stay but they wouldn't let me."

His appreciative teammates gave him a game ball.

When asked years later about his role and the significance of the game, the humble defensive star chuckled and said, "If you fire a BB gun in New York, by the time the news of it gets to Los Angeles, it was a Howitzer."

Art Donovan may have summarized the game best: "We started the greatest era in the history of the NFL, and I mean it. All my teammates will swear by it. We helped put major-league football on the map."

Donovan was right. The 1958 championship game was the beginning of an era. An era that was best defined by the gritty perseverance of one man: Johnny Unitas.

CHAPTER 15

THE "HUNT" FOR A NEW LEAGUE

HOW CAN ANYONE BE PROUD TO HAVE LOST A MIL-lion dollars?" Wayne Valley, part owner of the Oakland Raiders, asked at the 1962 American Football League owners meeting. "I propose we rename this league 'the Foolish Club,' because that's what we are."

Silence initially greeted Valley's remark. Then the room burst into laughter.

It wasn't that the AFL owners thought losing money was funny. It was just that Valley's sarcasm was the splash of cold-water humor the group needed. It reminded them that despite the grim financials for the 1961 season, they were precisely where they expected to be at that juncture.

Lamar Hunt, the man who'd convinced the others to join him as members of "The Foolish Club," never let them forget that moment. And, for the AFL's eight original owners, the moniker became their "badge of honor."

"I was an amateur photographer then and had taken some color pictures of several games [during the 1960 season]. I had a montage of eight photographs, each three by five, showing each team in action, and I sent them out as Christmas gifts one year. At the top was hand-lettered the phrase 'The Foolish Club.' "

Hunt's quest to become an owner of a pro football team began in 1958 when he attempted to purchase an NFL expansion team for his hometown, Dallas.

"I went to see Commissioner Bert Bell, late in 1958," he recalled. "He said the league really wasn't interested in expansion."

While the NFL may not have been ready to expand, it was in fact interested. Bell had recently appointed Chicago Bears owner George Halas and Pittsburgh Steelers owner Art Rooney to an expansion committee, with Halas serving as chairman.

Halas was a strong proponent of expansion. As early as 1956, he'd predicted the NFL would expand to sixteen teams, through successive grants of franchises to four cities, during the period 1960–65.

Although Bell discouraged Hunt, he urged him to seek out Walter and Violet Wolfner, owners of the financially struggling Chicago Cardinals. Bell intimated that the Wolfners might be in the market to sell or move their team to another city.

Hunt contacted the Wolfners, but the couple constantly equivocated.

During the course of conversations, the Wolfners mentioned a couple of people who had also tried to buy the Cardinals. One of those men was another Texas oilman, K. S. "Bud" Adams.

After a meeting with the Wolfners in January 1959, Hunt had a brainstorm—why not start his own league?

"It was a one-man thing for a while, until I called Bud Adams in Houston," he said. "He was the first person I contacted because I felt it was important to have a Dallas-Houston rivalry."

Lamar's brother Bunker set up the meeting in March 1959.

Adams was initially confused about what Hunt had on his mind.

"We talked about everything, but I couldn't figure out what he wanted," Adams remembered.

"It wasn't until I drove him back to Hobby Airport and, just as he was getting out of the car, he said, 'Bud, I'm thinking about starting a new league. Are you interested in joining me?' I said, 'Hell, yeah.'"

Encouraged, Hunt began to organize. He evaluated cities and identified men of means who might join him. His list included Denver minor-league baseball executive Bob Howsam, Minneapolis businessmen Max Winter, and H. P. Skoglund. Each of them had also unsuccessfully approached the Wolfners.

At the same time Hunt was looking to bring a pro team to Dallas, so too was Clint Murchison Jr., yet another rich Texas oilman.

Murchison had at various times in the 1950s attempted to purchase the 49ers, the Redskins, and the Cardinals.

In February 1959, Murchison met with Halas, who told him the NFL might look favorably upon franchises in Dallas and Houston, to begin play in 1961. He told Murchison to circle back with him in the fall and they'd discuss the formalities of applying for a franchise.

A few months later, in July 1959, Bell testified before the Senate Antitrust and Monopoly Subcommittee that a new league was planning to operate in six cities, and that the NFL welcomed the competition.

What the subcommittee didn't know was that Bell—who had been made aware of Hunt's plans for a new league just a few weeks earlier, by mutual friend and former Eagles quarterback Davey O'Brien—had asked Hunt for permission to mention his planned new league. Bell thought it would serve as a great example of the NFL's openness to competition, and Hunt thought it would be great publicity for his soon-to-be-announced league.

"The more teams and the more competition, the better," Bell told the lawmakers. He also said that he'd polled the twelve NFL owners and found that the idea of a rival league "hadn't met with a single objection." Bell then told the lawmakers he was meeting with representatives of the proposed new league the following day, which was true.

The fact was, he could have had a meeting right then and there. Hunt, according to biographer Michael MacCambridge, unbeknownst to the senators "sat silently in the back of Room 318 of the Senate office building listening." As Hunt would later describe, he "got to hear the actual birth of the American Football League, as told by Bert Bell."

Bell did meet with Hunt and O'Brien the next day.

During their meeting, Hunt emphasized that he wanted to maintain a friendly relationship with the NFL. He again proposed that Bell serve as commissioner of both leagues and that they hold a common player draft. He also suggested both leagues work together on a single television contract.

Although Bell rejected Hunt's offers, he offered plenty of advice, telling the men that while another league was possible, they had a lot of hard work ahead.

"It will take them three or four years to build qualified teams," he told the press after the meeting. "They'd have to make television arrangements, draw up contracts, draft players, secure stadium rights, arrange publicity, get their franchises, and [address] many other details."

If Bell's cautionary public assessment was meant to discourage Hunt, it didn't work. A few days later, on August 3, Hunt and Adams announced their intention to form a league. Two weeks later, on August 14, Hunt introduced the charter members of his new league.

Hunt presented himself as owner of the Dallas franchise. Howsam was there for Denver; Adams for Houston; Winter and a third partner, Bill Boyer, represented Minneapolis–St. Paul; Barron Hilton, son of the hotel tycoon, signed for Los Angeles; and Harry Wismer, a former minority owner of the Redskins and well-known radio announcer, signed for New York. Willard Rhodes of Seattle attended but announced he'd been unable to secure a playing site and was withdrawing, at least for the time being.

Eight days later, in a meeting in Los Angeles at the Beverly Hilton, the owners gave their new enterprise a name—the American Football League (AFL). It was a name that, according to AFL publicist Jack Horrigan, took a long time to be accepted. For the first half of its life the AFL was almost universally referred to as "the Other League."

Responding to the AFL's progress, Halas asked Hunt and Adams to meet him in Chicago. They agreed. Howsam came along as well.

Halas got right to the point.

"Lamar, I'll give you the Dallas franchise in the NFL. Bud, I'll give you the Houston franchise. But I don't want anything to do with Denver," Howsam recalled Halas saying.

Taken aback by the blunt offer, the three men asked for time to discuss it.

After a long review, Hunt and Adams assured Howsam that they were sticking with him and the other AFL owners.

On October 14, 1959, NFL owners gathered in Philadelphia to attend the funeral of Bell, who had died three days earlier of a heart attack while attending a game between the Eagles and Steelers—two teams he once coached and owned.

While in Philly, the owners called a special meeting and authorized Halas to explore expansion options and "make any moves he deemed wise." The vote was 11–0, with the Redskins' George Preston Marshall abstaining.

Less than a week later, Halas, along with committee member Rooney, announced that the NFL would expand into the key AFL cities of Dallas and Houston in 1960.

Murchison and a minority partner, Bedford Wynne, a well-connected, sports-minded Dallas attorney, were introduced as applicants for the Dallas franchise. Although Murchison's original plan was to apply for a franchise for 1961, Halas moved up the timetable by a year to "more effectively compete with the AFL Dallas team." Murchison was even willing to include Hunt as a partner.

The Houston applicant was identified as Craig Cullinan Jr., grandson of J. S. Cullinan, founder of Texaco.

Although the Halas-Rooney announcement was intended to sound like a done deal, it was not. Under pressure from some of his fellow owners—specifically Marshall and the Wolfners—Halas later acknowledged that Murchison and Wynne and Cullinan would have to secure stadiums and make formal applications for their franchises before the upcoming January meeting. At that time their applications would be considered by the full membership.

Meanwhile, Ralph Wilson Jr., a Detroit insurance and trucking executive and minority owner of the Lions, contacted Hunt to express his interest in a Miami franchise.

"I read in the paper that Lamar Hunt was starting a new league and one prospective site was Miami. So I called him cold and introduced myself and said I had a home in Miami and would he consider me for the franchise down there?"

Hunt told him he'd better act fast because others were interested. Wilson took Hunt's advice and flew to Dallas the next day.

When Wilson failed to secure a lease for the Orange Bowl, he decided to go back home and just forget the whole thing.

Hunt wasn't giving up so quickly. He called Wilson and suggested he consider any one of five other locations: Buffalo, St. Louis, Cincinnati, Louisville, or Atlanta.

Wilson called Nick Kerbawy, a longtime friend and former GM of the Lions, and veteran sportswriter Eddie Hayes and asked them which one would they pick.

Both said Buffalo.

After hastily scheduled meetings with Buffalo civic leaders who pledged their support, Wilson was back on board. In late October he was awarded the AFL's seventh franchise.

Shortly after hearing the news, Halas made another offer; he told Hunt and Adams that Dallas and Minneapolis could join the NFL in 1960, and Houston and Buffalo would be added in 1961.

It was a tempting proposition.

"Bud and I sat down," Hunt later told Horrigan. "Obviously, we were being asked to leave the American Football League in its embryonic state in return for the NFL franchises we'd originally wanted. But we both agreed that we made a commitment to the other fellows in the AFL and we felt we had to live up to our commitment."

The two men's loyalty to their partners wasn't shared by one owner.

At the new league's fall meeting in Minneapolis, a ten-man group from Boston, led by businessman Billy Sullivan, had just been approved as the holder of the AFL's eighth franchise when Harry Wismer announced that New York newspapers were reporting that Minneapolis was defecting to the NFL.

The report was initially denied by owner Max Winter.

"I'm with you guys one hundred percent," he told Hilton.

The next day he announced he was withdrawing from the AFL.

Winter's sudden change of heart was the result of the NFL's decision to drop Houston as a franchise applicant after Cullinan was unable to secure a playing site and meet other league requirements. Minneapolis was now the leading contender to replace Houston in the NFL expansion derby.

H. P. Skoglund, one of Winter's two partners, continued to insist that Minneapolis was sticking with the AFL.

"We will be playing football in the American Football League next year and we have no intention of going into the National," he said.

Skoglund even posed for an Associated Press photo depicting the eight AFL owners huddled up at the Minneapolis meeting with their hands together in a show of unity.

The photo's caption read: "All for one."

With rumors flying, the AFL owners still managed to address their other two agenda items: a player draft and a television policy.

In what would become a model for future television contracts, the owners agreed to a cooperative plan that would divide television revenues equally among its members.

As for the draft, Hunt summed it up well: "We were ill prepared."

Recognizing their collective lack of experience, the owners recruited the league's only team personnel guys to run the draft for the entire league: Dallas general manager Don Rossi, Denver general manager Dean Griffing, Houston director of player personnel John Breen, and Los Angeles general manager Frank Leahy.

The quartet of personnel professionals provided the owners with a list of the eight top-ranked college players at each offensive position. Each team would then pull one name out of a box until all the teams had a player for each offensive position. Then the process was repeated until each team had three full offensive squads.

But before the unusual selection process began, the owners agreed that each team would also select one "highly publicized player" from their region. The hope was that such high-profile territorial "bonus picks" would become the cornerstones of their teams and major gate attractions.

LSU running back and Heisman Trophy winner Billy Cannon was the most acclaimed college star. His rights were awarded to

Adams's Houston team, which led to one of the most famous signing stories of all time—one that Adams loved to tell—as well as a lawsuit from the NFL.

Cannon was the subject of an intense interleague recruiting battle between Houston and the NFL's Los Angeles Rams. Pete Rozelle, the Rams' general manager, was rumored to have signed the LSU star, even though he still had one game—the annual Sugar Bowl—of college eligibility remaining.

"I got in touch with Billy's trainer," Adams said, "and I told him that if Billy had signed with the Rams with one game left, I'd pay him [Cannon] twice what he got.

"I was at home at the time with my wife [Nancy], and I told her I was going to get a collect call from Baton Rouge real quick, and I did."

True to his word, Adams offered Cannon a contract that would double his $10,000 signing bonus as well as each of his three one-year $15,000 contracts. Adams told him he'd meet him at the Sugar Bowl to finalize the deal.

Adams signed Cannon under the goalpost after the Sugar Bowl, a publicity coup for him and the new league.

Afterward, Adams invited Cannon to drive back to Houston with him.

"I was driving Nancy's new Cadillac. I wanted him to meet her, and I was going to show him around and celebrate.

"We were at my house, and Nancy was fixing us some dinner. Billy told me his father had worked in a factory in Baton Rouge all his life and never had any money and had always wanted a Cadillac before he died. I could tell he wanted that one.

"Well, I gave Billy the keys and told him to go out the front door. He did. In a few minutes, Nancy came out from the kitchen and asked where Billy had gone. I told her back to Baton Rouge. She asked how he was getting back to Baton Rouge. I told her he got in the car and left. She said, 'Do you mean my car?' I told her 'Yes.' Naturally, she wasn't too happy about it. I told her I'd buy her a new one the next day."

And he did.

Cannon wasn't the only player signed on the Sugar Bowl field that day. Two other prominent players, Charlie Flowers and Johnny Robinson—both of whom had already signed with NFL teams— signed AFL contracts after the game.

The signings were beautifully orchestrated by Adams. All three renounced their NFL agreements a day or so before the game. Then, after the game was over and their college eligibility fulfilled, Cannon signed with Houston, Flowers with Los Angeles, and Robinson with Dallas.

It wasn't only a major public relations win for the AFL, but also an embarrassment for the NFL.

Adams was sometimes perceived as the aggressive counterbalance to the mild-mannered Hunt.

"Bud is somewhere between me and George Marshall," Hunt once said.

Their good-cop, bad-cop relationship was needed and effective.

Troubled by the threats posed by their new rivals, the NFL executive committee gathered at the Kenilworth hotel in Miami Beach three days before the official start of the league's mid-January annual meeting. Halas presented his expansion plan: Dallas would be admitted in 1960 and Minneapolis–St. Paul in 1961. Two other franchise applications—St. Louis and Miami—were tabled for future consideration.

Murchison and Wynne were ready to go in Dallas, while Winter's Minneapolis group was relieved to learn they had an extra year to prepare.

Winter had committed to the NFL several weeks earlier; his partners, Skoglund and Boyer, insisted they'd remain loyal to the AFL.

But once the Minneapolis Stadium Commission indicated its preference for an NFL tenant, Skoglund and Boyer rejoined Winter.

While Halas was certain Dallas and Minneapolis were the most logical expansion cities, he wasn't sure he had enough votes to deliver on his promises.

NFL bylaws required unanimous support before the league could expand. Marshall and the Wolfners were considered definite no votes.

While Marshall expressed strong opposition in general, he was particularly opposed to Dallas. The Redskins were the "team of the South," and Dallas would hurt his television and radio rights.

In a very public display of dissension, the Redskins' owner shared his objections: "The only reason for expansion I've heard from other owners is that we could destroy the new league," he told the Associated Press.

"If that is the only reason, then we are guilty of monopolistic practices. No one can give me an intelligent reason for adding a couple new franchises."

Marshall insisted he wasn't opposed to expansion per se.

"I would prefer to see the AFL operate for at least three years and see what happens," he said. "It would be proof that the NFL is not a monopoly. If the AFL succeeds, it will help the NFL. If it failed, it wouldn't hurt anyone but the owners of that league."

While the Wolfners also expressed concern about lawsuits and antitrust violations, their primary objection was that expansion would reduce the number of locations they might bargain with to relocate their franchise. And, like Marshall, they were concerned about how a Dallas team would affect their southern TV audience.

A frustrated Halas attempted to allay fears of antitrust action. The veteran owner explained that the expansion plans were "a culmination of five years of planning," not a reaction to the new league.

"Our intent always has been to expand when competition among our clubs began to equalize itself on an extremely high level. We have now reached that plateau," he said.

In a naked ploy to stymie the opposition, pro-expansion owners pushed through a bylaws amendment allowing expansion if approved by a ten-twelfths majority vote, rather than unanimous consent. It was a plan Halas had been shopping around for some time.

But even with the bylaws change, it appeared Halas might not have the votes. Two owners who had previously indicated support of his plan—Rams owner Dan Reeves and 49ers owner Vic Morabito—were wavering, questioning Halas's maneuvering. And Wellington Mara of the Giants was also thought to be uncommitted.

Mike Brown, owner and cofounder of the Cincinnati Bengals, attended the volatile meeting with his father, Paul, who was part of the Cleveland contingent. Brown later described how emotional Halas had become about the issue.

"I gave my word," Brown recalled a choked-up Halas saying as he pleaded for support.

He also said how his father told the other owners they owed Halas their support.

Edwin Anderson, president of the Lions and a strong Halas supporter, reminded the owners that they had authorized Halas to "make any moves he deemed wise."

"Anyone other than Marshall"—who abstained in the 1959 authorization vote—"who votes against expansion is reneging on a moral commitment," Anderson said.

In the end, Reeves, Morabito, and Mara supported Halas. Marshall, the vociferous leader of the opposition, also relented and voted yes. The Wolfners abstained.

To get Marshall's vote, certain conditions, including a $600,000 payment over two years, imposed on both new members, was negotiated.

"I fought for the conditions and when they passed I found some of the members had slipped, so I had to talk in favor of expansion. It brought out the laughs," Marshall said.

"It took a great load off Halas's shoulders," Anderson said. "When the vote was completed, I reached over and shook George's hand. There were tears in his eyes."

An appreciative Halas had some kind words for his longtime rival from Washington. "In the clutch, the old pro joined up," he said.

While Halas was pleased with his success, the AFL owners and recently hired commissioner Joe Foss were anything but. "An act of war" was how Foss characterized the NFL's expansion plans.

"We are looking into possible courses of action through the courts, Congress, or any other means," Foss said. "The AFL will definitely take action."

Hunt was equally blunt:

"Antitrust laws are designed to foster competition and not kill it off. It's pretty clear who has the monopoly here, and it is certainly the National Football League, and not the AFL."

With the last-minute defection of Minneapolis, the AFL scrambled to add a replacement franchise. Applications from Atlanta, Oakland, and San Francisco were all considered.

While Atlanta was considered the front-runner, Barron Hilton successfully campaigned for Oakland.

On January 30, 1960, the eight-team AFL—the Boston Patriots, Buffalo Bills, Denver Broncos, Houston Oilers, Dallas Texans, Los Angeles Chargers, New York Titans, and Oakland Raiders—was complete and ready to compete on and off the field.

A little more than five months later, on June 9, the AFL signed a five-year television deal with the American Broadcasting Company. The contract was for $1,785,000, with graduating increases each subsequent year of the contract. The cooperative revenue-sharing plan was a major step toward the league's eventual success.

Then, on the heels of that announcement—as Foss had warned and Marshall had feared—the AFL filed a $10 million antitrust lawsuit against the NFL.

While the AFL would eventually lose that case, the league won back-to-back interleague player-dispute cases. Within days of each other, two Los Angeles judges ruled in favor of the AFL regarding the signings of Billy Cannon and Charlie Flowers. The rulings enabled them and Johnny Robinson to play for their respective AFL teams.

Both leagues were emboldened by their courtroom victories. But they were just the opening salvos of what would become a costly, years-long war. And despite the back-and-forth battles between the leagues, the AFL kicked off its inaugural season on September 9, when the Denver Broncos defeated the Boston Patriots 13–10.

The "Hunt" for a new league was officially over, and the Foolish Club was a reality.

"I don't know what part of this venture is business and what part is personal with me now," Hunt said after his Texans played their first game. "I just know it is very important that I succeed."

Hunt's AFL did succeed. Over the next decade, the league would introduce pro football to new markets and fans, develop new stars, increase player opportunities, implement new ideas, and play 616 games, before merging with and improving the NFL in 1970.

In 1960 that all looked improbable, if not impossible.

CHAPTER 16

A COMPROMISE CANDIDATE, CONGRESS, AND TV

A LTHOUGH MUCH OF THE FOCUS OF THE NFL'S 1960 annual meeting was on expansion and the challenge of the AFL, the most heated, divisive, and time-consuming debate centered on who would replace Bert Bell as NFL commissioner.

While the club owners knew it would likely be a contentious debate, no one expected it would take seven days and twenty-three ballots before a decision was made.

A dozen or so candidates were rumored to be in contention, but only three men were in the running—Austin Gunsel, the league's treasurer and acting commissioner; Marshall Leahy, a San Francisco attorney and chief legal counsel for the 49ers; and Edwin Anderson, president of the Detroit Lions. Of those three, the clear favorites were Gunsel and Leahy.

The old guard, led by Redskins owner George Preston Marshall, favored Gunsel, a former FBI agent. Aligning with the often-recalcitrant Marshall were Frank McNamee of the Eagles, Carroll Rosenbloom of the Colts, and, in later rounds, Art Rooney of the Steelers. That group favored a football man from within the ranks. And they wanted the league office to stay in the East.

Supporting Leahy—a man more aligned with the league's newer ownership groups—were Vic Morabito, owner of the 49ers; Dan Reeves of the Rams; and the Chicago Cardinals' Walter Wolfner. This group felt the commissioner's office had routinely favored their counterparts on the East Coast. They favored a candidate from outside the ranks. And their choice—Leahy—pledged to move league headquarters to San Francisco.

Leahy could also number the owners of the Packers, Browns, Lions, and later the Giants among his supporters.

From the beginning, Bears owner George Halas had decided to abstain from all voting on the issue. He feared that taking a side might hamper his ability to get the votes he needed for his expansion plan, which was scheduled for a vote at the same meeting. Halas knew he was one or two votes shy and didn't want to make any last-minute enemies. Whoever emerged as commissioner would be okay with him.

"All we ask is a reasonable facsimile of Bell," he told the *Detroit Free Press*. "A man who will be honest, capable, courageous, and industrious."

The clubs supporting Leahy were determined to get their man. Not only did they repeatedly reject Gunsel, but they refused to consider any of the other candidates. They needed nine votes and they knew they were close.

The first vote resulted in seven for Leahy, four for Gunsel, and an abstention by Halas.

On the second ballot Leahy appeared to be making progress. Rooney voted for him, giving him eight votes. Halas, who could have ended it, passed again, something he'd do twenty-one more times.

Gunsel lost more ground on the third vote and by the fifth most of his supporters had flipped to Anderson.

Just before the sixth ballot, Rosenbloom nominated his popular general manager, Don Kellett—fresh off back-to-back championships with the Colts—as an alternative. Another divided vote resulted. It was obvious the Leahy supporters were not going to compromise.

As the hours, days, and debate continued, tempers flared.

"You people are being ridiculous," Rosenbloom told Leahy's supporters. "If God Almighty came down from heaven and agreed to serve as commissioner, you'd vote for Leahy."

On the twentieth ballot, the vote remained the same. The "solid seven," as the Leahy supporters were known, wouldn't budge. But the opposition—the "fearless four"—was just as stubborn.

Finally, Cleveland's Paul Brown had had enough. A Leahy supporter, he realized that the single-mindedness and egos at play were just too strong. Something had to give.

That's when Reeves, a staunch Leahy supporter, approached Brown with an idea.

"This will never end if we don't do something," he said. Then he suggested Brown consider nominating Pete Rozelle, the Rams' thirty-three-year-old general manager.

"I will not vote against Leahy," Reeves told Brown, "but if you put Pete up, I promise I'll leave the room and not vote at all."

Brown agreed and immediately sought out Giants owner Wellington Mara as an ally. Mara approached Rooney, who in turn sought advice from his son Dan. The younger Rooney knew Rozelle and thought he'd be a good compromise. His father agreed and joined the Brown-Mara alliance.

Then, in a brilliant tactical move, Brown, without consulting the others, reached across the aisle to Rosenbloom. Hinting he might already have enough support, Brown offered Rosenbloom the opportunity to be the dealmaker. He asked Rosenbloom to do the honors and nominate Rozelle. Wanting to end the impasse, and emerge as the guy who got it done, Rosenbloom agreed.

Brown and Mara then decided they'd better share their plan with Rozelle. They found him in his hotel room.

"I just looked at them," Rozelle later recalled. Stunned, he wondered if he was the right choice.

"You'll grow into the job," Brown assured him. He advised Rozelle to talk it over with Reeves, and leave the rest to him and Mara.

In the final session of the seventh day of the January 26 meeting, Rozelle was asked to leave the room. The young Rams executive was so far off everyone's radar as a candidate that the ever-watchful press corps paid no attention to him as he exited the meeting room.

Not wanting to wander too far, Rozelle camped out in a nearby men's room pretending to wash his hands whenever anyone entered.

As Rosenbloom began his Rozelle nomination presentation, Reeves—as promised—left the room. A vote was taken, and at

10:35 p.m. Pete Rozelle—the compromise candidate—was elected NFL commissioner.

The vote was eight in favor, one against, and three abstentions. Halas, Anderson, and Reeves abstained and the 49ers' Morabito voted in Leahy's favor.

Immediately after the vote, Rozelle and the press were ushered into the meeting room. Rozelle was warmly welcomed by applauding owners.

Fresh from his long stay in the men's room, the new commissioner turned to the surprised sportswriters, held up his hands, and said: "As you know already, I come to this job with clean hands."

Rozelle was the ideal compromise candidate. He was acceptable to the Leahy block because he was from the West Coast and understood their challenges. He was acceptable to the Gunsel faction because he was a favorite of Bell, who three years earlier had recommended him for the Rams' general manager position.

"I may have been picked because I was the only one who hadn't alienated most of the people at the meeting," Rozelle later said.

When Cameron Snyder of the *Baltimore Evening Sun* asked him if he thought he was a "compromise candidate," Rozelle said, "No, of course not. How could I be a compromise candidate? It just took 23 ballots to find me."

The new commissioner wasted no time establishing himself as a take-charge leader. He immediately announced he would keep the league office in Philadelphia for one year and then relocate to New York. That evening he conferred with Gunsel and convinced him to stay on as the league treasurer.

At the opening session the following day, he made clear his attitude concerning expansion, calling it a "must" for the league.

Two days later, Halas got his votes and the league added Dallas for the 1960 season and Minneapolis–St. Paul for 1961.

Even with the contentious issue of expansion out of the way, Rozelle knew he faced several other pressing challenges, including the threat of the rival league, the need for a league-wide television strategy, and related antitrust exemption negotiations.

+ + +

IMMEDIATELY AFTER the Dallas expansion was announced, AFL commissioner Foss delivered his "act of war" accusation.

Dallas, he insisted, was a "one-team town," and the AFL was already there and ready to go. An NFL franchise in the AFL headquarters city was evidence of the NFL's plan to "continue their monopoly in pro football," Foss said. He threatened to go to Congress or the courts or use any other means to stop the NFL invasion.

Rozelle, with just two days on the job, responded: "It's unfortunate that the AFL commissioner feels obliged to continue threats while the NFL would much prefer to develop a harmonious relationship with the 'proposed' new league."

It was typical Rozelle. As one national writer later noted, Rozelle was famous for confronting his problems with a standard formula: "Get all the information you can. Leave the other fellow with his dignity. Whenever possible use tact, not toughness. And allow room for the human touch."

Rozelle's response to Foss perfectly fulfilled that description. It was brief, on point, and diplomatic.

Halas, fresh off his expansion victory vote, was more Halas-like:

"The AFL people crying over the fight over the Dallas franchises should read the record," he said. Quoting Bert Bell's 1957 testimony before the House Judiciary Committee, Halas pointed out that the NFL had long planned to expand. Houston, Dallas–Fort Worth, Miami, Minneapolis, and Buffalo were all places Bell mentioned in his testimony as "crying for football teams."

No "harmonious relationship" offer from Halas, just counterpunches.

Dallas Cowboys president and general manager Tex Schramm—who had hired Rozelle in 1952 as a public relations specialist for the Rams—appreciated Rozelle's communication skills.

"He was able to accomplish things because he was able to bring diverse groups of egotistical, strong-minded owners and managers together and do things that were necessary to be done for the betterment of the league. Not necessarily the individual clubs," he said.

Rozelle was the "glue" that made it all work, Schramm said.

"To have a man that had his background and understanding with dealing with people, dealing with the media, the new world of television, and promotion was the most fortunate thing that ever happened to the league."

Even with Rozelle's measured response to Foss, it didn't take long for the AFL-NFL war of words to escalate. But, without losing sight of the challenge posed by the rival league, Rozelle knew he also had to focus on the other pressing issues: television and centralizing the league's operation.

To help accomplish both, the media-savvy and public relations–conscious commissioner moved the league's offices to New York City, the media capital of the world, a few months earlier than planned.

In 1960, NFL games were broadcast on three different networks, with each team negotiating its own deal. Baltimore and Pittsburgh were on NBC. Cleveland was on the Independent Sports Network. The other nine teams were on CBS, which also held rights options for 1961 and 1962.

Rozelle understood that teams negotiating separately was an unsustainable model. After nearly a year of study and discussions with individual teams, sponsors, and the networks, Rozelle reported his findings to the club owners at their January 1961 meeting.

Sponsors, he said, were concerned over diminished ratings that they attributed to "dilution" caused by individually negotiated games on multiple networks. Rozelle pointed out that such deals essentially put the league in a position where it was competing against itself. And, he reported, the AFL—carried on yet another network, ABC—was cutting into their market.

Rozelle feared that ratings drops for some of the weaker teams foreshadowed the possibility that they would lose their individual TV contracts.

His solution was a single-network approach where all fourteen teams—including Dallas and Minnesota—would share equally in television revenue.

"With only seven home games and a forty percent share of the road gate, each team, especially a losing one, needed TV money," he argued.

A team could land all the top draft choices, but the league's balance of power couldn't be maintained if every team didn't have the cash to sign the top picks.

If the league were to broadcast only the week's top game, the money would be better, but fans would lose road game telecasts.

"We can't let that happen," he said. "That would be letting down the people who stuck with us during the lean years."

The good news, Rozelle reported, was that CBS had tentatively offered a two-year, $9.3 million deal for all NFL regular-season games in 1962 and 1963.

He strongly recommended the offer be accepted.

"The big-city people—Halas, Reeves, the Maras—went along," Rozelle later said. "If Green Bay lost its television money, they wouldn't have a balanced league. It was an altruistic decision on their part."

Getting the "big-city people" to go along was no small accomplishment. And initially, some, like the Rams' Dan Reeves, opposed it.

"I had a big argument with Reeves," said Dan Rooney. "He [Reeves] said it wasn't fair," and shouldn't pass. Rooney warned Reeves that if he voted against the plan, he'd make sure that when the Rams played in Pittsburgh, they'd be blacked out.

"That's cutting your own nose off," Reeves replied. To which Rooney countered, "So we're going to cut your nose off, too."

"From then on," Rooney smiled and said, "he called me 'Bad Dan' . . . but that's the way it happened. There was a lot of discussion that took a lot of effort and thoughts in getting this together and Pete [Rozelle] had a lot to do with that."

Adding to some of the initial opposition, Rozelle openly expressed to the owners the likelihood that the Justice Department would challenge the legality of the single-network contract. And so it did.

On July 20, 1961, US district court judge Allan Grim ruled the agreement violated his 1953 judgment that upheld the league's "blackout rule"—the right to prohibit televising home games that were not sold out—but barred a single-network deal by the league.

Rozelle had hoped the judge might recognize the changing dynamics of the media since his earlier ruling. He did not.

A single-network policy, Grim ruled, restricted the rights of individual clubs to negotiate their own deals and was therefore a violation of antitrust laws.

Disappointed but undeterred, Rozelle huddled with the league attorneys. Together they decided legislation, not litigation, was the solution. Rozelle was about to become pro football's "chief lobbyist."

In late August, Rozelle testified before the House Antitrust Subcommittee on a bill he helped advance that would permit single-network contracts.

Rozelle told the subcommittee that unless the NFL could negotiate such a contract, only fans of teams in large metropolitan cities would be assured of seeing their teams on television. That, he pointed out, would be very unpopular with the folks back home.

On September 24, the Senate passed the Sports Broadcast Act of 1961. It was signed into law by President John F. Kennedy on September 30.

The new legislation, while very good news for the NFL, was equally well received by the rival AFL. Although "the other league" had already played the 1960 season under a single-network contract, it too would have been in jeopardy had the landmark bill not passed and been signed into law.

The impact of the Sports Broadcast Act was immediate.

In 1963, NBC was awarded exclusive network broadcasting rights for the AFL championship game for $926,000, and it later signed a then-whopping five-year, $36 million deal to begin the 1965 season.

Not to be outdone, CBS submitted the winning bid of $28.2 million per year for the NFL's 1964 and 1965 regular-season games. The network also paid $1.8 million for the rights to the NFL championship games for those same seasons.

"I didn't think it would go this high," a pleasantly surprised Rozelle said.

Smaller markets, like Green Bay, rejoiced.

"What Pete Rozelle did with television receipts," Packers coach Vince Lombardi said, "probably saved football in Green Bay." Rooney called it the "cornerstone of the success of the league."

Rozelle's vision of transitioning from a fraternity of independently operating sportsmen to a centralized, revenue-sharing league was officially under way.

CHAPTER 17

TOUGH DECISIONS

WHEN PETE ROZELLE WAS NAMED NFL COMMIS-
sioner, some veteran NFL observers questioned whether the
young soft-spoken Californian could handle the strong-willed
owners who hired him.

During his first three years as commissioner, Rozelle's accomplishments included leading the league's successful defense against
the AFL's $10 million antitrust suit; securing legislation that al-
lowed a single-network television arrangement; and presiding over
the successful launch of the two expansion teams. He was instru-
mental in facilitating the Cardinals' move to St. Louis. He helped
orchestrate a winner-take-all closed auction between the feuding
owners of the Los Angeles Rams that allowed one partner—Dan
Reeves—to buy out the three others. And, in 1962, with pressure from the NAACP and the federal government, he persuaded
Redskins owner George Preston Marshall to end his practice of
segregation and integrate his team.

But in early 1963, Rozelle faced the biggest challenge of his
young career, when Bears owner George Halas told reporters that
he'd asked Rozelle to investigate published reports of a possible
betting scandal involving a "member of a midwestern franchise."

Halas's less than subtle implication was directed at Paul Hornung, star halfback of the Green Bay Packers.

The announcement came—not coincidentally—on the same
day that news leaked that Bears fullback Rick Casares had submitted to two lie-detector tests as part of the unconfirmed gambling
investigation.

"Gossip columnists have come up with the disturbing rumors of wrongdoing and talks of federal investigations," Halas said. "I thought we should clear the atmosphere, so I took the matter to the commissioner."

The Bears boss speculated it might be much ado about nothing. Possibly just a matter of "fraternization with the wrong type of person."

Halas's announcement surprised Rozelle. And it complicated matters. Unbeknownst to most, Rozelle was not only aware of the allegations, he was already well into his own investigation.

Halas had put the commissioner in an awkward position. While he understood the seriousness of the rumors and his obligation to be forthright, he also knew he had to be cautious. It was as important to protect the innocent as it was to expose the guilty. And it was his job to protect the integrity of the league.

With Halas going public, Rozelle knew he would now be asked to comment endlessly on every piece of gossip and innuendo that arose. He knew this would slow his investigation, make it more difficult to get cooperation from reluctant sources, and possibly harm the league in the court of public opinion.

Rozelle tried to downplay the gravity of Halas's remarks:

"Our office maintains constant surveillance. . . . This investigation is just one of three or four we are conducting at the moment," he said.

Four days later, the Associated Press reported that Hornung and Detroit Lions star defensive tackle Alex Karras were a part of the rumored probe.

The AP report listed four "concrete developments": that Hornung was a friend and potential business associate of Abe Samuels, a "lumber company owner and duplicating machine executive" who admittedly bet heavily on pro football games; that Samuels employed Bears assistant coach Phil Handler as a salesman during the off-season and was "acquainted with" Bears fullback Rick Casares; that a business partner of Karras had been questioned about gambling, presumably by the FBI; and that a federal investigation was being planned.

The *Chicago American* reported that Samuels had admitted to betting up to $90,000 during a single football season.

The allegations drew an immediate denial from Halas.

"Phil never bet on a game in his life," Halas said of his coach, arguing that Handler had been working for the lumber company for fifteen years. And, he pointed out, Samuels was only a one-eighth owner in the company. "I see nothing wrong with Phil working there," he said.

Casares, already angry that his name had been linked to the lie-detector tests, vociferously defended himself.

"I've done nothing wrong but take a couple of tests," he said.

Casares said he took the tests only after being told it was for "the good of the league."

"All I got out of it is this rotten publicity. I was told that taking the tests would be strictly confidential. Then a couple newspaper guys not only find out about the tests, but the exact questions asked and everything else."

According to the AP, the questions included: Did he ever attempt to shave points? Intentionally fumble? Was he ever asked to throw a game or intentionally cause a penalty? And, had he concealed information from the commissioner?

To each question Casares said he responded no.

In denying any wrongdoing, Hornung told the *American* that he knew Samuels, but while the two were friendly, he said the only dealings he had with him involved a potential business opportunity. Samuels once offered him a duplicating machine franchise, which he decided against.

Handler and Casares were ultimately cleared of all charges.

Karras didn't fare as well.

In early January, both the *Detroit News* and the *Detroit Free Press* reported that Karras's Detroit business partner, Jim Butsicaris, had been questioned about gambling by the FBI. Their joint business venture was a bar that Rozelle would later describe as a "hotbed of illegal gambling."

Rather than proclaim his innocence, a defiant Karras admitted during a national television interview that he had bet on games, including ones in which he'd played. Later he backed off a bit by saying he "never bet more than a pack of cigarettes or a couple of cigars with close friends." He also claimed he "never talked to or even knew a bookie."

Throughout the investigation, Rozelle remained tight-lipped. So much so that the press accused him of trying to bury the story.

Finally, on January 18, two weeks after Halas's announcement, he broke his silence. In a meeting requested by wire service representatives, Rozelle denied he had any intention of covering up anything.

He compared his inquiry to that of a government investigation: "If you observe how all governmental investigations are conducted, you'll find that they are not conducted in the full glare of publicity. The NFL is not comparing itself to the U.S. government, but the principle is the same."

Rozelle refused to release the names of people his office had contacted or planned to contact, saying it could damage the investigation. He said releasing information would make it difficult to promise confidentiality.

"If I violate such pledges I will not get cooperation in the future," he said. He didn't offer any explanation as to whether he knew how the Casares interviews leaked.

Finally, on April 17, 1963, the most in-depth investigation in NFL history came to an end. In front of an overflow crowd of assembled media, Rozelle announced that Hornung and Karras were suspended indefinitely, Hornung for betting and Karras for betting and associating with people described as "known hoodlums."

And that wasn't all.

Five other Detroit players—guard John Gordy, defensive back Gary Lowe, middle linebacker Joe Schmidt, linebacker Wayne Walker, and defensive end Sam Williams—were each fined $2,000, the maximum penalty allowed, for betting $50 on the 1962 NFL title game at a social gathering arranged by Karras.

"There is absolutely no evidence of any criminality," Rozelle said. "No bribes, no game-fixing or point-shaving. The only evidence uncovered in this investigation, which included 52 interviews with players on eight teams, was the bets by the players penalized. All of these bets were on their own teams to win or on other NFL games."

"I was sort of expecting this," Hornung said when informed of his suspension.

Later, in a handwritten statement, he said: "I made a terrible mistake. I realize this now. I am truly sorry. What else is there to say?"

Hornung also said that he had placed his bets through Barney Shapiro, whom he said he met in 1956 in San Francisco and that the two became close friends.

"I was betting above the board with a friend and only as a friend," Hornung said.

According to Rozelle's investigation, Hornung began placing bets in 1959 and stopped in 1962. Asked why he discontinued betting, Hornung said, "I realized it wasn't the right thing to do."

Karras was less contrite.

"I haven't done anything that I'm ashamed of and I am not guilty of anything."

Rozelle said that the violation by the other five players "should be put in its proper perspective." He called their infraction "an act that cannot be condoned because of the strict rules of the NFL, but one that should in no way adversely affect the reputation of those involved." In other words, they violated the rules, but it appeared to be a one-time occurrence, not a pattern of behavior.

Rozelle told Murray Olderman of the Newspaper Enterprise Association that the toughest part of his decision was the inclusion of Joe Schmidt among the five men fined $2,000. Rozelle said he respected Schmidt as one of the game's great competitors and among its finest citizens.

Apparently, it was a sentiment shared by others. When investigators filed their reports, they appended a line: "Joe Schmidt is a gentleman."

Rozelle told *Sports Illustrated* the decisions he made were the hardest of his life.

"I thought about it at length," he said. "The maximum penalty for a player would be suspension for life. That would be for failure to report a bribe attempt or for trying to shave points. This sport has grown so quickly and gained so much of the approval of the American public that the only way it can be hurt is through gambling."

Rozelle also said that Hornung's and Karras's violations were "continuing, not casual." That, he said, factored into his decision.

The commissioner also announced that Detroit would be fined $4,000. The Lions' violation was broken into two separate charges and fines, though related. The first $2,000 was for the failure of coach George Wilson to notify the proper league authorities of police reports of players associating with known crime figures. The second $2,000 was for allowing unauthorized individuals on the sidelines during games.

The $4,000 fine seemed small compared to the $2,000 fines of the five players. But they were the maximum the commissioner could levy under league regulations.

For more than four months Rozelle willingly took the heat for his deliberate investigation. He wanted to prove that the league—through the commissioner's office—could police itself, clear up rumors beyond reasonable doubt, and satisfy even the watchful eye of the Senate subcommittee that was at that time assembling evidence of interstate gambling on amateur and professional sports.

Rozelle was frustrated because he knew things he couldn't discuss publicly.

For example, when Karras complained on national TV that he only bet "cigars and cigarettes" on games, Rozelle had evidence of Karras having placed multiple $100 bets on NFL games. And when General Manager Edwin Anderson said that not a single Detroit player had been under suspicion of association with gamblers or unsavory characters, Rozelle knew the chief of police had already shared his report of Lions players "mingling with known hoodlums."

In the end, Rozelle's approach proved successful. Club owners, sportswriters, fans, and even Hornung's coach, Vince Lombardi, praised Rozelle's actions.

"The commissioner had no other alternative," Lombardi said. "If allowed to continue, it could lead to more serious consequences."

Cleveland Browns owner Art Modell said Rozelle's "decisive and forceful action" made the NFL a stronger organization.

Even Senator John McClellan, chairman of the Senate subcommittee investigating sports gambling, commended the NFL "for taking the right action."

Most important, Rozelle's handling of the scandal won the support and respect of the league's owners. The respect for the office of the commissioner grew in the eyes of the public and the NFL owners. He was no longer seen "as a boy playing his part," according to Cowboys president Tex Schramm. "He gained once and for all everybody's complete respect."

In an analysis of Rozelle's actions, *Sports Illustrated*'s Tex Maule wrote, "Each of the big professional sports in America is administered by one man. . . . They are hired by owners, fired by owners and are manipulated like puppets by the owners whenever important decisions have to be taken."

But Rozelle, Maule wrote, "does not seem to fit this string-dance pattern. He has just suspended Paul Hornung of the Green Bay Packers, the biggest star in pro football, and Alex Karras, an All-Pro tackle who was the key to the Detroit Lions' superb defense. . . . He took this action without accepting any advice or pressure from the club owners who elected him."

Maule said he hoped Rozelle would continue to be a strong commissioner. "In his strength may lie the future of professional football," he wrote.

After a rough four months dealing with the betting scandal, Rozelle was finally able to return to the business of football. After all, there was still a season to be played, a champion to be crowned, and a war with "the other league" to be waged.

Then, on November 22, 1963, everyday life in America came to a screeching halt as the stunning news from Dallas hit the newswires and airwaves. President John F. Kennedy was dead. The victim of an assassin's bullet.

Shock, sadness, anger, and fear consumed the American public. A stunned nation could only ask why and wonder how such a thing could happen.

Now all sense of normalcy was gone. Radio and television provided round-the-clock coverage of the unfolding crisis. The country was in shock.

Was it a plot? Were there others involved? Was it an attack from a foreign power and would there be more to follow? There were many more questions than answers.

That evening Rozelle was faced with a tough question of his own. Would the NFL play games on Sunday as scheduled?

There was no easy answer.

Would playing the games be disrespectful? Or could they be a part of the needed return to normalcy?

There was support for both arguments.

Rozelle sought and listened to the advice of several trusted allies. Some he called, while others called him. Pierre Salinger, the president's press secretary, with whom Rozelle had a close relationship, was one of the first advisors he sought. Salinger assured Rozelle that he believed President Kennedy would not have wanted the games canceled.

Rozelle also called Pittsburgh's Dan Rooney.

"Pete thought Salinger was right," Rooney told biographer David Halaas. "Remember, this was at the height of the Cold War. We didn't know whether the assassination was part of a Soviet-backed conspiracy or the work of a madman."

The fact that neither Dallas nor Washington was playing at home that weekend helped Rozelle as he began to lean toward playing the games.

Cleveland owner Art Modell, whose team was hosting Dallas, said he believed the games should be canceled.

Time was not on Rozelle's side. Visiting teams were preparing to fly to host cities. The media and fans were demanding an answer.

The back-and-forth calls continued until early Saturday morning, when Rozelle told Rooney the games would go on.

"I told him, 'Okay, Pete, I disagree, but I'll support you.'"

That was the attitude of several other club owners—they questioned the decision, but trusted Rozelle's judgment.

Rozelle issued a brief statement:

"It has been traditional in sports for athletes to perform in times of great tragedy. Football was Mr. Kennedy's game. He thrived on competition."

As Rozelle's announcement hit the early editions of newspapers across the country, it became apparent that the NFL was virtually alone in its decision. Almost all major college and pro sports announced cancellations and postponements. And, making matters worse for Rozelle, the AFL—after considering canceling just the Patriots-Bills game scheduled to be played in Kennedy's home city of Boston—canceled all games. They were made up later in the season.

The AFL "made the right decision," Modell would later say.

Although the NFL games were played, none were televised. CBS canceled all weekend sports programming.

Rozelle attended the Cardinals–Giants game at Yankee Stadium. He went down to the pressroom after the game to take questions and explain his decision.

"Was it the money?" someone asked.

"Money had nothing to do with it," Rozelle said. According to published reports, since CBS chose not to televise the games, they were obligated to pay the league $320,000 regardless.

"I went to church this morning and paid my respects, and I'm sure so did most the people who came to Yankee Stadium," Rozelle said. "There's been criticism. There'll be more criticism this week. There has already been more than I anticipated, but believe me, I did this because I did not feel it would be disrespectful."

The decision was tough on players as well.

"Nobody wanted to play," Eagles Hall of Fame receiver Tommy McDonald told *Sports Illustrated* in 2003. "There wasn't anything you could do about it, but there was no way anybody wanted to go out and play a game that weekend. I'm a guy who wears his emotions on his sleeve, and I couldn't stop crying."

Several prominent sportswriters were highly critical. Red

Smith of the *New York Herald Tribune* was particularly tough: "In the civilized world, it was a day of mourning. In the National Football League, it was the 11th Sunday of the business year, a quarter-million-dollar day in Yankee Stadium."

Mel Durslag of the *Los Angeles Herald Examiner* was equally caustic, calling the decision "a sick joke."

Although Rozelle would later say he regretted his decision, longtime league communications executive Joe Browne spoke with Rozelle on several occasions about his decision.

He may have come to regret the uproar his decision caused, the negative publicity the league and owners received, Browne said, "But down deep in his heart, I believe he thought he made the right decision. . . ."

Although several club owners and many sportswriters criticized Rozelle's decision, fans still showed up for the games. Attendance at the seven games played was typical of the weeks prior. The only conspicuous drop in attendance was in Minnesota, but that was weather related.

Even so, the atmosphere was significantly different. There was no pregame activity, no halftime shows, and player introductions were eliminated. The games were played. The fans showed up. But any sense of "normalcy" was absent.

In the world of public opinion, it was like a championship fight that ended in a draw. Although it was a difficult and emotional decision, Pete Rozelle survived the fight and retained his title.

CHAPTER 18

A CEASE-FIRE AND A MERGER

T HE FIRST THREE YEARS THE NFL DIDN'T PAY THAT much attention to us," AFL commissioner Joe Foss once said. But what Foss saw as a lack of attentiveness was really an intentional wait-and-see approach by the NFL and Pete Rozelle.

Although none of the NFL club owners completely dismissed the AFL, some felt that the difficult challenges the upstart league faced would ultimately do them in.

Former commissioner Bert Bell's prediction in 1959 that it would "take them [the AFL] three or four years to build qualified teams" seemed to advance the notion of the league's unlikely success. Bell's laundry list of projected difficulties—television contracts, player contracts, drafting players, stadium rights, publicity, and franchises—may have fostered a sense of "Don't worry, it won't happen."

But what Bell and others didn't anticipate was the AFL's player-signing strategy and its cash reserves.

While not all AFL owners had the financial strength of oilmen Lamar Hunt or Bud Adams, the AFL's five-year television contract with ABC gave the "other league" two important assets—national exposure and money to help in a player-signing war.

And although the AFL did sign plenty of unwanted or unsigned NFL players, it did not raid NFL rosters, thus avoiding sure-to-follow legal challenges. The new league's strategy was to compete for and sign draft picks. That was a wide-open—but expensive—opportunity.

Initially the results were mixed.

"I remember that first tryout camp we had," Los Angeles Chargers head coach Sid Gillman once recalled. "Every bartender in Los Angeles thought he could play football. These gorillas would be outside every day standing in their cleats lined up for inspection."

With rosters composed primarily of rookies, free agents, and NFL castoffs, the AFL played its first season. While not always a thing of beauty, the overall quality of play surprised even league detractors. But while the play may have been deemed acceptable, attendance was not. League losses were reported to be more than $3.5 million (roughly $8.4 million in today's dollars).

The Chargers' 1960 home-game attendance was so bad that Barron Hilton moved the team south to San Diego. "If we don't make it here," Hilton said, "then we don't make it. I won't move again."

The other West Coast team, the Oakland Raiders, also struggled. Among its many challenges was its lack of a home. During their first year, the Raiders played four home games in San Francisco's Kezar Stadium and three in Candlestick Park. They played exclusively at Candlestick in 1961. But from 1962 through 1965 the vagabond team played in Frank Youell Field—a run-down 22,000-seat stadium named, appropriately enough, after an area undertaker.

It was not a great start, and if not for Bills owner Ralph Wilson the Raiders might have folded after their first season.

Shortly after the 1960 season, Raiders managing general partner Wayne Valley told Wilson he wasn't going to be able to field a team the next year.

"Wayne, if you drop out, this league will fail," Wilson said. Valley told Wilson he'd need $400,000 to play another year or two.

Wilson agreed to foot the bill.

In exchange Valley gave Wilson 20 percent of the team.

"I never had anything to do with operating the team," Wilson later said. "But they managed to stay in."

It was pretty much the same story in Denver, where owner Bob Howsam sold his franchise to local contractors Cal Kunz and brothers Alan and Gerry Phipps.

"We weren't prepared to lose that kind of money," Howsam said, "because we didn't have it."

While these were serious concerns, the worst was yet to come. The New York Titans, the league's marquee franchise, were a financial disaster that came close to killing the AFL.

"A man's ego can be a laughable thing," wrote Dick Young of the New York *Daily News*. "It can also be quite sad—and terribly self-destructive. Such is the case of Harry Wismer, who made the gargantuan mistake of trying to sell Harry Wismer for three years. From the inception of the Titans, the star of the show has been Harry Wismer."

Midway through the 1962 season, the league was forced to take over operations of Wismer's team.

Unable to pay his bills, the other owners—particularly Adams—dug into their pockets to keep the team operating.

After months of negotiations, a federal bankruptcy referee approved the sale of the Titans in March 1963 to a group of five "wealthy executives," headed by David "Sonny" Werblin, president of Music Corporation of America. The other investors: Leon Hess, head of the Hess Oil & Chemical Company; Philip Iselin, president of Korell, a New York textile firm; Townsend Martin, an investment banker; and Donald Lillis, a Wall Street broker.

The well-heeled, high-profile ownership group was welcome news for the owners, with Boston Patriots owner Billy Sullivan describing them as "one of the greatest sports groups in the world" and the Titans as "one of the strongest sports franchises."

Werblin correctly foresaw how football would evolve:

"Football is just like show business," he said. "You must have a good producer, director, and some outstanding talent in order to put a hit show together."

To that end, Werblin hired former Colts coach Weeb Ewbank as his producer, renamed his new show "the Jets," and began looking for talent to sign.

While the Titans fiasco was without a doubt the AFL's low point, the team's transformation into the New York Jets marked the beginning of a league surge.

In their book, *The Other League: The Fabulous Story of the American Football League*, Jack Horrigan and Mike Rathet—both veterans of the AFL front office—cited four "breakthrough events" in 1962–63 that began the league's turnaround. They were: Werblin's purchase of the Titans; the signing of eight number-one draft picks; Hunt's Dallas Texans relocating to Kansas City; and Al Davis's ascension as general manager and coach of the Raiders.

There was a good feeling in the AFL camp by this time, a feeling that AFL commissioner Foss shared with a reporter during a trip to Chicago. "Everything will get better from here," he said.

Early on, the NFL's Rozelle felt he had more pressing issues to deal with than a back-and-forth exchange with the unproven AFL. His focus was on getting a TV deal, working the single-network legislation through Congress, and settling the gambling investigation.

And he was successful. His emergence as a take-charge leader during that tumultuous period earned him *Sports Illustrated*'s Sportsman of the Year in 1963—the first nonathlete to receive the prestigious award.

So it's easy to see how some owners may have been lulled into believing that the AFL wasn't much of a threat. After all, they were enjoying the financial fruits of a lucrative television contract, an expanded fourteen-game season, increased attendance, and exciting football. Things were going well.

But Rozelle knew better. Although he didn't feel the NFL was at risk of losing many of its star players, he conceded that if the AFL survived, the NFL "would have a serious problem with rookies." Rozelle understood that the signing of rookies—something the AFL saw as their best chance for success—would be the battleground.

"With the Hornung case behind us and the American League starting to spend real money in their drafts," Rozelle told author Jerry Izenberg, "I'd have to say that 1964 and 1965 were the years we finally decided to go to war."

+ + +

"I'VE BEEN babysitting for about ten days," Baltimore Colts scout and former star running back Buddy Young said. "I've been following this guy around talking to him about the advantages of playing in the National Football League."

Young's remarks came when the Chicago Bears announced at a press conference the signing of University of Kansas running back Gale Sayers.

What was a Colts scout doing at a press conference announcing the signing of the Bears' first-round pick?

Turns out the league had asked Young to use his influence as a former player to convince Sayers to sign with the NFL.

Young said the league believed the AFL wanted Sayers so badly that it might consider kidnapping him.

"I was just ordered to keep him in the NFL."

It was dubbed "Operation Hand-Holding."

"Hand-holders" or "babysitters" were hired by the NFL to stay with high-profile probable draft picks, often hiding them in hotels and motels ahead of the actual draft meeting. The babysitters made sure no one from the AFL found any of them until they'd been signed. The AFL did pretty much the same thing, but more on a team-by-team basis rather than through a coordinated league effort.

And as you'd expect, there were stories of exotic gifts, vacation retreats, fast cars, and of course wild women and booze.

Some were even true.

Two rookie signings—one in 1965, the other in 1966—garnered nationwide attention and even a message from outer space.

First, in 1965, Sonny Werblin signed Alabama star quarterback Joe Namath. Namath was the first overall pick in both leagues. The Jets outbid the NFL's Chicago Cardinals for his services.

"The biggest player contract in the history of sport" was how Werblin described the Namath signing. The reported price tag was a then-staggering three-year deal for $427,000.

Later that year, astronaut Frank Borman, while circling the earth aboard the Gemini 7 spacecraft, delivered his daily message back to earth. "Tell Nobis to sign with Houston," the astronaut said.

"Nobis" was Tommy Nobis, the first overall pick in both 1966 drafts, who was being sought by the AFL's Oilers and the NFL's expansion-team Atlanta Falcons.

This time the NFL won.

No official figures were released for the Nobis contract. Nobis later said his agreement included a signing bonus, deferred over several years, "in the neighborhood of a couple hundred thousand dollars." His actual annual contract was a more modest five-year deal, starting at $25,000 and accelerating by $5,000 each of the next four years for a total of $145,000.

Oilers owner Bud Adams reportedly sweetened his failed attempt to sign the Texas star by offering him a Phillips 66 dealership and one hundred head of cattle.

Although the Oilers' package was thought to have been worth more, it was the personal touch by Falcons owner Rankin Smith that impressed the Texas linebacker. Smith sent his private plane to pick up Nobis's parents in San Antonio to bring them to Atlanta to be wined and dined.

"My family and I weren't used to that kind of treatment," Nobis said. "All of a sudden we were somebody and it was all because of football."

Well, maybe. The special treatment was more likely the result of two competing football leagues wanting the same thing: the best available player.

The Nobis and Namath signings were examples of just how crazy the bidding wars had become. Everybody had an opinion about the war. Even pro football legend Red Grange—the NFL's first big-salaried superstar—weighed in on the Namath deal.

Grange, who made $100,000-plus in 1925, warned of how some less-fortunate players might respond to the well-paid rookies. He offered: "I shudder when I think of all the punishment that boy [Namath] is going to take," he said. "I know in my case, I didn't have trouble with my teammates, but the other teams—well, they almost killed me."

"The bidding wars were ruining us," Dan Rooney said in his autobiography. "The AFL teams seemed to have money to burn."

As if the bidding wars weren't enough, on May 17, 1966, at a league meeting in Washington, DC, Rozelle delivered a bombshell: Giants owner Wellington Mara had signed kicker Pete Gogolak away from the AFL Buffalo Bills.

Gogolak, who introduced soccer-style kicking to pro football, had played out his option with the Bills and, in so doing, was a free agent who could sign with either league. His signing, however, ended the unwritten agreement between the leagues not to sign each other's players.

Of course, AFL owners—particularly Wilson—were furious, but so too were NFL owners. They saw the move as an escalation of the already expensive player-signing war.

"I think good judgment was not used," said George Halas. "I consider it derogatory to pro football. Many others [owners] did not like it either."

Some owners, such as Dan Reeves and Art Modell, openly questioned Rozelle's authority to approve a contract that would have such a negative impact on the entire league. Things got so heated that Rozelle had to call a time-out in the hopes that cooler heads would prevail.

What the owners didn't know then was that while both leagues were gearing up for more warfare, secret peace talks between Hunt and Dallas Cowboys president Tex Schramm were also under way.

Rozelle told his old friend Rooney about the negotiations, then swore him to secrecy.

Rooney asked Rozelle if he was sure a merger was a good idea.

Rozelle's answer was simple and succinct: "We have to have it."

+++

THE HUNT-SCHRAMM talks weren't the first of their kind. As the cost of players rose, some informal talks took place.

The most substantive occurred in 1965, when Wilson and Colts owner Carroll Rosenbloom were quietly dispatched by their leagues to discuss a possible merger.

The two met several times in January in Miami, where both had winter homes. "I went up there [to Rosenbloom's home] must have been 10 or 12 times to talk with him to see if anything could be worked out," Wilson recalled. According to him, several of Rosenbloom's original proposals were included in the final merger agreement, including the sharing of television revenue and interleague preseason games. Both men felt playing preseason games for a few years "until things softened up a little" would allow both sides time to work out the necessary details of a complete merger.

Perhaps concerned that history had overlooked his counterpart's contribution to the peace talks, Wilson said in 2012 that "Carroll was the one who came up with most of the ideas."

While no immediate action was taken by either league, things soon began to move quickly.

On April 6, Hunt and Schramm agreed to a "top secret" meeting that had all the makings of a scene right out of a cheesy spy novel.

"We agreed to meet at the Texas Rangers statue at Love Field in Dallas," Hunt said. The two sat in Schramm's car in the airport parking lot, where, according to Hunt, "Schramm outlined the generalities of a plan that he thought might be doable."

After a couple of hours the two men went their separate ways, with a plan to meet again. Hunt, like Schramm, did not disclose the meeting to most of the other owners. Both felt that with the animus as high as it was, the fewer in the know the more likely something positive might happen.

The following day, at the AFL annual meeting in Houston, Foss resigned as commissioner. Most believed he was forced out because of his failure to get Atlanta as an expansion team, and his failure to adequately respond to the NFL's successful hand-holding program.

Al Davis, the young, aggressive general manager and head coach of the Raiders, was named his successor.

In just three years Davis had converted the Raiders from doormats to contenders. His take-no-prisoners attitude was thought by some to be just what the league needed. Davis was convinced the AFL could win the war and he wasn't the least bit inclined to seek peace between the leagues.

"As we learned here," Wayne Valley said, announcing Davis's

appointment, "Al is his own boss, his own guy. He doesn't wear any man's saddle."

Truer words were never spoken.

"Give us about three months to get organized, and we'll drop a bomb somewhere and get everybody really excited," Davis promised after his appointment.

It didn't take three months. Davis immediately put the NFL on alert. No longer were rookies going to be the sole focus of the player-signing war. Davis initiated a plan to raid NFL rosters for veteran players by offering bonuses to sign contracts that would go into effect after they played out their NFL contract options.

Just two weeks after Davis was named commissioner, the Raiders announced that they'd signed Rams quarterback Roman Gabriel to a contract that would become effective in 1967, after his option year had expired.

Davis then opened similar negotiations with more than a dozen high-profile NFL players, including Bears all-league tight end Mike Ditka and 49ers quarterback John Brodie.

The gloves were off.

Meanwhile, Schramm and Hunt continued their talks and began to selectively share their progress with a few owners. Fearful that Davis's hard-line stance might jeopardize a potential agreement, he was intentionally kept in the dark—something Davis never got over.

Then, on May 30—less than two weeks after the Gogolak signing—Schramm and Rozelle finalized their idea of an acceptable merger plan. They presented it to Hunt the next day.

Schramm warned Hunt that while the NFL owners supported the plan, if he tried to revise it too much, the deal would "blow up."

Hunt flew to New York to meet with Wilson and Sullivan, the other members of the AFL's merger committee. Together they constructed a twenty-six-point list of differences, mostly concerning the fate of the two New York and Bay Area franchises.

Initially, Werblin and Valley opposed the merger, not wanting to share their markets with NFL franchises. But in a maneuver reminiscent of George Halas's 1960 NFL bylaws amendment that allowed expansion approval by a ten-twelfths majority vote, Hunt pushed through a similar change. A two-thirds majority replaced a unanimous approval provision for the merger. Werblin and Valley could not block the merger.

Finally, on June 8, 1966—and after much negotiating—Rozelle, Hunt, and Schramm appeared together at a press conference in New York's Warwick Hotel and announced that the two leagues had agreed to merge.

Even Halas, who had initially tried to crush the AFL, said he was delighted with the terms of the merger.

Under the agreement, Rozelle would be the commissioner of both leagues; the leagues would play an annual world championship game beginning after the 1966 season; all existing franchises would remain at their present sites; an annual combined player draft would be held; interleague preseason games would be played beginning in 1967; and a single league schedule would start in 1970. Also, two franchises would be added by 1968, one in each league, with the franchise fee from both to be paid to the NFL.

Several AFL owners were upset by the decision to charge the AFL owners an $18 million indemnity fee to be paid out over a twenty-year period. The Jets' Sonny Werblin insisted that the NFL should pay, not the AFL. But Hunt convinced the group that paying $2 million per team over twenty years was not such a bad deal, since much of the money would come from accrued interest.

The indemnity ended up going to just two NFL teams: $10 million to the Giants and $8 million to the 49ers, for agreeing to share the lucrative New York and Bay Area markets.

While both leagues had come to terms, there remained one huge potential stumbling block: unless Congress enacted antitrust protection legislation, the merger could dissolve.

Although owners from both leagues worked to convince officials of the merger's value, it was Rozelle who most successfully worked the halls of Congress.

Rozelle sought and received help from Illinois Republican and minority leader Everett Dirksen and Louisiana Democrat Russell Long. After much political wrangling, the two called their own "end-around" play circumventing opponents of the merger and attached the NFL exemption amendment to a popular investment tax credit bill that had already been approved by the House. On October 21, the now-forgotten tax bill and pro football's antitrust exemption became law.

For the AFL, the merger gave them two big things they wanted—an interleague championship game and interleague preseason games. But there was one more thing the upstarts insisted upon—realignment. And while they got that, too, it didn't come easy.

Immediately following the announcement of the merger, both leagues began working through the merger's various details.

The complexities led former NFL executive director Don Weiss—whose job it was to reconcile the leagues' constitutions—to remark that "about the only thing the National Football League had in common with the American Football League was that they both played a game called football."

Much of the discussion during the first six months centered on the planned world championship game. Where would it be played? Which of the two leagues' TV networks would broadcast the game? And, what it would be called?

Ultimately, it was decided the game should be played at a neutral site in a stadium with a maximum capacity. The 105,000-seat Los Angeles Coliseum was the logical choice. And, in a Solomon-like decision, Rozelle worked out a mutually beneficial deal whereby both CBS and NBC would broadcast the game.

As for what to call the game, it would be called the AFL-NFL World Championship Game.

The game's name became the Super Bowl quite by accident. In the AFL-NFL joint committee meetings, there was constant confusion over which championship game was which—the AFL Championship Game, the NFL Championship Game, or the new AFL-NFL World Championship Game. During one such meeting, Hunt, attempting to clarify which game he was speaking about, referred to the AFL-NFL Championship Game as "the Super Bowl."

He later called it "corny," acknowledging that it was just something that popped into his head, and that he was probably thinking of a toy his children played with called a Super Ball.

Rozelle had a different take on the name. According to Weiss, he absolutely hated it. But the press and the public embraced "Super Bowl" from the start. And although official league documents and publications stuck to the "AFL-NFL World Championship Game" through the first three games, by game four it was officially the "Super Bowl."

The merger's last major stumbling block was realignment. The AFL had ten franchises and the NFL sixteen. Since the full merger didn't go into effect until 1970, the two leagues seemed content to kick the proverbial can down the road until the last minute.

But when serious discussions did finally begin in 1969, the NFL surprised the AFL by suggesting that the two conferences might remain in the existing 16-10 alignment. AFL owners proclaimed that they'd never contemplated a 16-10 alignment when they agreed to the merger.

Somewhat surprisingly, Hunt sided with a compromise version in which the AFL would remain a ten-team conference. That plan called for a ten-team conference with the stipulation that as new franchises were granted, they'd be added to the AFL until both leagues were equal. Hunt's acceptance of that idea was no doubt fueled by his profound pride in the "other league's" success and the appeal of retaining—even if only symbolically—the league's logo and identity.

But other owners, including Paul Brown of the new Cincinnati Bengals franchise, were strongly opposed to the 16-10 plan. Brown famously said that he hadn't paid $10 million "to be in the AFL." His plan was to be a part of the NFL by way of the merger.

After a series of unproductive meetings, the ownership groups finally narrowed their options to three possibilities.

One plan was to completely realign without any regard to any team's league of origin. The second was to take intact certain divisions from each league and randomly locate them. The third was to move three NFL teams to the AFL.

Eventually, option three was selected. The tough part was which three teams would voluntarily leave the NFL for the AFL. Rozelle sweetened the pot by announcing that any team willing to shift would receive a $3 million bonus, payable by the other owners.

The AFL owners were concerned as to which teams might ultimately join their ranks.

"The AFL was very firm that they wanted two teams that were
meaningful . . . Cleveland and Pittsburgh were the two teams they
[wanted]," Dan Rooney recalled. "Now, Baltimore was saying
they'd go and there were others too who said they'd go, but they
[AFL] wanted to make sure that we didn't just give them teams that
didn't matter to them."

While Rooney remained opposed to the AFL plan, Modell
quietly let Rozelle know he would consider it if certain conditions
were met. His stipulations were that Rooney's Steelers had to join
him, and that the Browns would be in the same division as Pittsburgh and Cincinnati.

"I would not have moved unless the Steelers moved," Modell
said.

Before Modell shared his plan, Rooney and his father, Art,
along with Giants owner Wellington Mara, paid Modell a visit in
his hospital room, where he was suffering from a bleeding ulcer.
Modell had been admitted after collapsing in the lobby of the meeting hotel.

"I can't see us moving," the younger Rooney kept repeating
as he paced back and forth in Modell's hospital room. It was then
that Modell shared what he had told Rozelle. Art Rooney listened
and considered Modell's plan, but Dan remained steadfastly opposed. "I just can't see it," he said. It was Mara who helped prod
the younger Rooney along.

"I considered Wellington like my big brother," Dan Rooney
said. Mara counseled him to "take it easy" and at least listen to
Modell's plan. "You may get what you want," Mara told him. The
elder Rooney also reminded his son that it would be better to receive money than pay it.

Following their visit, the Rooneys, after a quick dinner, returned
to the NFL offices. But before joining the other owners, who were
still negotiating and lobbying one another's support for one or the
other realignment options, they went to Rozelle's office.

"He [Rozelle] hands me a piece of paper, and on it was Pittsburgh, Cleveland, Cincinnati, and Houston," Dan recalled. "So, I look at it. My father said, 'What was that?' I handed it to him and said, 'That's your new division.'" And with a nod of acceptance to his father, Dan Rooney gave his blessing. The Steelers joined the Browns in what would become the Central Division of the American Football Conference.

By then Rozelle had also worked it out that Baltimore would join the Bills, Patriots, Dolphins, and Jets in the AFC's Eastern Division. With the Colts having just lost to the Jets in Super Bowl III, it appeared that an instant rivalry had been born.

While Rooney was the necessary cog to make the realignment work, the unexpected hero was Modell.

"He [Modell] didn't do it because he's a martyr, nor did he do it for the money as some erroneously believe," wrote Milt Richmond of the United Press International. "He did it for the corniest reason in the world—'for the good of all'—and there are those who take that to mean for his own good as well. Art Modell isn't going to bother arguing the point."

Paul Brown, who was once fired by Modell, also sang his praises. "I just feel that it's all to his credit," he said. "It was his decision that what is best for pro football is best for everyone."

Once the three NFL teams agreed to what may have been the most significant franchise shifts in NFL history, it took only about forty-five minutes for the AFL to complete their league's realignment. But there was no solution in sight on the NFL side. The senior circuit was at a stalemate, divided over five different alignment possibilities.

Finally, a frustrated Rozelle resorted to an unscientific method to end the impasse. He placed five slips of paper—each one inscribed with one of the five possible alignments—into a glass vase. He then instructed his secretary to pull one of the slips. She handed it to Rozelle, who read it aloud, and that was that. The issue was settled. Realignment was complete. The merger was done.

The war was over.

CHAPTER 19

SUPER BOWLS I–IV

M UCH TALKING HAS BEEN DONE OF LATE BY THE public and the press as to when the American and National Football Leagues will meet in a championship game," AFL commissioner Joe Foss wrote to NFL commissioner Pete Rozelle in a letter dated December 6, 1963. "I feel strongly that the time has arrived for the inauguration of such an annual game."

Not surprisingly, Rozelle didn't share Foss's assessment and politely ignored the invitation.

The fact was, Foss didn't anticipate or really want the NFL to accept his offer—at least not then. His dispatch was meant to foster a growing belief that the young league was approaching a level of play that would make an interleague championship game possible—and competitive.

The letter was more a profile-raising stunt than a serious invitation. And it wasn't the first time Foss, or others in the league—such as Titans owner Harry Wismer—had made such an overture.

"If the NFL had paid attention to Ole Harry's cries for a championship game in those first couple of years," Foss said some years later, "we'd never have lived to see the day of any merger. They'd have handed us our head."

But, as Foss's letter suggested, the AFL was maturing quickly. By the mid-1960s, many observers felt the young league had come of age. And, when the merger became official, the leagues were poised to inaugurate their agreed-upon interleague championship game series. The sporting world would soon be able to judge for itself whether league parity was at hand.

The AFL-NFL World Championship Game series would begin after the 1966 season. That meant that four championship games would be played before the merger was complete in 1970. Four games for the two rival leagues to battle for world championship bragging rights. Four games for the AFL to prove that it belonged. Four games to set the stage for pro football's future.

These four games were like four quarters of a game. The winner would be crowned the champion—the superior league.

The first Super Bowl quarter pitted AFL founder Lamar Hunt's Kansas City Chiefs against the Green Bay Packers—winners of four NFL titles in the previous six seasons.

The Packers, a veteran squad coached by the already legendary Vince Lombardi, featured balance and discipline on both sides of the ball. What they lacked in youth and offensive speed, they made up for with power and preparation. The team was Lombardi's masterpiece.

Kansas City, while younger than the Packers, had a veteran quarterback in Len Dawson, a game-breaking wide receiver in Otis Taylor, and an innovation-minded coach in Hank Stram.

Stram's stack defense, in which linebackers were positioned directly behind defensive linemen, was famous for shutting down the opponents' running game and dared quarterbacks to throw the ball. Stram called his "moving pocket," in which the quarterback rolls out to his right or left, surrounded by blockers, the offense of the future.

As different as Lombardi and Stram were, both preached the importance of a "winning attitude."

"Winning isn't everything, it's the only thing," or some variation of that, and "Show me a good loser and I'll show you a loser" are just two examples attributed to the oft-quoted Lombardi.

Stram talked about winning in a *New York Post* article the day before Super Bowl Sunday.

"Winning is all I ever think of," he said. "It's funny, but most people think of ways to lose or things that will make them lose. Not me. I'm looking for a way to win."

That attitude became part of his team's DNA.

"I don't ever recall any game I ever played I didn't think we were going to win," Dawson told an NFL writer.

While Stram was known for his attention to fashion and a wisecracking demeanor, Lombardi was all business and a notorious taskmaster. Packers defensive tackle Henry Jordan once said, "When he says, 'sit down,' I don't even bother to look for a chair."

Building up to the game, Lombardi was his usual confident self. But when he returned to his hotel room after the first day of practice in Los Angeles, the coach found two telegrams awaiting his attention. One was from Bears owner George Halas, the other from Giants owner Wellington Mara. Both men wished the coach well, and both made it a point to remind him he was "representing the NFL."

Suddenly Lombardi realized he wasn't just playing to win, he was playing to preserve the reputation of the entire league. For NFL owners—some still simmering over the merger agreement—"winning" was definitely "the only thing."

If Lombardi was feeling the pressure, his players didn't seem to notice. "If Hank Stram were as smart as Vince Lombardi," said Packers guard Fuzzy Thurston before the game, "he'd be God."

But Stram was a confident man, too. When asked about league superiority, he adroitly offered that the battle between the leagues had been fought on paper for seven years and now "it was time to settle it on grass."

Surprisingly only 61,946 seats were sold in the 100,000-plus-seat Coliseum for the first AFL-NFL championship game. Some blamed the exorbitant ticket prices—twelve dollars for the good seats, eight and six dollars for second-tier seating.

The disappointing stadium attendance was more than offset by the more than 51 million viewers who tuned in to the CBS-NBC simulcast.

On the field, the Packers scored first on a six-play, 80-yard drive, capped by a 37-yard pass from quarterback Bart Starr to thirty-four-year-old backup receiver Max McGee, who was inserted in the lineup after starter Boyd Dowler reinjured his shoulder earlier in the drive. McGee, who had spent the previous night on the town, told his roommate Paul Hornung, "I haven't played enough to be in shape. What happens if Boyd gets hurt tomorrow?"

What happened was McGee—who had caught just four passes through the entire regular season—caught seven Starr passes for 138 yards and two touchdowns.

But even with McGee's strong performance, the Packers only led the Chiefs 14–10 at halftime. Stram's stack defense and the Chiefs' play-action passes on offense had the Packers playing "cautiously."

At halftime, Lombardi asked McGee—who planned on going into coaching the next season—what he thought the Packers' offensive strategy should be in the second half. "I told him, 'We got it.' It'll work better in the second half than it did in the first."

While his offense may have stayed the course, Lombardi decided to open his defensive attack. On the Chiefs' first possession of the third quarter, linebackers Dave Robinson and Lee Roy Caffey blitzed and hit Dawson as he attempted to pass. Packers safety Willie Wood caught Dawson's errant throw and returned it 50 yards to the Chiefs' five-yard line. On the next play, running back Elijah Pitts ran it in for a score.

Wood's interception changed the tempo of the game. The Packers cruised to a 35–10 victory.

"I thought Kansas City's Len Dawson did a fine job," Wood said after the game. "But after we got that quick six in the second half, he had to play our game. Then I knew we had them."

In the winner's locker room, a relieved Lombardi was repeatedly asked to compare the Chiefs to other NFL teams.

"They're a good football team," he said, "but it doesn't compare with the National Football League teams."

There was an immediate supportive chuckle from the members of the media surrounding the popular coach.

"That's what you wanted me to say . . . I said it," Lombardi declared. Then, perhaps trying to sound more gracious in victory, he clarified. "I think the Kansas City team is a real top football team, but it doesn't rate with the 'top teams' of the NFL. That's what I'm saying."

First quarter: NFL 1–AFL 0

+ + +

THE PACKERS repeated as NFL champs in 1967 and returned as the NFL representative in Super Bowl II. The AFL's champion was the Oakland Raiders.

This time around, Lombardi had a more congenial pregame approach, as did Raiders coach John Rauch. Neither wanted to provide the other with bulletin-board material. Both coaches went out of their way to praise the other.

Lombardi, who AFL loyalists thought had disparaged the Chiefs after Super Bowl I, praised the Raiders as a team with "excellent speed, agile linebackers, small but very quick linemen, and very fast defensive backs." He even said the Raiders could match his team in defensive speed. "If there is one difference between the defensive teams," he said, "it's that the Green Bay linebackers are a little bigger." Hardly chest-pounding bravado.

Raiders coach John Rauch was equally laudatory. He called the Packers "fantastic" and said they "didn't have a weak spot." He also recognized their winning tradition.

"There's no doubt there's a certain mystique about them. . . . I hope that doesn't bother us," he said.

Careful not to be overconfident, Lombardi told the press, "I never have gone into a game I didn't think I could win. But I always go into every game scared, and I go into this game scared."

The Packers' first two possessions resulted in field goals, the second of which came at the end an 8:40 drive. And while the Raiders held the Pack to just six points, Green Bay countered by not allowing the Raiders a single first down in their first possession of the first quarter.

The game's first touchdown came in the second quarter on a magnificent 62-yard pass-catch play between Starr and Dowler.

Down 13–0, Raiders quarterback Daryle Lamonica temporarily stopped the bleeding when he connected with Bill Miller on a 23-yard touchdown pass. But shortly before the half, Oakland's Roger Bird fumbled a fair catch, giving Green Bay the ball at midfield. With one second remaining on the clock, Don Chandler kicked his third field goal of the afternoon. To add insult to injury, the kick hit the crossbar and bounced over. It would be that kind of day for the Raiders. They went to the locker room down 16–7.

Prior to the game there had been speculation that Lombardi might be coaching his last game with the Packers. Realizing the rumor was likely true, Jerry Kramer, the Packers' veteran guard, gathered some of the other veteran players in the locker room at halftime. "Let's play the last thirty minutes for the old man," he said. "Maybe this is it for him."

Although the Raiders kept the score close in the first half, it was a different story in the second. A reinvigorated Packers team took control of the game.

On their second possession of the third quarter, Starr led the team on an 82-yard, 11-play drive that ended with a two-yard touchdown run by Donny Anderson. Twice Starr kept the drive alive with third-down conversion passes.

Then, in the fourth quarter, Green Bay's All-Pro cornerback Herb Adderley intercepted a Lamonica pass and raced 60 yards for a touchdown.

"Biletnikoff was running a turn-in pattern," Adderley said. "It was a good pass, but I was playing the ball deliberately. If I hadn't gotten to the ball, we would have been in trouble."

Although Lamonica responded with a 23-yard touchdown pass to Miller, it was too little, too late. Green Bay was once again victorious, this time 34–14 over their AFL opponent.

"What Jerry said at halftime moved us all," said Packers veteran tackle Bob Skoronski after the game.

While the score was again one-sided, postgame comments from the winner's locker room were less harsh than they'd been the previous year.

"Maybe Kansas City had better personnel, but this Oakland team gave us a fight all the way," Packers tackle Ron Kostelnik said. "They never quit."

Packers defensive lineman Henry Jordan said the Raiders were "as good as some NFL teams." He added, "Next year, it will go right down to the wire."

As for Lombardi, he diplomatically answered questions about the game, but headed off questions about his retirement, saying, "I've got no special announcement planned for today."

A few days later, he did. Lombardi said he was stepping down as coach to devote his time exclusively to his role as the team's general manager.

Second quarter: NFL 2–AFL 0

+ + +

IT MAY have been the most outrageous prediction in sports history. It was certainly the most notorious. Three days before Super Bowl III, New York Jets quarterback Joe Namath told the Miami Touchdown Club, "We're going to win Sunday. I guarantee you."

Namath's cocky words were dismissed by almost everyone as just another ridiculous statement by the brash AFL quarterback. Sure, he was a great talent. But the Jets? The AFL? Heck, they were 18-point underdogs to the NFL's 13-1 Baltimore Colts. And didn't the NFL win the first two interleague championship games by lopsided scores?

All true. But this was Broadway Joe Namath, the grinning, camera-ready guy that Jets owner Sonny Werblin paid $400,000 to turn his franchise around.

"I think he was underpaid," a jubilant Werblin would say after that now-historic Super Bowl.

Although Namath was the focal point of the game, the Jets' win was a team effort. From the start, Jets coach Weeb Ewbank set out to establish a strong ball-control running game, featuring running backs Matt Snell and Emerson Boozer. But Ewbank also spotted a weakness in the Colts' secondary: veteran cornerback Bobby Boyd seemed to have lost a step and the Colts' defense tried to protect him by rolling their coverage toward him.

Ewbank expected the Colts would double-cover their All-League receiver Don Maynard. "That meant George Sauer, our other receiver, might have a big day," Ewbank said. He did. He caught eight passes for 131 yards.

Going into the game, the Colts believed Maynard was still nursing a leg injury that might affect his play.

"I had a sore hamstring," Maynard later explained. He stayed out of the last game of the season against Miami to recuperate. While the rest helped him, Ewbank felt he needed to convince the Colts that he still had his deep weapon.

So, on the second play of the Jets' second possession, Maynard ran a go-deep pattern. He easily beat Boyd and safety Rick Volk. Although Namath's pass was too long, the play proved that Namath and company could go deep against the "bomb-proof" Colts.

"The rest of the game, Maynard had them scared," Snell recalled. Namath didn't throw to him again, but Maynard continued to line up very wide, forcing Baltimore to play a zone defense and cheat his way.

"I call that smart football," Maynard said. "You entertain the corner and the safety, weave at them, and make one commit and then the other, and you can make them play your game."

Ewbank also made a critical adjustment on defense. He moved a linebacker into the defensive line, making a five-man front, something the Colts were likely not expecting.

"They looked vulnerable on defense on film," Colts head coach Don Shula said. "They were not overly impressive from what we could see. We really felt we could run and pass freely." And in the early going, that looked to be the case.

On their first drive, Colts quarterback Earl Morrall, the NFL's regular-season MVP, directed a quick drive to the Jets' 19-yard line. But things suddenly fell apart. First, wide receiver Willie Richardson dropped a sure touchdown pass in the end zone. Then Morrall overthrew reserve tight end Tom Mitchell, who was also open. On third down the Jets' defense forced Morrall out of the pocket and tackled him for no gain. Placekicker Lou Michaels's 27-yard field goal attempt was no good. It was the beginning of what would become one of Morrall's worst performances in his long career.

The Colts couldn't catch a break. Sauer fumbled a Namath pass in the first quarter and the Colts recovered. But a Morrall pass intended for Mitchell was tipped and cornerback Randy Beverly intercepted.

In the second quarter, Namath, Sauer, and Snell accounted for most of a 12-play, 80-yard drive that ended with a 4-yard touchdown run by Snell and a 7–0 lead that stood until halftime. Snell would finish the game with 121 yards on 30 carries.

After both teams missed field goals, the Colts' Tom Matte ran a then–Super Bowl record 58 yards to the Jets' 16. But Morrall was intercepted for a second time. Then, after gaining possession with 25 seconds remaining in the first half, the Colts tried a flea-flicker play.

Morrall handed off to Matte, who tossed the ball back to Morrall, who then threw his third interception, this time to defensive back Jim Hudson. As if that weren't bad enough, Morrall failed to see flanker Jimmy Orr all alone in the end zone frantically waving his arm in the air. "We were simply lucky," Ewbank said of Morrall's missed opportunity.

At halftime, Shula struggled with whether he should make a change at quarterback. Veteran Johnny Unitas had lost his starter job because of an elbow injury. Unitas told Shula he was ready to play. But the coach stayed with Morrall.

After a Matte fumble, the Jets added a Jim Turner field goal to make the score 10–0. Following yet another failed Colts drive, Turner added his second field goal.

Down 13–0, Shula had seen enough. He turned to Unitas and said, "Get something going for us."

Ewbank—who coached the Colts to the famous overtime victory in the 1958 NFL championship game on the arm of the quarterback he now faced—knew firsthand what his old friend could do.

"All of a sudden I was scared to death," he would later confess. "All of us were. We'd seen him [Unitas] make so many big plays for so long."

Namath was no exception. "I looked up at the clock and saw 6:11 [time remaining]," he said. "The only time I talked to the Good Lord or prayed before a game or during a game was to keep us healthy or help us do our best. I never prayed to win a game," Namath recalled. "But I do remember looking up at the clock that day and saying, 'Oh please God, let that clock run.'"

Unitas—rusty from lack of playing time—went three-and-out on his first series. But following another Jets field goal, the legendary quarterback got hot. Suddenly the Colts were on the Jets' 25-yard line and "Johnny U" was in control.

Orr ran toward the Jets' end zone. Unitas, clearly in pain, fired a shot. It was short, and Beverly grabbed his second interception. But Unitas wasn't done. When the Colts got the ball back he orchestrated an 80-yard drive that included a fourth-down conversion, three Jets penalties, and three tries from the Jets' one-yard line. With 3:19 left in the game, the Colts scored on a one-yard run by Jerry Hill. After recovering a last-hope onside kick, Unitas drove the Colts to the Jets' 19 before a fourth-down pass attempt fell incomplete in the end zone.

The day and a 16–7 victory belonged to Namath, the Jets, and the AFL.

Namath wanted to be sure the world understood that.

"Are you one of those NFL writers?" Namath asked each reporter who approached him in the Jets' locker room after the game. "Well, listen," he'd say. "The AFL is here to stay, and you'd better believe it. I guarantee it."

Third quarter: NFL 2–AFL 1

+ + +

WHAT AN act to follow. First Lombardi's Packers destroyed the AFL's Chiefs and Raiders in Super Bowls I and II. Then a young brazen Jets quarterback delivers on a "guarantee" of victory for his team and league. The pressure the Kansas City Chiefs felt— especially quarterback Len Dawson—cannot be fully appreciated. Here they were again, this time facing the Minnesota Vikings, a two-touchdown favorite.

"It's different than when we played in the first Super Bowl in 1967," Dawson told the Associated Press's Will Grimsley. "In the 1967 game against Green Bay, I think we were a bit tight. Green

Bay was a glamour team. Many of us were awed by the tradition of the National Football League.

"The mystery is gone now. We have played the NFL teams. We know what they are. We should be more poised and relaxed."

But Dawson, while putting on his best face, was anything but relaxed. Five days earlier, NBC broke a story linking Dawson and other professional football players to a federal investigation into organized gambling. The investigation centered on Donald "Dice" Dawson—no relation, just a well-known Detroit gambler who had been under surveillance by the FBI.

Dawson had been introduced to the Detroiter several years earlier and admitted that he'd spoken to him on the phone twice. The first time was after he'd been sidelined with a leg injury and the second was after the death of his father. Neither call, he said, involved football.

In his book *The Making of the Super Bowl,* NFL executive director Don Weiss recalled how both the league office and the FBI treated the issue.

After "extensive interviews over a two- to three-day period," Weiss said it was clear that Dawson was innocent. Commissioner Rozelle held a press conference and cleared him of any wrongdoing. More important, the FBI dismissed the allegations as being "without foundation."

Dawson also got support from a most unlikely person. Prior to the game, Hank Stram received a telephone call from the White House. President Richard Nixon wanted him to tell Dawson that he knew "he had done nothing wrong."

"I told Lenny what the president said, and he was very touched by it," Stram said.

Still, Dawson admits he didn't sleep much before the game. His roommate Johnny Robinson could see the toll the allegations had taken.

"Whenever I looked at him," Robinson said, "it wasn't the easygoing Len Dawson I saw. He was tense; he wanted to be in solitude. It was a tremendous pressure week for him. He aged five years during the week."

+ + +

THE JETS' win in Super Bowl III was thought by NFL partisans to be a fluke. They were convinced the heavily favored Vikings would reestablish NFL dominance.

The Vikings were a formidable crew. Best known for their defense and led by a front four of Carl Eller, Alan Page, Gary Larsen, and Jim Marshall, the Vikings' defense was nicknamed the "Purple People Eaters" and led the NFL in fewest points allowed. On offense they had quarterback and league MVP Joe Kapp, who, though not a pretty passer, was a confident and inspirational leader and was not at all reluctant to run with the ball.

Minnesota's ground-based offense featured Joe Kapp and running backs Dave Osborn and Bill Brown. Though not a flashy offense, they led the NFL in scoring, averaging 27.1 points per game. They scored more than 50 points in a game three times during the regular season.

"We line up in basic formations and take it right to you," Vikings coach Bud Grant said of his team's offensive philosophy. But Grant ultimately relied on his defense. "Defense wins football games," he said. "Offense sells tickets."

The 1969 Chiefs were a better team than the one that represented the AFL in Super Bowl I. In addition to being more experienced and highly motivated, the recent addition of top-drawer players like linebackers Jim Lynch and Willie Lanier and tackle Curley Culp was significant.

Stram called his versatile offense a "dictator offense." He said he used twenty formations during Super Bowl IV, ranging from the tight end–I to the shotgun. In most plays tight end Fred Arbanas would line up behind Dawson and then shift left or right, making Minnesota's defense "delay momentarily." The offense would then look to capitalize on that slight hesitation.

It turned out that Stram's "triple stack defense"—not Minnesota's feared front four—would rule the day.

The Vikings simply could not run against the likes of defensive tackles Buck Buchanan and Culp and defensive ends Aaron

Brown and Jerry Mays. Three times they sacked Kapp, and they held him to just nine yards rushing. They dominated the smaller Vikings offensive line and shut down the run. If a Vikings ballcarrier did somehow get past them, linebackers Lanier, Bobby Bell, and Lynch were there to contain.

"The mighty Vikes' ground attack was stalled all afternoon as they moved the sticks only twice overland," wrote the *Pittsburgh Post-Gazette*.

The Chiefs also picked off two Kapp passes to stop drives and added a third when Gary Cuozzo replaced an injured Kapp in the final few minutes of the game.

Although Dawson's passing stats—12 of 17 for 142 yards— appear modest, he masterfully used every weapon in the Chiefs' offensive arsenal. Three drives in the game's first half resulted in three Jan Stenerud field goals. And a touchdown following a Vikings fumble on a kickoff return gave the Chiefs a 16–0 halftime lead.

Finally, with 10:28 remaining in the third quarter, Minnesota got on the scoreboard when Osborn finished a 69-yard drive with a four-yard touchdown run. But the Chiefs responded immediately with another touchdown.

Enjoying success throwing underneath the Vikings' coverage, Dawson connected on a short pass to Otis Taylor that went for a 46-yard score.

"That thing was just a little pass," Dawson said. "It's really not designed to go all the way. Otis is just a great athlete. He made the last forty yards on his own."

That was the final scoring play of the game. The Chiefs, with their 23–7 victory over the Vikings, were Super Bowl champions.

The victory also validated the Jets' Super Bowl III win and proved the AFL was for real.

Super Bowl IV was officially the last game played by an AFL team. And it was sweet justice for long-suffering AFL fans that it was Lamar Hunt's Chiefs that won it. The significance of the win was not lost on Stram.

"I think there always will be a strong attachment among the

people who were in this league from the beginning," he said. "I think there always will be a strong rivalry; football is such an emotional game."

"This is the last year for the American Football League," an understandably reflective Bobby Bell said. "We had a lot more to play for than people think. . . . We played this one for ourselves. We've got a lot of pride."

For Dawson, the game was vindication.

"The entire week was an ordeal," Dawson said. "I've never been through anything like it before. I am glad the ordeal is over. It's a big load off my back.

"It's a satisfying thing," he added, "because we had to live with that thing in 1967. Until today."

By 1970, the four quarters of the interleague championship game were complete.

The final score: NFL 2–AFL 2

The game is now officially in overtime.

CHAPTER 20

MONDAY NIGHT FOOTBALL

THE NATIONAL FOOTBALL LEAGUE CONTINUED TO prosper during the 1970s as pro football solidified its place as America's most popular sport. The merger between the American and National Football Leagues and the resulting realignment of franchises were accepted more quickly and enthusiastically by the public than almost anyone had expected.

Pete Rozelle told club owners at their spring meeting in 1971 that the previous year had been the best in league history. More people watched or attended NFL games than ever before.

Although Rozelle didn't flaunt it, a significant part of that success was attributable to a new television deal he negotiated with ABC.

Rozelle had long desired to have the NFL on all three major television networks on prime time. As early as 1964, he had considered a proposal from ABC president Tom Moore to schedule some NFL games on Friday nights. But that idea fizzled when Rozelle and Moore were reminded that in much of America (though maybe not Manhattan), Friday night belonged to high school football. Not only would the public be outraged, but Rozelle risked damaging his antitrust lobbying efforts in Congress.

With Fridays eliminated and no network interest in disrupting their Saturday evening entertainment schedule, Rozelle asked, "What about Mondays?"

ABC wasn't interested. *Ben Casey*—the network's popular medical drama—was moving to Monday nights, starting with the upcoming fall season.

Rozelle remained convinced that Monday night football was a good idea. In 1966 he convinced a reluctant CBS to experiment with broadcasting four Monday night games. The gambit worked. Ratings were strong enough that Rozelle felt he had enough ammo to continue his pursuit.

NBC took a one-game shot at the Monday night option in 1968. But when the game ran long and delayed the start of *The Tonight Show,* the network—not wanting to antagonize Johnny Carson, their most popular star—withdrew from further prime-time football discussions.

Rozelle immediately gave ABC another shot. He already had the enthusiastic support of Roone Arledge, the network's highly respected and innovative sports producer, who had just been named president of ABC Sports. Arledge and Rozelle had been quietly discussing the possibility for some time. But when ABC president Tom Moore was replaced by Elton Rule, Arledge was told the network thought the risk was not worth taking.

The prospect of prime-time football appeared dimmer than ever.

Rozelle had one more card to play. In October 1968, Cleveland Browns owner Art Modell, chairman of the NFL's television committee and a Rozelle ally, met with executives of the upstart Hughes Network. Taking advantage of the new network's desire to establish themselves in the sports broadcasting business, Modell negotiated a $9 million offer from the Howard Hughes–owned network.

Armed with the argument that Hughes could sell the NFL package one station at a time to many independent ABC affiliates, the network relented. On May 26, 1969, the NFL accepted ABC's offer of a three-year deal worth $8.5 million per year. The NFL thus became the first sports league with a regular series of national telecasts in prime time.

Although the offer was less than the Hughes offer, ABC's distribution was significantly better than the Hughes Network's. Not only that, but the upstart network had to rely on the less-popular UHF broadcast frequency to reach audiences in several markets.

The agreement was good for both parties. As authors Marc Gunther and Bill Carter wrote in their book *Monday Night Mayhem,* "Arledge knew better than anybody what sports could do for television. Rozelle knew better than anybody knew what television could do for sports."

Arledge was committed to making ABC's *NFL Monday Night Football* the best sports programming on network television. He saw the game as more than just football. As Sonny Werblin had said years before, football was entertainment. Now it was prime-time entertainment. And Arledge gave the game the full showbiz treatment.

While most Sunday NFL games were covered by four or maybe five cameras, Arledge's approach called for using as many as nine cameras, including one on a sideline cart and two handheld minicams. Every game, no matter how important it might have been, looked and felt like a playoff game. And the stadium lights against a dark sky provided a different city every week with the glitzy look of a Hollywood premiere.

The commercial possibilities opened the door to a new and lucrative audience, as Bob Cochran, the league's broadcast coordinator, told the *Los Angeles Times:* "We could reach more women, and that would help with advertising. Right now, our commercials are all for hard goods sold to men. Get more women interested and you might find Tide in there."

Monday Night Football did, in fact, draw large numbers of women viewers. In the mid-1970s, they comprised 36 percent of all viewers.

And then there was the broadcast team. Tradition was that a television broadcast team consisted of a play-by-play announcer and a color commentator. The play-by-play guy probably cut his teeth in radio and the color commentator was usually a former player expected to provide expert analysis of what the audience had just witnessed. It was a tradition as cut as it was dried.

Arledge challenged tradition and went with a three-man booth. And not just any three men. The original play-by-play announcer was the well-known voice of college football and other sports, Keith

Jackson. He was joined by the outspoken radio-TV commentator Howard Cosell and the likable former Dallas Cowboys quarterback Don Meredith.

The rationale for including Cosell was best articulated by ABC executive Dennis Lewin. Arledge wanted the production to be, above all, entertaining.

"We wanted to show people that pro football was more than a game of X's and O's. If we wanted X's and O's, we wouldn't have had Cosell."

In the program's second year, Jackson was replaced in the booth by Frank Gifford, who had been approached to be a part of the original team but was unable to get out of his contract with CBS.

It was the trio of Gifford, Meredith, and Cosell that launched ABC's program to pop-culture status. Their unique in-game banter and distinct personalities were sometimes more engaging than the game itself.

Halftimes were different, too. No marching bands on this network. ABC's halftime—which their research showed was the most popular part of their telecast—was a recap of highlights from the games played the previous day. Nowhere else could you see highlights of other games so soon; 24/7 cable sports and the internet were more than a decade away.

But it wasn't just the previous day's game highlights that captivated the audience. It was Cosell's trademark voice-over narration—argumentative, opinionated, and often at odds with his colleagues' views—that made it memorable.

Cosell was frequently the target of fans' anger when the network failed to feature their teams' highlights. The charge was inevitably "bias." But Cosell was immune to criticism. He gloried in it, which enraged his critics even further. Cosell was the man the fans loved to hate, and catnip to the network that sponsored him.

Like every broadcast team, the Monday night trio had to learn how best to play off one another. Jackson (and later Gifford) had to get used to the idea that they were the responsible traffic cop assigned to set the stage for Cosell's and sometimes Meredith's outrageous comments. Cosell had to learn to temper his remarks and not make outlandish statements, though it was sometimes hard to tell. And Meredith—who was affectionately referred to as "Dandy Don"—was told to hold back a little on the good-old-boy humor and offer more expert analysis.

The beauty of it was that none of them followed the script. Broadcasts could be argumentative, silly, and sometimes even informative. By midseason each broadcaster had his own supporters and detractors, and no one was happier than ABC, which saw the games' ratings go through the roof.

Cosell once summarized the roles to which he felt he and his colleagues had risen in their first year, in his inimitably Cosellian manner: "What do people talk about on Tuesday morning? They talk about me and Dandy and even Keith. We have become, if I may continue to tell it like it is—which is my nature—bigger than the game."

Meredith's quick wit on more than one occasion provided just enough humor to balance Cosell's sometimes witless orotundity.

One such occasion was during an October game in Minnesota that first year. With the camera focused on the Vikings' ever-stoic head coach, Bud Grant, Meredith quipped, "If Bud Grant and my old coach Tom Landry were in a personality contest, there'd be no winner."

Eventually, America figured it out. *Monday Night Football* was different. It was entertainment. And a ratings bonanza.

Fittingly, *Monday Night Football* made its debut in Modell's Cleveland Municipal Stadium. Modell was not only intimately involved in the ABC package, but he played a significant role in the negotiations between all the networks during the postmerger transition. At the owners' winter meeting in March, he proudly said that the ABC, NBC, and CBS contracts were "the largest sports broadcasting rights package in television history."

Still, several of his fellow owners were skeptics right up until the inaugural kickoff. But on September 21, 1970, when a record crowd packed Municipal Stadium for the first Monday night game, which matched the New York Jets with Broadway Joe Namath against one of the AFC's three new members, the Cleveland Browns, even the skeptics were beyond pleased.

Television—and football—history was made that night when the Browns defeated the Jets 31–21.

History of a different sort was made after the Browns' Homer Jones returned the second-half kickoff 94 yards for a touchdown. Who better than Jones to have a big play in the inaugural Monday night game? After all, it was Jones who in 1965, as a member of the New York Giants, brought entertainment to the end zone for the first time when he unveiled the touchdown celebration maneuver he called "the spike."

Monday Night Football was Pete Rozelle's "spike."

THE IMMACULATE RECEPTION

WHEN DON SHULA'S BALTIMORE COLTS LOST TO the AFL's New York Jets in Super Bowl III, more than a few NFL owners—especially the old guard—were beside themselves.

Dan Rooney, son of Pittsburgh Steelers founder-owner Art Rooney, remembered a tense postgame gathering of some NFL notables.

"I had dinner with Wellington Mara, Art Modell, Tex Schramm, and Vince Lombardi," he recalled in his autobiography. "They were furious, almost ready to throw [Colts owner] Carroll Rosenbloom out the window. . . . Lombardi criticized the Colts coaching staff, including Shula, listing the could'ves and should'ves that would have won the game."

Lombardi couldn't have known at the time that Chuck Noll, one of Shula's top assistants and a target of Lombardi's anger, was scheduled to be interviewed by Rooney the next day for the position of Steelers head coach.

Although Rooney Sr.—known universally as "the Chief"—was years away from officially turning over the reins to his eldest son, Dan, the younger Rooney was for all intents and purposes running the organization. His father had already entrusted him with much of the team's decision-making duties, including the search for a new coach.

Less than two weeks after Super Bowl III, Rooney announced that Chuck Noll would be the Steelers' new coach, the fourteenth in the team's notoriously underwhelming thirty-six-year history.

Two days later—under Noll's direction—the Steelers selected Joe Greene, a 6-4, 275-pound defensive tackle from North Texas State, as their first-round pick in the 1969 NFL draft.

Those two decisions did more to shape the fortunes of the Steelers organization than anything else before them.

"The organization needed a strong head coach and a plan for the future," Rooney said. "That coach and plan came in the person of Charles Henry Noll."

And in Greene, Noll and the Steelers organization had a cornerstone player on which they could build a dynasty.

Although Noll had been with the team only two days, he was well prepared for the draft, having been intimately involved in the Colts' preparations.

Initially, Rooney's brother, Art Rooney Jr., who oversaw the Steelers' scouting department, worried that he and Noll might not see eye-to-eye when considering prospective draft picks. But Art couldn't have been more pleased when Noll expressed his enthusiasm for Greene. Both had targeted him as the best possible choice for the Steelers.

The Pittsburgh media was less enthralled with the Steelers' selection of the small-school North Texas State tackle in the first round. The *Pittsburgh Post-Gazette* sarcastically headlined its post-draft story "Steelers Select . . . Joe Who?"

But Greene wasn't "Joe Who" for long. Although the Steelers finished 1-13 in 1969, Greene was named to the NFL's All-Rookie Team.

To the average fan, the Steelers—often referred to as the city's "lovable losers"—may not have looked much different from previous teams. But the Rooney brothers, team insiders, and many of the players saw an immediate difference.

Noll, they could see, had a plan and the discipline to stick with it. He focused on building through the draft. Working with the scouting cooperative known as BLESTO—the Bears, Lions, Eagles, Steelers Talent Organization—and the team's own scouting department, Noll was quietly reshaping the city's lovable losers into a respectable, competitive team.

Even with their abysmal 1-13 finish, the Steelers found themselves tied with the equally bad Bears. A coin toss determined which of the two would select first in the upcoming draft. The Steelers won. Noll selected a player he believed could do for his offense what Greene had already done for his defense. He drafted Louisiana Tech quarterback Terry Bradshaw.

By 1972, the Steelers had assembled an impressive lineup, several of whose members, like Greene, hadn't played at major colleges and universities or had binders full of admiring news clips. While the team boasted a number of graduates of traditional football factories like Notre Dame, Penn State, and the University of Southern California, the roster also included a number of players from small, southern black colleges and universities like Grambling, Florida A&M, and Prairie View.

A former newspaper editor named Bill Nunn was the man most responsible for the presence of these unheralded black players.

Nunn was the sports editor of the *Pittsburgh Courier*, one of the country's largest and most respected black newspapers. For years he'd covered black college football, writing about the athletes from historically black colleges and universities (HBCUs), who had been overlooked or ignored by mostly white sportswriters from major newspapers and NFL scouts. Each year Nunn named a Black College All-America Team. And although he'd occasionally get queries from a few NFL teams, the hometown Steelers were never among them.

After reviewing one of Nunn's Black College All-America Team stories, Rooney asked a *Courier* reporter why Nunn never attended Steelers games. Nunn sent word back that he "didn't like the way the Steelers did business." Taken aback, Rooney asked for a meeting. Reluctantly, Nunn agreed.

When they met, Nunn didn't hold back. He told Rooney that he didn't feel a reporter from a black newspaper was "particularly welcome" in the Steelers' press box. He said he was especially annoyed that over the years his hometown team had never contacted him about the Black College All-America Team.

"I don't think you'll ever be a winner," Nunn told Rooney.

Impressed by Nunn's candor, Rooney acknowledged that his frustrations were legitimate. But what happened next stunned Nunn.

"Well," Rooney said, "why don't you join us, scout for us?"

Shocked, Nunn initially turned him down, saying he already had a job. But Rooney persisted and eventually convinced him to scout for the team on a part-time basis.

"From the beginning," Rooney said, "Nunn was more than a scout." He quickly earned the trust and friendship of Noll, Rooney, and his brother Art Jr., and became the confidant to many of the team's players. In 1969 he joined the Steelers on a full-time basis.

While Nunn scouted major schools, including the Big Ten, his focus was on the largely untapped talent coming out of HBCUs. Those schools produced such future stars as defensive end L. C. Greenwood (1969), cornerback Mel Blount (1970), defensive tackle Ernie Holmes (1971), and wide receiver Frank Lewis (1971).

In the meantime, Noll and his scouting department during those years drafted tight end Larry Brown (1971), linebacker Jack Ham (1971), guard Gerry "Moon" Mullins (1971), defensive end Dwight White (1971), defensive back Mike Wagner (1971), and running back Franco Harris (1972).

It all came together in 1972 when the team that Noll and company had quietly put together took the field. Without knowing, they'd launched what became a massive change in the culture, attitude, and winning tradition of a franchise and the city it had grown up in.

"The thing that really put us over the top was Franco Harris," Greene recalled in a 2018 interview. "He just made us a better ball club, because he could really carry the football. And he was a winner. The way he went about his workouts and practice—Franco was the earliest guy there and the last guy to leave. He set the tempo. He was a good teammate."

With Bradshaw and Harris leading the offense and a defense led by Greene, the 1972 Steelers went 11-3 in the regular season.

After years of expecting and accepting the "same ol' Steelers," fans finally had something to cheer about. For the first time since

1947, and only the second time since the team was founded in 1933, the Steelers made the playoffs.

"The town caught on fire, and gave everybody nicknames," Bradshaw remembered. "You know, 'Franco's Italian Army,' 'Gerela's Gorillas,' 'The Steel Curtain,' 'Mean Joe Greene.' It really gave the team some identity."

+ + +

IT WAS two days before Christmas and Steelers fans filled Pittsburgh's Three Rivers Stadium. Bundled up in team-colored winter regalia and chanting, "Here we go Steelers, here we go," the proud legion of patient Pittsburgh loyalists sensed that their time, their destiny, had finally arrived.

All that stood in the way of that destiny were the fearsome Oakland Raiders.

The game was an early defensive battle. Neither team scored in the first half. The Steelers, however, changed their tactics at the start of the third quarter. Bradshaw came out passing and led a 12-play, 78-yard drive that ended with an 18-yard field goal by kicker Roy Gerela.

Midway through the third quarter, Raiders coach John Madden decided to pull quarterback Daryle Lamonica. The coach said Lamonica, who was struggling, was weakened by a recent attack of the flu. He was replaced by Kenny Stabler.

Late in the fourth quarter, Mike Wagner recovered a Stabler fumble. Gerela added another field goal, this time from 29 yards out. It was beginning to look like six points might be enough to carry the day.

But in the end, the Steelers and their beleaguered fans needed a little divine intervention to win the day.

"Late in the game, with probably a minute or so to play, Kenny Stabler came into the game," Greene recalled. "He scrambled—no, he stumbled—for about 40 yards and a touchdown that put them ahead 7-6. We got the football back somewhere around (their own) the 35- or 40-yard line and threw three incomplete passes.

"It had been such a fabulous year, I kept telling myself, 'This cannot end like this way.'"

With just 22 seconds left in the game and facing a fourth-and-ten from their own 40, it looked like the Steelers' playoff hopes were over.

Disappointed, the Chief rose from his press box seat and headed to a private elevator. He wanted to get to the locker room before the media, so he could console and congratulate his players. It had been a fantastic season and he didn't want them to forget that.

Meanwhile, on the field, the down-but-not-out lovable losers lined up for a final play. It had been a daylong defensive struggle. Greene and his "Steel Curtain" defensive line mates—White, Greenwood, and Holmes—had controlled the line of scrimmage. Ham had made an important interception. Safety Glen Edwards had a drive-stalling fumble recovery, as did Wagner. And kicker Gerela contributed the two field goals. Now the game and the team's fate rested squarely on the shoulders of Bradshaw and the rest of the Steelers' offense.

"I didn't have to pep 'em up," Bradshaw said after the game. "They all knew what we had to do."

But so did the Raiders. And they were just as determined. One more stop, and a few more seconds, and they would fly home and prepare for the AFC championship game.

Bradshaw called the play and broke the huddle. He took the snap and dropped back. The Raiders' defense came crashing through. Bradshaw scrambled. One Raider grabbed Bradshaw's shoulders. He wriggled free.

On the run, with the clock ticking down, Bradshaw looked for primary receiver Barry Pearson, who was running a post pattern toward the center of the field. Running back John "Frenchy" Fuqua, seeing his quarterback scrambling, cut across the middle to make himself a possible target. Harris—who was assigned to stay in and block—also started looking for an open spot. Bradshaw spotted Fuqua and fired the last pass of the game.

The ball, Fuqua, and Raiders safety Jack Tatum all converged at the same spot at the same time.

"Oh no," thought Harris as he saw the ball come flying out of the melee. But then he realized it was coming his way, some ten yards away from the collision. Remarkably, impossibly, Harris somehow snagged the ball in full stride just inches off the stadium turf and raced down the near sideline 60 yards for a touchdown.

"I think I was probably ten yards away around the fifty," Greene recalled. "And when he [Harris] caught it I ran. I think I beat him to the goal line," he said with a chuckle. "There's no way I really did, but it was such a euphoric moment."

Bedlam broke out in the stadium. Art Rooney, the Chief, the team's beloved patriarch, may have been the only man in the stadium to miss the most memorable play in his team's history. He was in the elevator, on his way to what he thought would be a mission of consolation, when Harris made his Immaculate Reception.

But with all the chaos on the field, there was still no signal from the officials, who were now huddled up. The game wasn't over. Five seconds remained on the clock. Was destiny about to become disaster?

Up in the press box, the sideline phone rang. Dan Rooney answered it. Referee Fred Swearingen demanded to speak to Art McNally, director of officiating, who was in the press box.

Rooney passed the phone to McNally. He couldn't hear what Swearingen was saying. But he did hear McNally's words: "Well, you have to call what you saw. You have to make the call. Talk to your people and make the call!"

The rule was simple. If the ball bounced off Jack Tatum—the defender—and Harris caught it, it was a touchdown. If it bounced off, was tipped, or was first touched by an offensive player—Fuqua—it was an incomplete pass.

"I was dazed," Fuqua said about the play. "I looked around and I hear people cheering. I couldn't imagine what happened. I hadn't seen Tatum coming. He gave me a good lick. Everything was dizzy."

When he got up off the turf, Fuqua saw Harris at the five-yard line.

"I was trying to figure out how he got the ball when he was supposed to be on the other side of the field," he told reporters after the game.

Finally, after an eternity, Swearingen stepped away from the huddled-up group of officials and raised his arms high into the air. Touchdown!

It took ten minutes for stadium security to clear the field so Gerela could add the extra point and the final five seconds could be played. The Steelers kicked off and had only to bat down one Stabler pass to end the game.

A stunned Raiders coach John Madden suggested that McNally, not the on-field officials, had made the call.

"If the officials really knew what happened," he said, "they'd have called it right away. But first they went into a huddle. That has to mean they didn't know. They called upstairs to Art McNally, NFL supervisor of officials, and he said it was a touchdown. He better have seen the replay," Madden warned. "He better not have made the decision on his own."

As the downcast Raiders prepared for a long trip home to the coast, the Steelers' locker room was a madhouse.

"The locker room was so crowded with sportswriters," Greene remembered. "It was just amazing, because prior to that the reporters that were in our locker room were local, which amounted to maybe three or four on a good day. . . . They were all over the place."

All thoughts of consolation were replaced by words of euphoric congratulation when Art Rooney made his way through the locker room.

"When I saw him come in, I think he was kind of surprised by all the hullaballoo that was going on," Greene said. "I don't know who told him we won the game, but nevertheless it was just really exciting, it was just a wild place."

As meaningful as the win was for the Steelers organization and the Rooney family, it may have been even more important for the city of Pittsburgh and the legion of Steelers fans who had stuck with their lovable losers.

Dan Rooney put the win in historical perspective.

"It's hard to explain," he said, "how much the Steelers meant to the people of Pittsburgh at this time. The old days of the steel mills and thriving industry were fast disappearing. As the factories and steel mills closed, tens of thousands of industrial workers found themselves laid off. . . . We thought steel would be here forever. It was our identity, our character—it was the name of our team. Our self-confidence as a people had been shaken to its core. Pittsburgh's sports teams helped restore some of that old confidence.

"The Pirates won the pennant and brought home the World Series trophy in 1971. Now it was the Steelers' turn to step up and show everyone what Pittsburgh could do."

A devout Catholic, Dan Rooney thought talk of an "Immaculate Reception" sounded just a little sacrilegious, though he eventually came around and agreed with Chuck Noll's final assessment of the play: "Well, if Frenchy didn't touch the ball . . . and Tatum didn't touch the ball . . . well, the rulebook doesn't cover the hand of the Lord."

Case closed.

CHAPTER 22

A STARTING QUARTERBACK

ALTHOUGH IT WASN'T FUNNY AT THE TIME, FORMER Grambling State University quarterback James "Shack" Harris can now chuckle when he recounts his start in pro football.

"The Buffalo Bills thought so much of me they drafted me in the eighth round and sent the ball boy to the airport to pick me up."

It was 1969 and "Shack"—short for Meshack, a biblical nickname his Baptist minister father gave him—had just finished a stellar collegiate football career at Grambling. In four seasons, he threw for 4,915 yards and 53 touchdowns, and led the Tigers to three consecutive Southwestern Athletic Conference championships.

At six-four and 215 pounds, with a strong arm and a pocket presence that confounded defenses and impressed scouts, he was a prototypical pro quarterback prospect. All the measurables would make him an early pick in the 1969 AFL-NFL draft.

But as his eighth-round selection suggests, there was a problem. Harris was black and—with few exceptions—black men didn't play quarterback in pro football. Even though significant progress had been made in the 1960s in opening the doors of opportunity to African American players, there were still challenges.

As the *Shreveport Times* wrote one week before the draft: "For various reasons, Negro quarterbacks just don't seem to be drafted by the pros. If they are, they are quickly switched to other spots."

It was called "stacking," the placing of athletes in certain positions based on racial stereotypes. Back then, the quarterback position was considered a "thinking man's" position, reserved for white players.

Since the beginning of the NFL in 1920, only five African Americans had ever played quarterback and none for more than a few games and most for just a few plays.

The first was Fritz Pollard—one of only two blacks in the NFL when it was founded in 1920. Pollard, a halfback, occasionally lined up as a quarterback during his seven-year Hall of Fame career with the Akron Pros, Milwaukee Badgers, Hammond (Indiana) Pros, and Providence Steam Roller.

Willie Thrower—a quarterback at Michigan State—became the first African American to play quarterback in the NFL's modern era. On October 18, 1953, Thrower completed 3 of 8 passes for 27 yards for the Chicago Bears in a game against the San Francisco 49ers.

It was Thrower's only NFL appearance. He was waived three weeks later.

That same year, George Taliaferro—a veteran of seven very good seasons with the Los Angeles Dons, New York Yanks, Dallas Texans, Baltimore Colts, and Philadelphia Eagles—started two games at quarterback for the Colts after starter Fred Enke was injured. When Enke returned, Taliaferro returned to his halfback position.

Two years later, on October 23, 1955, Charlie "Choo-Choo" Brackins went 0 for 2 passing for the Green Bay Packers in the closing minutes of a game against the Cleveland Browns. Brackins, a three-year starting quarterback at Prairie View A&M, was the first player from an historically black college to play quarterback in the NFL. He was placed on waivers after his one-game appearance.

The fifth African American to play quarterback in the pros was Marlin Briscoe, a quarterback from the University of Nebraska at Omaha.

The Broncos drafted Briscoe as a defensive back in the fourteenth round of the 1968 AFL-NFL draft. But after starter Steve Tensi was sidelined with a broken collarbone and the Broncos were on the verge of losing their third straight game, Denver coach Lou Saban turned to Briscoe.

With ten minutes remaining and down 20–7 to the Patriots,

Briscoe orchestrated two scoring drives that pulled the Broncos to within 3 points. Although they lost, Briscoe's play created a buzz in Denver.

The following week, Briscoe became the second African American quarterback in the modern era to start a game and the first to do so in the AFL. Briscoe went on to play quarterback in eleven games, starting seven.

But despite his impressive rookie season, Briscoe wasn't invited to compete as a quarterback in 1969.

Disappointed, he asked Saban for his release and the coach obliged.

After a couple weeks with the Canadian Football League's BC Lions, Briscoe decided he wanted to return to the States. He contacted a few coaches he felt might remember him in a positive light.

"I'd beaten Buffalo once and almost beat Oakland, and Raiders coach John Rauch was now in Buffalo," Briscoe said.

Rauch told him he was set at quarterback but he was looking for receiver help, and if he was interested, he'd give him a shot. Although Briscoe had never played receiver at any level, he accepted the offer. He not only made the team, he was named an All-Pro the following year.

By the way, Buffalo's quarterbacks in 1969, when Briscoe reported as a wide receiver, were veteran AFL All-Stars Jack Kemp and Tom Flores, and a promising rookie named James Harris.

+ + +

HAD ATTITUDES changed enough by 1969 that Harris might be given a fair shot? Could coaches, scouts, and management look beyond racial stereotypes and see a black quarterback leading their team? Or better yet, could they simply see him as just a quarterback?

Grambling coach Eddie Robinson, already a black college football legend, was hopeful but skeptical. While he publicly professed to believe the pros had progressed to the point where they'd "accept a Negro quarterback," he had doubts.

Robinson had by then sent more than seventy Grambling

players to the AFL, NFL, and Canadian Football League—a number that would increase to more than two hundred by the time he retired in 1997—but never a quarterback. Harris, he hoped, would be his first.

"I think he is the finest quarterback in the nation, bar none," Robinson said at the time.

Responding to the *Shreveport Times*' assertion that the pros' unwritten law regarding black quarterbacks would be on trial in the upcoming 1969 draft, Robinson responded: "I don't know about the 'unwritten law.' The only thing I ask is that they give him a chance at quarterback. Once he gets those black hands under the center, I think they're going to see as fine a pro quarterback prospect as there is."

Robinson shared the story of Mike Howell, another Grambling quarterback who was drafted in 1965 by the Browns.

"He had one of the strongest arms of anybody," Robinson said. "The Browns needed a defensive back and that's what they drafted him for," Robinson said, giving Cleveland the benefit of the doubt.

"With Harris, though," he said, "it's different. He has never played anything else."

In other words, if you draft Harris, you're drafting a quarterback. Period.

Some scouts told Harris that if he'd consider playing another position, like running back, receiver, or tight end, his draft status would improve.

But Harris had already decided—if he played pro football, it would be as a quarterback.

"I heard Martin Luther King say that one day it will not be the color of your skin; it will be the content of your character," Harris said. "That's when I decided I wasn't going to switch. I started thinking, Blacks are going to play quarterback."

Harris kept his word and pro scouts kept theirs. He was passed over on the first day of the draft.

Frustrated and angry by the slight, Harris told Robinson that with segregation the way it was and there being no black quarterbacks in the pros, he didn't think going to Buffalo made any sense.

Robinson listened, then offered advice.

"He told me that if I didn't try, don't come back to Grambling and say I didn't make it because I was black. I will never forget that."

+ + +

IMMEDIATELY UPON his arrival at Buffalo, Harris was taken to the Bills' downtown offices.

Inside the drab converted office space, a quartet of Bills execs were waiting. For Harris—who had grown up in the segregated South and attended an all-black high school and college—it was frightening.

"I'd never had an open conversation with white people before," he said.

The conversation that day was pretty much one-way. It began with Harris being told he would likely play receiver with the Bills. Then it moved quickly to contract talk.

"Your coach wants too much," he was told, referring to Robinson, who'd been negotiating on Harris's behalf. A new contract and a pen to sign with was pushed in his direction.

Caught off guard, Harris told the Bills' hierarchy that he had to call his mother before he'd sign anything. Not realizing they were being outmaneuvered, they told him to go ahead.

"I called Coach Robinson," Harris said with a smile. "I don't know what he told them, but they backed down."

The Bills eventually agreed on an $8,500 signing bonus and a $12,500 salary. Payroll figures were not made public back then, but *U.S. News & World Report* estimated in 1969 that the average salary was about $25,000 a year and at least half the players made $20,000 or better.

Although the Bills brought in eight different quarterbacks for tryouts during training camp, Harris battled through the competition. And he battled through injury. He used a painful muscle pull in his stomach as a reminder and motivator.

"In those days," he said, "if you were hurt, you could get cut."

The hard work paid off. The day before the season opener,

against the reigning Super Bowl champion Jets, Rauch assessed Harris's progress: "Right now, Harris is doing the best job throwing," Rauch said. "He still has a long way to go, but he's come along well in handling the team. He has a fine football mind, and when things go bad he doesn't seem to rattle or panic."

Rauch said the rookie reminded him of the Los Angeles Rams' Pro Bowl quarterback Roman Gabriel.

Whether he intended to or not, Rauch's statement debunked several racial stereotypes associated with a black quarterback:

Harris had the necessary skills—"best job throwing." He was a leader—"he's come along well in handling the team." He was smart—"a fine football mind." And he was poised—"doesn't seem to rattle or panic."

Harris appreciated Rauch's confidence. He knew his coach would be judged harshly should his decision not pan out.

"If I start I'll do my best and be happy," Harris told the press. "Anytime a rookie quarterback starts, that's the big pressure. It doesn't matter what color I am; I'm a rookie."

Three pro football milestones occurred when the Bills kicked off their 1969 regular season:

- Kemp began his final season before launching a political career that saw him rise to the Republican Party's nominee for vice president of the United States in 1996;
- O. J. Simpson, the first running back to rush for 2,000 yards in a season, made his rookie debut;
- And, almost unnoticed, Harris became the first African American quarterback to start a regular-season opener in pro football history.

All three incidents were notable. But to have a black man named the starting quarterback in a season opener, the key leadership position on a team—that was groundbreaking.

But as significant as it was, Harris knew he had to do more; otherwise he'd just be the sixth name on that short list of black quarterbacks who had almost made it. And unfair or not, he knew "as good as" would not be good enough.

Harris's pro debut didn't go as well as he'd hoped. Nursing a pulled groin muscle, he was in constant pain and under heavy pressure from the Jets' defense. Late in the third quarter, after it became apparent the injury was too much to play through, he was replaced by Kemp. The Bills lost 33–19.

After the game, Jets quarterback Joe Namath caught up with Harris and walked with him to the locker rooms. "Don't worry," Namath told him. "There will be more bad days. I know, I've had them."

Despite a rough start, Rauch announced that, providing his injury improved, Harris would start in week two. But the nagging injury persisted. Finally, in week four he was cleared to play. But by then Kemp had reestablished himself as the starter.

Then, two weeks later, while playing in relief of Kemp against the Raiders, Harris tore ligaments in his knee. His rookie season was over.

In 1970, the Bills struggled, and Harris played only sparingly. Rauch was fired and was replaced by assistant coach Harvey Johnson. The next year, Harris started only two games. Then, in 1972, Johnson was replaced by Saban.

Harris admits that by then the stress and constant pressure of wanting to succeed were affecting his game.

"I was struggling, probably holding on to the ball too long because I didn't want to make a mistake," he told William Rhoden in the book *Third and a Mile.* "I knew if I had a bad game that was the end of it."

The Bills—as a team—were in total disarray. Three losing seasons and three head coaches.

When Saban arrived, he made it known that he didn't want to carry two young quarterbacks—the Bills had drafted San Diego State quarterback Dennis Shaw in 1970—so Harris was released.

With no team offering him a tryout before the start of the 1972 season, a discouraged Harris took a job in Washington, DC, working for the US Department of Commerce.

"At first, I tried to stay in shape, but I stopped working out. That's when the Rams called."

The call was from Tank Younger, a Rams scout and former star fullback who played college football at Grambling under Coach Robinson.

Younger, with encouragement from Robinson, convinced Rams coach Tommy Prothro and new team owner Carroll Rosenbloom to sign Harris to the team's taxi squad.

Harris—after a year away from the game—slowly worked himself into shape.

The Rams' starting quarterback in 1973 was veteran John Hadl, who had played the previous eleven seasons with the Chargers. Adding youth to their team, the Rams drafted Youngstown State quarterback Ron Jaworski in 1974.

Then, creating even more uncertainty as to Harris's future, the Rams fired Prothro and hired Chuck Knox as his replacement.

"I was trying to figure out how I fit," Harris told *ESPN The Magazine* in 2014. "Hadl was the present, Jaws [Jaworski] was the future. Then, Chuck [Knox] gave me the news."

Knox had made a midseason trade. Hadl was a Green Bay Packer and Harris was the Rams' starting quarterback. News spread fast, and one of the first calls Harris received was from Robinson.

"When Coach Robinson called he was happy for me. But right away—and this is why he was such a good coach—he was stressing preparation. Coach Robinson would say, 'You're just going to get one opportunity. You must be ready for it.'"

In his first start as a Ram, Harris showed he was ready. He completed 12 of 15 passes for 276 yards and three touchdowns and ran for a fourth in a 37–14 rout of the 49ers.

Harris led the Rams to seven wins over the final nine games of the 1974 season, followed by a division title and their first playoff win in twenty-three years. His passer rating (85.1) was the highest in the NFC, and he was not only selected to play in the Pro Bowl, but also named the game's MVP. All firsts for an African American quarterback.

But even with his mounting successes, Harris was still looked at by many as a "black quarterback." Some expected him to fail—others hoped he would.

In both Buffalo and Los Angeles, Harris was heckled and received hate mail and death threats. One threat in 1975 while with the Rams was considered serious enough to warrant police protection.

In 1975, *Sport* magazine put Harris on its cover with the headline "Will James Harris Be the First ___ to Play Quarterback in the Super Bowl?" A footnote explained the blank was "Los Angeles Ram" but everyone understood it to mean "Black."

Even the Rams' front office at times seemed to want Harris to fail. Often overruling Knox, management brought in other quarterbacks to compete or, more accurately, unseat Harris as the starter. Candidates included Pat Haden, Joe Namath, and Vince Ferragamo.

Harris was 21-6 as a starter and 1-2 in the playoffs.

"But it still wasn't enough for the Los Angeles Rams organization to accept me as a quarterback, not a black quarterback," Harris said. "Chuck Knox was supportive, but the owner was going over his head."

Finally, in 1977, the Rams traded Harris to San Diego, where he finished his playing career in 1981.

Hoping to land a coaching job, Harris found no opportunity in either pro or college football.

Then, in 1987, while operating a small business with his brother back home in Munroe, Louisiana, Harris got an offer.

"Coach [Ray] Perkins gave me a scouting job down in Tampa," Harris said. Another opportunity and again he was ready.

Over the next twenty-six years, Harris climbed from being a scout to working as a front-office executive for several NFL teams. Along the way he was assistant general manager for the New York Jets; a player-personnel executive for the Baltimore Ravens (where he helped put together the team that would win Super Bowl XXXV); vice president of player personnel for the Jacksonville Jaguars; and senior personnel advisor for the Detroit Lions.

Throughout his long pro career, particularly as a player, there were times when Harris felt like being "as good as" or even "better than" just didn't matter. But even then—and often unknowingly—he was making a difference.

Warren Moon, then a quarterback at Hamilton High School in Los Angeles, remembered watching Harris: "I was a huge Rams fan to begin with . . . and to suddenly have an African American quarterback I could look up to, was a great thing," Moon said.

Doug Williams, another Grambling quarterback, had a special relationship with Harris.

"Let me tell you about James Harris," he said. "James Harris served as my other older brother. . . . With all the things he went through as a quarterback, not one time did Shack mention how tough it was. He didn't want me thinking I couldn't do it because I was black."

Harris was once asked if players he scouted or helped bring to the pros knew his story.

In his characteristically unassuming manner, he shrugged and said, "Not really."

While Harris appreciated how his sacrifices and hard work helped pave the way for others after him, his humility didn't allow him to take the credit he deserved.

"I only hoped that my play could be a ray of hope to young black kids," he said.

Harris didn't care much about who knows his story, not compared to the pleasure he took in seeing Warren Moon become the first African American quarterback enshrined in the Pro Football Hall of Fame and seeing Doug Williams win MVP honors in a Super Bowl.

Even with the game "stacked" against him, James "Shack" Harris made a difference. He helped bring the game out of its segregated past and into a future where no one marvels at the color of a quarterback's skin. Today, in the NFL, there are only "quarterbacks."

THE PERFECT COACH FOR A PERFECT SEASON

S HULA, YOU KNOW WHAT YOUR PROBLEM IS? You're uncoachable."

It's hard to believe anyone would say that to the only coach in NFL history to post a perfect 17-0 regular- and postseason record—but it's true. Making it even more remarkable is that the assessment came from Hall of Fame coach Paul Brown—even if he said it when Shula was a lowly ninth-round rookie defensive back at the time.

Brown's comment may have stung him, but, like every other seeming roadblock he faced in football, it didn't stop him.

Shula was drafted out of nearby John Carroll University in 1951.

The Browns were Shula's hometown team. He grew up in Painesville, just thirty miles from Cleveland Stadium. He was as excited as he was intimidated to be on the same football field as the players he'd idolized all his life.

"Otto Graham was my hero of all heroes," Shula said of the Browns' Hall of Fame quarterback.

"After I was drafted, I didn't hear from them [the Browns]," he said. "I thought they forgot about me." Finally, Brown's secretary called and told him to report to training camp the following morning.

"I get invited into his office at eleven thirty, and he comes in and introduces himself and says, 'Here's your contract.' I signed it as fast as I could. I thought they were going to take it back and say, 'We changed our mind.'"

Reminded during a 2015 interview of Brown's "uncoachable"

comment, Shula laughed. He acknowledged that Brown could be an inspirational figure in a young player's life:

"He would—in different ways—inspire you. Like letting you go, release you, waive you. That inspired you."

Fortunately, Brown saw something in Shula, as he did with another John Carroll rookie halfback, Carl Taseff, whom the Browns drafted in the twenty-second round. The two long-shot college teammates were the only rookies to make the Browns' 1951 squad.

Brown sometimes couldn't tell the rookies apart.

"I'll never forget in one of our scrimmages, he was standing behind the offense and watching as fullback Marion Motley plowed through the hole. I'm the only thing between him and the goal line. I said, 'Oh, I've got to do it.' So I put my head down, wrapped my arms up around him, and made the tackle.

"Paul says, 'Nice tackle, Taseff.' I jumped up. 'No, no, no, I'm Shula. I'm Shula!'

"He said—as only Paul could say it—'I'll try to remember.'"

Shula and Taseff played just one season together in Cleveland before both were traded to the Colts.

"I'm in a drugstore and I buy a paper and open to the sports page and my picture is on the page. . . . That's how I found out I was traded," he said.

The following year Shula and Taseff were reunited with Browns assistant coach Weeb Ewbank, who'd left Cleveland to become the Colts' head coach.

The reunion lasted three seasons, until Shula was released following the 1956 season. After one season with the Redskins, Shula retired as a player and almost immediately went into coaching.

His coaching debut was inauspicious. He got a job as an assistant backfield coach at the University of Virginia, where the football team posted a single win.

At season's end, Shula bumped into Blanton Collier, another former Browns assistant who had snagged the head coaching job at the University of Kentucky. Collier offered him an assistant coach's job and Shula took it.

Collier was a great teacher, for whom no detail of the game was too small. Shula remembered attending a clinic for high school coaches where Collier demonstrated how to take the snap from center and put it down for the kicker.

"He spent half an hour explaining it. . . . He covered every possible thing that could happen and taught it the right way."

After a year with Collier, Shula returned to the pros as a defensive assistant to George Wilson's Detroit Lions. The Lions posted winning records in each of Shula's three seasons with the team, and each year his reputation grew. Ironically, in 1962, the Lions— led by Shula's defense—beat Vince Lombardi's Packers 26–10. It was the Packers' only loss of the season.

Two months later, Colts owner Carroll Rosenbloom surprised the football world by naming Shula to replace Ewbank as Baltimore's new head coach. At thirty-three, he was the youngest head coach in NFL history.

His youth could prove awkward at times.

"I had some player-coaches with me that really helped me in that transition of me coaching guys who were much better than I was as a player," Shula said.

"I hired Gino Marchetti as a player-coach, Bill Pellington as a player-coach. . . . They would be in my coaches' meetings and then would have to go out and practice."

Marchetti, who'd recommended Shula for the job to Rosenbloom, was especially helpful.

The position of player-coach was familiar to Shula; it was a position his teammates often thought fit him, though they didn't always appreciate his "help."

"If somebody looked like they weren't sure what they were supposed to do, I didn't hesitate to tell them what I thought they should be doing," Shula said.

"I just felt it was my responsibility to do it, because I knew all of the assignments and I wanted to make sure they knew theirs."

Shula knew he had to prove himself as head coach. Being young was one thing, but having played with or against some of his new charges—including the legendary Johnny Unitas—he knew he had to earn their respect.

"It was tough," he said. "He [Unitas] was a much better player than I ever was. So, now, all of a sudden, I'm his coach. I had to prove myself in every meeting and every practice."

Shula was a well-known taskmaster. No one—not even guys like Unitas—got a break.

"I had two and three and four extra practices a day, and they complained about it. And then we started to win. That's when they bought into it."

Under Shula, the Colts enjoyed seven consecutive winning seasons. In only his second season, he guided the team to a 12–2 record and advanced to the 1964 NFL championship game. Their opponent was the Browns. Their coach was Shula's friend and mentor Blanton Collier.

The Colts, led by league MVP Johnny Unitas and a defense that allowed the fewest points in the NFL, were favored to win. But it wasn't to be. Collier's Browns shut the Colts out 27–0.

Four years later, the Colts were favorites once again to beat another top team coached by another old friend—Weeb Ewbank. But Super Bowl III belonged to Joe Namath and the Jets.

For Ewbank, it must have felt like déjà vu. Here he was facing the Baltimore team he'd led to victory in the classic 1958 NFL championship game, the game in which a young Unitas guided his team to an amazing win. Now Super Bowl III provided a showcase for another young star in Namath, while an injured and aging Unitas barely got on the field.

Shula left the Colts after the Super Bowl defeat to join a struggling new franchise that he would build into a perfect football machine.

+++

THE MIAMI Dolphins had won just three games the season before Shula was hired. Again, his path intersected with yet another coach who played a role in his young career.

This time it was George Wilson, the man who'd given him his start in Detroit. The current circumstances weren't congenial.

"He [Wilson] was just a great guy to work for and I just thought the world of him," Shula said. But he was sworn to secrecy while his contract to replace Wilson as the Dolphins' head coach was being negotiated.

Wilson was upset when he discovered the situation. Shula remembered Wilson saying, "I just wish you would have told me what was going on."

"He was probably right," Shula later confessed. "Somehow I should have let him know that I was in the hunt or that they were talking to me."

Shula wasted little time in changing the struggling Dolphins' culture. One of his first moves was to hire his old friend Carl Taseff as defensive backs coach. The John Carroll teammates coached together for the next twenty-four years.

In his first year with the Fins, Shula posted a 10-4 regular-season record. In just his second year, the Dolphins made it to Super Bowl VI, where they lost 24-3 to the Dallas Cowboys.

After back-to-back winning seasons, the young Dolphins team had clearly understood and accepted Shula's oft-stated philosophy that "hard work equals success."

Every NFL team begins every season with high hopes. But if any team ever hopes to achieve an undefeated season, they don't say so out loud, at least not in the beginning. The football gods can be a fickle, heartbreaking crew.

But as a season progresses and the wins start to accumulate, the unlikely begins to seem at least possible. Talk of going undefeated might be heard, if only in a whisper.

The 1972 Dolphins roster included six future Hall of Fame players—linebacker Nick Buoniconti, fullback Larry Csonka, guard Larry Little, quarterback Bob Griese, center Jim Langer, and wide receiver Paul Warfield.

With such a crew, going undefeated might seem more possible than usual. But it was contributions of some lesser-knowns that often made the difference for the 1972 Dolphins. And that was particularly true on defense.

Although the defensive unit was very good, it lacked the offense's obvious star power. It was the defense's relative anonymity and an unfortunate remark by Cowboys coach Tom Landry that earned them their "No-Name Defense" nickname.

After Super Bowl VI, Landry said during an interview that he couldn't remember the names of any of Miami's front four. The news clip was immediately posted on the Dolphins' bulletin board. The nickname emerged shortly thereafter.

Eventually, due to their outstanding play, the "No-Names" became household names. By the end of the season, defensive tackle Manny Fernandez, safety Jake Scott, defensive ends Bill Stanfill and Vern Den Herder, safety Dick Anderson, and Buoniconti were as well known as the team's offensive stars.

But even with all the talent on both sides of the ball, luck still had a big role to play that season.

"Sure, luck means a lot in football," Shula said. "Not having a good quarterback is bad luck."

In week five against the San Diego Chargers, it looked like just such luck had befallen the Dolphins. Griese suffered a dislocated ankle and a broken fibula. The recovery time was six to eight weeks. The best-case scenario for Griese's return looked to be week 11 or 12.

That's when Shula turned for help to the man whom most folks blamed for losing Super Bowl III.

Earl Morrall was thirty-eight years old. If he was remembered as the goat of Super Bowl III, he was also the guy who saved the Colts' season in 1968 when Unitas injured his throwing arm.

Shula, who had picked the veteran signal caller up off waivers from Baltimore, still had faith in Morrall.

"Anytime that he has been asked to step in and do it, he did it," Shula said. "He didn't look pretty doing it. He wasn't a gifted player, talent-wise. But he was just a guy that knew how to compete and knew how to win."

Morrall—with some heavy-duty help from running backs Larry Csonka, Mercury Morris, and Jim Kiick—kept the unbeaten streak going through the remainder of the regular season. Csonka and Morris became the first teammates in NFL history to each rush for 1,000 yards in the same season.

And the No-Name Defense did its part, too. Three wins were by shutout and opponents were held to an average of twelve points per game for the final nine regular-season games.

Griese returned to the roster in early December. Even though he knew his starter wasn't ready to play, Shula hoped he'd be ready for the playoffs.

Wanting to get a sense of where he was in his recovery—and with a comfortable 16–0 lead—Shula put Griese in for the final nine minutes of the season against the Colts.

Encouraged but not convinced by Griese's performance that day, Shula stuck with Morrall in the AFC divisional playoff game against the Browns the next week. He later admitted that after a Kiick fumble had stalled a drive, he was tempted to play Griese.

But he didn't. The Dolphins squeaked by the Browns 20–14. Shula raised more than a few eyebrows when he said Morrall would start against the Steelers in the AFC championship game.

At the same time, Shula seemed to leave the door open for a Griese return.

"Each week he's getting more and more time to heal and get back in the groove," he said.

Like the veteran quarterback that he was, Morrall remained confident.

"You know you've done it before," he told the *Pittsburgh Press*. "You've got the confidence, you've got the experience from the past and it means something. I think the other ballplayers know what I've done in the past."

Neither team's offense put any points on the scoreboard in the first quarter of the championship game. Then, early in the second, the Steelers got a lucky break when quarterback Terry Bradshaw fumbled into the end zone and Steelers tackle Gerry "Moon" Mullins fell on the loose ball for a touchdown.

The same lucky break had a downside when Bradshaw was injured on the play.

The Dolphins soon made some luck of their own when, facing a fourth-and-five on the Steelers' 49, punter Larry Seiple saw the Steelers' defense drop back to cover rather than trying to block the punt.

With no pressure from the defense, Seiple took off on a 37-yard run, putting the ball on the Steelers' 12. That set up Miami's tying touchdown—a nine-yard pass from Morrall to Csonka.

With the score tied 7–7 at halftime, Shula decided to make the switch. "Do you think you're ready?" he asked Griese. He didn't have to ask twice.

The Steelers took a 10–7 lead in the third quarter with a 14-yard field goal from Roy Gerela. With 10:50 left in the quarter, Griese entered the game. Three plays later he threw a quick slant pass that Warfield broke for 52 yards.

Two plays after that, Steelers linebacker Jack Ham intercepted Griese. But defensive end Dwight White was offside. So instead of a turnover, the penalty yardage made it Miami's ball, first-and-10 on the Steelers' 13. Then, on fourth down from the two, Shula opted to forgo an easy game-tying field goal and instead put the ball in Kiick's hands. He barreled in for the go-ahead score.

As Joe Falls of the *Detroit Free Press* later wrote, the Dolphins looked like an entirely different team under Griese's guidance.

Griese said it was all in a day's work.

"We just drove on them when we had to."

Early in the final quarter, Maulty Moore, a Dolphins backup tackle, blocked a Gerela field goal attempt. The Dolphins recovered and Griese executed a 49-yard scoring drive that put Miami ahead 21–10.

With just 7:25 left to play, Bradshaw—to the delight and resounding applause of the hometown crowd—returned to the Steelers' huddle. He quickly engineered an exciting drive that ended with a sensational one-hand touchdown grab by Al Young that pulled the Steelers to within four.

But it was too little, too late. Although the Steelers' defense got the ball back to the offense twice, two drive-ending interceptions ended any hope the Steelers had for a win.

The Dolphins were the proud possessors of a perfect 14-0 regular season. But Shula reminded his troops in the locker room that even a 16-0 record wouldn't mean a thing if the Dolphins lost the Super Bowl.

"We're going for 17-0 two weeks from now," he said. "We've been to the Super Bowl and we want to get there again and win. That's our goal."

Shula didn't offer his usual "hard work equals success" sermon. He didn't need to. Everyone in that locker room knew that was how they got to where they were.

Even though the Dolphins were 16-0, they were two-point underdogs in Super Bowl VII. Their opponent, the ageless Washington Redskins, were a solid team led by a strong defense that had played very well in their two playoff games. Loaded with veterans, the team was known as the "Over the Hill Gang."

Coach George Allen, who Hubert Mizell of the *Tampa Tribune* said "would scheme for the edge in a crocheting contest with his grandmother," praised the Dolphins to the skies.

"Miami is the best team in history," he said. "I don't know how the oddsmakers favor us."

While "best team in history" may have been a little over-the-top, the fact was the Dolphins' backfield was certainly one of the best in modern-day history. Csonka rushed for 1,117 yards in the regular season, Morris added 1,000 more, and Kiick contributed another 521. Their 2,960 combined rushing yards were the most by a team in a single season in NFL history.

"Miami has the finest three-man rushing bunch ever," said Allen as he added to his inventory of flattery.

"I'm honored George thinks so much of our team. I'm sure he's sincere and not just setting us up," Shula said with a sly grin.

When not trying to out-compliment each other, the two coaches agreed on one thing: the game would be decided by the defenses.

It was a matchup of young Miami defenders—ranked number one in the NFL—against a "battalion of Redskin graybeards" who were the best in the National Football Conference.

The coaches were right. It was a low-scoring game. But as Dolphins guard Bob Kuechenberg said afterward, it was "the most lopsided seven-point victory I ever saw."

The Dolphins built a 14–0 lead in the first half with Griese connecting with Howard Twilley for a 28-yard touchdown just before the end of the first quarter. Then Kiick ran for a one-yard touchdown in the second quarter. Kiick's score came after a short drive set up by an interception of Redskins quarterback Billy Kilmer. It was one of three interceptions of Kilmer, two by Scott, the game's MVP.

Defensively the Dolphins smothered Kilmer. In addition to the three picks, he was sacked twice and harassed all afternoon by the Dolphins' front four.

"Fernandez was all over the field," safety Anderson said. "He was uncontrollable," added Buoniconti.

On offense, Griese was judicious. He threw just 11 times and completed 8 for 88 yards. But it was Csonka and company—and outstanding play by an offensive line led by guard Larry Little—that controlled the tempo and the clock.

Csonka carried the ball 15 times for 112 yards and Morris and Kiick combined for an additional 22 carries for 72 yards.

"Our objective," said Warfield, "was to throw in running situations and run in throwing situations. I think that surprised them somewhat."

The victorious Dolphins locker room was jubilant, mixed with an air of righteous indignation. Buoniconti was the most talkative.

The eleven-year veteran had lobbied hard for more than two seasons for the recognition he felt his team and coach deserved.

"Shula's an absolute winner, maybe the greatest this game has ever known," he said. "His ego is very large and some of it rubs off. I've seen coaches who say they're out to win every game, but this guy steps up and really means it. This has a great effect, especially on the younger guys. Before the season, nobody talks about going undefeated. No player does. We talk about splitting with the Jets and the Colts and things like that. But Shula doesn't talk that way. He believes. And we did it."

Seventeen and oh. Not bad for someone deemed "uncoachable."

A RULES CHANGE, AND THE DECADE OF THE RUNNING BACK

T'S HARD TO BELIEVE THAT THE PLACEMENT OF little white lines four inches wide and two feet long could—and did—change the way the game of football was played. The white stripes that run parallel to the sidelines and are precisely placed at one-yard intervals for the full length of the field are called "hash marks." And they helped define the game in unexpected ways.

Hash marks officially found their way onto pro football fields in 1933. That's when the NFL implemented the ten-yard inbound provision. Whenever a play ended near the sideline, the ball was moved inward to the nearest hash mark for the next snap. Prior to that, an out-of-bounds ball was moved just one yard from the sideline and spotted there. Every other play began from the dead-ball spot. As a result, teams were often forced to run plays just to move the ball toward the middle of the field, rather than using their downs to advance the ball.

Although it was 1933 when the NFL officially added the hash marks, the league experimented with placing a downed ball 15 yards from the sideline a year earlier, during the now-famous 1932 Chicago Bears–Portsmouth Spartans indoor game played at Chicago Stadium to settle the 1932 league title. Based on that one game, Bears owner George Halas and Redskins owner George Preston Marshall successfully lobbied their fellow owners to permanently move the hash marks ten yards from the sideline.

Ever since, the league has periodically gone through what might be called "hash mark creep."

In 1935 the league voted to move the hash marks in an additional five yards, to 15 yards from the sidelines. In 1945 they moved them in 20 yards. Each time, the idea was to give the offense more options and maneuverability by providing more playable real estate.

And that was where the hash marks stayed until 1972, when the league moved them once again, to 23.5 yards from the sideline.

This time the inward shift was triggered by the emergence of dominant defenses, as was demonstrated by the Chiefs in Super Bowl IV. Coaches and league officials agreed that the increase was enough to aid beleaguered offenses, which in the previous three seasons had seen a 100-touchdown scoring drop-off.

The league thought the hash mark change would benefit quarterbacks by giving them more room to move. In 1971, for example, NFL teams called the most running plays per game in eleven years and threw the fewest passes in twelve.

But the rule change had the opposite effect. Runners, not passers, benefited most from the change. Rushing statistics were up in 1972 while passing stats were down.

In 1972, the first year with the new hash mark rule, a record ten running backs—O. J. Simpson (1,251), Larry Brown (1,216), Ron Johnson (1,182), Larry Csonka (1,117), Marv Hubbard (1,100), Franco Harris (1,055), Calvin Hill (1,036), Mike Garrett (1,031), John Brockington (1,027), and Eugene "Mercury" Morris (1,000)— all rushed for more than 1,000 yards.

The Dolphins' tandem of Csonka and Morris became the first pair of teammates to both rush for 1,000 yards in the same season. It was a milestone that would be matched in 1976 by Steelers running backs Harris and Rocky Bleier.

Also, in 1972 Green Bay Packers running back John Brockington became the first NFL player to rush for more than 1,000 yards in each of his first three seasons (1971-73).

Even the Bears' Bobby Douglas managed to rush for 968 yards in 1972. And he was a quarterback.

Atlanta Falcons running back Dave Hampton was, for a brief time, the eleventh running back in 1972 to gain at least 1,000 yards. Late in the Falcons' season finale against the Chiefs, Hampton's season-rushing total had reached 1,001 yards. But on his last carry of the game he was dropped for a six-yard loss and finished the season with 995 yards. It's not known if his contract included a 1,000-yard rushing bonus.

Jets running back John Riggins missed the century mark in 1972 by 56 yards. But he was just getting warmed up. He went on to eclipse the 1,000-yard mark three times in the decade (1975, 1978, 1979) and twice more in the 1980s.

While 1972 featured the rushing exploits of an impressive stable of runners, the focus in 1973 was on one man, Orenthal James Simpson.

Simpson, the former University of Southern California star and 1968 Heisman Trophy winner, got off to a slow start as a pro with the 1969 Buffalo Bills. It wasn't until 1972—the year of the hash mark—that "the Juice" registered the first of his five consecutive 1,000-yard seasons.

That year he gained an impressive 1,251 yards. But the next year, 1973, he obliterated the 1,000-yard standard of excellence by rushing for an amazing 2,003 yards.

Though others have since added their names to the 2,000-yard club, Simpson remains the only player to do so in 14 games. His 143-yard rushing average per game in 1973 is a single-season best, as are his rushing attempts (332), 100-yard games (11), and 200-yard games (3).

Although 1973 was a season to remember for the elusive running back, some say that in its totality, Simpson's 1975 campaign was even better. That year he gained 1,817 yards rushing, added 426 more receiving, and scored a then-record 23 touchdowns.

As of this writing, only ten players in NFL history averaged 125-plus rushing yards per game in a season. And only two, Simpson and the immortal Jim Brown, did it twice.

Another great running back made his NFL debut in 1975. After a relatively pedestrian rookie season in which he rushed for 679 yards, the Bears' Walter Payton had the first of his ten seasons of rushing more than 1,000 yards.

In 1977, the last of the NFL's 14-game seasons, Payton made a serious run at Simpson's single-season rushing record.

Although his 1,852 rushing yards total fell short of the record, it was the third best in a 14-game season behind only Simpson (2003) and Brown (1963). In that same season, the man they called "Sweetness" bested Simpson's single-game rushing record by two yards when he gained 275 against the Minnesota Vikings.

That same year, Heisman Trophy winner Tony Dorsett made his NFL debut with the Cowboys. He didn't disappoint. The five-eleven, 192-pound running back gained 1,007 yards rushing. And that was just the beginning. Dorsett would break the 1,000-yard mark in eight of his first nine seasons in the league. The only interruption to his streak came in 1982, during the strike-shortened nine-game season, which, ironically, was the only season he led the NFC in rushing.

While the increased running room created by the expanded hash mark placement helped speedy, elusive runners like Simpson and Dorsett, there was one back who didn't seem to care where the ball was placed.

Earl Campbell created his own space.

Campbell burst onto the NFL scene in 1978, rushing for a league-best 1,450 yards. He was the first rookie to lead the league in rushing since Brown did so in 1957.

One of the most powerful and punishing runners ever to set foot on the field, Campbell gained more than 200 yards in a game four times during his eight-year career. But his most famous performance came in a Monday night game against the Dolphins in his rookie season.

The *Chicago Tribune*'s David Israel described the one-man show that mesmerized the TV audience that night: "Campbell scored four touchdowns; he gained 199 yards on 28 carries; he got a go-ahead touchdown on a 12-yard sweep around the right side; he got the winning touchdown on an 81-yard sweep around the right side; and then he dashed off the field to change his clothes in the private telephone booth beneath the Astrodome stands."

If Campbell was Superman on game day, off the field he was Clark Kent.

"He's so humble," said Oilers guard Conway Hayman. "The only reason you know he is a star is the way outsiders and the press treat him. There are few guys in this world like Earl Campbell."

"SUPER" DEFENSES

W HILE THE 1970S WERE "THE DECADE OF THE Running Back," they were also "the Decade of the Defense." During the 1970s, dominant defenses emerged across the league.

Miami had the No-Name Defense. The Broncos had the Orange Crush and Minnesota the Purple People Eaters. The Chiefs' vaunted stack defense was still formidable and the Oakland Raiders—well, they were still the Oakland Raiders.

They were all formidable. But Tom Landry's two Doomsday Defenses and Chuck Noll's Steel Curtain were easily the best.

What's been called Dallas's "Doomsday I" included defensive tackle Bob Lilly, safety Mel Renfro, cornerback Herb Adderley— all future Hall of Famers—as well as linebackers Chuck Howley and Lee Roy Jordan. These stalwarts played from the latter half of the 1960s through the first half of the 1970s.

Doomsday II featured future Hall of Fame defensive tackle Randy White and Jethro Pugh, as well as defensive ends Harvey Martin and Ed "Too Tall" Jones, and safeties Cliff Harris and Charlie Waters. They enjoyed their heyday from the latter half of the decade into the early 1980s.

Pittsburgh's Steel Curtain featured Hall of Fame defensive tackle "Mean" Joe Greene and Ernie Holmes, and defensive ends Dwight White and L. C. Greenwood. They were backed up by linebackers Jack Lambert, Jack Ham, and Andy Russell. Lambert and Ham and cornerback Mel Blount are all in the Hall of Fame as well.

Veteran sportswriter Rick Gosselin, a student of NFL defenses, has written that nine Super Bowl champions of the 1970s finished in the NFL's top ten in defense and that eight finished in the top five.

"A dominating defense became as vital to the Super Bowl championship as a franchise quarterback," he wrote.

During the decade, the NFC's Cowboys and the AFC's Steelers played in the Super Bowl a combined nine times. The Cowboys played in five Super Bowls and won two of them. The Steelers played in four Super Bowls and won all four, two at the expense of the Cowboys. In both of those games, the margin of victory was just four points.

Although both Super Bowls were exciting, Super Bowl X was special. This was the showdown that propelled defense into the consciousness of football fans. While the game was hyped as Terry Bradshaw versus Roger Staubach, it was also a stunning defensive battle.

The Cowboys' path to Super Bowl X was reminiscent of Franco Harris's controversial "Immaculate Reception."

Two weeks earlier, in the NFC divisional playoff game against the Vikings, the Cowboys, down 20–14, took possession on their 15 with 1:51 left to play. A few plays later, facing fourth-and-16, Staubach hit Drew Pearson at the 50 for a first down. After an incomplete pass, Pearson told Staubach he could beat his man. Staubach told him to run the same route he'd run for the first down, only this time to go deep.

With twenty-four seconds on the clock, Staubach, under pressure, launched a desperation pass to his streaking receiver. Pearson was covered by Vikings cornerback Nate Wright. Both men could see that Staubach's pass was coming up just short of the goal line. Both slowed down, trying to adjust to the ball's flight. Pearson cut inside Wright and as the two struggled to adjust, Wright fell. Pearson reached back and caught the ball, pinning it against his hip before finally pulling it to his chest and running the final five yards for a touchdown.

A stunned Vikings home crowd went berserk, calling for an offensive pass interference call.

Both players said there was contact. Each blamed the other. Both coaches were sure they knew what had happened. Landry said Wright slipped. Vikings coach Bud Grant said he was pushed.

But the only call that mattered was the one made by the nearby official, who spoke with his arms: touchdown. Dallas won 17–14.

After the game, an elated Staubach said he didn't see the controversial catch.

"I got knocked down on the play," he said. "I closed my eyes and said a Hail Mary."

Thus was born an immortal football phrase: From that day forward, every last-minute desperation pass ever thrown would be called a Hail Mary.

So Super Bowl X wasn't just a clash between the Steel Curtain and Doomsday defenses, but a holy war between a team that won big from a Hail Mary and one that won on an Immaculate Reception.

Although the teams could be said to have benefited from a form of divine providence, both teams understood that defense would determine the outcome. Both coaches made that clear before meeting in Super Bowl X.

"If you play perfect offense, you can get beat 40–38," Noll said. "But with perfect defense, the worst you can do is 0–0."

Noll's philosophy was simple. "You have to first avoid losing."

Landry agreed. "Nobody gets to the Super Bowl without a super defense," he said. "Pittsburgh and Dallas have both . . . a great offense, a great defense. But when that happens, defense usually steals the show."

On game day, the Cowboys won the coin toss and elected to receive. Ex–Steelers running back Preston Pearson stood ready to field the kick.

Anticipating that the Steelers would go after their former teammate with a little more enthusiasm than usual, Landry called for Pearson to field the kickoff, then hand the ball off on a reverse to rookie linebacker Thomas Henderson.

It worked perfectly.

Henderson, who had exceptional speed for a linebacker, had to beat just one player on his way to the end zone: kicker Roy Gerela. Gerela drove Henderson out of bounds after a 53-yard return, but cracked a rib in doing so. He would miss two field goals and an extra point during the long ensuing game.

Even with Henderson's big return, the Steelers' defense forced the Cowboys to punt on their first series.

The Cowboys responded in kind. But Steelers punter Bobby Walden muffed the fourth-down snap and was buried under a pile of Cowboys at the Steelers' 29-yard line.

The Cowboys took advantage of the break and drew first blood when Staubach hit Pearson on a crossing pattern for a touchdown. Before the first quarter was over, Bradshaw answered with a 7-yard touchdown pass to tight end Randy Grossman. That score was set up by a leaping 32-yard reception by wide receiver Lynn Swann, a questionable starter since he had suffered a concussion just two weeks earlier in the AFC championship game. Before the game was over, Swann would make four critical catches that accounted for 161 yards and a touchdown.

With the score tied at seven, Dallas's flex defense kicked into high gear. The Steelers' offense struggled, but their defense—without superstar Joe Greene for most of the game due to a pinched nerve in his neck—picked up the slack.

A Dallas field goal in the second quarter gave the Cowboys a 10–7 lead at halftime.

The third quarter was a back-and-forth, scoreless defensive struggle. Staubach was under constant pressure. The Steelers' defense sacked the usually elusive quarterback seven times during the game and intercepted him three times. Defensive end L. C. Greenwood accounted for three of those sacks.

Still, the Cowboys hung on to their slim three-point lead.

In some of the pregame hype surrounding Super Bowl X, much was made of the idea that previous Super Bowls had been dull. The insinuation was that fans wanted offense and lots of it.

Noll said before the game that the alleged dullness was all in the eye of the beholder.

"If it ends up 7–3 on Sunday, it will perhaps take someone who truly knows football to fully enjoy it."

Landry sang from the same hymnal.

"I guess the dullness of the game depends on the person watching it," he said. "I usually find them fairly interesting to watch. I find it interesting to see how a team controls another team during the early stages of the game and then how that team finally breaks through to totally dominate and win. I guess some people don't find that interesting."

Landry's comments were prophetic. While the Steelers' offense struggled through much of the first three quarters, with 12:28 left in the game, they broke through.

Steelers reserve running back Reggie Harrison penetrated the Cowboys' line and blocked Mitch Hoopes's punt out of the end zone for a safety.

The Steelers were down by only one, 10–9.

"That blocked punt changed the momentum," Landry said after the game. "I thought we had a good chance to win it in the second half before this thing happened."

Two minutes later Gerela—wearing a corset to protect his ribs—kicked a 36-yard field goal that made it 12–10 Pittsburgh.

On the Cowboys' next possession, Staubach targeted Pearson again, but this time safety Mike Wagner was ready, and intercepted Staubach. Gerela added another field goal from the 18, giving the Steelers a 15–10 lead.

With under four minutes left in the game, the Steelers wanted to run as much time off the clock as possible. But facing a third-and-four, on their own 36, Bradshaw knew he had to pass. He called "69 Maximum Flanker Post," a deep pass to Swann.

Anticipating a pass, the Cowboys blitzed. Linebacker D. D. Lewis and safety Cliff Harris came flying in. Bradshaw evaded Lewis but was hit hard by Harris and lineman Larry Cole just as he released his pass. At the other end of the field, Swann had blown past cornerback Mark Washington. With Harris blitzing, Washington had no safety help. Swann hauled in Bradshaw's pass for a

64-yard touchdown. The Steelers were up with what appeared to be a comfortable 21–10 lead.

Steelers president Dan Rooney was spotted on the sidelines accepting a congratulatory handshake from Commissioner Pete Rozelle. But if anyone could appreciate the adage "It ain't over until the fat lady sings," it was Rooney.

Just about as fast as you could say "Immaculate Reception," the Cowboys roared back. Staubach orchestrated a five-play, 80-yard touchdown drive that used just one minute and eleven seconds. Staubach's touchdown pass was a perfectly thrown 34-yarder to Percy Howard. It was the only pass Howard caught during his eight-game NFL career.

Down 21–17, Dallas's Doomsday Defense rose to the challenge, holding the Steelers to just one yard on their next possession.

Facing a fourth-and-nine from the Cowboys' 41, Noll decided that, rather than punt, he would have running back Rocky Bleier run laterally and try to take as much time off the clock as possible. He was tackled at the 39-yard line after a two-yard gain.

"We already had botched one punt and they can score a touchdown on a blocked punt," Noll said after the game. "I had confidence in our defense. We were giving them the ball with no time-outs and I figured our defense could do it."

With 1:22 remaining, Staubach needed to move his team 61 yards. Sixty-one yards against the Steel Curtain.

Staubach quickly scrambled for one first down and then passed for another. Suddenly the Cowboys were on the Steelers' 38 with 22 seconds left in the game, exactly the number of seconds that had been on the clock three years earlier when the Steelers pulled off their Immaculate Reception.

Staubach missed on his next two passes.

With just three seconds left, Steelers fans were holding their breath and Cowboys fans were praying for another Hail Mary. But there would be no miracle. Staubach's last-ditch pass was batted away by safety Mike Wagner and caught on the rebound by safety Glen Edwards.

The Steel Curtain had rung down on Dallas and its Doomsday Defense.

Landry admitted afterward he was "a little surprised" when the Steelers didn't punt.

"They gave up field position, but we were out of time-outs. That's a judgment thing," he said.

"Noll's always had a lot of confidence in his defense. Of course, you're taking a chance. We could have hit one like we did in Minnesota."

Rooney admitted that was exactly what he feared. "I was really worried," he said. "I kept thinking about what they did to Minnesota."

"That was the most interesting game you've seen in ten years, wasn't it?" Cowboys running back Preston Pearson asked rhetorically in the locker room.

Noll was asked if their back-to-back Super Bowl wins were the beginning of a dynasty, along the lines of Green Bay or Miami.

"I leave those judgments to the historians," he said with a smile.

Historians agree that, while that game was many things, it wasn't dull.

ROZELLE FIGHTS
THROUGH THE NFL'S LOST DECADE

THE FIRST CENTURY OF THE NATIONAL FOOTBALL League breaks down neatly into ten distinct decades, 1920 through 2020. And while a case could be made for any of the ten-year periods as being the "most successful," the decade of the 1970s would have to be a top contender.

The 1970s began with the AFL-NFL merger and a unified, two-conference, twenty-six-team league. Two franchises—Tampa Bay and Seattle—were added in 1976. That same year, the San Diego Chargers and the Philadelphia Eagles played in Tokyo, in the first preseason game played outside the continental United States.

Sweeping rule changes were adopted in 1974 to facilitate the passing game and increase scoring.

In 1977, Pete Rozelle successfully orchestrated the largest single television package ever negotiated, reported to be a four-year, $650 million deal, roughly twice what the expiring network contracts paid.

During the 1970s, Pittsburgh, Cincinnati, New England, Philadelphia, Buffalo, Detroit, Kansas City, New Orleans, Dallas, and the Giants all moved into new stadiums.

There were historic, memorably exciting games, like the Raiders' 37–31 double-overtime win over the Colts on Christmas Eve, 1977. There were memorable plays, like Franco Harris's "Immaculate Reception" in 1972's AFC divisional playoff against the Raiders. And any number of individual records were set, such as Walter Payton's 275-yard single-game rushing performance against the Vikings in 1977.

Yes, it would be hard to beat the successes of the 1970s.

But as good as things were during the decade, some fractures in the NFL armor were beginning to emerge that would crack wide open during the 1980s.

Two problems rooted in the 1970s—an unresolved stadium lease in Oakland and unsettled labor-management disputes with the league—would present the NFL with some of its most serious challenges.

A third challenge, not rooted in the 1970s but just as disruptive, was the creation of yet another rival league, the United States Football League.

Together these three challenges so dominated the NFL's attention during the 1980s that it's come to be known as the NFL's lost decade. It took a great deal of skill and leadership to keep the NFL train on its tracks.

In 1977, Al Davis began negotiations with the Oakland–Alameda County Coliseum for a new stadium lease that included demands for much-needed—and expensive—facility improvements.

Knowing the Raiders had enjoyed a string of thirteen consecutive years of sold-out games, the members of the Oakland Coliseum Commission were not particularly responsive to Davis's requests. The commissioners felt he lacked leverage in the negotiations.

But things changed fast.

In 1979, Rams owner Carroll Rosenbloom, who was also unhappy with his stadium deal, announced that he would move his team thirty-five miles down the road to Anaheim at the end of the season. Rosenbloom was well within his rights to make the move, since it was within his seventy-five-mile protected territory.

Suddenly the Los Angeles Coliseum was without a tenant, and Davis was no longer without leverage. By December he was in serious discussions with Coliseum officials.

But one serious obstacle remained for Davis. Under NFL rules, a move beyond the seventy-five-mile protected territory would require the approval of 75 percent of the owners.

"I believe that any organization that sold every ticket it had for the last thirteen years and made millions of dollars from people in this area can't just get up and move," said Jack Maltester, president-elect of the Oakland Coliseum Commission.

"Maybe Al Davis will try," he said, "but I can't see the National Football League approving it."

On January 18, fearing he might not have the necessary votes, Davis made an unprecedented preemptive strike.

"I reserve the right to move my team if I desire," he told the Associated Press.

While the league wanted the Raiders to remain in Oakland, the owners were more concerned about Davis's open challenge to the league's authority, according to Steelers owner Dan Rooney. Davis's action threatened the league's fundamental powers.

Jay Moyer, the NFL's general counsel and later the league's executive vice president, recalled a meeting scheduled in late 1979 with the Oakland commissioners, Davis, Rozelle, and himself.

"We were dressed and ready to go when Rozelle got a phone call from one of the commissioners," Moyer recalled. The message was short and to the point. "Al says if you guys come, he won't meet."

It was no secret; Davis and Rozelle did not get along. Their hostility toward each other was as long-standing as it was obvious.

Davis's resentment went back to 1966, when Rozelle became the commissioner of the merged AFL and NFL a few months after Davis had been installed as AFL commissioner.

"He [Davis] was loudly opposed to the merger," columnist Dave Anderson wrote in the *New York Times*. "He wanted to win the war. But when the armistice suddenly was signed, without his consent, Davis had no job, no league and no love for Pete Rozelle."

On January 19, 1980, the news media were standing by to grill Rozelle at the annual commissioner's Super Bowl press conference. The number one topic that day was what Rozelle was going to do about Davis and the "I reserve my right" threat he'd made the day earlier.

Rozelle said he had no choice. It was his job to uphold the league's constitution and to see that a vote of the owners was taken.

If Davis balked, Rozelle said he would "take any actions available to me to prevent such a move, unless the owners vote their approval of it."

At the league's winter meeting in early March, the owners voted 22–0 against Davis and his potential move to Los Angeles.

Davis did not attend the session, and five teams—Los Angeles, Philadelphia, Cincinnati, Miami, and San Francisco, most with stadium issues of their own—abstained.

Davis later called the owners' decision "a business conspiracy" and said he and his attorney, former San Francisco mayor and Justice Department antitrust lawyer Joseph Alioto, would ignore it.

He also said the team would "take the only other remedy open to us."

Shortly thereafter, the Raiders joined the Los Angeles Coliseum Commission in an antitrust suit they had filed earlier against the NFL, challenging the league's team-transfer rule.

The league and the Raiders battled for months in Los Angeles courtrooms.

The first of two lengthy trials ended on August 14, 1981, with a hung jury. After fifty-five days of testimony and deliberation, jurors singled out one fellow juror as the reason they failed to reach a consensus.

Angered by the results, Davis claimed that the juror was an "NFL plant." He also repeated another unsubstantiated charge, that Rozelle was blocking his move to hold on to the Los Angeles market for himself.

Rozelle scoffed at the suggestion.

A second trial was held in the spring of 1982. After twenty-three days, the jury sided with Davis and the Los Angeles Coliseum. It was a severe legal blow to the NFL and devastating news to the city of Oakland and to Raiders fans.

Jay Moyer spoke for Raiders fans everywhere when he said they should not have been abandoned "just because the owner of the team thought he could make a lot more money somewhere else."

"We certainly lost this round," a subdued Rozelle said after the verdict. "We'll see what happens in the future."

What happened was the Raiders moved to Los Angeles and two years later, buoyed by the ruling, the Baltimore Colts moved to Indianapolis.

In the Colts case, the league found itself in a damned if we do, damned if we don't situation.

If the league tried to stop the team from moving, it faced the possibility of an antitrust suit from Indianapolis. If they gave the move an official blessing, they'd be in antitrust trouble in Baltimore.

"We said 'hands off,'" Moyer recalled. Colts owner Robert Irsay was told to make his own decision. And he did.

On March 28, 1984—in the dead of night—fifteen moving vans loaded with all the team's belongings pulled out of the Colts' training facility at Owings Mills, Maryland, headed for Indianapolis, where the Colts have played ever since.

There was one more franchise shift during the decade, though it was less contentious. The owners approved the transfer of the St. Louis franchise to Phoenix in 1988. This time the club's owners followed all the league's internal requirements and the owners approved it.

While addressing these problems during the first half of the decade, the NFL was concurrently working through major challenges from the NFL Players Association and its executive director, Ed Garvey.

In February 1977, the NFL and NFLPA—following a three-year battle that included a failed players strike in 1974—approved a five-year collective bargaining agreement.

That agreement, which was set to expire in 1982, allowed the continuation of the college draft through 1986 (a US district court had earlier declared the draft illegal). It included a no-strike, no-suit clause, and instituted a forty-three-man active player limit. The agreement reduced pension vesting from five years to four, increased minimum salaries along with preseason and postseason pay, and provided improved insurance and medical benefits. The agreement modified player movement rules and reaffirmed the commissioner's authority to discipline players.

Although labor peace was achieved, both sides were left

wanting. Almost immediately the two groups began posturing for the next round of negotiations.

In January 1980, Rozelle was asked what he thought the decade of the eighties might bring. It wasn't prosperity or exciting football that Rozelle foretold: the future would be all about labor problems.

"The key will be how the new collective bargaining agreement reads after it is hammered out following the 1981 season," he told the *Palm Beach Post.* "Naturally, the Players Association will be seeking more freedom for its players, similar to what baseball players now have." Then, with a hefty dose of alarmist messaging, he added, "I'd be surprised if team sports will survive as we know them now, with total free agency."

But in the end, Rozelle would not be directly involved in labor issues in the 1980s. That responsibility would belong to the NFL Management Council, an ownership committee established in the early 1970s as a counterpart to the NFLPA.

In a move originally designed to free Rozelle up from the constant haranguing and personal attacks of Garvey and the NFLPA, the council removed Rozelle from the negotiating table.

"That aggravated Ed Garvey no end," Moyer said.

"Ed always tried to position himself on a level with Pete Rozelle. His theory was that he [Garvey] represented the players and the players were the game. Rozelle just represented the owners."

The NFL made it clear that they saw it differently. Rozelle represented all aspects of the league—the players, the owners, and the fans. Garvey and the NFLPA would be handled by a league committee, not its chief executive officer.

"Ed banged his head against the wall for many years on that," Moyer said with a smile.

Paul Tagliabue felt the council's decision to insulate Rozelle made sense in the beginning.

But hard-liners on the committee—the Cowboys' Tex Schramm and Tampa Bay owner Hugh Culverson—felt Rozelle was too soft on players, and a split developed; instead of protecting Rozelle, the committee excluded him.

The committee and Jack Donlan, its executive director, took a more aggressive approach.

Donlan had a reputation as a tough negotiator in the airline industry.

Machinists' Union representative Wilbur Spurlock remembered Donlan.

"The NFL owners could not have found a better man," he said in 1982. "If they want to try to break the players . . . Donlan is the tool to do it."

Rozelle, for his part, felt the council had gone rogue.

The refusal to compromise by Donlan, Schramm, and Culverson on management's side with the equally stubborn NFLPA leadership culminated in two strikes in the 1980s.

The first began at midnight September 20, 1982, following a Packers-Giants Monday night game. It ended fifty-seven days later when the parties finally ratified a new collective bargaining agreement.

The strike reduced the season to nine games. A special playoff system was developed, with the Redskins and Dolphins representing their conferences in Super Bowl XVII.

The Redskins won the game 27–17, but no one won the 1982 labor-management playoff battle. The owners reportedly lost $450 million and the players' union made no significant free agency gains at the bargaining table.

Even though the agreement again extended the NFL draft and left the veteran free-agent system basically unchanged, Rozelle felt the effects of the fifty-seven-day strike were an "extreme negative" for the league. His personal frustration grew.

With no free agency gains for the NFLPA, Garvey resigned under pressure in 1983. He was replaced by former Raiders All-Pro guard and future Hall of Famer Gene Upshaw.

The strike was costly. Both sides insisted such a work stoppage would never happen again.

But it did.

+ + +

WHEN THE new collective bargaining agreement ended in 1987 with free agency demands still unresolved, the players' union called the decade's second strike. It began two weeks into the season.

Negotiations got off to a poor start, as reported by *Newsday*:

"Upshaw said that Schramm was very direct about free agency during the talks yesterday.

"'Tex made it very clear,' Upshaw said. 'He said the owners are the stewards of the game, and the players are only transient workers. The players come and go, but the game is the most important thing. I guess you have to relate that comment to something that it reminds me of: They are the ranchers and we are the cattle and they could always get more cattle.'"

Upshaw's analogy fired up the NFLPA base and was repeated in several newspapers, which attributed it as a direct quote from Schramm rather than Upshaw's analogy.

Dan Rooney was at the meeting and during a 2014 interview confirmed that the "We are the ranchers" remark was made by Schramm.

"Gene and I were sitting at the end of the long table. We could look at each other and he would just shake his head. When Schramm said that, I thought they'd blow up. I thought there might be some punches thrown. Gene just looked at me and said, 'What is this?'"

Whatever it was, the council ultimately validated the remark when they announced the striking players would be supplanted by "replacement" players.

Week three of the NFL was canceled as teams scurried to find, sign, and prepare replacement players who then played in weeks four, five, and six.

Approximately 15 percent of the active players chose to cross the NFLPA picket lines. The majority who didn't cross were openly resentful toward those who played in what became known as the "scab games."

The replacements came from every walk of life. Some were former Canadian Football League players, others were castoffs from NFL training camps. Some were refugees of the recently failed

United States Football League. And still others were just guys living the dream of playing in the NFL.

In union towns like Philadelphia and New York, animosity toward the games and players was very high, while in other cities, like Dallas, not so much. But, overall, the scab games were an embarrassment to the league.

The first day after the strike was called, Upshaw mentioned a "mystery man" who he said could bring a quick end to the strike. It was a short-lived secret. One day later it was confirmed that Rozelle was the "mystery man."

Union spokesman Frank Woschitz told the news media that the mystery man—Rozelle—had met for an hour and a half with Upshaw and Donlan and that the two had made plans for further talks.

While the Rozelle-Upshaw meeting didn't bring peace, it did at least bring the principals back to the negotiating table. Also, somewhat lost in the news was the announcement that Pittsburgh Steelers president Dan Rooney—long considered a voice of reason—had joined the NFL's negotiating team.

"I wanted to negotiate this thing in good faith," Rooney said in his autobiography. "But Schramm and Culverson were adamant. They were ready to lock the players out and go on with the season using retired pros, collegiate has-beens and NFL wannabes."

The final replacement game was played on October 19, a matchup between the Redskins and the home-team Cowboys. While the Cowboys had several big-name players cross the picket line, the Redskins and the Eagles were the only teams not to have any defections. In a minor victory for the striking players, Washington beat Schramm's Cowboys 13–7.

The twenty-four-day players' strike ended with the players returning in time for the seventh week of the season, but still without a collective bargaining agreement.

After the failed strike, the NFLPA turned to the courts and filed an antitrust suit challenging what it called the NFL's restrictive work rules. The courts found that the league was exempt from particular antitrust laws because the restrictions were contained in the collective bargaining agreement.

Realizing their options were limited, the players voted in 1989 to decertify their union and operate as an association. As the 1980s came to an end, so too did the way the NFL and the NFLPA negotiated their differences. The NFLPA decided its future success would be determined in courtrooms, not boardrooms.

+++

AT A press conference on May 11, 1982, just four days after the Los Angeles Coliseum–Oakland Raiders antitrust trial ended—New Orleans businessman Dave Dixon announced the formation of the new United States Football League. The USFL would begin play the next year as a twelve-team league in major US cities.

But the big news was that, unlike previous upstart leagues that tried to compete with the NFL, the USFL would operate as a spring league, playing a February-to-July schedule, thus avoiding direct competition with the NFL fall schedule.

John Bassett, owner of the USFL's Tampa franchise, saw the wisdom of avoiding head-to-head competition with the NFL: "When you have to compete with the kind of television money and success the NFL has had, for us to think of going head-to-head with them would be like the Argentinians taking on England *and* Russia."

Realizing it would take time and patience for the new league to develop, Dixon announced that the USFL would make several necessary allowances. It would have a modest $1.2 million salary limit per team, it would not sign college underclassmen, and it would not get into a bidding war for NFL veterans.

The USFL's pledge sounds strikingly like the NFL's 1920 charter members' announcement of the three reasons why a league was needed: to combat players' high salary demands; to protect college eligibility; and to keep players from jumping from one team to another.

As the saying goes, "The more things change . . ."

If the USFL's salary cap sounds low, consider that NFL team salaries in 1982 ranged from $3.5 million for the Atlanta Falcons to $5.7 million for the Pittsburgh Steelers.

Within weeks, the spring league announced it had secured a two-year television deal from ABC worth $18 million for a "game of the week." They also signed a two-year cable-TV deal with ESPN worth $12 million. At about the same time, former ESPN president Chet Simmons was named league commissioner.

The timing for a spring football league wasn't that outrageous of an idea, according to Paul Tagliabue, the NFL's then–outside legal counsel.

"Commissioner Rozelle had secured a huge television contract [reported to be $2.1 billion over five years] in 1982," Tagliabue said. "[I]t was seen by the sports community in general as an affirmation that football was king, and the fan interest was incredible."

But while the USFL's founding tenets were sincere and made a lot of sense, they were also short-lived.

On February 23, the USFL's New Jersey Generals grabbed headlines when the team signed University of Georgia running back and Heisman Trophy winner Herschel Walker.

Walker, who was a junior, signed a three-year, $5 million deal. While reaction in Athens, Georgia—home of the Georgia Bulldogs—was disbelief, in South Hackensack, New Jersey, where the Generals maintained their offices, it was pandemonium. Generals tickets were suddenly the hottest in town.

"I think he [Walker] has made our league," Dixon told the Associated Press. "I think we're on a credibility level with the NFL at this moment. I thought that would take two or three years to achieve."

Simmons compared the Walker signing to another historic contract. "I think we're more ready for Herschel Walker than the AFL was for Joe Namath," he told reporters.

So much for salary control and college-eligibility concerns.

Walker's signing had two immediate impacts. It helped encourage reluctant draft picks to consider the USFL as a reasonable alternative to the NFL and it created a new benchmark for salaries in both leagues.

The USFL successfully completed its debut 1983 season despite some last-minute shuffling of franchises and owners. The average attendance was 25,000, which was close to what Dixon had projected. But the financial losses—primarily due to several teams abandoning the recommended salary cap—were higher than expected, reportedly close to $40 million.

Initially, the NFL insisted that it was neither opposed to nor concerned by a spring league. Although Rozelle was a great believer in the seasonality of sports and had previously expressed his concern about the potential oversaturation of pro football, he also said that if the USFL was patient, spring football might work.

"I don't ever recall him [Rozelle] saying they're doomed if they'd stick to their original plan," Moyer said years later. "But it became apparent relatively soon that there were going to be pressures to deviate from that original plan, as we all witnessed."

The USFL's second season saw more franchise shifts and new teams, with the league expanding from twelve to eighteen teams. There were also major ownership changes, including, most notably, the purchase of the Generals by a New York City real estate developer named Donald Trump.

In addition to these changes, several teams signed prominent NFL players, including Browns quarterback Brian Sipe and Buccaneers quarterback Doug Williams. Teams also opened their checkbooks and signed several high-profile draft picks, including quarterbacks Jim Kelly and Steve Young and defensive lineman Reggie White.

But at season's end, not much had changed from the previous year. Television ratings and attendance totals were only slightly better, and league-wide losses were again reported to be more than $40 million.

In late August 1984, Simmons made official what many believed was already in the works. The USFL would play one more season of spring football and then shift to a fall schedule in 1986. The plan lacked unanimous owner support but was pushed through by a small, aggressive group led by Trump.

Several news outlets not only questioned the wisdom of the shift, but wondered whether a fall schedule was the league's real goal.

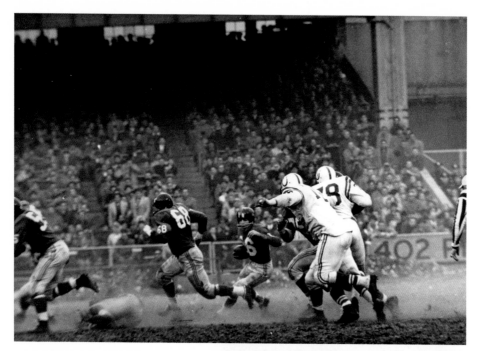

New York Giants halfback Frank Gifford was one of seventeen future Hall of Fame players, coaches, and administrators involved in the 1958 NFL Championship Game between the Giants and the Baltimore Colts. The Colts won the thrilling overtime game 23–17.

During his nine years with the Baltimore Colts, Weeb Ewbank coached six future Hall of Famers: Johnny Unitas, Raymond Berry, Lenny Moore, Art Donovan, Jim Parker, and Gino Marchetti. Shown here with their coach are Unitas, Berry, and Moore.

The New York Giants 1958 coaching staff included two assistants—Vince Lombardi (front row, left) and Tom Landry (back row, left)—who would go on to have Hall of Fame careers as NFL head coaches.

The eight original owners of the American Football League (pictured here with AFL commissioner Joe Foss, seated, right) called themselves "The Foolish Club." The moniker was a badge of honor for the band of owners of the upstart league that challenged the established NFL in the 1960s.

The Boston Patriots and the Denver Broncos made history on Friday, September 9, 1960, as the participants in the first AFL game. The Broncos defeated the Patriots 13–10.

The AFL had its first public relations win over the NFL when, in 1960, LSU running back and Heisman Trophy winner Billy Cannon signed with the new league's Houston Oilers over the NFL's Los Angeles Rams.

Minnesota Vikings quarterback Fran Tarkenton was well known for his ability to "scramble" out of trouble. On this play he had good reason to scramble, as he was being pursued by two of the game's most ferocious defensive players, Chicago Bears legends Dick Butkus and Doug Atkins.

Pete Rozelle (center) was a surprise choice as NFL commissioner in 1960. Rozelle negotiated the first league-wide television contract, managed the AFL-NFL merger and the league realignment that followed, and developed the Super Bowl into the world's most successful single-day sporting event. Pictured with Rozelle at his hiring announcement are (left to right) NFL owners George Halas (Chicago Bears), Frank McNamee (Philadelphia Eagles), and George Preston Marshall (Washington Redskins), and Eagles executive Joe Donohue.

On June 8, 1966—after much negotiating—Tex Schramm, Pete Rozelle, and Lamar Hunt appeared together at a press conference in New York's Warwick Hotel and announced that the AFL and NFL had agreed to merge, ending the costly war between the two leagues.

Kansas City Chiefs head coach Hank Stram and Green Bay Packers coach Vince Lombardi were all smiles prior to the start of Super Bowl I. By game's end, only Lombardi could smile. His Packers defeated the Chiefs 35–10.

Just three days before Super Bowl III, Joe Namath announced, "The Jets will win Sunday. . . . I guarantee it." When Namath and the Jets delivered a 16–7 victory over the 171/2-point favorite Baltimore Colts, the stature and credibility of the rival AFL was put on the same level as the established NFL.

Monday Night Football made its debut in 1970. ABC broke with tradition and featured a three-man broadcast team, with commentary by Howard Cosell and Don Meredith and play-by-play by Keith Jackson. Jackson was replaced by Frank Gifford in year two.

This piece of turf was removed from Three Rivers Stadium by Franco Harris from the exact spot where he made his famous "Immaculate Reception" in the closing seconds of the 1972 AFC Divisional Playoff Game.

Fritz Pollard—one of only two blacks in the NFL when it was founded in 1920—occasionally lined up as a quarterback during his seven-year Hall of Fame career with the Akron Pros, Milwaukee Badgers, Hammond (IN) Pros, and Providence Steam Roller. But it wasn't until 1969 that a black man was named the starting quarterback in a season opener. That pioneering first belongs to Buffalo Bills rookie quarterback James Harris.

Don Shula, the winningest coach in NFL history, was accorded the game's highest honor—election to the Pro Football Hall of Fame. This photo was taken immediately following his formal enshrinement, on July 26, 1997.

Thought by many to be the greatest running back of all time, Jim Brown led the NFL in rushing yards eight times and was All-NFL eight of his nine years in the league. His career rushing mark of 12,312 yards was the most by a running back at the time of his retirement.

Defensive tackle Bob Lilly was the first-ever draft choice of the Dallas Cowboys and the foundation for the team's great defensive unit that became known as the "Doomsday Defense."

The Pittsburgh Steelers' Steel Curtain defense and the Dallas Cowboys' Doomsday Defense entered Super Bowl XIII as the league's two best. During the regular season, the Cowboys had allowed only 107.6 rushing yards per game and the Steelers had allowed 107.8. What was expected to be a defensive battle ended up being a 35–31 shootout and the Steelers' third Super Bowl win.

Three of the most influential individuals in NFL history—Commissioner Pete Rozelle, Chicago Bears owner George Halas, and NFL counsel Paul Tagliabue—appear together before a 1981 House subcommittee to support antitrust legislation to allow the NFL to operate as a single enterprise, then comprised of twenty-eight teams.

A smiling Pete Rozelle (center) poses for a photo with President Lyndon Johnson (second from right) at the White House after the president signed a bill that included an antitrust exemption allowing the AFL-NFL merger. House minority leader and future president Gerald Ford is next to Johnson.

Michael Irvin—the first-round pick of the Dallas Cowboys in 1988 and the emotional leader of the famed Cowboys' "triplets"—delivers his Hall of Fame enshrinement speech in Canton, Ohio, in 2007.

Gene Upshaw was the first lineman who played guard exclusively to be elected to the Pro Football Hall of Fame. After his playing career, Upshaw distinguished himself as the executive director of the NFL Players Association.

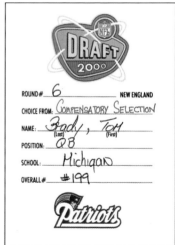

Michigan quarterback Tom Brady was a sixth-round "Compensatory Pick" of the New England Patriots in the 2000 NFL Draft and the 199th player selected overall.

Two NFL commissioners, Paul Tagliabue (center-right) and Roger Goodell (center-left), on the Houston Texans sideline with team owner Bob McNair (far left) and New England Patriots owner Robert Kraft (far right).

NFL commissioner Roger Goodell (left) and NFL Players Association executive director DeMaurice Smith hold up copies of their newly negotiated Collective Bargaining Agreement, which had been signed during a brief ceremony conducted on the front steps of the Pro Football Hall of Fame on August 6, 2011.

New England Patriots head coach Bill Belichick (left) and owner Robert Kraft came to Canton to honor former Patriots wide receiver Randy Moss at his 2018 Hall of Fame enshrinement.

Vito Stellino of *The Baltimore Sun* wrote: "There is a lot of talk about a scenario in which the NFL absorbs four or five of the strongest teams in the league and the rest simply disappear," he wrote. "There is a belief that some of the owners, like Trump, are just using the USFL as a vehicle to blast their way into the NFL."

"They were cagy about their stated objective," Moyer said. "I don't know that they ever admitted that they wanted to do something other than play successfully and compete against the NFL in the fall, but we know that some of them had the view—particularly Trump—that 'we're going to get one, two, three franchises, we're going to force the NFL to take us and the rest of these guys can go pound salt.'"

Adding fuel to fire, the USFL announced in mid-October it was suing the NFL for $1.7 billion on antitrust grounds.

+ + +

WHILE THE USFL managed to muddle its way through its final spring season, the real clash of titans wasn't on the playing field, but again, in the courtroom. It was a place that had become all too familiar to Rozelle.

"The United States Football League suit—as baseless as it is—comes as no surprise to anyone following sports," Rozelle told the Associated Press when the suit was announced.

"Antitrust litigation has been a part of the game plan of every 'second' league in modern professional sports history," he said.

But, Rozelle said, this case was a "transparent effort" by the USFL to blame their well-documented problems and failures on the NFL. He further claimed, as some in the media had already speculated, that "treble-damage antitrust lawsuits figured as much in USFL plans as did making their league a business entertainment success."

Trump confirmed Rozelle's belief when he told the news media the league's financial losses would be "recouped in full with treble damages." The antitrust suit, he said, was the "single most important aspect of the drive to make this league survive."

The suit was filed on behalf of the USFL by Trump's mentor,

New York attorney Roy Cohn, best remembered as Senator Joseph McCarthy's chief counsel during the infamous McCarthy House Un-American Activities Committee hearings in 1954.

Cohn was only briefly involved in the case before turning it over to another well-known New York attorney, Harvey Myerson. Of Myerson, *Fortune* magazine once wrote: "He carries his clients safely across a high wire with no net below."

The USFL's suit boiled down to a claim that the NFL conspired to monopolize professional football and impede the growth of the USFL by pressuring the three major television networks to not negotiate with the USFL for the fall season.

The NFL contended that their television contracts were not exclusive and the USFL was founded as a spring league and did not seek television contracts for the fall. It was the USFL's mismanagement that created its financial problems and inability, the league argued.

The NFL also denied that it had promised any USFL owner a franchise if they pulled their support from the USFL.

Prior to the start of the trial, at least one NFL owner argued at the league meeting that the owners should seriously consider discussing a settlement. Tagliabue, representing the NFL's defense team, said it would be a huge mistake to settle, since the suit was a "sham claim."

Moyer, who was also at the meeting, remembered that Tagliabue's remarks nipped the question of settling in the bud.

"Paul was very levelheaded. It was not the least histrionic at all. It was very matter-of-fact and sensible and everybody responded to it."

Dan Rooney often credited Tagliabue's standing firm as a turning point.

"No question," Moyer said. "This was the feeling Pete Rozelle had and that all of us had, that if you yield to this, there will never be an end to it. And if you continued to yield to demands like that [absorbing some franchises], you're going to have a fifty-two-team league someday."

Rozelle and twenty-seven NFL teams were named as defendants

in the antitrust suit. Raiders owner Al Davis was spared, since he had agreed to testify against the NFL.

Davis was originally expected to testify about his antitrust suit against the NFL, but in a pretrial motion, presiding judge Peter Leisure ruled that Davis's Oakland case was unrelated and could not be admitted into evidence. Davis did, however, testify for the USFL. Not about Oakland, but about New York.

Davis claimed without evidence that Jets owner Leon Hess intended to move to New Jersey with the understanding that the league would not allow another team into New York, which, according to Tagliabue, was "completely hogwash."

The NFL owners were furious when Davis testified against them.

"At least in Los Angeles he was fighting for his own franchise," Art Modell said. "I could respect that, but I can't respect this."

The owners particularly resented Trump's scheme to get a third franchise in New York. "He is trying to get into the NFL on the cheap," Modell said.

But it didn't matter what Modell or any of the NFL owners thought. It came down to what the jury thought.

The trial lasted forty-two days and included testimony from forty-three witnesses. After thirty-one hours of deliberations, over five days, the jury found the NFL nominally liable for one antitrust violation and awarded the USFL one dollar in damages—which, as an antitrust settlement, was trebled to three dollars.

While the jury found the league was "in a monopolistic position," since it was the only football league in America prior to the USFL, the NFL didn't injure the USFL.

Tagliabue called the decision "about as resounding a victory as you could get."

"The USFL," Rozelle said at the time, "shot themselves in the foot."

Trump called the verdict a "great moral victory." But USFL commissioner Harry Usher—on the job only since January 1985— had a more accurate assessment. "It's like a death in the family."

Usher had often acknowledged during the trial that damages

were very important to the league's future. "Without substantial damages," he told the *New York Times*' Dave Anderson, "the USFL dies."

And so it did. On March 10, 1988, in a unanimous 3-0 decision, the Second Circuit Court of Appeals in New York upheld the original jury's verdict. Judge Ralph K. Winter said the USFL "sought through the court decree the success it failed to gain among football fans."

+++

DURING THE 1980s, Rozelle spent much of his time in courtrooms, battling the NFLPA, Davis, and the USFL.

In the USFL suit, Moyer said that Rozelle "had to carry fifty years of NFL history on his shoulders and be ready to answer any hostile questions that were directed at him regarding any aspect of that history."

And it was much the same in the Raiders case. Rozelle—the man who was the face of the NFL—was made the focus of most of Davis's attacks.

It took a toll. Almost exactly a year after the USFL suit was settled, Rozelle—the man who forever linked pro football and TV, managed a merger of two leagues, and introduced NFL football to broad new audiences—retired.

Moyer, a modest man who played an important role during his many years with Rozelle, said that the 1980s may have been brutal, yet under Rozelle's leadership, "the train stayed on the tracks."

"I can't find a weakness in his leadership style," his admiring friend and colleague said. "I can't find a negative thing to recall about Pete Rozelle. He was one of the best human beings I've ever known. Smart, beautiful in working with people. He was a people person in the highest and best sense of the term. You had to work to dislike Pete Rozelle or anything he did."

THE 49ERS STRIKE GOLD

THERE'S NO DENYING THERE WAS PLENTY OF OFF-the-field turmoil during the 1980s. But those difficult times were in many ways overshadowed—at least from the fans' perspective—by on-the-field excitement. There were unforgettable games, remarkable player performances, and imaginative, innovative coaching.

Records no one thought could ever be broken fell like leaves from an autumn tree during the 1980s.

Bears running back Walter Payton eclipsed Jim Brown's 12,312 career rushing yards and then some. "Sweetness," as he was known, finished 1987 with an amazing career record of 16,726 yards.

And in 1984, Rams running back Eric Dickerson rushed for 2,105 yards, breaking Bills superstar O. J. Simpson's single-season record of 2,003.

Young quarterbacks like San Francisco's Joe Montana, Denver's John Elway, and Miami's Dan Marino passed their teams to playoff victories in the 1980s.

Redskins wide receiver Art Monk set a new single-season reception record with 106 catches. And it was during the 1980s that 49ers wide receiver Jerry Rice began his twenty-year assault on the NFL record book.

Over on the defensive side of the ball, Giants linebacker Lawrence Taylor and Eagles defensive end Reggie White redefined the way their positions were played.

It was a great time for innovative coaching. Forty-Niners coach

Bill Walsh and Redskins coach Joe Gibbs emphasized offense, while Giants coach Bill Parcells and Bears coach Mike Ditka showcased defense. All four won Super Bowl rings during the decade.

And there were never-to-be-forgotten games like the Chargers' 41–38 thrill-a-minute overtime victory against the Dolphins in the 1981 AFC divisional playoff game.

In that one, Chargers tight end Kellen Winslow put on a one-man show. In addition to blocking a Dolphins field goal attempt on the last play in regulation, Winslow—despite suffering from a pinched nerve in his shoulder, dehydration, severe cramps, and a gash in his lower lip that required stitches—recorded a playoff-record 13 receptions for 166 yards and a touchdown.

In another famous matchup—the 1986 AFC championship game—Elway led his Broncos on a 98-yard march against the Browns to tie the game 20–20 with 37 seconds left in regulation. That masterful fifteen-play series is known today simply as "the Drive." He continued to work his magic in overtime that day by driving 60 yards in nine plays to set up the game-winning field goal.

The 1980s featured many memorable performances, many great teams, but the 49ers were the team of the decade. They had one of the best coaches in NFL history in Walsh, one of the greatest quarterbacks in Montana, and the game's all-time leading receiver in Rice, all of them since enshrined in the Hall of Fame. And they had a slew of great defensive players as well, including three more future Hall of Famers in defensive end Fred Dean, linebacker Charles Haley, and defensive back Ronnie Lott. Put their talents all together and you get a recipe for Super Bowl wins.

+++

ARGUABLY, THE 49ers team of the 1980s began in 1977. That's when thirty-year-old Edward J. DeBartolo Jr. of Youngstown, Ohio, an executive with the Edward J. DeBartolo Corporation, one of the country's largest public real estate development businesses, founded by his father, Edward J. DeBartolo Sr., purchased the failing franchise. At the time, the 49ers had only made the playoffs four times (1957, 1970, 1971, 1972) since 1950, when the franchise joined the NFL as a part of the merger between the NFL and the All-America Football Conference.

Although a novice at running a pro sports team, DeBartolo took control and immediately began to shake things up.

Just a week after being approved by the NFL as the new owner, DeBartolo hired Joe Thomas as general manager and announced that first-year coach Monte Clark, who had guided the team to its first winning season (8-6) since 1972, was "resigning."

DeBartolo explained that the terms of Clark's contract conflicted with Thomas's role as GM. Unwilling to relinquish whatever those duties were, Clark was forced to resign.

Thomas had been director of player personnel for the Vikings from 1961 to 1965 and the Dolphins from 1965 to 1971, and was general manager of the Colts from 1972 to 1977. A well-regarded personnel man, Thomas had an outstanding reputation for building those franchises into winning organizations.

But his personnel magic never took effect in San Francisco. The 49ers went 7-23 during Thomas's first two seasons. The team seemed disorganized. During those two years, three more head coaches were hired and fired. Thomas fired Ken Meyer and Pete McCulley. The third to go, Fred O'Connor, was fired by DeBartolo, who also fired Thomas.

One day after Thomas's departure, DeBartolo announced the hiring of Bill Walsh as head coach and director of football operations. Counting Clark, Walsh was the 49ers' fifth coach in just twenty-two months.

Although DeBartolo said he'd considered several men for the job, his focus was on only one candidate.

"Honest to God, within ten minutes I knew this was the guy," DeBartolo said after their one and only meeting.

DeBartolo said that after Walsh's two years as Stanford's head coach and a ten-year tour of duty as an NFL assistant coach, Walsh was ready to be a head coach.

Time would prove DeBartolo's words prophetic.

Walsh's years as an assistant coach began in 1966, when he was a backfield coach for the Raiders. In 1968 he went to Cincinnati, where, under head coach Paul Brown, he built a reputation as an elite offensive coach with a special talent for schooling quarterbacks. During his eight seasons with the Bengals, Walsh directed much of the offense and was widely praised for his tutelage of quarterbacks Greg Cook, Virgil Carter, and Kenny Anderson.

Walsh was viewed by many as the heir apparent to Brown in Cincinnati. But when Brown decided in 1975 that it was time to pass the torch, he chose another assistant—Bill Johnson. Walsh was devastated.

Brown later explained that Johnson had been his assistant for eight years, and though he thought Walsh was a brilliant coach, "he was from California, and I always thought he would want to go back."

Brown was right. Although Walsh would gladly have remained in Cincinnati, he quit the Bengals days after Johnson was anointed, accepting a job as an assistant with the Chargers.

"The way it was done was not as civilized as it should have been," Walsh later said. "Brown didn't tell me. The TV people came to my house and told me. So that wasn't very good. . . . [T]he minute that happened, my wife and I knew we'd have to leave and go someplace to start over. And we did."

Following a one-year stint with the Chargers, Walsh was hired by Stanford. In two years he turned a mediocre team into a solid winner, with victories in the 1977 Sun Bowl and the 1978 Bluebonnet Bowl. But when DeBartolo called and offered him a chance to be a head coach in the NFL, Walsh didn't hesitate.

DeBartolo gave Walsh full control of the team. He would decide which players to draft, whom to keep, and whom to let go.

In his first draft, Walsh hoped to find some young difference makers who might contribute sooner rather than later. Only two players selected that year made any impact at all. But both those players made a hell of an impact.

Walsh used his third-round pick in the 1979 draft to select Notre Dame quarterback Joe Montana. Then, in the tenth round, a round where you usually find backups and kickers, he took a chance on a Clemson wide receiver named Dwight Clark.

Montana and Clark would soon be more than difference makers. They became major parts of the foundation of a dynasty, a dynasty that introduced itself in one game and on one play remembered today as "the Catch."

+ + +

WALSH'S 49ERS got off to a slow start. They finished 2-14 in 1979 and 6-10 in 1980. Montana didn't earn a starter's berth until late in the 1980 season. Although he had promising moments, Walsh wasn't quite sure that Montana was on track to be the franchise quarterback he had hoped for.

Meanwhile, the team's revamped front office—headed up by John McVay—continued collecting needed pieces for the team's rebuilding program. They made several key defensive picks, starting with linebacker Keena Turner in 1980.

But the big score on defense came in the 1981 draft. That year, the 49ers hit a mother lode of talent. Four of the 49ers' first five picks were defensive backs. Three—Ronnie Lott, Eric Wright, and Carlton Williamson—became starters as rookies. Lott went on to play his way into the Hall of Fame.

The three rookie defensive backs, along with second-year cornerback Dwight Hicks, became the 49ers' starting secondary.

That same year, the Niners signed veteran linebacker Jack "Hacksaw" Reynolds, a former first-round pick of the Rams, and in a midseason trade with the Chargers landed defensive end Fred Dean, another of their future Hall of Famers.

The defensive moves paid off immediately. Only three times during the 1981 season did San Francisco yield more than 20 points in a game. Lott, Hicks, and Dean were ultimately named to the Pro Bowl.

On offense, Montana and Clark emerged as a formidable pass-catch combo. Montana racked up more than 3,500 passing yards and 19 touchdowns, while Clark led the team with 85 receptions.

They were the main cogs in Walsh's horizontal passing game, an offensive style he had designed during his years in Cincinnati.

When Walsh arrived in Cincinnati, the expansion-team Bengals were short on talent. Quarterback Virgil Carter was athletic but lacked a strong arm. Walsh devised a system of short, quick, timed throws to make the most of Carter's skill set.

He drew on Paul Brown's game strategy, which called for the offense to make 25 first downs per game and control the ball with short passes and selective runs. As opponents adjusted to stop the short game, Walsh would lull them into a false sense of security and go for a big play downfield.

Walsh's famous West Coast Offense was a refined version of that short-passing attack. There were option reads by receivers and breakout patterns at the end of routes. It included a lot of underneath crossing patterns and running backs being used as receivers. In 1985, running back Roger Craig, the perfect player for Walsh's offense, became the first player in NFL history to rush for more than 1,000 yards (1,050) and catch passes for more than 1,000 yards (1,016) in the same season.

The name West Coast Offense was coined by Giants coach Bill Parcells after his defensively oriented team defeated the 49ers 17–3 in the 1985 wild-card playoff game.

"What do you think of that West Coast Offense now?" Parcells sneered after his team's win.

Walsh initially resisted the West Coast Offense moniker—perhaps because it was first uttered as an insult—but as others continued to use it, and the offense continued to earn praise, he eventually accepted it.

"It is an umbrella term for precision-timed passing, variable formations, and the exploitation of each player's skills," Walsh would explain.

And—like George Halas's T-formation of four decades earlier—it required a certain kind of quarterback, someone who had great instincts and could throw with a keen sense of timing and control. For Halas it was Sid Luckman. For Walsh it was Montana.

"What I have is recognition," Montana once said. "The ability to see everything on the field. Position the other team to death. Keep the ball alive and keep it moving forward. Then, at the right moment, knock them on their ass."

The 49ers finished the 1981 regular season with a 13-3 record. Walsh was named Coach of the Year. His team was back in the playoffs after a ten-year drought. Their opponent in the divisional playoff game was the 9-7 Giants.

They beat the Giants in that game 38–24. Although the offense played well, the defense, particularly the secondary, struggled.

"If we make the same mistakes next week against Dallas that we made today," Wright said, "it's over," a sentiment echoed by fellow cornerback Ronnie Lott.

Walsh didn't disagree, but he had high praise for Montana and the offense.

Montana completed 20 of 31 attempts for a career-high 304 yards. Receiver Freddie Solomon had six catches for 107 yards and Clark caught five for 104 yards. In all, Montana threw to eight different receivers. Solomon's performance was particularly impressive when you consider he was battling the flu and playing with a 101-degree fever.

The following week, the 12-4 Cowboys came to San Francisco looking to avenge the 45–14 pounding the 49ers had given them in week six. These were *the Cowboys*—America's Team!—who in the last eleven seasons had been to five Super Bowls and won two. They were cocky. But the 49ers were unfazed. They didn't think the 45–14 whipping was a fluke. "They didn't respect us," Montana said.

As Gary Myers said in his book *The Catch*, the NFC championship game was memorable "more for its dramatic moments than for its artistic beauty."

There were six lead changes during the game and nine turnovers—six by the 49ers, including three Montana interceptions. Few teams have ever recovered from that many turnovers. As if the turnovers weren't bad enough, Lott, who had cautioned his teammates against making mistakes, was nailed for two costly pass interference calls that led to Dallas touchdowns.

But the 49ers continued to hang tough.

Trailing 27–21, they were on their own 11-yard line with 4:54 left in the game—89 yards away from heading to their first-ever Super Bowl.

Now it was up to Montana. He had to do what he did best— keep the ball alive and keep it moving forward. And he had to forget about the interceptions. That was history. The only thing that mattered now was 89 yards away.

"Eighty-nine yards to go against America's Team," Clark said he thought to himself. "I don't know if this is really possible."

Montana's task resembled the one faced by another skinny third-year quarterback from western Pennsylvania. In 1958, Johnny Unitas needed to lead his Baltimore Colts on an 80-yard overtime drive to claim the NFL championship. He did it in 13 plays.

Montana directed a 13-play, 83-yard drive that put the ball on the Dallas six-yard line. It was textbook Montana.

Facing a third-and-goal with 58 seconds remaining, Walsh summoned Montana to the sideline. Run "sprint right option," he told his quarterback.

It was a play—like all Walsh's plays—that the team had practiced ad nauseam, a pass play designed to go to Solomon. Walsh had used it in the first quarter when Montana and Solomon connected for the game's first touchdown, an eight-yard toss.

"Bill never lets a quarterback forget about fundamentals," Montana said. "A lot of teams work on it until camp is over and then forget about it. We work on it constantly."

When Clark got to the line of scrimmage, he saw that the Dallas secondary was doubling up on him. That's what was supposed to happen. He was the decoy. Safety Michael Downs and cornerback Everson Walls had Clark in their sights. Walls had already intercepted Montana twice and recovered a fumble. Nothing would have made him happier than to shut down Montana again.

When Montana took the snap from center Fred Quillan, he rolled to his right as the play was designed. But Solomon had slipped before he could make his break. That slight variation in timing threw everything off. A crowd of Cowboys, including Ed

"Too Tall" Jones, Larry Bethea, and D. D. Lewis, came bearing down on Montana. He couldn't see Solomon, but he knew where to look for Clark, whose job was to run a left-to-right drag, then cut deep into the end zone along the back line.

Walsh's fundamentals were never more important. Clark had to be where he was supposed to be, where Montana expected him to be.

"I couldn't see anyone except Too Tall," Montana said after the game. Knowing it was third down and he would have another shot, Montana had to make a split-second decision to either trust the play call and his decoy receiver or run the ball out of bounds before Too Tall clobbered him.

"My job was to find Joe and, once he found me, slide along the end line," Clark said.

Montana, running laterally and backward at the same time, jumped off his back foot and threw the ball high into the end zone. Clark never saw the ball leave Montana's hand.

"The throw was high, just like it had to be," Clark said. "I didn't think Joe was gonna get it off. I thought it was too high and I'm not much of a jumper. But I guess I can go just as high as I need to in a championship game," he said.

"It was unbelievable," Montana said. "He jumped three feet off the ground. It was just a great catch."

Montana may have been the only man in the stadium who didn't see the catch in real time. Bethea had pushed him to the ground just as he released the ball. He had to wait to see it on TV in the locker room.

"All I know is that when we got the ball the last time I was confident we could move. We all were," Montana said.

While the 49ers and their playoff-starved fans were ecstatic with their 28–27 lead, there were still 51 seconds on the clock.

Could "the Catch" get upstaged by another Dallas Cowboys "Hail Mary"?

In the Cowboys' huddle, quarterback Danny White reminded his teammates, "All we need is a field goal." When Drew Pearson caught White's first pass, it looked like he was on his way to a

75-yard touchdown. But Wright made a desperate grab and caught Pearson by the jersey, stopping him at the San Francisco 44 with 38 seconds remaining. One more pass and Dallas would be in field goal range.

But on the next play, backup defensive lineman Lawrence Pillars broke through the line and nailed White, causing him to fumble. Defensive end Jim Stuckey fell on the ball. It was over. The San Francisco 49ers were NFC champions and the Catch was football history.

"It was a hell of a play," Cowboys defensive tackle Randy White said afterward. "Call it luck or anything you want, but they made the play when they had to. More power to them. I hope they win the Super Bowl."

They did, beating Walsh's former team, the Bengals, 26–21, in Super Bowl XVI.

During the ensuing decade the 49ers played in five NFC championship games and three more Super Bowls (XIX, XXIII, XXIV) and began a run of sixteen consecutive seasons (1983–98) with ten or more wins.

And it all started with the Catch.

TAGS! YOU'RE IT

PETE ROZELLE'S DECISION TO RETIRE AS COMMIS-
sioner in early 1989 caught the owners by surprise. Although
he acknowledged to his staff that he'd made the decision the
previous October, Rozelle secretly didn't want to be a lame-duck
commissioner during the upcoming season.

Reaction was immediate.

Giants owner Wellington Mara perfectly captured the feeling
among the owners.

"Our task will be to try to find the replacement for the irreplace-
able man," he said. "I think Pete Rozelle will forever be the standard by which all sports commissioners will be judged."

Mara reflected on how just before Rozelle's election in 1960, his
father, Giants founder Tim Mara, had been "dazzled" by an offer
to purchase the team for $1 million.

By contrast, he noted how Jerry Jones had just paid $140 mil-
lion for the Dallas Cowboys.

"He [Rozelle] had the unique ability to get people all on the
same page in a business where you could depend on twenty-eight
different people all going in different directions," said Chiefs owner
Lamar Hunt.

People who knew Rozelle also knew the job had exacted a toll
on him.

"At every turn there are new brush fires to stamp out," wrote
Bill Lyons in *The Philadelphia Inquirer*. "His tan has faded, his
hairline receded, and furrows of concern have been plowed into
his face. Clearly it isn't fun anymore."

A search committee of Mara, Browns owner Art Modell, Hunt, Bills owner Ralph Wilson, Packers president Robert Parins, and Steelers president Dan Rooney was formed. All had twenty years or more in the NFL. They recommended Jim Finks, who'd played for the Steelers in the 1950s. More recently Finks had been an executive with the Vikings (1964–73), Bears (1974–82), and Saints (1983–84).

But Finks's approval was blocked in July by a group of eleven "new guard" owners. Suddenly there was a divide between the younger and older owners.

According to the *Chicago Tribune,* Bears president Michael McCaskey had warned the members of the committee that they had made a terrible blunder by not including the newer owners. Those men, including Jerry Jones, the Broncos' Pat Bowlen, and Vikings president Mike Lynn, wanted a younger, CEO-like administrator rather than a "football guy" with less experience in the business community. Their choice was forty-eight-year-old attorney Paul Tagliabue, one of the commissioner's closest advisors.

Tagliabue's role as outside legal counsel to Rozelle and the league made him an influential force. Tagliabue had been intimately involved in virtually all NFL matters since 1969.

League staffers and insiders were very familiar with Tagliabue. Whenever there was a major issue, Rozelle would be certain to seek out his advice. "What does Paul think?" was a familiar refrain within the league office, one former staffer said.

While Tagliabue was a definite NFL insider, he was not as well known by the owners as Finks. But Finks and Tagliabue had a long relationship that went back to the early 1970s, when Tagliabue represented the league in a lawsuit filed by the NFL Players Association in Minnesota.

"He has taken a very low profile in this league, so he wasn't very well known by the owners," Finks told the Minnesota *Star Tribune* in 1989. "But he was very well known to me. I knew, for at least 20 years, that every major decision Rozelle was faced with, he advised the commissioner."

The battle between the owners raged for more than seven

months. After the Finks nomination was blocked, an expanded committee came back with two additional candidates, who were quickly dismissed. It was either Finks or Tagliabue. Neither side would budge.

Fearing his candidacy had caused too big a disruption, Tagliabue reached out to Rozelle.

"I called Commissioner Rozelle and said, 'Look, if I'm part of the problem here, just count me out, because I'm perfectly happy doing what I'm doing.'"

Rozelle didn't want to hear it.

"Just don't you worry about it," Tagliabue remembered him saying. "It's for me to worry about it, not you."

Somewhere along the line, Modell suggested that the commissioner position should be split between a commissioner and a deputy commissioner for business operations.

The idea didn't get very far.

Tagliabue knew Rozelle would oppose anything that would dilute the authority of the commissioner. He shared Rozelle's opinion that there was no clear line between what was football and what was business.

They both believed the game was the product, and the commissioner was responsible for the integrity and quality of the product, and that would ultimately drive the value of the business operations.

With no solution to the stalemate in sight, Rozelle took on the role of peacemaker and appointed a new, five-man committee that included two hard-liners from each side, with Steelers president Dan Rooney serving as committee chairman. The old guard was represented by Mara and Modell. Lynn and Bowlen represented the new guard.

Rooney was in a tough spot. Finks was a friend and Rooney originally supported him as the committee's choice. But he also knew Tagliabue and thought he would be a better fit to handle the league's business and legal affairs, especially in labor relations. Realizing that Finks probably didn't have enough votes for approval, Rooney threw his support behind Tagliabue.

"I was afraid we were going to lose him [Tagliabue], and he was the one who could get elected," Rooney later told the *Pittsburgh Press*.

As committee chairman, Rooney saw himself more as a mediator than a partisan. His levelheaded voice of reason was well respected among his fellow team executives, old and new.

"Hey, if we keep fooling around," he told the committee, "we're going to lose both of these guys and they are the best two candidates."

The impasse may well have been more about the differences between the owners than the candidates.

"I don't believe there was any question the initial process was too much for Finks to overcome," Jones later said. He added that one of the reasons the new guard rallied behind Tagliabue was that they felt he would be very acceptable to many Finks supporters.

Jones echoed Rooney's warning. "The threat of losing both candidates was the leverage that made it happen," he said.

"The truth of the matter is that Paul Tagliabue is as much old guard as anyone," Modell later admitted. "Paul Tagliabue and I have worked together for years."

So, 219 days after Rozelle announced his resignation, the committee unanimously recommended Tagliabue. Then, by a vote of the full membership that Rozelle later said was "slightly less than unanimous," Tagliabue was elected NFL commissioner.

When asked about the ownership divide, he said, "To me, this is a minor problem of bringing people back together. I told Pete [Rozelle] I hope we talk about right guards and left guards, not old guards and new guards."

Little did anyone realize at the time that a major part of Tagliabue's legacy would be his unparalleled success at "bringing people back together," manifested by seventeen years of labor peace between the owners and players.

+ + +

THE DAY after Tagliabue was named commissioner, he received a telephone call from maverick Raiders owner Al Davis. After a few pleasantries, Davis, who had battled the NFL and then–legal counsel Tagliabue in an ugly antitrust lawsuit, got to the point. He was calling to offer some friendly advice.

"Al said, 'Look, we're going nowhere with the Players Association,'" Tagliabue recalled. Davis told him he thought the league's management council, which was led by Jack Donlan, was going about it all wrong.

Davis reminded Tagliabue that NFLPA executive director Gene Upshaw was a great offensive lineman and that the first thing offensive linemen learn is that if someone slaps you in the head, "you slap him back twice as hard."

The management council, Davis said, had been slapping Upshaw in the head for years. They did it during the player strikes in 1982 and 1987, and were doing it now.

"Stop slapping him in the head," Davis told Tagliabue. "Sit down with him, go to dinner, have a drink, and get to know him. He'll respect you. You played sports, he played sports. But you're never going to get anywhere by slapping him in the head, other than to have a headache because he'll slap you back twice as hard."

"It was good advice," Tagliabue said.

Curiously, the morning Tagliabue was named commissioner, and before Davis called him, the Associated Press had asked Upshaw about Tagliabue's hiring.

"I've never believed that Paul Tagliabue is interested in prolonging conflict," he said. "In fact, if the situation were different, I wouldn't mind having a beer with him. He realizes that in sports there are many things to do beyond litigation."

Coincidence? Maybe.

Tagliabue had made it clear from the beginning that he would insist on being directly involved in all labor negotiations. He had seen how the management council's exclusion of Rozelle had undermined his authority and hurt negotiations.

In his first owners' meeting as commissioner, Tagliabue began consolidating his authority. He got the owners to agree to strip the management council, NFL Properties—the league's business unit—and NFL Films of their independent status. All three were placed under the commissioner's authority. Tagliabue also made sure he would direct the league's labor policy.

The management council's Donlan resigned a few months later.

By the time Tagliabue became commissioner, the Players Association—frustrated by the lack of progress in negotiations and the hostile relationship between them and the management council—had already decertified as a union. So, while the NFL no longer faced the threat of work stoppages like those in 1982 and 1987, it faced potentially more serious challenges in the form of antitrust litigation brought on by the NFLPA on behalf of the players.

Tagliabue understood that new approaches for signing and paying players were needed. He also believed there was a need for some form of a salary cap.

"If you talked to the management council about salary cap," Tagliabue said, "it was almost like an 'expletive deleted.'"

The mere mention of a salary cap implied to the owners on the management council that you were going to agree to some form of free agency, which they were adamantly opposed to.

"You had to talk about wage scales, you had to talk about other ideas, but if you used the words 'salary cap,' you were digging a hole for yourself at the beginning of the discussion," Tagliabue said.

It was clear to Tagliabue there had to be some major labor changes; otherwise, if left in the hands of antitrust courts, "the league would lose control of its future."

"The NBA had reached an agreement on a salary cap and had a new structure," Tagliabue said, "and at least some of us felt that that was the direction in which the NFL had to go. But it wasn't easy to get there."

When Tagliabue took office in 1989, the league had already instituted a limited free-agency program they called "Plan B." Under the plan, the twenty-eight NFL clubs were permitted to "protect" thirty-seven players on their rosters, while the remaining twenty-two, consisting mostly of aging veterans and backup players, were given free agency.

Plan B was implemented by the owners without negotiating with the Players Association and was immediately panned by them.

"Free agency in that system is illusionary and a bad package for the players," Upshaw said. "They [the owners] know they are running the risk of later being found in court to have violated the law."

While the league knew the players would not support the flawed plan, the hope was that it might be a system that could be defended in any antitrust suits.

To no one's surprise, the NFLPA challenged the plan in court. Their argument was that the plan was still restrictive. The best players, who had the most to lose, would never benefit from a system like Plan B.

"The plan didn't address the heart of the problem," Tagliabue said. "You were addressing the edges of the problem, not the core."

The presiding judge suspended the trial for two weeks, urging everybody to try to reach a settlement.

"At that time, we could not get an agreement among ourselves, much less with the Players Association," Tagliabue recalled. "The Players Association was ready to reach an agreement, but the owners were not."

On September 10, 1992, after a thirty-six-day trial, a jury ruled that Plan B violated federal antitrust laws.

Looking back, Tagliabue said the two-week hiatus had been a missed opportunity because the agreement that was finally reached that fall was not as good as the system that could have been agreed to earlier.

Eventually, after a lengthy period of negotiations, the two sides felt they were at a place where an agreement was possible. The deal included a salary cap and free agency, with the caveat that each team could exempt one "franchise" player from free agency, provided he was offered a contract equal to the average salary of the top five players at his position. This assured teams that they could protect their star player and he would be financially rewarded.

"That became the ultimate selling point," Tagliabue said. "It created the dynamic that everyone would be riding an upward wave."

On December 15, Upshaw and Players Association lawyer Jim Quinn joined Tagliabue at the league owners meeting, where they spent two days explaining the plan to a seven-member committee that had the authority to render a decision. The committee included Davis, Mara, Rooney, Bowlen, Bengals team executive Mike Brown, Redskins president John Kent Cooke, and Rams president John Shaw.

But at the end of the two-day marathon meeting, it appeared that only three committee members were prepared to accept the deal. According to the Associated Press, there was "more dispute among the various factions of owners than with the player representatives."

Upshaw and Quinn left the meeting empty-handed and disappointed.

After they left, Tagliabue took the proposal to the full membership. He carefully explained the details of the plan and stated his firm belief that it was a good, workable deal.

Tagliabue emphasized how recent financial successes and potential future revenue streams would support the deal.

He used the recently negotiated $3.6 billion television contract as an example of the league's growing business strength. That contract increased each team's annual revenues from $17 million per year per team to $31 million. And he reminded owners that with labor peace, the league could move forward with its expansion plans, something that had been delayed due to the uncertainty of the antitrust ruling.

Tagliabue said those factors "gave everybody, including the union, an understanding that there would be growing revenues that would fund the new system and it would be to everyone's advantage to have a bigger pie."

Tagliabue's arguments carried the day. Although the owners had many concerns, it was agreed that it was better to work with the players than to leave it to the courts to decide.

A tentative seven-year agreement was announced on December 22, 1992, and finalized two weeks later. The new collective bargaining agreement—the first since 1987—provided players with unlimited free agency after playing four years in the league, subject to the single-franchise-player stipulation. In return, the recertified NFLPA agreed to a salary cap based on a percentage of revenues.

The 1993 collective bargaining agreement was extended by the players and owners in 1998 and then again until 2002 and then through the 2006 season.

Uninterrupted labor peace and the restructuring of the league operations during Tagliabue's tenure were the foundation for incredible league growth.

"Paul took over at a time when we had serious problems," Rooney told his biographers Andrew Masich and David Halaas. "But he was up to the challenge."

Rooney felt that Tagliabue's most important achievement was the way he changed the relationship between the league and the Players Association. He felt that Tagliabue and Upshaw had developed a sense of trust and respect for each other.

Although the two did develop a very good relationship, Tagliabue is quick to add that, almost from his first day on the job, Rooney and Mara pushed him to "get out and meet with the players."

He listened and quickly scheduled three meetings: one in Pittsburgh, one in New York, and a third in Philadelphia. He had mixed results.

"I went to a meeting with the Giants. . . . It was on Friday afternoon during what Bill Parcells called his 'beer and pizza hour.' "

"That was not a good setting." He chuckled as he retold the story. The informal talk had shifted to free agency and there was no shortage of differing opinions from players.

"It almost ended up a pizza fight," Tagliabue said. "People almost started throwing pizza pie at each other. All hell broke loose."

In the future the commissioner did a little more advance work on his team visits. No more pizza and beer.

But Tagliabue felt the meetings were important. The feedback to Upshaw was positive. "It helped Gene to be able to go back to the players and say, 'This is not the same old same old,' " he said.

Although Tagliabue felt Upshaw was a "very hard-headed business person," he believed that as a former player and team leader, he knew and understood the dynamics of the game. It was something he hadn't seen in Upshaw's predecessor, Ed Garvey.

Upshaw understood the disparities in the way players were being paid. "Offensive linemen were paid far less than quarterbacks, yet quarterbacks were dependent on them to succeed," Tagliabue said.

"The fact that Gene was a great player and a teammate and competitor with men who had become coaches in the NFL was just as important," Tagliabue said.

"He would talk to Art Shell, who was coaching the Oakland Raiders. He would talk to people like [Steelers head coach] Bill Cowher and [Kansas City head coach] Marty Schottenheimer all throughout his tenure. He'd use the fact that he was a former player to talk to coaches about what kind of [labor] system might work."

"Upshaw saw nothing wrong with capping the high end of the spectrum, in terms of player compensation, as long as you raise the minimum salary dramatically, and as long as you gave free agency to the players who were in the midpoints or the lower ends of the spectrum."

"There were owners who by that time felt Gene Upshaw and I could get an agreement by going to dinner and having a glass of wine," the commissioner joked. That of course was not the case.

While Tagliabue held Upshaw in high regard, the feeling was mutual.

"When he began the fight to bring free agency to the NFL, Gene didn't realize that he would soon find himself working with a partner in Paul," Art Shell, Upshaw's former teammate and longtime friend, said. "Not because Paul was an advocate for free agency, but because Paul could see that it was inevitable that free agency would come to the NFL and he was determined to have it be a positive development for the game and the fans.

"Paul never stopped listening to Gene, never turned his back on true engagement and negotiation, and never tried to make the players walk away from their goals.

"I know if Gene were alive today, he would be Paul's strongest advocate."

While he says he's proud of his accomplishments as commissioner, Tagliabue has said that getting labor peace and installing the salary cap, free agency, and franchise player rules were his most significant achievements.

The basic system that Tagliabue and Upshaw negotiated in 1993 is still in place today. It's a system that enables teams to keep their most outstanding players. It allows teams to have sustained periods of success. And it limits the movement of superstars, who are most important to the teams and their fans.

While Tagliabue readily admits that there have been "changes in the economics" of the agreement, at its core it is the same.

In addition to the years of labor peace, Tagliabue oversaw some of the most significant changes and successes in NFL history, including the addition of four new teams, the expansion of network and cable television contracts, the adoption of the instant-replay system, creation of the first year-round twenty-four-hour television channel dedicated to the NFL and football, establishment of the first internet site by a major sports league, major new stadium development, international expansion of the game, league realignment, and increased league-wide revenue sharing.

"Where the players and owners had been enemies during the '80s," Tagliabue stressed, "I think we created a partnership that was very real . . .

"We transformed that into an era [the 1980s] of growth and innovation and change and expansion and service to the fans with new stadiums, new TV, and lots of other things."

"Many people talk about the NFL commissioners who solved problems," Rooney said. "Tagliabue avoided problems. He solved them before they arose—that was his brilliance."

"I guess I view what you do as a commissioner in two steps," Tagliabue said in a 2014 interview. "Anticipate the future and innovate for the future. If you can anticipate the future, you don't have to be reactive. That's not the position you want to be in." One of his favorite sayings over the years that supports that philosophy: "If it ain't broke, fix it anyway."

All it took was someone with a talent for bringing people together.

CHAPTER 29

JERRY JONES BUYS A TEAM, FIRES A COACH, AND GIVES BIRTH TO "THE TRIPLETS"

JERRY JONES HAD ONLY ONE LONG-RANGE GOAL when he graduated from the University of Arkansas in 1965. He wanted to own a pro football team. Twenty-four years later, on February 25, 1989, he bought one. But the former captain of the 1964 national champion Arkansas Razorbacks didn't buy just any football team, he bought "America's Team," the Dallas Cowboys.

"I've always wanted to be involved," Jones said at a press conference announcing his purchase. "But, I never dreamed, in my fondest imagination, that the team that everybody in America knows stands for the NFL . . . I never dreamed I could be a part of that team. That's very humbling to me."

The press conference announcing the transfer of the Cowboys' controlling ownership from H. R. "Bum" Bright to Jones was delayed for nearly an hour while Jones and Cowboys president Tex Schramm met with Cowboys coach Tom Landry.

The visit wasn't a social call. Jones was there to tell Landry— the only head coach in the Cowboys' twenty-nine-year history— that he was being relieved of his duties. University of Miami coach Jimmy Johnson—Jones's teammate at Arkansas—would be Landry's replacement.

While news had already leaked about the Johnson hiring, Landry had not been officially informed of his dismissal.

Bright offered to tell Landry himself. But Jones quickly vetoed that idea.

"I can't do this unless I face him personally," he told Bright.

It was an awkward meeting, to say the least.

"I was basically just trying to say something you just can't say," Jones later said.

There really was no good way to terminate a living legend who had coached twenty consecutive winning seasons from 1966 to 1985, played in five Super Bowls, and won two of them.

But the team had fallen on bad times, suffering three consecutive losing seasons. Still, Landry was clearly hurt by the decision.

"No one had to tell me," he told the Associated Press two days after the visit. "I would have had to be pretty stupid not to know when they got on the airplane to come see me. They could have saved the trip because all they did was tell me I was fired.

"Sure, the firing could have been handled better, but I won't get upset over it," the ever-stoic coach said.

Although Jones didn't offer any excuses for the way he handled Landry's firing, it wasn't helped by the fact that news of Johnson's hiring was prematurely leaked by a news outlet. That clearly complicated the already delicate situation.

Naturally, the coaching change was on everyone's mind when Jones finally arrived at the press conference. The new owner didn't mince words: "The fact is, I wouldn't be an owner if Jimmy Johnson was not the head coach," he said.

He told the press he would be a hands-on owner and would have "an understanding" of virtually every aspect of the franchise operations, "from socks to jocks."

"There's no way in the world that with my enthusiasm and love for what I'm getting ready to do, and the kind of price I'm paying, that I can look in the mirror if I don't plan to be a part of everything," he said. "I want to understand that everyone associated with it is giving it everything that they can."

Brad Sham, the Cowboys' longtime play-by-play announcer and radio talk-show host, listened to the press conference live on the telephone and later reflected.

"It's not like everyone was celebrating the great ownership regime of Bum Bright. People want to forget how much the public wanted Landry out the last couple of years."

Sham remembered the Cowboys' 3-13 team in 1988 as the worst

Cowboys team he'd ever seen. He remembered how callers to his nightly radio talk show said the game had passed Landry by. Every night, Sham said, it was the same story—until he got fired. "Then," Sham said, "the same people were calling saying, 'How could they fire Tom Landry?'"

Landry, disappointed as he was, acknowledged the team's three-year slump. Although the Cowboys had won the NFC East in 1985 with a 10-6 record, the aging team dropped to 7-9 the following year, then 7-8, and finally 3-13.

"I probably should have gotten out," Landry told the Associated Press, "but I really enjoyed the challenge of bringing a team to that game [the Super Bowl]. In fact, I probably enjoy the challenge of it more than the actual game."

Many of Landry's former players were upset with his firing but also understood that it was an unfortunate part of the business of football. How it was handled was the rub.

Trying to make sense of the move, Bob Lilly, the Cowboys' first-ever draft choice and Hall of Fame defensive tackle, said, "He is going out on a business deal. He didn't get fired. It happens all the time in business. Still, it's the end of an era. . . ."

+++

SO, HOW was it that this oilman from Little Rock, Arkansas, emerged victorious from a deep list of potential buyers?

More familiar names, such as Jerry Buss, owner of the NBA's Los Angeles Lakers, had been rumored to have the inside track on the ownership derby.

"We probably talked to seventy-five different people," Bright told reporters. "Seriously to about fifteen, intensely to about five, and we have made a deal with one, Jerry Jones of Little Rock."

Bright added that he and Jones shook hands on the deal two days earlier, and then "got the lawyers in." But the handshake, he insisted, was all that was necessary. Jones was "as square as a graham cracker," he said. "The guy will do what he says he will do."

Part of Jones's strategy in buying the team was to keep a low profile and keep his coaching plans to himself. He didn't want

Bright to think he was quite as serious as he was. Although he'd been negotiating for five months, he purposefully kept his name out of public speculation until December.

Had he been more public, Jones later said, he might not have been so heavily criticized for firing Landry. But, he feared, any public indication that he already had a replacement coach in mind would have tipped his hand and strengthened Bright's bargaining position.

"I had to avoid letting them [the Cowboys] know," Jones said. "It's not good business being quoted in the *Dallas Morning News* saying, 'I want this more than I want my next breath.'"

So, who was this outsider who now owned the proud Texas franchise?

Jones was born in Los Angeles in 1942. His father, J. W. "Pat" Jones, moved the family to Little Rock three years later, where he purchased a fruit stand. His was at first a modest success story. He developed the fruit stand into a grocery store. But the family lived in an apartment upstairs.

A natural-born showman and grassroots promoter, the senior Jones—dressed in a white suit and a cowboy hat—would walk through his store and chat with his customers. He built a stage in the middle of the store where he hosted country music acts, a local radio show, and amateur talent contests. After school, nine-year-old Jerry, wearing a dress shirt and bow tie, would come to the store and greet shoppers as they entered. Occasionally he'd earn a tip for pushing a cart or packing a bag of groceries for a customer.

Pat Jones eventually sold the grocery business and started an insurance company—Modern Security Life—in Springfield, Missouri.

Jones, like his father, had a strong entrepreneurial spirit. While attending the University of Arkansas, he made small-business investments.

"I owned a small interest in several oil wells," he told *Forbes* magazine in 2012. "I sold life insurance to businessmen and sold shoes to students in fraternities." Sportswriters called Jones "the Razorback businessman."

In 1965, fresh out of college, Jones went to work in his father's insurance company. But it was a temporary stop. He was already focused on his goal of owning a pro football team and taking steps to ensure he would get one.

He started showing up at American Football League owners' meetings in the mid-1960s. He would hang out in the hotel hallways or lobbies—anywhere he thought he might be able to engage a team executive between meeting sessions. He made sure the football power brokers knew who he was and what he wanted.

One of the owners he met was Joe Robbie, who had just purchased the Miami Dolphins.

"I flew down to Miami to see him, just as he was moving into the Dolphins' office," Jones told *ForbesLife* in 2012. "In Miami, I literally helped push Joe's desk up the stairs of the Dolphins' office."

"It so happened that Barron Hilton was then looking to sell the San Diego Chargers," Jones said. "Joe [Robbie] called him right then and there."

Hilton told Robbie that he didn't have time for "tire kickers and dreamers." He insisted that if Jones was serious, he'd need to produce a $1 million line of credit. Then they could talk.

So where does a twenty-five-year-old with little money and a big dream get a $1 million line of credit?

Jones had recently received some financing for a small string of Shakey's Pizza Parlors back in Missouri. He asked that investment group if they'd provide the line of credit.

That group, the International Brotherhood Teamsters, agreed and sent the required letter of credit to Hilton. The Teamsters also loaned Jones $50,000 for a 120-day option to buy the team.

Jones got his meeting and was told the asking price for the Chargers was $5.8 million. He next visited another owner he'd met while crashing AFL meetings, Lamar Hunt.

"He treated me like a Rockefeller," Jones said, "even though I didn't have any money." But while Hunt was encouraging, he was also blunt about the financial risks involved in owning an AFL team.

"I knew the financials didn't look good," Jones said. "But I wanted to do it."

Confident in his ability to deliver, Jones went to his father for a loan. The senior Jones was immediately and adamantly opposed to his son's plan. He told him the risk was too great.

"Don't tell me I'm not involved," he remembered his father telling him. "Don't you tell me that. If you can't pay, I'm going to have to be looking after your well-being, and what I've got is relatively modest."

Reluctantly, Jones backed out of the deal. A few months later, following the AFL-NFL merger, Hilton sold the Chargers to Eugene Klein and Sam Schulman for $10 million, nearly double what Jones would have paid.

"He talked me out of an investment that doubled in price in six months," Jones said of his father. "It substantiated that I wasn't nuts in chasing the Chargers."

+ + +

ONE YEAR after losing his opportunity to purchase the Chargers, Jones found himself deep in debt after a land-deal investment collapsed. Jones had personally guaranteed loans he couldn't cover. Although he would eventually work through his financial difficulties, it challenged him in a way he'd not previously experienced.

"I had gone, in one year, from the can-do high of nearly buying a football team to being shaken to the core by the cold reality of what happens when you get upside down relative to cash flow," Jones told *ForbesLife*.

"I got so depressed," he said, "it was a real effort to leave home for work. My wife was very concerned about my mental state." Jones called the troubled times and financial difficulties his greatest education. It was a blessing, he said, that it came so early in his life.

"I've taken those lessons and applied them to everything I've done since then," he said.

While Jones's land deal was a disaster, one of his other business ventures, Jones Oil and Land Lease, a company he'd founded in 1970, was hugely successful. In the wildly speculative business of oil and gas exploration, his initial Oklahoma well ended up gushing. Over the next two decades he established offices all over the western United States and Canada.

By 1988, when Jones started thinking about making a run for the Cowboys, his personal wealth was said to be well over $200 million, maybe even double that, according to some in the energy business.

When Jones bought the Cowboys, he knew he was paying for the mystique of America's Team. But, in just the first few months, much of that mystique was gone. First Landry was fired. Schramm resigned a couple months later. Then Gil Brandt, another key executive, left after completing the all-important player draft. Those moves didn't exactly please or energize the Cowboys faithful.

As for the team mystique, it was a bit like the emperor's new clothes. When Jones purchased the team, Bum Bright's Cowboys were losing $1 million a month. The interest alone on the money Jones borrowed to buy the financially struggling team was costing him nearly $100,000 a day.

Jones never said how much he paid for the franchise, but he later quipped that he was going to need some lead in his back pocket "because I'm a lot lighter than when I came to Dallas."

While Jones made light of the price he paid, he understood that the Cowboys' mystique needed to fall in line with the team's income and expense entries. He immediately set out to find more and new ways to create revenue.

That's when he turned to sponsorships.

At the time, the Cowboys had just one sponsor, the team's media guide. Most of the luxury suites in Texas Stadium were without leases. In-house stadium deals were almost nonexistent.

"I found a whole bunch of new sponsors, generating revenue that hadn't been there before," Jones recalled. "I had my team now. And the cash flow turned the right way."

Jones's marketing strategy included major sponsorship and licensing contracts negotiated separately from the NFL. He signed stadium sponsorship deals with companies like Pepsi, Nike, AT&T, Dr Pepper, and American Express.

The NFL—which had league-wide sponsorship agreements with competitors like Coca-Cola—claimed such independently negotiated deals violated a 1982 trust agreement that authorized the league to negotiate the marketing of the team's logo and name. The result was that in 1995 the league filed a $300 million lawsuit against Jones, challenging his sponsorship practices. Jones countersued for $700 million, accusing the league of blocking teams from conducting their own marketing business.

Some speculated that the league's lawsuit was at least partially an angry reaction by the league to the way Jones revealed his Nike deal. Jones announced his deal in a press release distributed during a *Monday Night Football* game at Texas Stadium. The release was headlined "Cowboys' Owner Bucks NFL Again."

Three months later, the two sides settled their lawsuits, acknowledging that it was time to move forward and get past the costly litigation.

It was a victory for Jones. The settlement meant he was free to continue his existing Texas Stadium sponsorships and enter new ones with no obligation to share revenues. But it was also a victory for the other owners, many of whom quickly modeled their stadium deals after his.

While Jones was busy finding new ways to generate revenue, Johnson began a youth movement with the team personnel.

"We had the worst team in the NFL," Jones told the crowd attending his 2017 Pro Football Hall of Fame enshrinement ceremony. "So, we got the first pick in the [1989] draft. . . . That first choice was a no-brainer. It was Troy Aikman."

Aikman joined a Cowboys team that a year earlier had selected wide receiver Michael Irvin in the first round. For Irvin, it was a reunion of sorts; he had played for Johnson at the University of Miami.

While Johnson was excited about the pass-catch combination of Aikman and Irvin, he knew the team was still a long way from being a serious contender.

After an 0-4 start in 1989, Johnson came up with a radical idea to improve his team quickly. He knew Aikman, Irvin, and running back Herschel Walker—who had signed with the Cowboys in 1986 following the collapse of the USFL—were the best players he had. His best chance to build a winner quickly, he reasoned, would be to trade one of his best for draft picks and then select younger players that fit his system. Aikman was not a consideration. He was Johnson's first pick and the foundational rock upon which he'd build his team.

Initially, Johnson considered trading Irvin to the Los Angeles Raiders. But Raiders owner Al Davis surprised Johnson by convincing him he'd be a fool to do so. Davis told Johnson he'd need at least one good receiver to catch Aikman's passes.

That left Walker, who was not only coming off a great season—1,514 yards rushing and another 505 yards receiving—but a fan favorite.

"We were old and slow, and we needed to jump-start the rebuilding process," Johnson said. "I had to figure out a way to parlay our best asset into a whole team."

What resulted was a blockbuster deal between the Cowboys and the Minnesota Vikings. The complicated trade—the largest in NFL history—involved a combination of eighteen draft picks and players. The Cowboys gave the Vikings Walker, their third- and tenth-round picks in the 1990 draft, and their third pick in the 1991 draft. In return, Dallas got linebackers Jesse Solomon and David Howard, defensive end Alex Stewart, running back Darrin Nelson, cornerback Ike Holt, and Minnesota's first-, second-, and sixth-round picks in the 1990 draft.

But that wasn't all. Johnson had insisted that each of the players the Cowboys received had a conditional draft pick attached to him in the event he was cut before February 1, 1990. That's where the deal got complicated, and Johnson got what he really wanted—more draft picks.

Once the deal was done, Johnson indicated he had no intention of keeping the players. His plan was to release them and cash in on the conditional picks. Solomon, Howard, Stewart, and Holt were released and Nelson, who refused to report to the Cowboys, was traded to San Diego.

Eventually the outmaneuvered Minnesota Vikings general manager Mike Lynn worked out another deal with Jones and Johnson that allowed the Cowboys to keep the conditional draft picks *and* Solomon, Howard, and Holt. Minnesota got San Diego's fifth-round pick from the Nelson trade.

Jones not only approved the trade; he made it possible by agreeing to pay Walker a $1.25 million exit bonus. As leverage, Walker had threatened to retire rather than agree to the deal, forcing Jones to sweeten the pot. And if that wasn't enough, the Vikings also kicked in a Mercedes-Benz and a house comparable to Walker's Dallas home.

Over the next three seasons, Johnson mixed and maneuvered the Vikings' picks—three first-, three second-, one third-, and a sixth-round pick—along with the Cowboys' own picks. The result was the nucleus of what would become the 1990s Team of the Decade.

Among the picks the Cowboys made from 1990 to 1992 were defensive tackle Russell Maryland, running back Alonzo Highsmith, cornerback Kevin Smith, wide receiver Alvin Harper, safety Darren Woodson, and cornerback Clayton Holmes.

But it was a trade using one of the Vikings' first-round picks they acquired in the 1990 draft that led to the best draft move in Cowboys history. The Cowboys sent the Vikings' pick to the Pittsburgh Steelers to move up from the 21st pick in the draft to the 17th, where they then selected University of Florida running back Emmitt Smith.

While most of the Cowboys' picks resulting from the Walker trade became solid contributors, the addition of Smith was the biggest difference maker. In Aikman, Irvin, and Smith, the Cowboys had a triple-threat offense reminiscent of the team's earlier power trio of quarterback Roger Staubach, running back Tony Dorsett, and wide receiver Drew Pearson.

"The Triplets," as they became known, were the key to launching the on-the-field turnaround that Jones had promised but naysayers had doubted.

While the Cowboys finished 1-15 in 1989, the following year Smith made his pro football debut. It was clear that something special was beginning. Smith rushed for 937 yards and added another 228 yards receiving and earned NFL Rookie of the Year honors. And while his 937-yard rushing performance was impressive, it represented the second-fewest rushing yards he would gain in a season during his remarkable fifteen-year career. A consistent, workmanlike runner, Smith recorded eleven consecutive 1,000-yard seasons and retired as the game's all-time leading rusher with 18,355 yards.

Aikman, with the help of a rapidly improving offensive line, led a balanced offensive attack that featured big-play abilities, with Irvin on the outside as well as ball-control efficiency with Smith carrying the ball.

Although Aikman never threw for more than 3,500 yards or more than 23 touchdowns in any season, his astute play-calling, accurate passing, and superb game management enabled the Cowboys' offense to wear down opponents and then unleash that big-play moment that they seemed able to call up at will.

"My career certainly wasn't established based on passing statistics because of the nature of the team I played on," Aikman said in a 2012 interview. Instead the consummate team leader deferred to the team's success as his legacy.

"I'm very proud of the world championships and team accomplishments that we were able to have," he said.

Irvin was the most productive wide receiver in Cowboys history. "The Playmaker," as he was called, was a starter in the Cowboys' offense from day one. Although a knee injury sidelined him for ten games in 1989, he returned to the starting lineup in the fifth game of the 1990 season and quickly reestablished himself as Aikman's go-to guy.

The 1991 season was Irvin's breakout year, during which he caught an NFC-leading 93 passes for 1,523 yards. That same year

Smith rushed for a league-leading 1,563 yards. And even though a knee injury caused Aikman to miss the final four games of the 1991 regular season, the Cowboys returned to the playoffs. Aikman missed the team's wild-card victory over the Bears—their first play-off win in nine years—but he played poorly in relief of Steve Beuer-lein in the divisional championship game, a 38–6 loss to the Detroit Lions. But it was still a great season and an omen of things to come.

All three of "the Triplets" were voted to that year's Pro Bowl.

The next season began a streak of three Super Bowl wins over a four-year period. Led by the Triplets and an improved defense, the Cowboys were the NFL's dominant team through the next six seasons.

In 1992, Aikman had his best season statistically, throwing for 3,445 yards and 23 touchdowns. In the Cowboys' lopsided 52–17 win over the Bills in Super Bowl XXVII, he and Irvin connected on two touchdown completions in a span of just fifteen seconds. Aikman completed 22 of 30 passes for 273 yards and four touch-downs and earned game MVP honors. Irvin caught six passes for 114 yards and two touchdowns. Smith ran for 108 yards on 22 car-ries and became the first running back in history to lead the league in rushing and win a Super Bowl in the same season.

The following year the Cowboys repeated as Super Bowl cham-pions in another one-sided (30–13) win over the Bills. Smith, add-ing to his ever-growing list of accomplishments, became the only running back to win NFL MVP, the league rushing crown, and Super Bowl MVP.

Following the team's second Super Bowl season, a well-documented rift between Jones and Johnson ended with the coach and owner agreeing to part ways. It was about respect. Jones felt he deserved it; Johnson was reluctant to share it.

Los Angeles Times staff writer Bill Paschke summed it up well: "Shame on Jerry Jones for letting Tuesday's divorce happen. But triple shame on Jimmy Johnson for making it happen."

Johnson was replaced by another former Arkansas Razorback, Barry Switzer, who had been head coach at the University of Okla-homa for sixteen seasons.

In 1994 the Switzer-coached Cowboys finished with a 12-4 record and had high hopes for an unprecedented third straight Super Bowl win. But the dream of taking home another Vince Lombardi Trophy ended in the NFC championship game when the 49ers—after losing the two previous NFC title games to Dallas—finally defeated the Cowboys, 38–28.

The following year the Cowboys again posted an impressive 12-4 record. Smith had his best season, leading the league in rushing attempts (377), yards gained (1,773), average yards per game (110.8), and touchdowns (25).

In the NFC championship game against the Green Bay Packers, the Triplets were in complete sync. Aikman threw for 255 yards and two touchdowns, both to Irvin, and Smith rushed for career-playoff bests of 150 yards and three touchdowns in the Cowboys' 38–27 win. Two weeks later the Cowboys won a record third Super Bowl in four years by beating the Pittsburgh Steelers 27–17.

+ + +

BUILDING THE Cowboys into a winning, profitable franchise during the 1990s remains a highlight of Jerry Jones's long and successful ownership tenure.

"Taking it to the top after going through all those things buoyed me," Jones told the *Sports Business Journal* in 2017. "It allowed me to be very aggressive. It also let me feel good that I was on the right path and this was the best way to grow the NFL."

"As [Atlanta Falcons owner] Arthur Blank told me, 'you have led us, the owners, kicking and screaming, to the point where we are today.'"

CHAPTER 30

THE ROONEY RULE

I'd like to say a special thank-you to ten men—Willie Brown, Buck Buchanan, Earnel Durden, Bob Ledbetter, Elijah Pitts, Jimmy Raye, Johnny Roland, Al Tabor, Lionel Taylor, and Allan Webb. Now, those names might not be familiar to you, but those were the African American assistant coaches in the NFL in 1977, my first year in the league.
—TONY DUNGY, FROM HIS SPEECH AT THE 2016 PRO FOOTBALL HALL OF FAME ENSHRINEMENT CEREMONY

IT WAS A SMALL GROUP OF MEN, JUST TEN OF them, if you can believe that. Ten African American assistant coaches in the entire NFL. Many of them never got the chance to move up the coaching ladder like I did. But they were so important to the progress of this league."

Progress? Yes. But it was ever so slow. There were only two African American head coaches in the NFL's first eighty-nine years: halfback Fritz Pollard, who played and coached for a variety of now-defunct NFL teams in the 1920s; and Art Shell, who coached the Los Angeles Raiders some sixty years later.

In the league's early years, when few African Americans got to play, the omission of a black coach hardly seemed odd. But as the league fully integrated in the 1960s, 1970s, and 1980s, and rosters included more black players than white players, the lack of black coaches became painfully obvious.

+ + +

ON SEPTEMBER 30, 2002, attorneys Johnnie L. Cochran Jr. and Cyrus Mehri issued a critique of the league's poor minority hiring practices, titled "Black Coaches in the National Football League: Superior Performance, Inferior Opportunities."

The report noted that only five African American head coaches had been hired since 1989. It also said black coaches were held to a higher standard than their white counterparts and were consequently denied a fair chance to compete for head-coaching jobs.

The report showed that during the previous fifteen years, black head coaches had averaged 1.1 more wins per season than white coaches, led their teams to the playoffs 67 percent of the time, and won 1.3 more games in their final season than did white coaches before being fired.

"In case after case," the report's authors said, "NFL owners have shown more interest in and patience with white coaches who don't win than black coaches who do."

The spark that ignited the fire that was the Cochran-Mehri report was the 2002 firing of two African American head coaches: Dungy, by the Tampa Bay Buccaneers; and Dennis Green, by the Minnesota Vikings. It was Green's first losing season in ten years. Dungy, who had taken over a Bucs team in 1996 that had twelve double-digit-loss seasons in the previous thirteen years, was fired after taking the team to the playoffs four times.

Dungy was hired by the Indianapolis Colts the following season, but Green was out of coaching for two years before being hired by the Arizona Cardinals.

"We knew we had a problem," Steelers owner Dan Rooney said. "We knew we had to create an equal opportunity for African Americans to become head coaches."

The result was that in a meeting in New York on October 31, 2002, NFL commissioner Paul Tagliabue proposed the creation of a committee on workplace diversity, to be chaired by Rooney. The other committee members were Falcons owner Arthur Blank, Eagles owner Jeff Lurie, Broncos owner Pat Bowlen, and Rams part-owner Stan Kroenke.

"What we did basically, as a league, was reach a consensus that it was important to have an owner committee on workplace diversity and to work within that framework," Tagliabue said at the press conference announcing the formation of the committee.

The committee's goal was to find a way to institutionally or structurally increase the number of minorities in key positions.

"I don't think this is a thing you do and that's the end of it," Rooney said at the time. "We will develop ideas as we go along now and in the future."

Tagliabue added that coaching was just one aspect of the need for diversity. The need for more African Americans in front-office administrative positions—citing Baltimore Colts general manager Ozzie Newsome—was equally important. It requires "as much effort and focus as the coaching situation," he said.

Rooney praised Tagliabue for developing a variety of hiring initiatives but noted, "The commissioner doesn't hire our [front office] executives, we do. It is our responsibility."

That was not only a critically important line, but also one that was strategically planned by both men. They knew that any hope of ownership support for their workplace diversity plan meant it had to be a plan that the owners felt was their own. It could not be—no matter how well intended—presented as a directive from the league office. That would immediately be rejected by some club owners, even some who were already taking steps to improve club diversity. Many owners considered it a team issue and would have resented having the league office "force" them into compliance.

"There are some things owners have to do for themselves," Rooney said. "And do it because it's the right thing to do. And they have to be held accountable."

In other words, craft a policy but let the owners have input and ownership.

But both also realized that leadership at the club staff level was important, particularly on this issue. Front-office executives could help influence ownership contributions.

To that end, Tagliabue announced the formation of a complementary working group of club executives whose members included the Falcons' Ray Anderson, the Buccaneers' Rich McKay, the Colts' Bill Polian, the Ravens' Ozzie Newsome, and the Jets' Terry Bradway.

While both the diversity and the executive groups held several formal meetings with Tagliabue and Rooney, both also worked behind the scenes to make sure all voices were heard, including the Fritz Pollard Alliance, an advocacy group designed by Cochran, Mehri, and former Browns lineman John Wooten to promote opportunities for African Americans.

The diversity committee issued a preliminary report to the owners in late December, just seven weeks after its formation. Out of this report was born what's now known as the "Rooney Rule," which required teams to interview minority candidates for coaching vacancies. It was a mandatory policy, and it was unanimously approved by the owners.

Tagliabue later explained the importance of the unanimous vote.

"To get everybody to say, 'I agree,' then you're in the position that when they don't get it done, you can go back and say you're going to be fined or lose a draft choice."

Mehri said he was also pleased that it was mandatory and included a noncompliance penalty. But he was skeptical that it would ever be enforced.

That doubt disappeared when, in June 2003, Tagliabue fined the Detroit Lions $200,000 for not interviewing any minority candidates before hiring coach Steve Mariucci. The commissioner told the other teams that future failures to interview minority candidates could lead to fines of $500,000 or higher, as "conduct detrimental to the NFL."

The Fritz Pollard Alliance hailed Tagliabue's action.

"We are pleased that the rule now has teeth and hope today's announcement sends a strong message to owners to embrace inclusive hiring practices going forward," said Kellen Winslow, the alliance's executive director.

In a letter supporting Tagliabue's Hall of Fame candidacy, Wooten later said, "Paul did what real leaders do.

"He listened, he showed respect, and he and Dan Rooney led

the most significant change in hiring practices in professional sports that I have seen in my lifetime."

Wooten also said that this was not the first time Tagliabue had taken a controversial position when it came to racial equality.

In 1990 the club owners had voted to play the Super Bowl in Phoenix. "But when the state rejected proposals to make Martin Luther King's birthday a holiday, Paul Tagliabue took the extraordinary step of moving the Super Bowl out of Arizona."

To those who knew him, Tagliabue's concern for racial equality was nothing new. When he was hired as NFL commissioner, the Associated Press reported: "While he belongs to a prestigious law firm, friends say Tagliabue has taken a special pride in the public-interest work his firm does for no fee. He is especially proud of a victory for low-level government employees in a racial-discrimination case."

Tagliabue was never comfortable in the limelight, preferring instead to work behind the scenes.

In a 1986 letter from Pete Rozelle thanking him for his successful work on the USFL antitrust suit, Rozelle described his friend as "just being the usual dependable get-things-done Paul."

"He [Tagliabue] was the driving force behind the implementation of the Rooney Rule," Dungy said in 2017. "He had many behind-the-scenes meetings with owners, GMs, and coaches to see how we could better attack the problem. There is no doubt in my mind that I got head coaching interviews in the early 1990s because he asked owners to at least take a look."

Rooney, whose name is forever attached to this landmark policy, has stated on many occasions that the "rule" should really be known as the "Tagliabue-Rooney Rule."

THE NFL RESPONDS TO NATIONAL CRISES

*Athletic competition is about determination. It's about
resilience. It's about never giving up. It's about accepting a
blow and coming back and winning. There's a symbolism
in athletics about determination and work ethic. There's an
unwillingness to accept defeat that athletics represent.*

—PAUL TAGLIABUE

PAUL TAGLIABUE WAS IN HIS MANHATTAN OFFICE.
It was a beautiful, early-autumn day in New York, the kind of
day people write songs about. He was on a conference call when
his assistant came bursting into the room. She was almost hysteri-
cal, talking about low-flying planes over Manhattan.

Annoyed at the interruption, Tagliabue told her to calm down
and let him finish the call.

It was shortly after 9 a.m. on September 11, 2001.

When the unbelievable news began to drift out, Tagliabue—
like many others—thought a small private aircraft had gone astray
and crashed into one of the World Trade Center's towers. But it
was quickly determined to be a commercial aircraft. And not just
one but two. Then word came that the Pentagon was also hit.

"It was clear that between plane number one and plane number
two, this was not an accident," Tagliabue said. "It was something
much more significant. It quickly became clear that it was some
kind of an attack."

One of the first calls Tagliabue received that awful day was from
NFL Players Association executive director Gene Upshaw, who

had just dropped his kids off at school in Northern Virginia. He was driving to his Washington office when he saw black, billowing clouds of smoke coming from the Pentagon.

Upshaw wanted to know from Tagliabue if anyone who worked for the league or who had friends or relatives there might be trapped in the towers.

Tagliabue didn't know. For his part, he shared his concern for the family and friends of NFLPA members.

For those moments, football was the last thing on the minds of these two sports executives.

"We had employees who had spouses, brothers, sisters, cousins, working in those buildings," Tagliabue later recalled.

As the horror sank in, panic seized the staff. Questions that no one could answer and fear that no one had ever experienced gripped everyone.

One team executive called to ask what the league planned to do regarding the upcoming weekend's games. He was bluntly told that Tagliabue and Upshaw hadn't yet discussed the matter. They were "ensuring the safety of their employees and families first."

Within minutes of the attack, Tagliabue learned that two employees had family members working in the towers. One was out of town on league business and could only watch TV reports and worry if her husband was safe. The other rushed from the league office to the twin towers. He arrived just as the tower in which his wife worked collapsed. Stunned, he returned to the league office. Tagliabue and other staffers took him around the corner to St. Patrick's Cathedral, where together they prayed for a miracle. None was forthcoming. Both employees' spouses were among the attack's victims.

"It was darkness. It was hell," Tagliabue told sports journalist Peter King. "I've learned from that experience that when you're in the midst of a tragedy where there's loss of life, you're in darkness. I'd compare it to hell. What is required by people outside the immediate area of devastation is leadership and hope. Hope can bring some light to that dark and seemingly endless experience."

In the immediate aftermath of the attacks, confusion reigned.

Tagliabue, like millions of other Americans, wondered if the attacks were even over yet.

Despite the clamor and confusion, decisions needed to be made. Football decisions.

Tagliabue was on the phone constantly with several owners, particularly owners of the Washington and New York franchises. A few owners—stranded in the city—made their way to the league office, while others got through on the phone.

Some owners argued that postponing the games would be giving in to the terrorists. Others, notably Cleveland owner Art Modell, pleaded to postpone, perhaps remembering the negative fallout when Pete Rozelle didn't cancel games after the assassination of President Kennedy.

Players were also divided. Conference calls by Upshaw with team player representatives found eleven in favor of playing and seventeen opposed. They were divided over the same questions: was it too soon to play after such a tremendous loss of life or was not playing giving in to the terrorists?

Giants cornerback Jason Sehorn was particularly forceful in his opposition to playing that weekend.

"It's one thing to see it on TV," he said during one of the players' conference calls. "It's another thing, every day, to look from our practice field and see the towers gone."

Tagliabue listened to arguments and advice from players, owners, civic leaders, and government officials. But it was Dan Rooney, Wellington Mara, Carolina Panthers owner Jerry Richardson, and Upshaw whom he worked with most closely.

"Both Gene and I wanted to make sure that the league and the Players Association and all the teams were on the same page and that we came out of this in unanimity, even though different opinions were expressed along the way," Tagliabue said.

Many things had to be considered and the clock was ticking.

Security was a major concern. The league had made significant security improvements over the last decade, during the Gulf War in 1991 and following the bombings of the World Trade Center in 1993 and the federal building in Oklahoma City in 1995.

Tagliabue met with NFL director of security Milt Ahlerich to discuss stadium readiness for the eventual resumption of games. He also called on Lew Merletti, the Browns' security chief and a former director of the United States Secret Service, to head up a new security task force.

Publicly, Tagliabue was reassuring. "I'm very, very sure our stadiums will be secure for the players and the fans," he said.

Tagliabue didn't want to appear cowed by the terrorists, but he felt the enormous scale and nature of the attack was such that "a pause" was necessary.

He told the news media on September 13, "At a certain point playing our games can contribute to the healing process. Just not at this time."

"Our priorities for this weekend are to pause, grieve, and reflect," he said. "It is a time to tend to our families and neighbors and all those wounded by these horrific acts."

The games were canceled.

Almost immediately other sports leagues, teams, and organizations—many of whom had called Tagliabue for guidance—followed his lead.

Tagliabue later reflected on his decision: "I think if you're a chief executive, or you're the captain of the basketball team, or you're the principal of the school, you know that it's your responsibility to lead and to make decisions.

"Leadership is about lots of things, but it includes making decisions and making hard choices. It also means acting quickly in crises. . . . It was clear that we had a platform that was respected. We had a voice that would be listened to if we were saying intelligent things.

"I think the league can really set a tone and be a leader in ways that go quite beyond football games. At the time, the country was looking for leaders who were doing things that people felt needed to be done. Forget about your differences. Forget about your own needs. Focus on what you have in common with other people and focus on the needs of others. Make it your own responsibility to support others and be a good citizen."

The media had a lot of questions. Would the games be rescheduled? Or the Super Bowl?

Tagliabue's answer was simple: "Don't worry about replaying the week of games that we're canceling. In some way, we'll get that done. That's just a detail." His confident simplicity seemed reassuring.

One week later, the games returned. Stadiums were full of fans wearing red, white, and blue and waving mini American flags that were distributed as they entered the security-enhanced arenas. Homemade banners and signs declaring NEVER FORGET replaced the more typical placards exulting a favorite player or team.

First responders were at every stadium collecting donations for the families of their fallen brothers and sisters. Firemen's boots were passed through the stands for contributions.

In Kansas City, the Chiefs restarted the 2001 season in a game against the defending NFC champion New York Giants—a team that had become a universal symbol of hope not just for New York, but for the entire country.

"When the Giants took the field that day," Tagliabue said, "there was a roar of applause and it clearly was applause for the people of New York, not just the New York Giants football team. It was a roar of support for the people of New York, Washington, and America. It was a roar of applause for the New York City Police Department, the New York City Fire Department, and the New York City emergency personnel, plus our military. It was a roar of support for all the people that were working to deal with the aftermath of the attack twelve days earlier."

A pregame pageant featuring one hundred US Army soldiers carrying an American flag drew a standing ovation. Standing with the players and coaches on the sideline was Chiefs owner Lamar Hunt and Tagliabue. They and the players and coaches donned blue FDNY or NYPD caps.

In the Giants' locker room after their win over the Chiefs, the players wanted only to talk about the fans. Wide receiver Joe Jerevicius talked of an emotional visit he and some of his teammates had made earlier in the week to the site of the devastation.

"To have those guys [workers at the recovery site] hug you and break down on you and actually say, 'Guys, we need you to play this Sunday. We need you to divert our attention from what is going on here in the city . . . ' If that doesn't motivate you, I don't know what will," he said.

In Cleveland, Browns cornerback Corey Fuller and safety Earl Little ran out of the tunnel onto the field carrying a large American flag, while their teammates followed behind waving miniature versions.

"We just wanted everyone in New York and the rest of America to know that we're behind them 110 percent," Little said.

It was a scenario that was replayed in every NFL stadium. "U-S-A, U-S-A" rang throughout the NFL world. It was as unifying and healing as anything the government could have done.

"I think his leadership after the 9/11 attacks was his finest hour," the Giants' John Mara said of Tagliabue. "He made the decision not to play and coordinated the response, which I believe greatly aided our country's healing process."

While the nation looked to its political leaders for strength and a sense of security, it also looked to the private sector to help reestablish the all-important sense of normalcy that had been stolen by the attacks. Tagliabue's decision to pause and reflect resulted in one of the most remarkable demonstrations of American unity since the end of World War II.

NFL football stadiums became America's stage to say to the world, "We are unwilling to accept defeat."

+ + +

IN 2005, one specific NFL stadium—the Louisiana Superdome—became a symbol of both despair and triumph.

On August 29 of that year, it became the shelter of last resort for thousands of displaced New Orleans residents who'd lost their homes to Hurricane Katrina. In all, 1,833 hurricane-related deaths were attributed to the monstrous Category 5 storm.

Floodwaters from the storm's surge and the city's failed levees tore through neighborhoods, destroying thousands of homes and displacing tens of thousands of people. The Superdome became the shelter of last resort for some thirty thousand suddenly home-less people.

Initially, the Superdome was going to serve as a temporary shel-ter for some 850 patients with serious medical conditions who, of-ficials believed, would ride out the storm together with the city's health department staff.

Doug Thornton, an executive with SMG, the company that managed the stadium, had been through a similar scenario and was comfortable with that plan. But things changed drastically, and for the worse, as Katrina barreled toward the city. When the National Weather Service revised its forecast, Mayor Ray Nagin asked Thornton to open the Superdome as a refuge for potentially thousands.

Thornton agreed. But, he told Nagin, there was no way he could call in the staff he needed to run the facility.

"All of our employees had left town with the mandatory evacu-ation," he later told *USA Today* reporter Nate Scott. Thornton said he needed a contingent of National Guardsmen and a few hours on Sunday, August 28, to prepare.

"I thought it would be two days at most and we'd be out," said Lieutenant Colonel Doug Mouton of the 370 National Guard, whose troops arrived to assist the undermanned management staff. "That's been the history. With Hurricane George, it was thirty-six to forty-eight hours. Hurricane Ivan, it was less than that. Never did I think we'd be here for nearly a week."

Things went from bad to worse as floodwaters surrounded the Superdome and winds ripped a section off the roof, shredding the dome's protective waterproof skin. Water poured into the stadium and onto the field.

By the time the storm had subsided, and the water had receded enough for four hundred evacuation buses to get to the stadium, the thirty thousand temporary residents of the badly damaged Super-dome had been in the dark, hot, steamy stadium for nearly a week. Toilets had backed up; raw sewage and trash were everywhere.

"I can't describe the smell," one SMG staff member said, "but I'll never forget it."

As the storm receded and recovery efforts began, there were fears that the Superdome would be condemned and razed. But it passed a structural evaluation and it was declared sound. Even so, it might take two years to make the necessary repairs.

When Louisiana governor Kathleen Blanco signed an order to repair the stadium, she called it "a leap of faith."

"I knew we would lose the NFL franchise without a stadium," she later said. "But I had no idea if we could keep the team even if I committed to a renovation."

There was no chance the Saints could play in the Superdome in the 2005 season. Team owner Tom Benson was forced to take his team on the road. But when he did, there was plenty of speculation that he was also shopping for a new permanent home.

Prior to Katrina, Benson and state officials had been discussing the future of the Superdome and the Saints. Blanco desperately wanted to keep the team from moving. Press reports were that the two sides were at least in agreement that a renovated Superdome with additional amenities might be acceptable, rather than a new, more expensive stadium.

So, with the earlier fears of a Saints relocation still looming, suspicions grew to genuine concern when the team announced it would play in San Antonio while the Superdome was being repaired. San Antonio was the headquarters of Benson's automobile dealership business and was a city that had lusted after an NFL franchise for years.

Meanwhile, Tagliabue got involved. According to Dave Anderson of *The New York Times,* he demanded that the Saints play more home games at Tigers Stadium in Baton Rouge (four) than in San Antonio's Alamo Stadium (three), plus one at Giants Stadium, with the Giants as the visiting team.

The NFL declared the weekend of the Giants game, September 18–19, as "Hurricane Relief Weekend," which concluded with a telethon in conjunction with a *Monday Night Football* doubleheader on ABC and ESPN. In total, the NFL, its owners, teams, players, and fans contributed $21 million to the Hurricane Katrina relief effort.

After a meeting with Benson and Blanco on October 30 at the first Baton Rouge game, Tagliabue publicly declared that the league was still determined to see the Saints remain in Louisiana.

Behind closed doors, he was more specific. Tagliabue assured Blanco that the NFL would not abandon New Orleans in its time of greatest need, assuring her that he would personally work with Benson through the coming months.

The Saints, he promised, would always remain "an integral part of the fabric of New Orleans."

There was one catch. Tagliabue knew the Saints had to be in a permanent home by 2006. He did not want to lose the leverage he had to make New Orleans that place. He told Blanco the Superdome had to be game-ready for the opening of the 2006 regular season.

"We had nine months to complete a two-year project," Blanco later said, "and I agreed to his terms."

Nine months later, on September 25, in what can only be described as a Super Bowl–like atmosphere, the Superdome was reopened. A pregame musical performance by U2 and Green Day literally "set the stage."

"I never thought it would look this good this fast," Thornton was quoted as saying. "It's iconic for the people of New Orleans. This is our version of Ground Zero."

"We need this team," a fan dressed in Saints regalia told an Associated Press reporter on game day. "It crosses all lines. It's not Democrat or Republican. It's not rich or poor. It's not black or white. It's black and gold."

A sellout crowd cheered when their 2-0 Saints ran out of the tunnel onto the field to take on the 2-0 Atlanta Falcons.

"You literally felt the noise," Saints offensive tackle Zach Strief told ESPN. "It's loud in there a lot, moments where you can't hear anything. But that's just people screaming to make it loud. [This was an] emotional release."

The Saints wasted no time in rewarding their fans for sticking with them. The Falcons' first drive was a three-and-out. Then Steve Gleason, the Saints' special-teams maven, broke through the Falcons' line and smothered Michael Koenen's punt.

The ball bounded into the end zone, where Curtis Deloatch fell on it for a touchdown. Just ninety seconds into the game and everyone knew it was over. The Saints and New Orleans were back.

The Saints won the game, 23–3, and the stadium was their trophy. An appreciative team dedicated a game ball to the fans and the city.

"It meant a lot to them when the Saints didn't leave in their time of need," Saints rookie running back Reggie Bush said after the game. "When the people of New Orleans needed something to look to for confidence and something to be proud of, they looked to the Saints."

"The Saints lifted the spirits of a bedraggled, exhausted people who had labored so hard to bring order to our world," Blanco wrote. "The Superdome, once the image of despair, was now the symbol of victory."

Paul Tagliabue attended what one headline writer called the "Saints back home in the Dome game." But he wasn't there as NFL commissioner. Tagliabue had retired in July. He was there as a welcome guest.

James Carville, a longtime New Orleans supporter and political advisor to President Bill Clinton, had a thought.

"The city fathers should take down the statue of Robert E. Lee at Lee Circle in New Orleans and put up a statue of Paul Tagliabue."

KRAFTING A WINNER— THE NEW ENGLAND PATRIOTS

THERE WAS GOOD NEWS FOR FOOTBALL FANS IN Boston on January 21, 1994. The beloved New England Patriots had been sold for the second time in two years. Well, that was the news. The good part was that the sale was to a local buyer, Robert Kraft, who, unlike the current owner James Orthwein, planned to keep the team in New England. The sale by Orthwein to Kraft ended two years of speculation and fear that the Patriots would turn into deserters.

The Boston Globe described Kraft as a "businessman, philanthropist and sports fan" who, ever since the Boston Braves "broke his heart" by leaving town in 1953, wanted to own a professional sports team.

Born and raised in nearby Brookline, Kraft was a graduate of Harvard Business School and a Patriots season-ticket holder since 1971. "Section 217 on the old metal benches in Foxboro Stadium," he would brag. A proud New Englander through and through. Buying the Patriots was the fulfillment of a dream.

"Some people think it's pretty silly to spend so much money just for a game," he said. "But for those of you who aren't fans, let me tell you that this game holds the attention of this community and communities throughout the country from August to January. . . . It really impacts the psyche and the fabric of the community."

Kraft's dream to own the Patriots began to take shape in 1985, when he purchased an option on the land surrounding Sullivan Stadium, the Patriots' home field, located in suburban Foxborough, twenty-nine miles southwest of downtown Boston. Buying the underdeveloped parcel of land was a shrewd move as Kraft began to position himself to make a serious run at owning the Patriots.

In 1988, he took another step by paying $25 million to purchase Sullivan Stadium out of bankruptcy court. He outbid several prospective buyers, including then–team owner Victor Kiam.

But the real gem in the deal wasn't the aging stadium that everyone agreed was substandard for an NFL team; it was the lease agreement that included an "operating covenant" that required the Patriots to play all their home games there through 2001. The lease proved to be an unbelievably fortuitous acquisition for Kraft. It was a fact not missed by *The Boston Globe*: "Kraft had the money, the arena and, perhaps most importantly, the lease."

In 1994, Kraft was offered $75 million for that all-important lease. The offer came from Orthwein, who, two years earlier, on May 11, 1992, had purchased the Patriots from Kiam.

Orthwein knew the binding lease agreement would negatively impact the franchise's value and the interest level of prospective buyers. Kraft knew that if he accepted Orthwein's offer, the Patriots would be leaving town.

A lifelong resident of St. Louis and a major shareholder of Anheuser-Busch, Orthwein had no intention of being the long-term owner of the team. According to his hometown newspaper, the *St. Louis Post-Dispatch*, he purchased the franchise to protect a $30 million loan he'd made to Kiam's minority partner, Fran Murray.

Orthwein referred to himself as the franchise's interim owner. His stated goals were to stabilize the franchise, work to resolve the stadium issue, and find a local owner.

Although Orthwein did improve the team by signing head coach Bill Parcells and quarterback Drew Bledsoe to contracts, the stadium deal was still a mess, and nobody really believed that part about finding a local owner.

Compounding the locals' distrust was the fact that Orthwein was actively working to secure an expansion team for St. Louis, a city that lost its NFL team in 1988, when the Cardinals moved to Phoenix. Many feared that Orthwein would find a way to move the Patriots to St. Louis or sell the team to someone else who would.

But Kraft not only turned down Orthwein's $75 million offer, he countered with one of his own. He presented the beer baron with a then-record $172 million offer to purchase the Patriots. Orthwein accepted.

Although parties from Baltimore, Hartford, and St. Louis were also negotiating with Orthwein, it came down to Kraft and Stan Kroenke, who was representing the St. Louis group. Although Kroenke's bid was more than Kraft's, the deal contained contingencies requiring protection from the all-but-certain lawsuits that would follow if the team didn't honor the binding stadium lease agreement.

"There were a lot of people bidding and a lot of possibilities out of state. My hometown was one of them," Orthwein said. "This [Kraft's offer] was the cleanest, least complicated way to proceed."

"As much as we'd like to see NFL football back in St. Louis," Kroenke said, "it's clear that Mr. Kraft faces far fewer obstacles in purchasing the Patriots than does any other party, and we understand Jim Orthwein's decision in this regard."

Although Orthwein appreciated Kroenke's understanding, he knew football fans in St. Louis might not be as empathetic. "As of now," he said, "I'm not going to be the most popular man in the world there [St. Louis] for a while."

But for Kraft it was a celebration. "This is my hometown," he proclaimed. "I don't believe my hometown would have been the same if this team had left here."

Kraft waxed nostalgic about achieving his boyhood dream, but he also knew there was much work to be done. While owning the stadium played in his favor when it came time to buy the franchise, the reality was that it was an aging facility with no revenue-producing amenities and would be a major financial drag to the incoming owner. Even if he did own the lease.

Interestingly, Kraft shared one of the reasons he hadn't "pushed harder" to buy the Patriots in earlier years. It was the absence of a league-wide salary cap.

To Kraft, the NFL salary cap—which was implemented that

year—meant that teams were now on a level financial playing field. "An owner with a big ego just can't go out and outspend everybody else," he said.

Kraft understood that the new salary cap system not only addressed the upwardly spiraling player costs but also provided teams the ability to restrict a "star player" from the free agent market, as long as he was offered a contract equal to the average salary of the top five players at his position. That arrangement was reassuring for Kraft, who also understood the need and value of a "star player."

"I always worried that if you don't sign a star player you'd be perceived as a jerk in your own hometown," Kraft half-jokingly remarked.

Kraft's stated objective in buying the Patriots was to "help bring a championship to New England." It was a goal you'd expect to hear from every new owner. But, since this team had won just nineteen of its last eighty games, skepticism remained high that it would occur in the immediate future.

When Kraft bought the team, just about everything, including its troublesome stadium, was considered second-rate. Rookies visiting the stadium for the first time would proclaim their high school's locker room to be better equipped. Patriots veteran defensive back Ty Law once remarked that the stadium was so bad, he "looked forward to playing on the road."

But things were about to change. In Kraft's first year as owner, the team made the playoffs, ending an eight-year drought. That was followed by playoff appearances in four of the next five seasons. The hometown kid, it seemed, was delivering on his promise. Fans responded by purchasing tickets. By the start of his first season as owner, every home game was sold out, a feat that had never been accomplished in the team's thirty-four-year history. Since then, every Patriots home game has been a sellout.

The year 2000 was the start of the new millennium, and for the Patriots it was also a new beginning—a clean slate, so to speak.

That year the Patriots hired a new head coach, Bill Belichick;

began construction on a new and privately financed stadium (one of the first in NFL history); and drafted their franchise quarterback, Tom Brady.

Clearly, when the Patriots tabbed Brady as their sixth-round compensatory pick (199th overall) in the 2000 NFL draft, no one thought they'd just landed their future franchise quarterback. Brady wasn't on anyone's franchise-QB radar. Except for maybe his own.

Kraft has often shared the memory of his first encounter with the confident sixth-round pick. It was in the parking lot at Foxboro Stadium (formerly Sullivan Stadium). Brady, carrying a pizza, was coming out of a trailer that was being used as a temporary team shop when he spotted Kraft.

"He comes over and said, 'Hi, I'm Tom Brady,'" Kraft recalls. "I said I know who you are. You're our sixth-round draft choice out of Michigan. He looks me right in the eye and says, 'Yeah, and I'm the best decision this team has ever made.'"

Well, maybe so. But today even Brady would have to admit that hiring Belichick that same year might also qualify as a contender for the "best decision" the team ever made.

FAST-FORWARD TO October 1, 2018. The Patriots have just defeated their division rival Miami Dolphins 38–7. The lopsided win was important, as it ended an unusual two-game losing skid. But the game was also significant in a very different way. It was the Patriots' 300th win under the ownership of Robert Kraft. No other owner in NFL history had reached 300 victories faster. The milestone win came in the 432nd game of Kraft's 25th season of ownership.

How impressive is that? Well, by comparison, the Broncos reached 300 wins for owner Pat Bowlen in his 30th season (501 games), while the Raiders hit the mark for Al Davis in his 31st (495 games).

After the win, the first player to enter the locker room and greet Kraft was Brady. The two embraced in a quick congratulatory hug.

Then Belichick gathered the team for some postgame remarks. After a quick laudatory review, he shifted gears to acknowledge the boss: "Today was a special day for us, for Robert [Kraft]. His 300th win. The quickest to 300 by any owner."

Belichick's remarks were interrupted by spontaneous applause and shouts of "speech, speech, speech" by the players who had huddled around the popular team owner.

Obviously, winning requires good players and coaches. And it's no coincidence that the clear majority of the three hundred victories under Kraft's ownership came during the Belichick-Brady era. It was also significant that the wins came during the salary-cap era, an era that by design meant long-reigning dynasties would be the exception, not the rule. It is also an era during which Belichick is the only NFL coach to win five Super Bowls.

"Our family is just a vehicle and a custodian of this great asset," Kraft said after Belichick handed him the game ball from the three hundredth win. "It's the players and coaches that did it. So, thank you, this is a great thrill for me and my family and you're the reason it happened. I hope we're all together for four hundred."

In typical Patriots low-key fashion, the three-hundredth-win acknowledgment was short and to the point. It was just a pause in the otherwise fast-moving success story of an owner, coach, and quarterback. Together the Kraft-Belichick-Brady triumvirate has lifted the Patriots franchise from worst to first, fulfilling one of the greatest franchise revivals in the history of sport.

"Beginning in 2000 and throughout the decade," veteran Boston sports journalist Ron Borges wrote, "the Patriots not only had stable management, coaching and quarterbacking, but arguably some of the greatest examples of each in NFL history."

"It's unbelievable to me the consistency they've had," Giants owner John Mara told ESPN's senior writer Greg Garber. "They're in a league by themselves, and a lot of that starts with the owner. Obviously, they have a Hall of Fame coach and a Hall of Fame quarterback, but I think they have a Hall of Fame owner, too."

Kraft, Belichick, and Brady were the architects of a pro football dynasty that arguably should be at the top of any such list.

The success the Patriots attained during the first decade of the new millennium is unsurpassed. The team's 126 regular- and postseason victories are the most by any team in one decade in the history of the NFL. Their ten-year run of superlative play resulted in three Super Bowl titles (XXXVI, XXXVII, XXXIX), four conference titles, and seven playoff wins.

During the decade they set three significant NFL records for consecutive wins. From 2003 to 2004 they won 21 consecutive games, including playoffs. From 2006 to 2008 they won 21 consecutive regular-season games. And from 2001 to 2005 they won 10 consecutive playoff games.

Belichick was the first NFL coach to win 14 or more games in a season four times during one decade.

"That's unbelievable when you think about fourteen wins in a sixteen-game season," former Chicago Bears coach Mike Ditka said. "Doing it four times? That's truly amazing."

In 2007, the Patriots also became the first NFL team to win 16 games during the regular season and the only team to win 18 consecutive games in one season. Unfortunately, the streak ended with their 17–14 loss to the New York Giants in Super Bowl XLII.

Marv Levy, the Hall of Fame coach who took the Buffalo Bills to four consecutive Super Bowls, called what Belichick and Brady accomplished together "remarkable."

Levy, who presented quarterback Jim Kelly for enshrinement into the Hall of Fame and once said of Bills owner Ralph Wilson, "He wasn't my boss, he was my friend," understands the value of a good owner-coach-quarterback relationship.

+++

THE PATRIOTS' on-the-field dominance in the first decade of the 2000s almost ended before it began.

On September 11, 2001, the world as we knew it changed forever when a terrorist attack toppled the twin towers of the World Trade Center in Manhattan.

At the time, Kraft was moving full speed ahead on his long-term project to build a privately financed stadium when he had what he called a "blue steel moment." Anxious to get his massive stadium construction project started, Kraft—without the financing in place—had ordered $64 million worth of custom-made blue steel for the stadium.

With all the fallout and confusion following the terrorist attack, no one was sure what the future held, and what the worldwide economic effect might be on the financial community. Kraft couldn't wait. He had to trust his instinct.

"I wrote a personal letter to guarantee the money," he later recalled. "It's not like a roll of paper you could send back. It was custom-designed steel." Fortunately his personal guarantee worked out.

In addition to taking the personal financial risk of building a stadium, he admits he also bid nearly $57 million more than his financial advisors recommended when he purchased the Patriots. While considered by most to be a shrewd businessman, Kraft does put a lot of faith in his own instincts.

"Those things they don't teach you at Harvard Business School," he likes to say.

Jonathan Kraft has seen his father "follow his gut" many times. "I'm done from ever trying to persuade him otherwise," he told an interviewer in 2015. "When his gut instinct is strong, you just defer to him because he's always right."

And while New England was without a doubt the team of the decade in the 2000s, the team's dominance continued well into the next decade.

+++

IN 2016, Kraft told CSNBayArea.com that when he took ownership of the Patriots in 1994, he had a distinct vision for his franchise and that it was modeled after an earlier NFL dynasty.

"I wanted people to view us and look at us the way people looked at the 49ers," Kraft said.

In fact, almost immediately after his first NFL owners' meeting, Kraft set up a meeting with 49ers owner Ed DeBartolo Jr. and team president Carmen Policy. He wanted to learn from the masters.

"I went to my first owners' meeting and I met with them and they were very gracious and kind," Kraft said. "Probably the main lesson I learned from that—twenty-odd years later—is I always try to be very welcoming and kind to new owners coming in. Because I know it's a very exciting opportunity and adventure to come into the league. It's a great privilege."

Kraft and his son, Jonathan, visited DeBartolo and Policy in the 49ers' Bay Area headquarters. "I don't think anyone could've been more hospitable than Eddie was with the 49ers," Kraft said, "and it was at the height of their achievements."

"It's the right thing to do," DeBartolo offered. "They are your partners. I know it's very competitive. But you know what? Then you have to be one step ahead of everybody and you have to continue to forge on. I had no qualms about having fellow owners come out and see how we operate."

Others can attest to Kraft's "lessons learned" from DeBartolo.

"Robert was the first owner who called when it was announced that I had made a deal to purchase the Jaguars from Wayne [Weaver] and [his wife,] Delores," Jaguars owner Shad Khan said.

"Welcome to a life of experiencing the highest of highs and the lowest of lows—that's the NFL, and there is nothing like it," Kahn recalled Kraft saying. "And he was right."

Welcoming new owners isn't where the similarities between the Patriots and the 49ers end. Looking back, the similarities between the two franchises are striking.

During his 2016 Pro Football Hall of Fame enshrinement speech, DeBartolo said the turning point for his franchise was "when God blessed him with the good judgment to hire a gentleman by the name of Bill Walsh." That decision was then further enhanced by Walsh's decision to select Notre Dame quarterback Joe Montana in the third round of the 1979 draft.

Kraft's "good judgment" was to hire Belichick, and Belichick's decision to select Brady with a compensatory pick in the sixth round eerily parallels the 49ers' formula for success that also ended with multiple Super Bowl wins by both teams.

The 49ers' combo of DeBartolo-Walsh-Montana won three

Super Bowls (XVI, XIX, and XXIII) together in the 1990s. The Patriots' Kraft-Belichick-Brady trio won three (XXXVI, XXXVIII, and XXXIX) in the first decade of the 2000s. The Patriots now boast six Super Bowl wins and eight Super Bowl appearances with the same owner-coach-quarterback combo, the most in the history of the NFL.

"It's just almost unfathomable what they've accomplished," Levy said.

When former Patriots linebacker Tedy Bruschi asked Kraft during an interview for ESPN "how he keeps the Patriots team on track and moving forward no matter what the distraction," Kraft told him that it was all about "continuity" and surrounding himself with "good people."

"The job of ownership is to keep the continuity when you have something good. I think some people make change just for change's sake. I have a rule, we never break something down unless we can put something better in its place. And the Belichick-Brady combo has been pretty good."

THE LAST COMMISSIONER
OF THE NFL'S FIRST CENTURY

T TOOK SEVEN DAYS AND TWENTY-THREE BAL-
lots before Pete Rozelle was elected commissioner of the NFL in
1960. Paul Tagliabue was elected after a 219-day battle between
the league's old and new guard owners in 1989.

When Tagliabue decided it was time to retire in 2006, he
wanted the transition to his successor to go much more smoothly.

First, he told his friend Dan Rooney that he planned to step
down. He asked him to send a letter to the other owners just before
their March 20 annual meeting to let them know his intention and
that he would address them collectively at that time.

At that meeting Tagliabue said he would retire by the end of
July. Then, in his usual, organized fashion, he appointed a committee to find his replacement. Tagliabue had mastered the art of
building consensus through carefully constructed committees. He
understood the importance of inclusion.

The search committee would be co-chaired by Rooney and
Panthers owner Jerry Richardson. It included Patriots owner Robert Kraft, Raiders owner Al Davis, Chiefs owner Lamar Hunt, Jets
owner Woody Johnson, Cowboys owner Jerry Jones, and Bears
president Mike McCaskey.

The ownership group then hired an executive search firm to
assist in identifying qualified candidates. They delivered a list of
nearly two hundred. Based on what the owners' committee said it
wanted, that list was whittled down to nineteen contenders. The
committee reduced the list to eleven, then five. And on August 8,

after just five ballots, Roger Goodell—a career NFL executive—was elected commissioner.

He would be the last NFL commissioner of the league's first century.

Goodell's personal and professional pedigree was unquestionable. The forty-seven-year-old son of former U.S. senator Charles Goodell of New York, he had been Tagliabue's top assistant and was intimately involved in many important league initiatives.

"We've had the two greatest sports commissioners in the history of sports," Goodell said when he addressed the media, "Paul Tagliabue and Pete Rozelle, and I was fortunate to work for both."

"Roger got his MBA from Pete Rozelle and Paul Tagliabue," Kraft said after the announcement. "That's not a bad education."

"One of the delicate parts of the job," Kraft told *Boston Globe* reporter Ron Borges, "is the commissioner works for 32 owners. But in a way, he's our boss." The tough part, Kraft explained, somewhat tongue in cheek, was that "most of those 32 guys don't feel they have a boss."

Sometimes the job will require "pushing back," Kraft said, "putting the interests of the NFL ahead of an individual owner or team."

It was sage advice and something Goodell would have to face more than once.

Marc Ganis, a leading sports consultant, told the *Los Angeles Times* that Goodell's election validated the last seventeen years of Tagliabue's leadership and the NFL's standing as "a business and a sports property."

Goodell was the first career employee to rise through the NFL's ranks to its most important position.

His football odyssey began in 1982 as an intern at the NFL offices in New York. He then interned for a year with the New York Jets before returning to the NFL in 1984 as a public relations assistant.

In 1987 Rozelle elevated Goodell to assistant to the president of the American Football Conference. Three years later Tagliabue appointed him director of international development and club administration. He continued working his way up the executive ladder until 2001, when Tagliabue named him executive vice president and chief operating officer.

When Tagliabue announced he was stepping down in 2006, Goodell was seen as his logical successor.

While he had benefited from his tenure with both Rozelle and Tagliabue, his seventeen years with Tagliabue afforded him his greatest executive opportunities. Goodell played an integral role in many of the league's business decisions, including stadium development, league expansion and realignment, and the NFL's numerous lucrative television deals.

+ + +

WORKING FOR the NFL was a dream come true for Goodell. While a student at Washington & Jefferson College, he sent a letter to his father telling him that the one thing he wanted to accomplish in life besides making him proud was to become commissioner of the NFL.

Goodell's father, Charles, a former U.S. senator, died in 1987, before he could witness his son achieve his lofty goal. But as proud as his father would have been, he could have only equaled, not exceeded, the pride his son already felt for him.

When Senator Robert Kennedy was assassinated in 1968, New York governor Nelson Rockefeller turned to Representative Charles Goodell of Jamestown, New York, to fill his seat.

Considered a moderate-to-conservative Republican, Charles Goodell surprised his party by championing legislative efforts that were more closely aligned with moderate-to-liberal factions of his party. But when he became the first senator to voice his opposition to the Vietnam War, the Nixon White House—particularly Vice President Spiro Agnew—openly turned on him.

Hanging on a wall in Roger Goodell's New York office is a framed copy of the *Congressional Record* of September 25, 1969. It's the official record of his father's Senate floor speech denouncing the war in Vietnam.

"The war did not end that day," the *Globe*'s Borges later wrote, "but Charles Goodell's political career did."

"At a very young age, my four brothers and I learned the importance of integrity, character, and standing up for what is right, no matter the cost," Roger Goodell said.

+ + +

THE NFL brand was never stronger than when Goodell assumed his new role as commissioner. And while he was already a major contributor to that success, he had his sights set on future growth and opportunities for the league.

In his first press conference, Goodell said that he planned to focus on the game, innovation, and strengthening the league's thirty-two teams.

"Those are the things that made the NFL great in the past," he said. "I think they will help us keep our focus and make the game greater going forward." He described his job as "an awesome responsibility . . . not only to maintain the level of success the NFL has, but to build on that."

He also made it very clear from the beginning that he would not tolerate anything that could damage the "integrity of the game or its brand."

"Protecting the shield," as he would often describe it, became the driving force behind many difficult decisions Goodell faced, especially when it came to enforcing NFL conduct rules.

"I was the first owner to be fined by the new commissioner," Rooney, a Goodell supporter, recalled. "He hit me hard when I criticized the officials after our game against the Falcons on October 22, 2006."

Although he said he still "disagreed with the official's call," Rooney admitted that Goodell did the right thing by fining him. He said it established a precedent that no owner was above the league rules.

Goodell got off to a running start as commissioner. In his first twelve months, many of the projects he had been working on as the league's chief operating officer were coming to fruition.

He also introduced new initiatives he hoped to develop as commissioner.

Preaching the need for more transparency between the league office and member clubs, he visited each club during his first year. He christened a new stadium in Phoenix. He announced an expanded international business and marketing strategy that included playing one or possibly two international regular-season games each year between 2007 and 2011.

At the league's March 2007 annual meeting he announced a new revenue-sharing plan to help subsidize the league's lower-revenue teams. And, at the same meeting, he announced he was preparing a new player-conduct policy that would allow the league to penalize off-the-field offenders even before their cases had made their way through the legal system.

Goodell's announcement came on the same day that Las Vegas police announced they would seek felony charges against Tennessee Titans cornerback Adam "Pacman" Jones in connection with a February fight at a Las Vegas strip club that ended with a shooting (not by Jones) that left a man paralyzed.

Less than a month later, Goodell completed the revised player-conduct policy and acted. He suspended Jones for a year. In a separate action, he suspended Cincinnati Bengals wide receiver Chris Henry for eight games after Henry had been arrested four times in a fourteen-month span.

It was the beginning of a series of off-the-field behavior issues that the commissioner faced and addressed, and that reflected badly on the league and its players.

"It's a privilege to represent the NFL, not a right," Goodell said in a statement. "These players and all members of our league have to make the right choices and decisions in their conduct on a consistent basis."

That same year, Goodell disciplined yet another high-profile player, a coach, and a team.

He suspended Atlanta Falcons quarterback Michael Vick indefinitely after he pleaded guilty to federal and state charges of illegal dogfighting.

Vick served eighteen months in prison. After consulting with internal advisors, other players, NFL ownership, counselors, and people from animal rights groups, Goodell made the decision to conditionally reinstate the repentant quarterback. "I accept that you are sincere when you say that you want to, and will, turn your life around, and that you intend to be a positive role model for others," Goodell said in his letter to Vick informing him of the reinstatement. "I am prepared to offer you that opportunity. Whether you succeed is entirely in your hands."

Vick made the most of his second chance and played another seven seasons in the NFL with the Eagles (2009–13), Jets (2014), and Steelers (2015).

Patriots head coach Bill Belichick and the Patriots were disciplined after an investigation showed that Belichick had a team employee videotape New York Jets defensive coaches' play-calling signals from an unauthorized location during their game on September 9, 2007, at Giants Stadium.

While some—including Senator Arlen Specter of Pennsylvania—questioned the investigation for its haste and for the destruction of six tapes from the 2006 and 2007 preseason that may have been evidence of earlier wrongdoing, Goodell came down hard on Belichick and the Patriots. The coach was fined $500,000, the maximum allowed, and the Patriots organization $250,000. The club also forfeited their first-round pick in the 2008 NFL draft. "I misinterpreted the rule. . . . I take responsibility for it," Belichick said in February 2008. "Even though I felt there was a gray area in the rule and I misinterpreted the rule, that was my mistake and we've been penalized for it."

The videotaping scandal became known as "Spygate."

Goodell called the episode "a calculated and deliberate attempt to avoid long-standing rules designed to encourage fair play and promote honest competition on the playing field."

Spygate was the first of two investigations of the Patriots by the league. Seven years later, following their win over the Indianapolis Colts in the 2014 season's AFC championship game, allegations were made that the Patriots had deliberately deflated footballs used in the game by quarterback Tom Brady. That controversy became known as "Deflategate."

This time, following new investigation guidelines that were developed after Spygate, the league launched a four-month independent investigation that was headed by Ted Wells Jr., a litigation partner at a noted New York law firm.

In May 2015, after the Wells investigation concluded that it was "more probable than not" that Brady was "generally aware" of Patriots attendants deflating footballs prior to the game, he was suspended for four games.

Brady won an appeal that allowed him to play during the 2015 season. But in April 2016, the US Court of Appeals reversed that ruling, stating that the commissioner had "properly exercised his broad discretion under the collective bargaining agreement and that his procedural rulings were properly grounded in that agreement and did not deprive Brady of fundamental fairness."

Brady reluctantly fulfilled his four-game suspension by sitting out the first four games of the 2016 season. The Patriots finished that season as AFC champions and won Super Bowl LI in overtime, 34–28, over the NFC champion Atlanta Falcons. Brady was named the game's MVP.

"My first obligation is to uphold the integrity of the game," Goodell told NFL Network's Rich Eisen. "That's to uphold the rules of the game and make sure all thirty-two teams are operating under the same rules, all players are operating under the same rules, and you do that on a consistent basis. . . . I have to make sure that we continue to do the things that are necessary to protect the integrity of the game, and I will do that without compromise."

There were other cases of misconduct involving coaches, players, and teams to which Goodell responded. But one involving Baltimore Ravens running back Ray Rice received the most attention and criticism.

Rice was charged with aggravated assault resulting from a physical altercation with his fiancée in an Atlantic City casino elevator.

A security camera showed Rice dragging his seemingly unconscious fiancée out of the elevator.

Initially, Goodell suspended Rice for two games and fined him $529,000, the equivalent of a three-game salary. But the two-game ban drew widespread criticism of Goodell and the NFL's policy on domestic violence, prompting Goodell to send a lengthy letter to the owners admitting he "didn't get it right."

"I take responsibility both for the decision and for ensuring that our actions in the future properly reflect our values," Goodell said. "Simply put, we have to do better. And we will."

Goodell announced that, in the future, violations regarding assault, battery, domestic violence, or sexual assault involving physical force would result in a suspension without pay of six games for a first offense. A second offense would result in banishment from the NFL for at least one year.

But in the aftermath and circulation of a second video that captured the actual assault, the Ravens announced they were releasing Rice and the NFL suspended him indefinitely.

On December 10, 2014, as part of the follow-up to their promise to address domestic violence, Goodell announced that teams had unanimously endorsed a revised and strengthened Personal Conduct Policy for all NFL employees.

The role of the commissioner serving as the league disciplinarian didn't begin with Goodell. In fact, it went back to 1941, when commissioner Elmer Layden, under the league's revised constitution, was given the power "to discipline any persons connected with the league—club owner, stockholder, players, officials, or anyone else on the payroll of any club." It was also reported by the Associated Press that there would be no appeal process and fines for misconduct "may run as high as $25,000."

One might suggest things hadn't changed much in sixty-five years. And while that might be true, in 2016, John Mara, an owner of the Giants, offered a more contemporary explanation of Goodell's dilemma to *New York Times* reporter Ken Belson: "I think it's largely due to the social-media age and the fact that he had some high-profile cases and admittedly made some mistakes. . . . It's almost gotten to the point where no matter what he does, he faces an avalanche of a criticism."

+ + +

WHILE GOODELL'S disciplinary acts garnered a lot of media scrutiny, the commissioner was concurrently racking up numerous positive achievements, not the least of which were several lucrative television deals.

In 2010 the league had its best television season, with NBC's *Sunday Night Football* the number one prime-time program, averaging 21.4 million total viewers. Television rights fees had soared to more than $4 billion annually.

In that same year the NFL draft debuted a new three-day format that featured the first two days in prime time on NFL Network, ESPN, and ESPN2.

In 2014 the draft's three-day television coverage drew 45.7 million viewers. Then, in 2015, Goodell announced that the league was "taking the show on the road." The draft is now so popular that NFL cities compete for it, much like the Super Bowl. It has become a tentpole event on the growing calendar of the NFL's year-round programming.

The league's annual revenue more than doubled, from $6 billion when Goodell took office in 2006 to $13 billion before the end of his first decade as commissioner.

In 2008, both the NFL and the NFL Players Association had begun to prepare for potentially contentious collective bargaining discussions scheduled for the end of the 2010 season. The owners had earlier announced that they would exercise their option to opt out of the existing CBA, which meant labor peace could end following the 2010 season.

And that's what happened. On March 11, 2011, the NFL announced a lockout of its players following the Players Association's decision to decertify as a union and pursue court action against the league, rather than collectively bargain.

"The clubs believe that this step [the lockout] is the most effective way to accelerate efforts to reach a new agreement without disruption to the 2011 season," read an NFL statement.

"Any agreement reached from this point forward with the NFL will be as a result of the court system, not a collective bargaining agreement," the Players Association countered.

Adding a layer of complexity was the fact that both Goodell and the NFLPA's executive director, DeMaurice Smith, were negotiating their first labor agreement.

By the time the lockout ended on June 25, it was the longest work stoppage—135 days—in league history and the first since 1987.

"We know what we did to frustrate our fans over the last several months," Goodell said. "They want football and it's our job to give them football."

A formal signing of the ten-year agreement reached between the two former combatants was conducted on the front steps of the Pro Football Hall of Fame on August 6.

"There was a sense of relief from Smith and Goodell, who shook hands three times during the brief signing and even hugged after spending nearly half a year in tense negotiations, haggling over a new way to distribute the NFL's massive revenue stream," Will Graves of the Associated Press wrote.

The new agreement dealt with a variety of old and new issues. Chief among them was a reduction of the percentage of shared revenues the players would receive. This was a major bone of contention by the owners and a motivating factor for their opting out of the CBA.

The owners argued that with a larger percentage of the revenues they would be more likely to reinvest in costly but big-ticket revenue opportunities, such as new stadiums, more international games, new media, and other expensive ventures. In theory, that would create a larger pie. The players, while receiving a smaller percentage of the shared revenues, would ultimately earn more revenues from their piece of a larger pie.

It was essentially the same argument Tagliabue used in prior negotiations. "There was an understanding there would be growing revenues that could fund a new system," Tagliabue said about the previous deals, "and it would be to everybody's advantage to have a growing pie."

But to get to that point, the owners had to make concessions in other areas, such as a more player-friendly salary cap structure and modified veteran free agency. There were major improvements in player safety and health issues, including later training camps and a reduction of off-season team activities (OTAs) from fourteen to ten. And there were greater benefits for retired players as well, including the establishment of a new $620 million Legacy Fund, which would be devoted to increasing pensions for pre-1993 retirees.

The reaction to labor peace was immediate. Deals got done. Owners invested while players made more money and had greater security and better-quality-of-life benefits.

A record 107.4 million football-hungry fans tuned in to the league's "Kickoff Weekend" games on CBS, NBC, ESPN, and Fox on September 8, 11, and 12.

On the same day as the Thursday night 2011 season opener, and not coincidentally, the league announced that they had signed a new *Monday Night Football* contract with ESPN through the 2021 season. The deal was estimated to be $15.2 billion, a 73 percent increase over the old deal.

In December, the league's other TV partners—CBS, NBC, and Fox—agreed to new contracts through 2022. The agreements included an expansion of the Thursday night game package on NFL Network from eight to thirteen games. Although no financial terms were announced, the packages were reported to be worth a combined $27 billion over the length of the contracts.

The ten-year labor agreement made long-term TV deals possible. The certainty of uninterrupted NFL football, the number-one-rated live TV program, was welcomed by the networks and their sponsors. The ratings topped everything else the networks had to offer. Those ratings translated into advertising dollars, as well as viewership that benefited the networks' promotions and non-NFL programming.

In 2014, satellite TV in the form of DirecTV also signed a new contract and announced that it would expand its Sunday out-of-market game package. DirecTV's subscription programming makes every NFL game a "national" game.

In 2015, the NFL and Yahoo! combined for the first-ever live streaming of an NFL game when it broadcast real-time live video over the internet of the Bills and Jaguars game in London.

Within weeks of the new CBA, the owners approved a resolution to continue the NFL's commitment to play regular-season games in the United Kingdom through 2016. That commitment was expanded in 2015, with the league agreeing to play international regular-season games through 2025 and to consider games in other countries.

The league had played three games in London to sellout crowds in 2014, 2015, and 2016. In 2017, after having hosted four games in London, Mayor Sadiq Khan said: "London is the international home of the NFL and staging the equivalent of what would be half an American football team's home games in the city is a huge step towards my ambition of bringing a franchise to the capital."

That same year, the NFL announced it would play three regular-season games in Mexico from 2019 to 2021.

And NFL football returned to Los Angeles after a twenty-two-year absence in 2016, when club owners approved the transfer of the St. Louis Rams franchise to LA. With its return came plans for a $4.9 billion stadium, an entertainment district, and perhaps the next big thing in the NFL's evolution as a "business and a sports property."

While Goodell has been resolute in his commitment to "protect the shield," and the "things that made the NFL great in the past," he has been equally committed to the league's future. As the NFL closes out its first century, its brand has never been stronger. Innovation, new and renewed broadcast partners and media platforms, franchise and stadium stability, and year-round NFL football have all contributed to record revenues and an ever-growing fan base, all of which bodes very well for the league's future.

+++

JUST AS Roger Goodell is the last commissioner of the NFL's first century, so too is the 2011 CBA the century's last labor agreement. The next CBA won't be negotiated until after the 2020 season, the first season of the NFL's second century.

And while we can't know what the burning issues of the day will be in 2021, we can hazard a guess. As noted in the early chapters of this book, they will likely include the same three nagging problems the league's founding fathers faced in 1920 when they met in Canton: the need to combat players' salary demands, keeping players from jumping from team to team, and college eligibility issues.

And there will likely be those other two early-day and recurring problems—also referenced throughout this book—of sustainable markets and suitable stadiums. They too will likely remain issues to address. And probably not just in the United States.

The NFL has come a long way since that day in 1920 when fifteen men representing ten teams gathered in a Hupmobile showroom to discuss the future of play-for-pay football. And since that day there have been tens of thousands of players, coaches, and administrators, and millions upon millions of fans, who have contributed to make the founders' hundred-dollar dream the greatest sports success story of the last century.

Happy birthday, NFL.

Acknowledgments

SPECIFIC TO THE BOOK, I WANT TO GRATEFULLY acknowledge and thank my son Shaun, who worked tirelessly as my researcher and content developer. Whether it was gathering information, chasing down hard-to-find facts, or pushing me to be more succinct, his help was invaluable. Also, a special thanks to my brother Jeremiah, whose professional advice and copyediting made this a better book.

Many thanks to all my coworkers at the Pro Football Hall of Fame, who work every day to fulfill our mission statement, which is to *honor the heroes of the game, preserve its history, promote its values, and celebrate excellence EVERYWHERE*. A special thanks to Chris Schilling and Saleem Choudhry, who were always there to pick up the slack while I sometimes "borrowed time" to see this project through. And to David Baker, president and CEO of the Hall of Fame, thank you for your encouragement and support.

Notes

CHAPTER ONE: LEAGUE TALK

2 **"professional organization"**: Bob Braunwart and Bob Carroll, "1905: Challenge from Canton," *The Coffin Corner*: 8(4), 1986: 1–9.

2 **"professional coach"**: Ibid.

3 **"Even the most loyal"**: Bob Braunwart, Bob Carroll, "The Ohio League," *The Coffin Corner*: 3(7), (1980): 1–4.

5 **"tacit understanding"**: "Football Magnates Set No Limit on Salary to be Given College Stars," *Canton Evening Repository*, July 15, 1919.

5 **"If a team manager wants to pay $10,000"**: "Sky Limit in Players' Case in Grid Game," *Canton Daily News*, Jul. 15, 1919.

6 **"would be on hand when the bell rang"**: "Canton and Massillon Will Meet Twice in Football," *The Canton Daily News*, Aug. 5, 1919.

7 **"put a worthy challenger"**: "Bulldogs Appear in New York Nov. 9; Play Tigers 2 Games, Nov. 16 and 30," *Canton Evening Repository*, Aug. 5, 1919.

9 **"to form a grid league"**: "Plans Are Under Way to Form Grid League for 1920 Season," *Cleveland Plain Dealer*, Nov. 3, 1919.

9 **"Organization is the next step"**: Ibid.

9 **"Teams will enter agreements"**: Ibid.

9 **"We will be on the ground"**: " 'Grid' League Talk Leads to Canton Action," *Canton Daily News*, Jul. 13, 1919.

10 **"a real sure-enough league"**: "Plans Are Under Way to Form Grid League for 1920 Season," Cleveland *Plain Dealer*, Nov. 13, 1919.

CHAPTER TWO: A REAL SURE-ENOUGH LEAGUE

11 **"On August 21, 1920"**: "Pro Football Moguls Form National Body; Bulldogs to Open Oct. 3 With Pitcairn," *Canton Evening Repository*, Aug. 21, 1920.

11 **"national in scope"**: Ibid.

12 **"Professional Football Representatives from"**: American Professional Football Association, meeting minutes, Aug. 20, 1920.

14 **"Morgan O'Brien, a Staley engineer"**: George S. Halas, with Gwen Morgan and Arthur Veysey, *Halas by Halas: The Autobiography of George Halas* (New York: McGraw-Hill, 1979), 60.

15 **"Ten well-organized outfits"**: "Ten Cities in New Array of Football Foes," *Canton Repository*, Sept. 18, 1920.

15 **"We announced membership"**: Chris Willis, *Old Leather: An Oral History of Early Pro Football in Ohio, 1920–1935* (Lanham, MD: Scarecrow Press, 2005), 126.

16 **"promote good football and elevate"**: "J. Thorpe Heads Pro Grid Teams in New League," *Akron Evening Times*, Sept. 18, 1920.

16 **"provide for membership for every big city"**: "Ten Cities in New Array of Football Foes."

19 **"much against my will"**: "Professional Football Teams Form Organization to Elevate the Game," *Akron Beacon Journal*, Sept. 18, 1920.

19 **"He had what the rest of us lacked"**: Chris Willis, *Joe F. Carr: The Man Who Built the National Football League.* (Lanham, MD: Scarecrow Press, 2010), 136.

22 **"It long has been the thought there should be"**: Frank Menke, "News and Views of Sport," *Press and Sun-Bulletin* (Birmingham, NY), Aug. 17, 1921.

23 **"Within two years"**: "Professional End of Football Pays Stars Big Money," *The St. Louis Star and Times*, Aug. 28, 1921.

CHAPTER THREE: GROWING PAINS AND A NAME CHANGE

24 **"I'll give you $5,000 seed money"**: Halas et al., *Halas by Halas*, 70.

25 **"I could not believe such good fortune"**: Ibid.

25 **"Charles W. Harley, Edw. G. Sternaman, William Harley, and Geo. S. Halas"**: A copy of this handwritten agreement, between the four named parties to manage the Decatur Staley Football team, was shared with the author by the Sternaman family.

27 **"Stagg is wrong if he attempts"**: Ibid.

27 **"professional football that is a menace to college football"**: Jack Gibbins, "Pro Body Refuses to Take Blame for Scandal," *Akron Beacon Journal*, Feb. 1, 1922.

27 **"So why blame us for the Taylorville incident?"**: Ibid.

27 **"It is a harsh thing to say"**: "The Other Side of the Question," *Atlanta Constitution*, Feb. 13, 1922.

28 **"the action of the American Professional Football Association"**: "Football Pros Show Green Bay the Door; Tribune Story Cause," *Chicago Tribune*, Jan. 29, 1922.

28 **the "National Football League"**: "College Stars Barred by Pro Grid Magnates," *Dayton Daily News*, Jan. 29, 1922.

29 **"I lacked enthusiasm for our name"**: Halas et al., *Halas by Halas*, 92.

CHAPTER FOUR: RED GRANGE TURNS PRO

30 **"Golden Era"**: Joe Horrigan and John Thorn, eds., *The Pro Football Hall of Fame 50th Anniversary Book: Where Greatness Lives* (New York: Grand Central Publishing, 2012), 22.

31 **"One day late in October of 1925"**: Halas et al., *Halas by Halas*, 103.

32 **"a tour that I am interested in arranging for Red Grange":** Letter from C. C. Pyle to Dutch Sternaman, dated Aug. 9, 1925. This information as well as other primary source materials, including financial records and contracts relative to the Grange signing and "Barnstorming Tour" (some of which the author cited in an earlier book, *The Pro Football Hall of Fame 50th Anniversary Book: Where Greatness Lives*), were obtained from the Dutch Sternaman Collection, housed in the Pro Football Hall of Fame Ralph Wilson Jr. Research and Preservation Center.

32 **"publicity agent":** " 'Red' Grange, Besieged by Newspaper Men, Again Denies Having Turned Pro," *Cincinnati Enquirer,* Nov. 20, 1925. Also, "Report Grange and Father Agree on Playing Pro Game," *Hartford Courant,* Nov. 19, 1925.

32 **"all proposals the Illinois star":** "Pyle Laughs When Grange Denies Bond," *Tampa Bay Times,* Nov. 18, 1925.

33 **"It would be a violation of":** "Red Returns After a Talk with Father," *Stevens Point Journal,* Nov. 18, 1925.

33 **In a November 18:** Don Maxwell, "Red Worries, but Clings to Illinois Team," *Chicago Tribune,* Nov. 18, 1925.

33 **"In the morning, he":** Halas et al., *Halas by Halas,* 106.

33 **Interestingly, Halas made no reference to Grange:** Horrigan and Thorn, *The Pro Football Hall of Fame 50th Anniversary Book,* 30.

34 **"I'd rather that my boy agreed to something":** Ibid.

34 **The game contract, rewritten after Grange joined the squad:** This information as well as other detailed primary source materials, including financial records and contracts relative to the Grange signing and "Barnstorming Tour," some of which the author cited in an earlier book (*The Pro Football Hall of Fame 50th Anniversary Book: Where Greatness Lives*), was obtained from the Dutch Sternaman Collection, housed in the Pro Football Hall of Fame.

36 **"were four demands for each seat":** Gordon Mackay, "Red Grange Offers Problem for Those Who Delve into All-American Path," *The Philadelphia Inquirer,* Dec. 3, 1925.

36 **"There gathered at the Polo Grounds in Harlem yesterday afternoon":** Damon Runyon, "Grange a Lazy Pro, Observes Runyon, After Sunday Tilt," *El Paso Herald,* Dec. 7, 1925.

36 **"drew almost one hundred reporters"** Horrigan and Thorn, *The Pro Football Hall of Fame 50th Anniversary Book,* 30.

36 **"Red Grange had done what nothing else":** "Seventy-five Thousand See Red Grange Play in New York," *The Miami News,* Dec. 7, 1925.

36 **"lifted the promoters of the professional game":** Damon Runyon, "80,000 Will See Grange in L.A. Games," *The San Francisco Examiner,* Jan. 16, 1926.

37 **"I founded the Giants on brute strength":** Dave Anderson, "Sports of the Times; When Grange Put the Pros in New York," *The New York Times,* Nov. 26, 2000.

37 **"most bruising battles":** John Carroll. *Red Grange and the Rise of Modern Football* (Urbana and Chicago: University of Illinois Press, 1999), 112.

37 **"grew to twice its normal size":** Halas et al., *Halas by Halas,* 110.

38 **"Grange, as everyone knows, receives the lion's share"**: Horrigan and Thorn, *The Pro Football Hall of Fame 50th Anniversary Book,* 42.

38 **"but I'll be glad to quit"**: "Red Not Headed for Matrimonial Goal": *Asbury Park Press,* Jan. 12, 1926.

39 **"Twice during the tour Pyle gave"**: Halas et al., *Halas by Halas,* 116.

CHAPTER FIVE: FEBRUARY FALLOUT

40 **"I am firmly convinced the net result"**: President's Report, National Football League minutes of the annual meeting at the Hotel Statler Detroit, Feb. 6–7, 1926, Pro Football Hall of Fame Archives.

40 **"Just when it seemed our organization had gone fairly well"**: Ibid.

42 **"and believes his team will win"**: James Crusinberry, "Cards Challenge Bears to Match Red Against Red," *Chicago Tribune,* Dec. 9, 1925.

42 **"Have opportunity to play"**: Western Union Telegram, Dec. 10, 1925, copy in Dutch Sternaman Collection, Pro Football Hall of Fame Archives.

43 **"Am playing Milwaukee Thursday"**: Ibid.

43 **"No one is as sorry over what happened"**: Chris O'Brien, "Pros' Version of Grid Triangle," *Chicago Tribune,* Dec. 17, 1925.

44 **"According to our rules"**: Ibid.

44 **"come through with a team"**: Ibid.

44 **"he could pick up some extra players"**: Ibid.

44 **"I paid no more"**: Ibid.

44 **"Just before the game I learned"**: Ibid.

44 **"Now I know the mistake"**: Ibid.

44 **"things were moving fast"**: Ibid.

44 **"Anyway"**: Ibid.

44 **"Naturally, I wish to do anything about it"**: Ibid.

44 **"I have always tried to give"**: Ibid.

44 **"Those boys were blameless"**: James Crusinberry, "Folz Takes All Blame; O'Brien Admits Fault," *Chicago Tribune,* Dec. 17, 1925.

44 **"So was Chris O'Brien"**: Ibid.

45 **"under all penalties that the league could inflict"**: President's Report, National Football League minutes of the annual meeting at the Hotel Statler Detroit, Feb. 6–7, 1926.

46 **"to dispose of his assets at Milwaukee"**: Ibid.

46 **"While the penalties that were imposed"**: Ibid.

47 **"there be no championship awarded"**: Ibid.

48 **"I have control of Greater New York"**: John Kieran, "Tim Mara Keenly Awaits Invasion of Red Grange Local Promoter Back from Detroit Meeting, Explains League Has No Vote on Matter," news clip on file at Pro Football Hall of Fame.

48 **"The story that nineteen clubs voted in favor"**: Ibid.

48 **"Pyle's chin narrowly missed a massaging"**: Harry March, *Pro Football: Its Ups and Downs* (Albany, NY: J. B. Lyons, 1934), 119.

49 **"He [Pyle] took over the loquacious"**: Ibid.

49 **"We have most of the high-class"**: "Pro Football Forces Ready for Revolters," *Minneapolis Star Tribune,* Feb. 10, 1926.

49 **"Chris O'Brien stuck"**: March, *Pro Football: Its Ups and Downs,* 121.

49 **"His loyalty and stability"**: Ibid.

50 **"way out at the loose end of"**: Westbrook Pelger, "Pro Grid Season Dies Unwept as Gotham Shivers," *Chicago Tribune,* Dec. 6, 1926.

CHAPTER SIX: REDUCED, UNDER LIGHTS, AND INDOORS

51 **"The majority of present owners"**: Letter from Aaron Hertzman to Leo Lyons dated Feb. 24, 1961. Pro Football Hall of Fame Ralph Wilson Jr. Research and Preservation Center.

52 **"Class A" and "Class B"**: Minutes of the annual meeting of the National Football League held at the Astor Hotel, New York City, Feb. 5–6, 1927. Pro Football Hall of Fame Ralph Wilson Jr. Research and Preservation Center, 3.

52 **"any money in the League Treasury"**: National Football League minutes of the annual meeting held at the Hotel Statler Cleveland, Apr. 23, 1927.

53 **"33 giant projectors on poles 53 feet high"**: "Night Football Makes Debut Before 6,000 at Kinsley Park," *Providence Journal,* Nov. 7, 1928.

54 **"Nobody thought we could pull it off"**: Author interview with Pearce Johnson.

54 **"the end zones were dark"**: Ibid.

54 **"panicky feeling that the player"**: "NFL's First Night Game," Pro Football Hall of Fame website, Jan. 1, 2005, profootballhof.com/news/nfl-s-first -night-game.

54 **"a huge success"**: Julian Rubinstein, "Flashback," *Sports Illustrated,* Nov. 7, 1994.

54 **"We went ahead and had permanent"**: Ibid.

54 **"for all league daylight"**: Tony Latone player contract, on file at Pro Football Hall of Fame Archives.

54 **"to help pay the installation costs"**: Author interview with Pearce Johnson.

55 **"Lee, I'm out of chalk"**: Halas et al., *Halas by Halas,* 170.

55 **"It had snowed heavily in Chicago"**: Ibid.

55 **"Halas did much more than pay me"**: Ibid., 171.

56 **"The decision to bring the Bears and Spartans indoors"**: Wilfred Smith, "Bears Battle Spartans for Title Tonight," *Chicago Tribune,* Dec. 18, 1932.

56 **"After all, professional football"**: Ibid.

56 **"make possible a regulation drive"**: "Pros to Decide Championship Indoors," *The Minneapolis Star,* Dec. 16, 1932.

57 **"The scoring weapon"**: Arch Ward, "Charity Gets $20,000," *Chicago Tribune,* Dec. 15, 1930.

57 **"Players standing on their own goal lines"**: "One for the Comic Strip: Pro Title Game Proves Huge Joke but Bronko Bucks Plenty," *The Minneapolis Star,* Dec. 19, 1932.

57 **"It was the difference between sitting ringside"**: Will McDonough et al., *75 Seasons: The Complete Story of the National Football League, 1920–1975* (Atlanta: Turner Publishing, Inc., 1994), 43.

58 **"I lined up as usual"**: Halas et al., *Halas by Halas,* 169.

58 **"Actually, I was on my back"**: Ibid.

58 **"It wasn't like the Super Bowl is today"**: C. Robert Barnett, " The Portsmouth Spartans," *The Coffin Corner,* Vol. 2, No. 10 (1980).

59 **"If they only knew how near our football"**: Dick Cullum, "Carr Wants Team in New Structure. President of Circuit Here—Says All Pro Games Will Go Indoors Some Day, and Boom," unidentified news clip, 1933.

CHAPTER SEVEN: TELEVISION DEBUTS

61 **"spectacular stuff"**: Lou Niss, "Clark's New Subbing Policy Yields Results," *The Brooklyn Daily Eagle,* Oct. 23, 1939.

62 **"close to 50 yards in the air"**: Jim Campbell, "Pro Football's First TV Game, 1939," *Football Digest,* Oct. 1975.

62 **"I didn't know about it"**: Jim Campbell, "Pro Football's First TV Game, 1939," *Football Digest,* Oct. 1975.

62 **"It was late in October"**: Ibid.

62 **"We used two iconoscopes"**: Ibid.

63 **"We decided right away"**: Ibid.

63 **"Living in or near"**: Copy of letter dated Nov. 30, 1939, from Albert Morton, on file at Pro Football Hall of Fame Archives.

63 **"We offered to reimburse him"**: Ibid.

63 **"Who knows?"**: Ibid.

CHAPTER EIGHT: THE T-FORMATION AND THE MAN-IN-MOTION

64 **"I had grown up with the T"**: Halas et al., *Halas by Halas.*

65 **"The consequence was that I"**: Ibid., 136.

65 **"The change," Halas joked later:** Ibid., 139.

65 **"The idea was not to flatten"**: Robert Peterson, *The Early Years of Pro Football* (New York: Oxford University Press, 1997).

66 **"I did a good bit of inventing"**: quantcoach.com/Shaughnessy.htm.

66 **"In all my years in football"**: Andrew Schiff, "The Fascinating History of Jews Who Revolutionized the Game of American Football," *The Times of Israel,* Nov. 26, 2017.

67 **"front-runners, quitters and crybabies"**: Jeff Davis, *Papa Bear: The Life and Legacy of George Halas* (New York: McGraw-Hill, 2005).

67 **"We discussed for hours"**: Halas et al., *Halas by Halas,* 189.

68 **"Gentlemen, this is what George Preston Marshall thinks of you"**: Ibid., 190.

68 **"This is the story of a man"**: Wilfred Smith, "Sid Luckman's Generalship Key to Victory," *Chicago Tribune,* Dec. 9, 1940.

68 **"the second play after"**: Ibid.

68 **"It was the most humiliating"**: George Kirksey, "Bears Take to Redskins Like Honey," *The Columbus Telegram* (Columbus, NE), Dec. 9, 1940.

69 **"Take your Redskins back to Boston"**: "Rabid Rooters Pelt Marshall with Programs," *The Courier-Journal* (Louisville, KY), Dec. 9, 1940.

69 **"Those guys out there quit"**: Kirksey, "Bears Take to Redskins Like Honey."

69 **"The weather was perfect"**: John Thorn, with David Reuther, eds. *The Armchair Quarterbacks* (New York: Charles Scribner's Sons, 1982). Arthur Daley, "Bears 70, Redskins 0," *The New York Times,* Dec. 8, 1940.

CHAPTER NINE: THE NFL'S FIRST COMMISSIONER

70 **"We who have given a good deal of time"**: 1940 NFL press release.

71 **"fair and impartial administration"**: "Carr, President of Football League Dead," *Chicago Tribune,* May 21, 1939.

71 **"pro football's balance wheel"**: Ibid.

71 **"czar"**: Henry McLamore, "Today's Sports Parade," *Shamokin News-Dispatch* (Shamokin, PA), Feb. 2, 1939.

71 **"having to deal with the numbskulls"**: Ibid.

71 **"Why? Did you read"**: Ibid.

72 **"the only contribution Storck"** Author interview with Dan Rooney.

72 **"very accommodating to his hobby"**: NFL meeting minutes, Jul. 22, 1939, p. 26.

73 **"The owners picked three men"**: Walter Byers, "Showdown in Pro Football," *Liberty* magazine, Sept. 14, 1946.

73 **"wasn't even in on the signing"**: "Dissension Is On in the Pro Ranks," *The Cincinnati Enquirer,* Feb. 6, 1941.

73 **"We talked to them by telephone"**: "Pro Majority Defend Action Signing Layden," *Chicago Tribune,* Feb. 6, 1941.

74 **"Layden is the finest available man"**: Ibid.

74 **"The league owes a debt of gratitude"**: Ibid.

74 **"the league should be obligated"**: NFL meeting minutes, 1941.

74 **"the pros have borrowed Notre Dame's"**: Dick Hyland, "Behind the Line," *Los Angeles Times,* Feb. 6, 1941.

75 **"as important and imperative to the life"**: NFL minutes of Publicity Clinic, Aug. 28, 1941.

75 **"more reporter than propagandist"**: Ibid.

75 **"high, dignified plane"**: Ibid.

CHAPTER TEN: A WORLD AT WAR

76 **"We knew something was going on"**: Tony Barnhart, "The 1940's: NFL Goes to War," (reprinted by permission of the *Atlanta Journal-Constitution*), *The Coffin Corner*: Vol. 9, No. 8 (1987).

77 **"the most important meeting since"**: NFL press release, Feb. 28, 1942.

77 **"Until federal authorities decide"**: NFL press release, Mar. 24, 1942.

77 **"From Aristotle's time on down"**: Ibid.

78 **"For professional sports, the easiest method"**: NFL press release, May 13, 1942.

78 **"Football coaches have always been"**: NFL release exclusive to radio, May 7, 1942.

78 **"The bleeding hearts"**: Ibid.

79 **". . . The young man must be toughened"**: Ibid.

80 **"combined two bad teams"**: Interview with Al Wistert, NFL Films, 2004.

81 **"I was educated in America"**: Apr. 3, 1946, Death March *Today in History* blog at WordPress.com.

82 **"It cheered me up,"**: NFL Films Presents—1998, show #7.

82 "Hostilities have ceased": armyhistory.org/mario-tonelli, biography of Mario Tonelli, Jan. 27, 2015.

82 "I was stupid enough to think": NFL Films Presents—1998, show #7.

82 "I'm very grateful for Charley Bidwill": Ibid.

83 "There was antiaircraft fire all around": *Football and America* (Pro Football Hall of Fame publication).

83 "gallantry and intrepidity at the risk of": Congressional Medal of Honor citation.

83 "Jack suffered very little": John Gunn article PFRA quoted in jacklummus .com.

84 "It was horrible": Author interview with Ralph Wilson Jr.

84 "Ships were lying on their sides": Ibid.

84 "I was the first American to see Hiroshima": Ibid.

CHAPTER ELEVEN: THE NFL'S FOUR-YEAR WAR

85 "heads would roll": *PIC Magazine,* Oct. 1946.

86 "I organized the All-America conference because": Joe Hendrickson, "Pro Football War," *Esquire,* Aug. 1945.

86 "Old Navy men say I rooted for the war to last forever": Bob Oates, "He's Calling New Signals, This Time Against Particularly Threatening Foe," *Los Angeles Times,* Apr. 10, 1985.

87 "Anyone could become a great promoter": Byers, "Showdown in Pro Football," *Liberty* magazine, Sept. 14, 1946.

87 "All I know of new leagues": Edward Prell, "Pro Football Co-Operation Is Their Goal," *Chicago Tribune,* Apr. 21, 1945.

87 "the basis for a successful publicity campaign": Byers, "Showdown in Pro Football."

87 "The Chicago front office couldn't": Tommy Holmes, "Topping's Jump May 'Make' New League," *The Brooklyn Daily Eagle,* Nov. 7, 1945.

88 "It seems to me, that": Ibid.

88 "We have been doing business here": Jack Hand, "Disagreement of Field Dates Results in Action," *The Brooklyn Daily Eagle,* Dec. 6, 1945.

88 "We wish them luck": "Mara Burns Over Topping's Shift," *Brooklyn Eagle,* Dec. 6, 1945.

88 "right out of this town": Caswell Adams, "Giants Topping's Pet Peeve as He Discusses Grid Plans," *The Cincinnati Enquirer,* Dec. 31, 1945.

88 "player help": "Topping Puts Screws on New Grid Circuit," *The Pittsburgh Press,* Jan. 6, 1946.

89 "The vagueness and apparent ineptitude": "Elmer Layden, the Pro Grid Chief Quits, as Battle of Rival Leagues Flares," *Albuquerque Journal,* Jan. 12, 1946.

89 "We have been trying to imitate": "Rams, Pro Grid Champions, Will Move to Los Angeles," *The Pittsburgh Press,* Jan. 13, 1946.

89 "It was known that some club owners": Jerry Jurgens, "Bert Bell Named N.F.L. Czar, After Elmer Layden Resigns, Ready to Take on All America" *The Daily Times* (Davenport, IA), Jan. 12, 1946.

89 **"As the commissioner, he steered the league"**: Harry Boyle, "16 Mirrors of Sports," *Pittsburgh Post-Gazette,* Jan. 14, 1946.

89 **"The greatest damage to"**: Arch Ward, "In the Wake of the News," *Chicago Tribune,* Jan. 14, 1946.

90 **"more than one franchise in any city"**: "Elmer Layden, the Pro Grid Chief Quits."

90 **"By doing this, we are fixing"**: Ibid.

91 **"We intend to spare neither money"**: Larry Smith, "Pro Grid Heads Remove Rubber Band from Roll," *Sioux City Journal* (Sioux City, IA), Jul. 31, 1945.

91 **"keeping a watchful eye on the team"**: Bob Oates, "The L.A. Dons: 4 Decades Ago Maverick Football Team Made a Fleeting but Memorable Impact," *Los Angeles Times,* Dec. 26, 1986.

91 **"One night in New York, when the Rockets"**: Bob Oates, "The LA Dons," *The Los Angeles Times,* Dec. 26, 1986.

91 **"We learned later"**: Ibid.

93 **"I have explored every avenue"**: "Ingram Optimistic," *The Cincinnati Enquirer,* Dec. 17, 1948.

93 **"Maybe, we ought to let them"**: "Baltimore Franchise Blocks Merger of Football Leagues," *Hartford Courant,* Dec. 21, 1948.

93 **"common understanding"**: "Loop Moguls Confab Ends in Deadlock," *Democrat and Chronicle* (Rochester, NY), Dec. 21, 1948.

94 **"Look at it from this standpoint"**: "Marshall Glad to Have Colts in New League," *The Baltimore Sun,* Dec. 10, 1949.

95 **"The merger will get the club owners"**: "Pro Football Leagues Merge, End Four-Year War," *Chicago Tribune,* Dec. 10, 1949.

95 **"cast his lot"**: "Ram, Don Presidents Discuss Team Merger," *The Los Angeles Times,* Dec. 10, 1949.

95 **"get out of football"**: "Lindheimer Weighs Offer to Join Rams," *The Los Angeles Times,* Dec. 11, 1949.

95 **"These deals are the results of"**: "Cleveland Browns Get New Part-Owner," *Beckley Post-Herald* (Beckley, WV), Jun. 3, 1950.

95 **"It forced the old league"**: "AAC Life Short, but Turbulent," *Chicago Tribune,* Dec. 10, 1949.

CHAPTER TWELVE: THE CLEVELAND BROWNS' NFL DEBUT

97 **"The Eagles may chase us off"**: "Eagles Favored Over Cleveland," *The San Bernardino County Sun,* Sept. 16, 1950.

97 **"be on hand for"**: Ibid.

98 **"When I was with the [Chicago] Rockets"**: Stan Grosshandler, "All-America Football Conference," *The Coffin Corner,* Vol. 2, No. 7 (1980).

98 **"We never said we could beat the"**: Ralph Bernstein, "Browns Set for Eagles," *The Evening Sun* (Baltimore, MD), Sept. 16, 1950.

98 **"Money"**: Tommy Holmes, "Bert Bell Hails Prosperous Times," *The Brooklyn Daily Eagle,* Sept. 12, 1950.

98 **"I can't see any other difference between"**: "Bell 'Discovers' Grid Browns, *Akron Beacon Journal,* Sept. 13, 1950.

98 **"Not everyone hated the Browns"**: Shelby Strother, *NFL Top 40: The*

Greatest Pro Football Games of All Time (New York: Penguin Group, 1988), 36.

99 **"Brown put teaching into coaching"**: Author interview with Don Shula.

99 **"He brought the classroom"**: Ibid.

99 **"We watched old films"**: Strother, *NFL Top 40*, 36.

99 **"If we play the game we're capable of"**: Ralph Bernstein, "Browns Set for Eagles," *The Evening Sun* (Baltimore), Sept. 16, 1950.

100 **"We know they don't like us"**: Strother, *NFL Top 40*, 36, 37.

100 **"only slightly faster than sound"**: Rick Reilly, "Browns Destroy Eagles, 35–10, in Huge Upset," *Sports Illustrated*, Oct. 16, 1991, si.com/vault/1991/10/16/125163/the-author-returns-to-yesteryear-to-report-on-a-history-making-football-game-browns-destroy-eagles-35-10-in-huge-upset-qb-graham-stars-nfl-champs-embarrassed.

101 **"I think Paul wanted to make a point"**: Strother, *NFL Top 40*, 37.

101 **"We're happy," he said**: "Cleveland Browns Slap Eagles 35-10 for Mythical Grid Title," *The Press Democrat* (Santa Rosa, CA), Sept. 17, 1950.

101 **"act like you've been here before"**: Jerry Izenberg, *Rozelle: A Biography* (Lincoln: University of Nebraska Press, 2014), 48.

101 **"When you play football"**: "Otto Graham Gets French Trophy," *The Philadelphia Inquirer*, Sept. 17, 1950.

101 **"I've been playing with those guys"**: Ibid.

101 **"I never saw a team with so many guns"**: Ibid.

102 **"Graham," Kilroy added, "may be the best"**: .si.com/vault/1991/10/16/125163.

102 **"What a team"**: Lee Linder, "NFL's Commissioner Bert Bell Now Recognizes Browns—Great," *Argus-Leader* (Sioux Falls, SD), Sept. 18, 1950.

102 **"Mind you, I'm not partisan"**: Ibid.

102 **Then, as if suddenly remembering**: Ibid.

102 **"I lived in fear all week"**: Reilly, "Browns Destroy Eagles."

102 **"Four years of ridicule"**: Ibid.

CHAPTER THIRTEEN: THE NFL'S FINAL FAILED FRANCHISES

104 **"fraudulent surrender"**: "Judge Removes Two Pro Grid Clubs from List of Defendants in Suit," *St. Louis Post-Dispatch*, May 20, 1952.

106 **"equality with every other"**: John Chandler, "Collins Says He'll Keep Yank Franchise in N.Y.," *The Evening Sun* (Baltimore), Jan. 16, 1952.

106 **"Baltimore interests expressed"**: Will Grimsley, "NFL Rules Committee Rejects Extra Point Elimination Plan," *Clarion-Ledger* (Jackson, MS), Jan. 17, 1952.

107 **"The Giants now will be the only"**: Will Grimsley, "Texans Attempt Local Flavor for NFL Club," *Daily Press* (Newport News, VA), Jan. 21, 1952.

107 **"We have everything in Texas"**: Patrick Joyce, "Owners of Dallas Texans Say Football Is Natural as Oil-Cotton to State," *The Courier-Gazette* (McKinney, TX), Feb. 21, 1952.

107 **"There is room enough in Texas"**: Joe Horrigan, "Belly Up in Dallas," *The Coffin Corner*, Vol. 7, No. 3, 1985.

107 **"The Texans have not demonstrated":** Jinx Tucker, "Jinx Tucker's Hot Shots," *Waco Tribune-Herald,* Sept. 27, 1952.

108 **"In Texas, Negroes and Whites get along":** Joyce, "Owners of Dallas Texans Say Football Is Natural as Oil-Cotton to State."

108 **"Anticipating heavy demand":** Horrigan, "Belly Up in Dallas."

109 **"The Texans knocked out Jim Crow":** Mickey Herskowitz, "Once Upon a Time in Dallas . . . ," from *More Than a Game,* John Weisbuch, ed. (Englewood Cliffs, NJ: Prentice-Hall, 1974), 96–99.

109 **"go into the stands":** Horrigan, "Belly Up in Dallas."

109 **"We had a good time in spite of everything":** Ibid.

110 **"Once, we ran a couple of plays without":** Ibid.

110 **"Hell, I was a quarterback":** Herskowitz, "Once Upon a Time in Dallas," 96–99.

110 **"There!" he shouted:** Ibid.

110 **"We got all the breaks":** Horrigan, "Belly Up in Dallas."

110 **"I have been talking with the group":** "Baltimore Colts to Return to Pro Grid Wars in 1953," *Daily Press* (Newport News, VA), Dec. 1, 1952.

110 **"reconditioned franchise from":** Ibid.

111 **"the team would not be operated by":** "Baltimore Colts Are Due to Return to Pro Football," *The Daily Times* (Salisbury, MD), Dec. 1, 1952.

CHAPTER FOURTEEN: THE GREATEST GAME EVER PLAYED AND THE LEGEND OF JOHNNY UNITAS

113 **"We out-gutted them":** Norman Miller, "Did Loose Talk Sink Giant Ship," United Press International, Dec. 30, 1958.

114 **"Nobody wanted you guys":** Jack Mann, "Sudden Death in the Afternoon," in *The Armchair Quarterbacks,* 178–186.

114 **"In fourteen years, I heard them all":** Lou Sahadi, *Johnny Unitas: America's Quarterback* (Chicago: Triumph Books, 2004).

114 **"The kids at North Catholic":** Dan Rooney, as told to Andrew E. Masich and David F. Halaas, *Dan Rooney: My 75 Years with the Pittsburgh Steelers and the NFL* (New York: Da Capo Press, 2007), 46.

115 **"When the 1955 NFL Draft took place":** Ibid., 60.

115 **When the ninth round rolled around:** Author interview with Dan Rooney.

116 **"It might have been better":** Dan Rooney, *Dan Rooney: My 75 Years with the Pittsburgh Steelers and the NFL,* 63.

116 **"I always accused Johnny of writing it":** "Unitas Football's Top Athlete '60s," *The Boston Globe,* Feb. 3, 1970.

117 **"So," Ewbank said:** Strother, *NFL Top 40,* 52.

119 **"I told the squad at intermission":** "Out-Gutted Them, Says Colts' Spinney," *Elmira Advertiser* (Elmira, NY), Dec. 29, 1958.

119 **"It was third down, right":** Strother, *NFL Top 40,* 53.

120 **"Big Daddy fell on Gino":** Ibid., 54.

120 **"I made that first down":** "Out-gutted Them, Says Colts' Spinney."

120 **"A lot of players wanted to go for it":** Strother, *NFL Top 40,* 54.

120 **"We need this one":** Ibid., 154.

120 **"We were running what we call":** "Berry's Receptions Click in Most Crucial Moments," *The Daily Times* (Salisbury, MD), Dec. 29, 1958.

120 **"The real dramatics came when the Colts"**: Arthur Daley, "Overtime at the Stadium," *The New York Times,* Dec. 29, 1958.

121 **"We had the game locked up"**: Strother, *NFL Top 40,* 55.

122 **"I gave the guy an extra minute"**: Ibid.

122 **"There was no risk of interception"**: Ibid.

122 **"We just had to win because"**: "5-Year Plan of Ewbank Arrives Early," *Palladium-Item* (Richmond, IN), Dec. 29, 1958.

122 **"We out-gutted them"**: "Out-Gutted Them Says Art Spinney," *The Morning Herald* (Hagerstown, MD), Dec. 29, 1958.

123 **"We were only a few feet and seconds"**: "Colts Bring Maryland First NFL Title, Outlast Giants in Overtime, 23 to 17," *The Morning Herald* (Hagerstown, MD), Dec. 29, 1958.

123 **"I miscalculated"**: "5-Year Plan of Ewbank Arrives Early."

123 **"In the years to come, when our children's children"**: "New York Writers Endorse Colt Fans' Opinion," *The Daily Times* (Salisbury, MD), Dec. 30, 1958.

123 **"We thought he made it"**: "Movies Proof of Right Call in Crucial Play," *The Daily Times* (Salisbury, MD), Dec. 30, 1958.

123 **"The worst part about being hurt"**: Cameron Snyder, "Loop Title Caps Great Colt Year," *The Baltimore Sun,* Dec. 30, 1958.

123 **"If you fire a BB gun"**: Author interview with Gino Marchetti.

123 **"We started the greatest era in the history of the NFL"**: Lou Sahadi, *Johnny Unitas: America's Quarterback* (Triumph Books, 2004), xv.

CHAPTER FIFTEEN: THE "HUNT" FOR A NEW LEAGUE

124 **"How can anyone be proud"**: Michael MacCambridge, *Lamar Hunt: A Life in Sports* (Kansas City, MO: Andrews McMeel Publishing, LLC, 2012), 124.

124 **"I was an amateur photographer and had taken some pictures"**: "Lamar Hunt and the Foolish Club," *Chiefs.com,* April 4, 2015.

124 **"I went to see Commissioner Bert Bell"**: Jeff Miller, *Going Long: The Wild Ten-Year Saga of the Renegade American Football League in the Words of Those Who Lived It* (Chicago: Contemporary Books, 2003), 2.

125 **"It was a one-man thing for a while"**: Ibid., 3.

125 **"We talked about everything"**: Ibid., 3.

125 **"It wasn't until I drove him back to Hobby Airport"**: Randy Covitz and Kent Pulliam, "Chiefs Founder, AFL Pioneer Dies; Sports Visionary Was an Innovative Businessman Who Turned Daydreams into Reality and Transformed the Face of Pro Football," *Kansas City Star,* Dec. 14, 2006.

126 **"The more teams and the more competition"**: "Plans for 2nd Pro Grid League Aired During Senate Hearing," *Democrat and Chronicle* (Rochester, NY), Jul. 29, 1959.

126 **"sat silently in the back of Room 318"**: MacCambridge, *Lamar Hunt,* 97.

127 **"It will take them three or four years"**: "Second Pro Grid Loop Backer Talks with Bell," *Statesman Journal* (Salem, OR), Jul. 31, 1959.

127 **"Lamar, I'll give you the Dallas franchise"**: Miller, *Going Long,* 6.

128 **"make any moves he deemed wise"**: "Dallas Ready, So It Got Early Franchise in NFL," Minnesota *Star Tribune,* Jan. 29, 1960.

128 **"I read in the paper that Lamar Hunt"**: Author interview with Ralph Wilson Jr.

129 **"Bud and I sat down"**: Jack Horrigan, *The Other League: The Fabulous Story of the American Football League* (Chicago: Follett Publishing Company, 1970), 16.

129 **"I'm with you guys one hundred percent"**: Miller, *Going Long,* 12.

130 **"We will be playing football in the American Football League"**: "AFL Completes Player Draft, Awaits Salary War with NFL," *The Journal Times* (Racine, WI), Nov. 24, 1959.

130 **"We were ill prepared"**: Miller, *Going Long,* 12.

131 **"I got in touch with Billy's trainer"**: John McClain, "Bud Adams' AFL Venture More Than Meets the Eye," *Houston Chronicle,* Aug. 9, 2009.

131 **"I was at home at the time"**: Ibid.

131 **"I was driving Nancy's new Cadillac"**: Ibid.

133 **"The only reason for expansion"**: "Marshall to Sue if NFL Expands," Minnesota *Star Tribune,* Jan. 8, 1960.

133 **"I would prefer to see the AFL operate"**: Ibid.

133 **"a culmination of five years of planning"**: Ibid.

133 **"Our intent always has been"**: Ibid.

134 **"I gave my word"**: Author interview with Mike Brown.

134 **"Anyone other than Marshall"**: "Dallas Ready, So It Got Early Franchise in NFL."

134 **"I fought for the conditions and when they passed"**: "NFL Adds Dallas Team," *The Baltimore Sun,* Jan. 29, 1960.

134 **"It took a great load off Halas' shoulders"**: "Dallas Ready, So It Got Early Franchise in NFL."

134 **"In the clutch, the old pro joined up"**: Ibid.

134 **"An act of war"**: "NFL Move Is an Act of War," Minnesota *Star Tribune,* Jan. 29, 1960.

134 **"We are looking into possible courses of action"**: Ibid.

135 **"Antitrust laws are designed to foster competition"**: Ibid.

135 **"I don't know what part"**: MacCambridge, *Lamar Hunt,* 107.

CHAPTER SIXTEEN: A COMPROMISE CANDIDATE, CONGRESS, AND TV

138 **"All we ask is a reasonable facsimile of Bell"**: "Three Big Problems on Agenda," *Detroit Free Press,* Jan. 17, 1960.

138 **"You people are being ridiculous"**: Tex Maule, "The Infighting Was Ridiculous," *Sports Illustrated,* Feb. 8, 1960. si.com/vault/1960/02/08/583717/the-infighting-was-vicious.

139 **"This will never end if we don't do something"**: Izenberg, *Rozelle,* 48.

139 **"I will not vote against Leahy"**: Ibid.

139 **"I just looked at them"**: Ibid., 50.

139 **"You'll grow into the job"**: "Pete Rozelle, 1985 Enshrinee," Pro Football Hall of Fame News Release (#8, 4-1-85).

140 **"As you know already, I come to this job"**: Izenberg, *Rozelle,* 50.

140 **"I may have been picked because"**: Ibid.

140 **"No, of course not. How could I be a compromise candidate?:** "New Czar Rules with Organization," *The Evening Sun* (Baltimore), Sept. 23, 1960.

141 **"continue their monopoly":** "Senior Loop Admits Texans," *Oakland Tribune,* Jan. 29, 1960.

141 **"It's unfortunate that the AFL commissioner":** Ibid.

141 **"Get all the information you can":** "Pete Rozelle, 1985 Enshrinee," Pro Football Hall of Fame News Release (#8, 4 1-85).

141 **"The AFL people crying over the fight":** "Back at Foss," *The Minneapolis Star,* Jan. 29, 1960.

143 **"With only seven home games":** "NFL Wrestles Problem of Who Will Televise Games," *The Ogden Standard Examiner,* Feb. 19, 1961.

143 **"We can't let that happen":** Ibid.

143 **"The big-city people":** Phil Patton, *Razzle Dazzle: The Curious Marriage of Television & Football* (Garden City, NY: The Dial Press, 1984), 55.

143 **"I had a big argument with Reeves":** Rooney, *Dan Rooney: My 75 Years with the Pittsburgh Steelers and the NFL,* 97.

145 **"I didn't think it would go this high":** "CBS Obtains Video Rights," *The Baltimore Sun,* Dec. 25, 1964.

145 **"What Pete Rozelle did with television receipts,"** Bob Carter, "Rozelle Made NFL What It Is Today," ESPN.com.

CHAPTER SEVENTEEN: TOUGH DECISIONS

146 **"member of a midwestern franchise":** Jerry Izenberg, *Rozelle: A Biography* (Lincoln: University of Nebraska Press, 2014), 67.

147 **"Gossip columnists have come up with the disturbing rumors":** "NFL Betting Scandal Being Probed," *Journal and Courier* (Lafayette, IN), Jan. 5, 1963.

147 **"fraternization with the":** Ibid.

147 **"Our office maintains constant surveillance":** Ibid.

147 **"concrete developments":** "Outside Associations of NFL Players Are Investigated," *Leader-Telegram* (Eau Claire, WI), Jan. 8, 1963.

148 **"Phil never bet on a game in his life":** "Halas Gives Handler Okay," *The Baltimore Sun,* Jan. 11, 1963.

148 **"I've done nothing wrong":** "Bears' Fullback Admits Lie Test," *The Times Herald,* Jan. 6, 1963.

148 **Casares said he took the tests:** Ibid.

148 **"All I got out of it is this rotten publicity":** Ibid.

149 **"never bet more than a pack of":** "Lions' Alex Karras Admits NFL Betting," *The Times and Democrat* (Orangeburg, SC), Jan. 17, 1963.

149 **"If you observe how all governmental":** "Colts' Owner Probed on Bets, Denies Guilt," *The Philadelphia Inquirer,* Jan. 19, 1963.

149 **"If I violate such pledges I will not get cooperation":** Ibid.

149 **"There is absolutely no evidence":** Tex Maule, "Players Are Not Just People, *Sports Illustrated,* Apr. 29, 1963. si.com/nfl/2015/05/12/si-vault-paul -hornung-alex-karras-pete-rozelle.

150 "**I was sort of expecting this**": "Hornung's Fate Up to Him: Rozelle," *Chicago Tribune*, Apr. 18, 1963.

150 "**I made a terrible mistake**": Ibid.

150 "**I realized it wasn't**": Ibid.

150 "**I haven't done anything that I'm ashamed of**": Ibid.

150 "**should be put in its proper perspective**": Ibid.

150 "**Joe Schmidt is a gentleman**": Murray Olderman, "How Rozelle Handled NFL's Gambling Scandal," *Standard-Speaker* (Hazleton, PA), Apr. 20, 1963.

150 "**I thought about it at length**": Maule, "Players Are Not Just People."

151 "**continuing, not casual**": Ibid.

151 "**mingling with known hoodlums**": "NFL Suspends Karras, Hornung for Gambling," *The Times* (Shreveport, LA), Apr. 18, 1963.

152 "**The commissioner had no other alternative**": "Pro Football Backs NFL Commissioner on Suspensions," *The La Crosse Tribune*, Apr. 18, 1963.

152 "**decisive and forceful action**": Ibid.

152 "**as a boy playing his part**": Kenneth Rudeen, "Sportsman of the Year: Pete Rozelle," *Sports Illustrated*, Jan. 6, 1964. baltimoresun.com/news/bs-xpm -1996-12-07-1996342065-story.html.

152 "**Each of the big professional sports in America**": Maule, "Players Are Not Just People."

152 "**does not seem to fit this**": Ibid.

152 "**In his strength may lie**": Ibid.

153 "**Pete thought Salinger was right**": Rooney, *Dan Rooney: My 75 Years with the Pittsburgh Steelers and the NFL*, 104.

153 "**I told him, 'Okay, Pete, I disagree, but I'll support you.'**" Ibid., 104.

154 "**It has been traditional in sports**": "NFL Games to Be Played 'In Tradition,' Rozelle Says," *Green Bay Press-Gazette*, Nov. 23, 1963.

154 "**made the right decision**": Izenberg, *Rozelle*, 93.

154 "**Was it the money?**" Milton Gross, "Fan Just Didn't Know Why He Went to Football Game," *The Star Press* (Muncie, IN), Nov. 27, 1963.

154 "**Money had nothing to do with it**": Ibid.

154 "**I went to church**": Ibid.

154 "**Nobody wanted to play**": Charles P. Pierce, "Black Sunday: The NFL Plays After JFK's Assassination, *Sports Illustrated*, Nov. 19, 2014, si.com/ nfl/2014/11/19/black-sunday-nfl-plays-after-jfks-assassination.

155 "**In the civilized world, it was a day of mourning**": Red Smith Views of Sport, *The Herald Examiner*, Nov. 25, 1963.

155 "**But down deep in his heart**": Author interview with Joe Browne.

CHAPTER EIGHTEEN: A CEASE-FIRE AND A MERGER

156 "**The first three years the NFL didn't pay that much attention**": Horrigan, *The Other League*, 20.

156 "**take them [the AFL] three or four years to build**": "Second Pro Grid Loop Backer Talks with Bell," *Statesman Journal* (Salem, OR), Jul. 31, 1959.

157 "**I remember that first tryout camp we had**": Horrigan, *The Other League*, 20.

157 **"If we don't make it here"**: Ibid.

157 **"Wayne, if you drop out, this league will fail"**: Author interview with Ralph Wilson Jr.

157 **"I never had anything to do with operating"**: Ibid.

158 **"We weren't prepared to lose that kind of money"**: Michael MacCambridge, *Lamar Hunt: A Life in Sports* (Kansas City, MO: Andrews McMeel Publishing, LLC, 2021), 119.

158 **"A man's ego can be a laughable thing"**: Dick Young, New York *Daily News,* Nov. 13, 1962.

158 **"wealthy executives"**: "Five Executives Buy Bankrupt New York Titans," *Palladium-Item* (Richmond, IN), Mar. 16, 1963.

158 **"one of the greatest sports groups in the world"**: Jerry Nason, "Sullivan Hails Titans Owners," *The Boston Globe,* Mar. 16, 1963.

158 **"Football is just like show business"**: Marty Fischbein, "Sports Angles" *Asbury Park Press* (Asbury Park, NJ), Sept. 8, 1963.

159 **"Everything will get better from here"**: "AFL Turned Corner This Year," *Mt. Vernon Register-News* (Mt. Vernon, IL), Dec. 20, 1962.

159 **"would have a serious problem with rookies"**: Izenberg, *Rozelle,* 104.

159 **"With the Hornung case behind us"**: Ibid.

159 **"I've been babysitting for about ten days"**: Wendell Smith, "An Admirer of Coach Halas, for Many Years, Sayers Signs with Bears . . . Galimore's 'Eleven,'" *The Pittsburgh Courier,* Dec. 12, 1964.

160 **"I was just ordered to keep him in the NFL"**: Charles Chamberlain, "Task Force in NFL Assigned to Sign Talent": *The Gettysburg Times,* Dec. 2, 1964.

160 **"Operation Hand-Holding"**: Horrigan, *The Other League,* 24.

160 **"The biggest player contract"**: "Namath Signs $400,000 Pact," *The Morning Call* (Allentown, PA), Jan. 3, 1965.

160 **"Tell Nobis to sign"**: "Astronaut Tells Nobis to Sign with Houston 11," *The Star Press* (Muncie, IN), Dec. 12, 1965.

161 **"in the neighborhood of a couple"**: ajc.com/sports/. the-first-falcon-tommy-nobis-was-epic-and-barely-made-atlanta.

161 **"My family and I weren't used to that"**: McDonough, et al., *75 Seasons,* 201.

161 **"I shudder when I think"**: "Red Grange Fears for Namath," *The Fresno Bee,* Jan. 10, 1965.

161 **"The bidding wars were ruining us"**: Rooney, *Dan Rooney: My 75 Years with the Pittsburgh Steelers and the NFL,* 108.

162 **"I think good judgment was not used"**: Halas et al., *Halas by Halas.*

162 **"We have to have it"**: Author interview with Dan Rooney.

162 **"I went up there"**: Author interview with Ralph Wilson Jr.

163 **"until things softened up"**: Ibid.

163 **"Carroll was the one who came"**: Ibid.

163 **"We agreed to meet at the Texas Rangers"**: MacCambridge, *Lamar Hunt.*

163 **"As we learned here"**: George Ross, "Davis' Parting Words: Retain Pride," *Oakland Tribune,* Apr. 21, 1966.

164 **"Give us about three months to get organized"**: Horrigan, *The Other League,* 29.

164 **"blow up"**: MacCambridge, *Lamar Hunt,* 119.

166 **"about the only thing the National Football League had"**: Don Weiss, with Chuck Day, *The Making of the Super Bowl: The Inside Story of the World's Greatest Sporting Event* (Chicago: Contemporary Books, 2002).

168 **"The AFL was very firm that they"**: Author interview with Dan Rooney.

168 **"I would not have moved unless"**: "Rozelle Delayed Remap Word for 21 Hours in Hope of Making 'Package,'" *Green Bay Press-Gazette,* May 12, 1969.

168 **"I can't see us moving"**: Author interview with Dan Rooney.

168 **"I considered Wellington like my big brother"**: Ibid.

168 **"He [Rozelle] hands me a piece of paper"**: Ibid.

169 **"He [Modell] didn't do it because he's a martyr"**: Milton Richman, "Modell Unexpected Hero of Realignment," *Green Bay Press-Gazette,* May 12, 1969.

169 **"I just feel that it's all"**: Michael MacCambridge, *America's Game: The Epic Story of How Pro Football Captured a Nation* (New York: Random House, 2004), 258.

CHAPTER NINETEEN: SUPER BOWLS I–IV

170 **"Much talking has been done of late"**: AFL Commissioner Joe Foss wrote to NFL Commissioner Pete Rozelle in a letter dated December 6, 1963.

170 **"If the NFL had paid attention to Ole Harry's"**: Horrigan, *The Other League,* 24.

171 **"Winning is all I ever think of"**: Jack Lindberg. "Nice Guys Sometimes Finish First," New York *Daily News,* Jan. 15, 1967.

171 **"I don't ever recall any game"**: Ibid.

172 **"When he says, 'sit down' "**: John Crittenden, "The Book on Vince Lombardi," *The Miami News,* Jan. 9, 1968.

172 **"If Hank Stram were as smart as"**: Ibid.

172 **"it was time to settle it on grass"**: Bill Bryson, "No Fraud," *Des Moines Tribune,* Mar. 16, 1967.

173 **"I haven't played enough to be in shape"**: Ibid.

173 **"I told him, 'We got it' "**: Ibid.

173 **"I thought Kansas City's Len Dawson"**: "What They Said," *Des Moines Tribune,* Jan. 16, 1967.

173 **"They're a good football team"**: Vince Lombardi's postgame interview audio recording, Pro Football Hall of Fame Archives.

173 **"That's what you wanted me to say"**: Ibid.

174 **"If there is one difference"**: Ibid.

174 **"fantastic" and said they "didn't have a weak spot"**: "Packers, Raiders Mum," *The Troy Record,* Jan. 10, 1968.

174 **"There's no doubt"**: Ibid.

174 **"I never have gone into a game"**: Lee Remmel, "Packers Roster May Reach 39 by Super Bowl Kickoff," *Green Bay Press-Gazette,* Jan. 11, 1968.

175 **"Let's play the last thirty minutes"**: "Could Be It for Lombardi," *San Mateo Times,* Jan. 15, 1968, p. 22.

175 **"What Jerry said at halftime moved us all"**: Ibid.

175 **"Maybe Kansas City had better personnel"**: Larry Harris, "Raiders Better

Than Chiefs, but Still No Match for G.B.," *The Evening Sun* (Baltimore, MD), Jan. 15, 1968.

175 **"as good as":** Pat Livingston, "Raiders Cry Rematch After Super Bowl Mismatch," *The Pittsburgh Press*, Jan. 15, 1968.

176 **"I've got no special":** Ron Reid. "Green Bay Awes Raider Quarterback," *The Times* (San Mateo, CA), Jan. 15, 1968.

176 **"We're going to win Sunday":** Joe Willie Namath with Dick Schaap, "Namath Relished Colt Meeting," *The Palm Beach Post*, Nov. 21, 1969.

176 **"I think he was underpaid":** Charles Nobles, "Sonny Werblin: A Prophet with Honor," *The Miami News*, Jan. 4, 1969.

176 **"That meant George Sauer":** Strother, *NFL Top 40*, 101.

177 **"I had a sore hamstring":** Jim Sargent, "Don Maynard, Best Big-Time Receiver for New York's Titans and Jets," *The Coffin Corner:* Vol. 27, No. 1 (2005).

177 **"The rest of the game":** Strother, *NFL Top 40*, 102.

177 **"I call that smart football":** Sargent, "Don Maynard, Best Big-Time Receiver for New York's Titans and Jets."

177 **"They looked vulnerable on defense":** Strother, *NFL Top 40*, 101.

178 **"We were simply lucky":** Ibid., 102.

178 **"Get something going for us":** Ibid.,103.

178 **"All of a sudden I was":** Ibid.

179 **"Are you one of those NFL writers":** "AFL Now Here to Stay," *The News-Palladium* (Benton Harbor, MI), Jan. 13, 1969.

179 **"It's different than when":** Will Grimsley, "Stram Says Chiefs' Attitude 'Excellent,'" *The Journal and Courier* (Lafayette, IN), Jan. 9, 1970.

180 **"The mystery is gone now":** *Shreveport Times,* Fri, Jan. 9, 1970.

180 **"extensive interviews over":** Weiss, with Chuck Day, *The Making of the Super Bowl,* 170.

180 **"without foundation":** Ibid.

180 **"he had done nothing wrong":** Jack Crittenden, "Dawson, Not Huntley-Brinkley Wind Up as MVP," *The Miami News,* Jan. 12, 1970.

180 **"I told Lenny what the president said":** "Nixon Clears Dawson," New York *Daily News*, Jan. 12, 1970.

180 **"Whenever I looked at him":** "Super Pressure Keep Super Dawson Keyed for Kansas City Triumph," *The Manhattan Mercury* (Manhattan, KS), Jan. 12, 1970.

181 **"We line up in basic formations":** "1969: Super Bowl IV—Kansas City vs Minnesota Vikings," *Golden Football Magazine,* goldenrankings.com.

181 **"Defense wins football games":** "Nothing Fancy about Vike Offense," *Press Democrat* (Santa Rosa, CA), Jan. 11, 1970.

182 **"The mighty Vikes' ground attack":** Jack Sell, "Lenny Guides Chiefs to 23–7 Super Victory," *Pittsburgh Post-Gazette*, Jan. 12, 1970.

182 **"That thing was just a little pass":** Strother, *NFL Top 40*, 107.

182 **"I think there always will":** "Chiefs, Conquering Heroes, Fly Home 'Satisfied' With Victory," *The Indianapolis Star*, Jan. 13, 1970.

183 **"This is the last year for":** Jim O'Brien, "'We showed the doubters, played for ourselves'—Bell," *The Miami News,* Jan. 12, 1970.

183 **"The entire week was an ordeal":** "Dawson's Work Is Hailed," *Pittsburgh Post-Gazette*, Jan. 12, 1970.

183 **"It's a satisfying thing":** Lew Ferguson, "Kansas City Fans Greet Chiefs with Open Arms," *Asheville Citizens Times,* Jan. 13, 1970.

CHAPTER TWENTY: *MONDAY NIGHT FOOTBALL*

186 **"Arledge knew better than anybody":** Marc Gunther and Bill Carter, *Monday Night Mayhem: The Inside Story of ABC's Monday Night Football* (New York: Beech Tree Books, 1988), 31.

186 **"We could reach more women":** Charles Maher, "The Next Problem," *The Los Angeles Times,* Mar. 28, 1969.

187 **"We wanted to show people":** McDonough, *75 Seasons,* 243.

188 **"What do people talk about":** "Monday Nights Won't Be the Same," *The Daily Tribune* (Wisconsin Rapids, WI), Dec. 28, 2005.

188 **"If Bud Grant and my old coach":** Gunther and Carter, *Monday Night Mayhem,* 77.

188 **"the largest sports broadcasting rights package":** Meeting minutes from NFL Owners Meeting, Mar. 17–21, 1970.

CHAPTER TWENTY-ONE: THE IMMACULATE RECEPTION

190 **"I had dinner with Wellington Mara":** Dan Rooney, as told to Andrew E. Masich and David F. Halaas, *Dan Rooney: My 75 Years with the Pittsburgh Steelers and the NFL* (New York: Da Capo Press, 2007), 111.

191 **"The organization needed a strong head coach":** Ibid., 117.

191 **"Steelers select . . . Joe Who":** Rooney, *Dan Rooney,* 130.

192 **"didn't like the way the Steelers did business":** Ibid., 134.

192 **"I don't think you'll ever be a winner":** Ibid.

193 **"Well," Rooney said, "why don't you join us, scout for us?":** Ibid.

193 **"From the beginning," Rooney said:** Ibid., 135.

193 **"The thing that really put us over the top was Franco Harris":** Author interview with Joe Greene.

194 **"Late in the game, with probably a minute or so to play":** Author interview with Joe Greene.

195 **"I didn't have to pep 'em up":** Pat Livingston, "Steelers '72: Never Say Die," *The Pittsburgh Press,* Dec. 24, 1972.

196 **"I think I was probably ten yards away around the fifty":** Author interview with Joe Greene.

196 **"Well, you have to call what you saw":** Rooney, *Dan Rooney,* 4.

196 **"I was dazed":** Bob Smizik, "Frenchy Simply Dazed by It All," *The Pittsburgh Press,* Dec. 24, 1972.

197 **"I was trying to figure out how":** Ibid.

197 **"If the officials really knew what happened":** Jeff Samuels, "Stunned Raiders Swear They Should Have Won," *The Pittsburgh Press,* Dec. 24, 1972.

197 **"The locker room was so crowded":** Author interview with Joe Greene.

197 **"When I saw him come in":** Ibid.

198 **"It's hard to explain" he said, "how much the Steelers meant":** Rooney, *Dan Rooney,* 146.

198 **"Well, if Frenchy didn't touch the ball":** Ibid., 5.

CHAPTER TWENTY-TWO: A STARTING QUARTERBACK

199 **"The Buffalo Bills thought so much"**: Author interview with James Harris.

199 **"For various reasons, Negro quarterbacks"**: "Grambling's Robinson Billing Harris as Pro Quarterback," *Shreveport Times,* Jan. 21, 1969.

201 **"I'd beaten Buffalo once"**: William C. Rhoden, *Third and a Mile: The Trials and Triumphs of the Black Quarterback* (New York: ESPN Books, 2007), 94.

201 **"accept a Negro quarterback"**: "Grambling's Robinson Billing Harris as Pro Quarterback," *Shreveport Times,* Jan. 21, 1969.

202 **"I think he is the finest quarterback in the nation"**: Ibid.

202 **"He had one of the strongest arms of anybody"**: Ibid.

202 **"With Harris, though"**: Ibid.

202 **"I heard Martin Luther King say"**: Rhoden, *Third and a Mile,* 104.

203 **"He told me that if I didn't try"**: Jason Reid, "James 'Shack' Harris Is Prominent on List of Ground-breaking Quarterbacks," *The Undefeated,* Oct. 12, 2017.

203 **"I'd never had an open conversation"**: Author interview with James Harris.

203 **"Your coach wants too much"**: Ibid.

203 **"I called Coach Robinson"**: Rhoden, *Third and a Mile,* 110.

203 **"In those days"**: Ibid., 111.

204 **"Right now, Harris is doing the best job"**: "The Bills Could But . . .," *Democrat and Chronicle* (Rochester, NY), Sept. 14, 1969.

204 **"If I start I'll do my best"**: Ibid.

205 **"Don't worry," Namath told him:** Author interview with James Harris.

205 **"I was struggling"**: Rhoden, *Third and a Mile,* 116.

206 **"At first, I tried to stay in shape"**: Steve Wulf, "All Hell Broke Loose," ESPN.com, Jan. 20, 2014, espn.com/nfl/story/_/id/10294156/in-1974-james-harris-became-first-black-qb-start-playoff-game-espn-magazine.

206 **"I was trying to figure out"**: Ibid.

206 **"When coach Robinson called he was happy"**: Ibid.

207 **"But it still wasn't enough"**: Author interview with James Harris.

207 **"Chuck Knox was supportive"**: Rhoden, *Third and a Mile,* 124.

207 **"Coach [Ray] Perkins gave me a scouting job"**: Ibid., 125.

208 **"I was a huge Rams fan"**: Wulf, "All Hell Broke Loose."

208 **"Let me tell you about James Harris"**: Reid, "James 'Shack' Harris Is Prominent."

208 **"Not really"**: Wulf, "All Hell Broke Loose."

208 **"I only hoped that my play"**: Author interview with James Harris.

CHAPTER TWENTY-THREE: THE PERFECT COACH FOR A PERFECT SEASON

209 **"Shula, you know what your problem is?"**: NFL Films, "Ray Nitschke Luncheon," July 25, 1997.

209 **"Otto Graham was my hero of all heroes"**: Author interview with Don Shula.

209 **"After I was drafted, I didn't hear"**: Ibid.

209 **"I get invited into his office"**: Ibid.

210 **"He would—in different ways"**: Ibid.

210 **"I'll never forget in one of our scrimmages"**: Ibid.

210 **"I'm in a drugstore":** Ibid.

211 **"He spent half an hour":** Ibid.

211 **"If somebody looked like":** Ibid.

212 **"It was tough":** Ibid.

212 **"I had two and three and four":** Ibid.

212 **"He [Wilson] was just a great guy":** Ibid.

213 **"I just wish you would have told me":** Ibid.

213 **"He was probably right":** Ibid.

213 **"hard work equals":** Evan Grant, "Dolphins' Don Is Gone," *Florida Today* (Cocoa, FL), Jan. 6, 1996.

214 **"Sure, luck means a lot in":** Ibid.

214 **"Anytime that he has been":** Ibid.

215 **"Each week he's getting more and more":** "Dolphins Decide to Go with Earl," *News-Press* (Fort Myers, FL), Dec. 27, 1972.

215 **"You know you've done it before":** Jeff Samuels, "Morrall on Hot Seat Again," *Pittsburgh Post-Gazette,* Dec. 31, 1972.

216 **"Do you think you're ready":** Joe Falls, "Dolphin Punter Has OK to Run Ball Anytime—Shula," *Detroit Free Press,* Jan. 1, 1973.

216 **"We just drove on them":** Ibid.

217 **"We're going for 17-0":** "Fake Punt Not Planned," *The Montana Standard* (Butte, MT), Jan. 1, 1973.

217 **"would scheme for the edge":** Hubert Mizel, "Dolphins, Skins Battle Today for World Title," *Tampa Tribune,* Jan. 14, 1973.

217 **"Miami is the best team in history":** Ibid.

217 **"Miami has the finest three-man rushing bunch":** Ibid.

217 **"I'm honored George thinks so much":** Ibid.

217 **"the most lopsided seven-point victory":** John Crittenden, "The Greatest Team Ever to Play Football," *The Miami News,* January 15, 1973.

218 **"Fernandez was all over the field":** Ibid.

218 **"Our objective," said Warfield:** Al Levine, "Unprecedented Season Ends with Title, 14–7," *The Miami News,* Jan. 15, 1973.

218 **"Shula's an absolute winner":** Crittenden, "The Greatest Team Ever to Play Football."

CHAPTER TWENTY-FOUR: A RULES CHANGE, AND THE DECADE OF THE RUNNING BACK

222 **"Campbell scored four touchdowns":** David Israel, "Four Campbell TDs Rush Oilers Past Dazzled Miami," *Chicago Tribune,* Nov. 21, 1978.

223 **"He's so humble":** Tom Greer, "Campbell Souper, Oilers Top Miami," *Philadelphia Daily News,* Nov. 21, 1978.

CHAPTER TWENTY-FIVE: "SUPER" DEFENSES

225 **"A dominating defense became as vital":** Rick Gosselin, "The 1970's Defense Wins Championships," in *The Pro Football Hall of Fame 50th Anniversary Book: Where Greatness Lives,* eds. Joe Horrigan and John Thorn (New York: Grand Central Publishing, 2012), 153–180.

226 **"I got knocked down on the play"**: "Here's the History of the NFL's 'Hail Mary' Pass on Its 41st Anniversary," ABC-7 News (San Francisco), Dec. 28, 2016, abc30.com/sports/how-the-hail-mary-football-pass-got-its-name/1138071/.

226 **"If you play perfect offense"**: Hubert Mizell, "Coaches Aren't Dull; Teams May Be," *Tampa Bay Times,* Jan. 17, 1976.

226 **"You have to first avoid losing"**: Ibid.

226 **"Nobody gets to the Super Bowl without a super defense"**: Ibid.

228 **"If it ends up 7-3 on Sunday"**: Ibid.

228 **"I guess the dullness of the game depends"**: Ibid.

228 **"That blocked punt changed the momentum"**: Al Abrams, "At Long Last—A Super Win," *Pittsburgh Post-Gazette,* Jan. 19, 1976.

229 **"We already had botched"**: Vito Stellino, "Super Steelers Shatter Cowboys," *Pittsburgh Post-Gazette,* Jan. 19, 1976.

230 **"They gave up field position"**: "Noll Decision Against Punt a Good Call?," *Honolulu Star-Bulletin,* Jan. 19, 1976.

230 **"Noll's always had a lot of"**: Ibid.

230 **"I was really worried"**: "Block Punt Risk Reason for Fourth Down Play," *The Courier Express* (Dubois, PA), Jan. 18, 1976.

230 **"That was the most interesting game"**: Ibid.

230 **"I leave those judgments to"**: McDonough, Will, et al., *75 Seasons: The Complete Story of the National Football League, 1920–1975* (Atlanta: Turner Publishing, Inc., 1994).

CHAPTER TWENTY-SIX: ROZELLE FIGHTS THROUGH THE NFL'S LOST DECADE

232 **"I believe that any organization that sold"**: "Raiders-Oakland Marriage Seen at End," *Star-Gazette* (Elmira, NY), Jan. 18, 1980.

233 **"Maybe Al Davis will try"**: Ibid.

233 **"I reserve the right to move"**: Ibid.

233 **"We were dressed and ready"**: Author interview with Jay Moyer.

233 **"He [Davis] was loudly opposed"**: Dave Anderson, "Davis-Rozelle Firefight Could Engulf NFL," *The New York Times,* Dec. 21, 1980.

234 **"take any actions available"**: "Coliseum Commission Offers $15 million," *The Petaluma Argus-Courier* (Petaluma, CA), Jan. 19, 1980.

234 **"a business conspiracy"**: "Raiders Move Turned Down at NFL Owners' Meeting," *Los Angeles Times,* Mar. 11, 1980.

234 **"take the only other remedy open to us"**: Ibid.

234 **"just because the owner of the team"**: Author interview with Jay Moyer.

234 **"We certainly lost this round"**: "Jury Says Davis Can Move Raiders to L.A.," *Arizona Daily Star,* May 8, 1982.

235 **"We said 'hands off' "**: Author interview with Jay Moyer.

236 **"The key will be how"**: "Pete Rozelle: On the Record," *The Palm Beach Post,* Jan. 19, 1980.

236 **"That aggravated Ed Garvey"**: Author interview with Jay Moyer.

236 **"Ed always tried"**: Ibid.

236 **"Ed banged his head against"**: Ibid.

237 **"The NFL owners could not have found"**: "John M. Donlan: Executive Director, NFL Management Council," UPI Archives, Sept. 20, 1982.

238 **"Upshaw said that Schramm"**: Rich Hoffman, "NFL Talks More Unsettled," *Philadelphia Daily News,* Sept. 25, 1987.

238 **"We are the ranchers"**: Author interview with Dan Rooney.

238 **"Gene and I"**: Ibid.

239 **"I wanted to negotiate this thing"**: Rooney, *Dan Rooney,* 231.

240 **"When you have to compete"**: Curt Sylvester, "If Money Talks, USFL Will Out-shout Cynics," *Detroit Free Press,* Jun. 13, 1982.

241 **"Commissioner Rozelle had secured"**: Author interview with Paul Tagliabue.

241 **"I think he [Walker] has made"**: Mike Tierney, "What Does This Mean to the NFL . . . ," *St. Petersburg Times,* Feb. 24, 1983.

241 **"I think we're more ready"**: Dave Schreiber, "What This Means to the USFL," *St. Petersburg Times,* Feb. 24, 1983.

242 **"I don't ever recall him"**: Author interview with Jay Moyer.

243 **"There is a lot of talk about"**: Vito Stellino, "USFL Is Seeking Identity, Survival Through '87 Season," *The Baltimore Sun,* Aug. 24, 1984.

243 **"They were cagy about their"**: Author interview with Jay Moyer.

243 **"The United States Football League suit"**: "NFL Accused of Setting Up Secret Unit to Put USFL Out of Business," *St. Petersburg Times,* Oct. 19, 1984.

243 **"Antitrust litigation has been a part"**: Ibid.

243 **"treble-damage antitrust lawsuits"**: Ibid.

243 **"recouped in full with treble damages"**: Hal Bock, "Trump Blames Rozelle for USFL's Loss of $100 Million," Associated Press, Oct. 19, 1984.

243 **"single most important"**: Ibid.

244 **"sham claim"**: Author interview with Paul Tagliabue.

244 **"Paul was very levelheaded"**: Author interview with Jay Moyer.

244 **"No question," Moyer said**: Ibid.

245 **"completely hogwash"**: Author interview with Paul Tagliabue.

245 **"At least in Los Angeles he was"**: Dave Anderson, "USFL on Death Bed," *The New York Times,* Jul. 31, 1986.

245 **"He is trying to get into the NFL"**: Ibid.

245 **"about as resounding a victory as you could get"**: Author interview with Paul Tagliabue.

245 **"The USFL," Rozelle said at the time**: John Powers, "USFL Wins $1 in Antitrust Decision," *The Boston Globe,* Jul. 30, 1986.

245 **"great moral victory"**: Ibid.

245 **"It's like a death in the family"**: Ibid.

246 **"Without substantial damages"**: Dave Anderson, "It's the 4th Quarter and $1 Won't Buy Trump or the USFL More Time," *The New York Times,* Jul. 30, 1986.

246 **"sought through the court decree"**: "The U.S. Football League Lost Its Appeal for a . . . ," UPI Archives, Mar. 10, 1988.

246 **"had to carry fifty years of NFL history"**: Author interview with Jay Moyer.

246 **"the train stayed on the tracks"**: Ibid.

246 **"I can't find a weakness in his leadership"**: Ibid.

CHAPTER TWENTY-SEVEN: THE 49ERS STRIKE GOLD

249 **"Honest to God, within ten minutes"**: Gary Myers, *The Catch: One Play, Two Dynasties, and the Game That Changed the NFL* (New York: Crown Publishers, 2009), 34.

250 **"he was from California"**: Ron Borges, "Walsh Is the Old Master," *The Boston Globe,* Jan. 22, 1989.

250 **"The way it was done was not"**: Sam Farmer, "49ers Coach Reshaped Football," *Los Angeles Times,* Jul. 31, 2007.

252 **"What do you think of that"**: Ira Miller, "The 1970's Defense Wins Championships," in *The Pro Football Hall of Fame 50th Anniversary Book: Where Greatness Lives,* eds. Joe Horrigan and John Thorn (New York: Grand Central Publishing, 2012), 181–206.

252 **"It is an umbrella term"**: Randy Riggs, "There's Something in the Air at Nebraska—Footballs," *Austin American-Statesman,* Sept. 1, 2004.

252 **"What I have is recognition"**: Ron Borges, "Montana Wins Mind Games," *The Boston Globe,* Jan. 26, 1990.

253 **"If we make the same mistakes"**: "Cowboys Want to Abolish Their Cowboy Jinx in the Playoffs," *Tampa Bay Times,* Jan. 5, 1982.

253 **"They didn't respect us"**: Myers, *The Catch,* 4.

253 **"more for its dramatic moments"**: Ibid.

254 **"Eighty-nine yards to go"**: Will McDonough et al., *75 Seasons,* 250.

254 **"Bill never lets a quarterback"**: "Smart Quarterbacks Listen Closely When This Coach Discusses Offense," *The Philadelphia Inquirer,* Jan. 10, 1982.

255 **"I couldn't see anyone except"**: Strother, *NFL Top 40,* 177.

255 **"My job was to find Joe"**: McDonough et al., *75 Seasons,* 250.

255 **"The throw was high"**: Steve Wilstein, "Catch It, Dwight, Catch It," *Reno Gazette-Journal,* Jan. 11, 1982.

255 **"It was unbelievable"**: Ibid.

255 **"All I know is that when"**: "The San Francisco 49ers Are in the Super Bowl," *Ukiah Daily Journal* (Ukiah, CA), Jan. 11, 1982.

256 **"It was a hell of a play"**: "Dallas Shows Its Class in Defeat," *The San Francisco Examiner,* Jan. 11, 1982.

CHAPTER TWENTY-EIGHT: TAGS! YOU'RE IT

257 **"Our task will be to try"**: "Rozelle Is Praised by League Notables," *The Philadelphia Inquirer,* Mar. 23, 1989.

257 **"He [Rozelle] had the unique ability"**: Ibid.

257 **"At every turn there are new"**: Bill Lyon, "He's Had Fill of Football," *The Philadelphia Inquirer,* Mar. 23, 1989.

258 **"What does Paul think?"**: "Rozelle Relied on Successor," Minnesota *Star Tribune,* Oct. 27, 1989.

258 **"He has taken a very low profile"**: "NFL Owners Finally Agree: It's Tagliabue," Minnesota *Star Tribune,* Oct. 27, 1989.

259 **"I called Commissioner Rozelle and said"**: Author interview with Paul Tagliabue.

259 **"Just don't you worry about it"**: Ibid.

260 **"I was afraid we were going to lose"**: Steve Hubbard, "Rooney Key Figure in Tagliabue Vote," *Pittsburgh Press,* Oct. 27, 1989.

260 **"Hey, if we keep fooling around"**: Ibid.

260 **"I don't believe there was any question"**: Don Pierson, "Tagliabue Emerges as NFL Chief," *Chicago Tribune,* Oct. 27, 1989.

260 **"The threat of losing both candidates"**: Ibid.

260 **"The truth of the matter is that"**: Ibid.

260 **"To me, this is a minor problem"**: Ibid.

261 **"Al said, 'Look, we're going'"**: Interview with Paul Tagliabue on *Talk of Fame Sports Network,* Feb. 1, 2017.

261 **"you slap him back twice as hard"**: Author interview with Paul Tagliabue.

261 **"Stop slapping him in the head"**: Ibid.

261 **"It was good advice"**: Interview with Paul Tagliabue on *Talk of Fame Sports Network,* Feb. 1, 2017.

261 **"I've never believed that"**: "Rozelle Relied on Successor."

262 **"If you talked to the management council"**: Author interview with Paul Tagliabue.

262 **"You had to talk about wage scales"**: Ibid.

262 **"the league would lose control"**: Ibid.

262 **"The NBA had reached"**: Ibid.

263 **"Free agency in that system"**: "NFL Owners Set for Free Agency," *The New York Times,* Jan. 30, 1989.

263 **"The plan didn't address the heart"**: Author interview with Paul Tagliabue.

263 **"At that time, we could not"**: Ibid.

263 **"That became the ultimate selling point"**: Ibid.

264 **"more dispute among the various"**: "Tagliabue Convinces Owners to Negotiate Player Settlement," *The Newark Advocate,* Dec. 17, 1992.

264 **"gave everybody, including the union"**: Author interview with Paul Tagliabue.

265 **"Paul took over at a time"**: Rooney, *Dan Rooney.*

265 **"get out and meet with the players"**: Author interview with Paul Tagliabue.

266 **"When he began the fight to bring"**: Letter from Art Shell, dated Dec. 30, 2016, on file at the Pro Football Hall of Fame, supporting Paul Tagliabue's Hall of Fame election.

266 **"Paul never stopped listening"**: Ibid.

267 **"Where the players and owners had"**: Author interview with Paul Tagliabue.

267 **"Many people talk about"**: Rooney, *Dan Rooney,* 272.

267 **"I guess I view what you do"**: "Paul Tagliabue," Sports Broadcasting Hall of Fame, Inductees, sportsbroadcastinghalloffame.org/inductees/paul-tagliabue.

CHAPTER TWENTY-NINE: JERRY JONES BUYS A TEAM, FIRES A COACH, AND GIVES BIRTH TO "THE TRIPLETS"

268 **"I've always wanted to be involved"**: Paul Borden, "Man Who 'Always Wanted to Be Involved' Now Is, in a Big Way," *Courier-Post* (Camden, NJ), Feb. 27, 1989.

268 **"I can't do this unless"**: "Bright Says He Regrets Not Firing Landry Himself," *Deseret News* (Salt Lake City), Feb. 26, 1990.

269 **"I was basically just trying to say"**: Nick Patowski, "Turnover," *Texas Monthly*, Oct. 2012.

269 **"No one had to tell me"**: Denne H. Freeman, "Landry Says He's Done Coaching," *The Tampa Tribune*, Feb. 27, 1989.

269 **"Sure, the firing could have been"**: Ibid.

269 **"The fact is, I wouldn't be an owner"**: Borden, "Man Who 'Always Wanted to Be Involved' Now Is."

269 **"It's not like everyone"**: Calvin Watkins and Todd Archer, "Jerry Jones: Pretty Serious Risk," ESPN.com, Feb. 25, 2014.

270 **"the same people were calling"**: Ibid.

270 **"I probably should have gotten out"**: Freeman, "Landry Says He's Done Coaching."

270 **"He is going out on a business deal"**: Steve Tracey, "Former Cowboys Players Voice Regret Over Firing," *The Tampa Tribune*, Feb. 27, 1989.

270 **"We probably talked to seventy-five different people"**: Paul Borden, "Man Who 'Always Wanted to Be Involved' Now Is, in a Big Way," *Courier-Post* (Camden, NJ), Feb. 27, 1989.

271 **"I had to avoid letting them"**: "Jones Was Determined to Buy Cowboys," *The Lincoln Star*, Apr. 3, 1989.

271 **"I owned a small interest"**: "The Making of Maverick Jerry Jones, in His Own Words," *Forbes*, May 7, 2012.

272 **"I flew down to Miami to see him"**: Monte Burke, "When Jerry Jones Nearly Bought the Chargers and Learned About Business the Hard Way," *Forbes*, May 2, 2012.

272 **"It so happened that"**: Ibid.

272 **"tire kickers"**: Ibid.

272 **"He treated me like a Rockefeller"**: Ibid.

273 **"I knew the financials"**: Ibid.

273 **"Don't tell me I'm not involved"**: David Moore, "An Ever-Growing Snowball: The Inside Story of Jerry Jones Taking the Game, People He Loves for Wild Ride to Hall of Fame," *SportsDay*, July 2017.

273 **"He talked me out of an investment"**: Barry Horn, "Flashback: The Time Jerry Jones Almost Bought the Chargers," *SportsDay*, Sept. 2013.

273 **"I had gone, in one year"**: Jerry Jones, as told to Monte Burke, "When Jerry Jones Nearly Bought the Chargers and Learned About Business the Hard Way," *Forbes*, May 2, 2012, forbes.com/sites/monteburke/2012/05/02/when-jerry-jones-nearly-bought-the-chargers-and-learned-about-business-the-hard-way/#7925c2d61a38.

273 **"I've taken those lessons"**:.Ibid.

274 **"because I'm a lot lighter"**: Borden, "Man Who 'Always Wanted to Be Involved' Now Is."

274 **"I found a whole bunch of new sponsors"**: Jones, "When Jerry Jones Nearly Bought the Chargers."

275 **"We had the worst team in the NFL"**: 2017 Pro Football Hall of Fame Enshrinement speech.

276 **"We were old and slow"**: Steve Wulf, "The Run That Birthed Dallas' Dynasty," ESPN.com, Oct. 8, 2014.

278 **"My career certainly wasn't established"**: Author interview with Troy Aikman.

278 **"I'm very proud"**: Ibid.

279 **"Shame on Jerry Jones for letting"**: Bill Paschke, "Commentary: Jerry Jones Was Wrong, but Johnson's the Villain," *Los Angeles Times,* March 30, 1994.

280 **"Taking it to the top"**: *Sports Business Journal,* 2017.

280 **"As [Atlanta Falcons owner] Arthur Blank told me"**: Bill King, "The Lone Star: Jerry Jones," *Sports Business Journal,* May 22, 2017.

CHAPTER THIRTY: THE ROONEY RULE

281 **"I'd like to say a special thank-you"**: Tony Dungy's 2016 Pro Football Hall of Fame Enshrinement speech.

281 **"It was a small group of men"**: Ibid.

282 **"In case after case"**: Ron Borges, "Report Spelled It Out in Black and White," *Boston Sunday Globe,* Oct. 6, 2002.

282 **"We knew we had a problem"**: Author interview with Paul Tagliabue and Dan Rooney.

282 **"What we did basically"**: Commissioner Tagliabue Press conference/League Meeting, New York, Oct. 31, 2002.

283 **"I don't think this is a thing you do"**: Ibid.

283 **"as much effort and focus"**: Ibid.

283 **"The commissioner doesn't hire"**: Ibid.

283 **"There are some things"**: Author interview with Paul Tagliabue and Dan Rooney.

284 **"To get everybody to say"**: Ibid.

284 **"We are pleased that the rule"**: Mike Householder, "NFL Fines Millen $200,000 over Coach Search," *The Leaf Chronicle* (Clarksville, TN), Jul. 26, 2003.

284 **"Paul did what"**: Letter on file at HOF from John Wooten, written on Dec. 22, 2016, supporting Paul Tagliabue for Hall of Fame election.

285 **"But when the state rejected proposals"**: Ibid.

285 **"While he belongs to a prestigious"**: "Rozelle Relied on Successor," Minnesota *Star Tribune,* Oct. 27, 1989.

285 **"just being the usual"**: Letter, dated Aug. 4, 1986, on file at the Pro Football Hall of Fame from Pete Rozelle to Paul Tagliabue.

285 **"He [Tagliabue] was the driving force behind"**: Tony Dungy's 2016 Pro Football Hall of Fame Enshrinement speech.

CHAPTER THIRTY-ONE: THE NFL RESPONDS TO NATIONAL CRISES

286 **"Athletic competition is about"**: Author interview with Paul Tagliabue.

286 **"It was clear that between plane"**: Ibid.

287 **"We had employees who"**: Ibid.

287 **"ensuring the safety"**: Andrew Brandt, "Remembering 9/11: An NFL Executive's Story," *Forbes,* Sept. 11, 2011.

287 **"It was darkness"**: Author interview with Paul Tagliabue.

288 **"It's one thing to see it on TV"**: Peter King, "On the Spot Paul Tagliabue Wrestled with Whether the NFL Should Play On, and His Decree Shaped the Sports Weekend," *Sports Illustrated*, Sept. 24, 2001.

288 **"Both Gene and I wanted"**: Author interview with Paul Tagliabue.

289 **"I'm very, very sure our stadiums"**: King, "On the Spot Paul Tagliabue Wrestled with Whether the NFL Should Play On."

289 **"At a certain point playing"**: Mike Burton, "In Unprecedented Move, NFL Calls Off Week 2," *The Philadelphia Inquirer,* Sept. 14, 2001.

289 **"Our priorities for this weekend"**: Excerpt from official NFL Statement released to the press on Sept. 13, 2001.

289 **"I think if you're a"**: Peter King, "Paul Tagliabue's Post 9-11 Correspondence," *Sports Illustrated*, July 15, 2014.

289 **"Leadership is about a lot"**: Ibid.

289 **"I think the league can really set"**: Ibid.

290 **"Don't worry about replaying"**: Ibid.

290 **"When the Giants took the field that day"**: Author interview with Paul Tagliabue.

291 **"To have those guys"**: Dan Caesar, "Players Take the Field Amid Much Poignancy, Patriotism, Reflection," *St. Louis Post-Dispatch,* Sept. 24, 2001.

291 **"We just wanted everyone"**: Ibid.

291 **"I think his leadership"**: Letter from John Mara to Pro Football Hall of Fame Selection Committee, 2016.

292 **"All of our employees had left"**: Nate Scott, "Refuge of Last Resort: Five Days Inside the Superdome for Hurricane Katrina," *USA Today,* Aug. 24, 2015.

292 **"I thought it would be two days"**: Ibid.

293 **"I can't describe the smell"**: Glenn Guilbeau, "Saints Go Marching in Dome," *Shreveport Times,* Sept. 25, 2006.

293 **"a leap of faith"**: Letter from Louisiana Gov. Kathleen Babineaux Blanco to Pro Football Hall of Fame Selection Committee, supporting Paul Tagliabue for Hall of Fame election, dated Jan. 5, 2017.

293 **"I knew we would lose the NFL"**: Ibid.

294 **"an integral part of the fabric"**: Ibid.

294 **"We had nine months to complete"**: Ibid.

294 **"I never thought it would"**: Guilbeau, "Saints Go Marching in Dome."

294 **"We need this team"**: Paul Newberry, "Game Brings Spotlight to City," *The Morning Call,* Sept. 26, 2006.

294 **"You literally felt the noise"**: Mike Triplett, "Ten Years Ago, a Blocked Punt Symbolized the 'Rebirth' of the Saints and New Orleans," ESPN.com, Sept. 26, 2016.

295 **"It meant a lot to them"**: "Back Home in the Dome," *Enterprise-Journal* (McComb, MS), Sept. 26, 2006.

295 **"The Saints lifted the spirits"**: Letter from Louisiana Gov. Kathleen Babineaux Blanco to Pro Football Hall of Fame Selection Committee, supporting Paul Tagliabue for Hall of Fame election, dated Jan. 5, 2017.

295 **"The city fathers"**: Dave Anderson, "For Saving Saints, Tagliabue Deserves a Place in the Hall," *The New York Times,* Feb. 13, 2010.

CHAPTER THIRTY-TWO: KRAFTING A WINNER—THE NEW ENGLAND PATRIOTS

296 **"businessman, philanthropist"**: Richard Kindleberger, "At Long Last, Kraft Is a Team Man," *The Boston Globe,* Jan. 22, 1994.

296 **"Section 217 on the"**: Greg Garber, "Pats' Success Unmatched under Kraft," ESPN.com, June 20, 2015.

296 **"Some people think it's pretty silly"**: Dan Shaughnessy, "Local Boy Makes Good on His Promise to Himself and His Community," *The Boston Globe,* Jan. 22, 1994.

297 **"Kraft had the money"**: John H. Kennedy, "Stadium Covenant a Major Roadblock," *The Boston Globe,* Jan. 22, 1994.

298 **"There were a lot of people"**: Ibid.

298 **"As much as we'd like to see"**: "Another Letdown for St. Louis," *The Hartford Courant,* Jan. 22, 1994.

298 **" 'As of now,' he said"**: Alan Greenberg, "Home-Field Advantage Works for Kraft," *The Hartford Courant,* Jan. 22, 1994.

298 **"This is my hometown"**: Shaughnessy, "Local Boy Makes Good on His Promise to Himself and His Community."

299 **"An owner with a big ego"**: Greenberg, "Home-Field Advantage Works for Kraft."

299 **"I always worried that"**: Ibid.

299 **"help bring a championship"**: New England Patriots 2018 Media Guide, p. 8.

300 **"He comes over and said"**: Robert Kraft retelling his first encounter with Tom Brady, YouTube, published Mar. 12, 2013. youtube.com/ watch?v=CDGigFdAllo.

301 **"Today was a special day"**: Calli Remillard, "Watch Patriots Owner Robert Kraft Address the Locker Room after His 300th Win," Boston.com, Oct. 1, 2018.

301 **"Our family is just a vehicle"**: Ibid.

301 **"Beginning in 2000 and throughout"**: Ron Borges, "Prospering in the Age of the Salary Cap," in *The Pro Football Hall of Fame 50th Anniversary Book: Where Greatness Lives,* eds. Joe Horrigan and John Thorn (New York: Grand Central Publishing, 2012), 233–255.

301 **"It's unbelievable to me"**: Greg Garber, "Pats' Success Unmatched under Kraft," ESPN.com, June 20, 2015.

302 **"That's unbelievable when you"**: Borges, "Prospering," 241.

302 **"He wasn't my boss"**: Marv Levy, Pro Football Hall of Fame Enshrinement speech, Aug. 4, 2001.

303 **"I wrote a personal letter"**: Borges, "Prospering," 249.

303 **"Those things they don't teach"**: Ibid.

303 **"I'm done from ever trying"**: Greg Garber, "Pats' Success Unmatched under Kraft," ESPN.com, June 20, 2015.

303 **"I wanted people to view us and look"**: Matt Maiocco, "Robert Kraft Modeled the Patriots after Eddie DeBartolo's 49ers," NBCsports.com, Nov. 11, 2016.

304 **"I went to my first owners' meeting"**: Ibid.

304 **"I don't think anyone"**: Ibid.

304 **"It's the right thing to do"**: Ibid.

304 **"when God blessed him"**: Maiocco, "Robert Kraft Modeled the Patriots After Eddie DeBartolo's 49ers."

305 **"It's just almost unfathomable"**: Tereasa Walker, "4 Keys to the Patriots' Success during the Brady/Belichick Era," boston.com, Feb. 2, 2017.

305 **"The job of ownership is"**: *SportsCenter*/ESPN interview, Aug. 4, 2018.

CHAPTER THIRTY-THREE: THE LAST COMMISSIONER OF THE NFL'S FIRST CENTURY

307 **"We've had the two greatest"**: Sam Farmer, " 'Born, Bred' to Be the Commissioner," *The Los Angeles Times*, Aug. 9, 2006.

307 **"Roger got his MBA"**: Reaction Implies the NFL Scores with Its Selection," *The Cincinnati Enquirer*, Aug. 9, 2006.

307 **"One of the delicate parts"**: Ron Borges, "Goodell Is Where He Belongs," *The Boston Globe*, Sept. 22, 2006.

307 **Sometimes the job will require:** Ibid.

307 **"a business and a sports property"**: Alan Abrahamson, "Goodell Is Chosen as NFL Chief," *The Los Angeles Times*, Aug. 9, 2006.

309 **"The war did not end"**: Borges, "Goodell Is Where He Belongs."

309 **"At a very young age"**: From Roger Goodell statement regarding the opening of The Robert H. Jackson Center's exhibit, honoring the life of Charles Goodell.

309 **"Those are the things that"**: D. Orlando Ledbetter, "Goodell Selected to Head NFL," *The Atlanta Constitution*, Aug. 6, 2006.

309 **"I was the first owner"**: Dan Rooney, as told to Andrew E. Masich and David F. Halaas, *Dan Rooney: My 75 Years with the Pittsburgh Steelers and the NFL* (New York: Da Capo Press, 2007), 275.

310 **"It's a privilege to represent"**: "NFL Comes Down Hard on Pacman, Henry," *Daily Record* (Morris County, NJ), Apr. 11, 2007.

311 **"I misinterpreted the rule"**: Mike Reiss, "Belichick and Pioli Speak Out," *The Boston Globe*, Feb. 18, 2008.

311 **"a calculated and deliberate attempt"**: "Belichick Draws $500,000 Fine, but Avoids Suspension," ESPN.com, Sept. 14, 2007.

312 **"properly exercised his broad"**: US Court of Appeals ruling, Apr. 25, 2016.

312 **"My first obligation is to"**: Roger Goodell interviewed on *The Rich Eisen Show* on NFL Network, Feb, 2, 2014.

313 **"didn't get it right"**: Tom Pelissero, "Goodell Turns Up Focus on Domestic Violence," *USA Today*, Aug. 29, 2014.

313 **"I take responsibility both"**: Ibid.

313 **"to discipline any persons"**: Tom Siler, "Future of Pro Football Now in Hands of Layden," *Dixon Evening Telegraph* (Dixon, IL), Apr. 7, 1941.

313 **"may run as"**: Ibid.

313 **"I think it's largely due"**: Ken Belson, "Roger Goodell's Power Play," *The New York Times*, Sept. 8, 2016.

314 **"The clubs believe that"**: Simon Evans, "NFL Announces Lockout of Players," Reuters, Mar. 12, 2011.

315 **"Any agreement reached from this"**: Ibid.

315 **"We know what we did"**: Sam Farmer, "Player Reps Accept League Proposal for 10-year CBA," *The Orlando Sentinel*, Jul. 26, 2011.

315 **"There was a sense of relief"**: Will Graves, "Signing of Deal Ends Labor Dispute," *Pittsburgh Post-Gazette,* Aug. 6, 2011.

315 **"There was an understanding"**: Author interview with Paul Tagliabue.

317 **"London is the international home"**: "NFL to Play Four Games in UK in 2017," NFL Media Release, 2017.

Bibliography

Carroll, Bob. *The Ohio League, 1910–1919.* North Huntingdon, PA: Pro Football Researchers Association, 1997.

Carroll, Bob, Michael Gershman, David Neft, and John Thorn, eds. *Total Football II: The Official Encyclopedia of the National Football League.* New York: HarperCollins, 1999.

Carroll, Bob, and Bob Gill. *Bulldogs on Sunday, 1919.* North Huntingdon, PA: Pro Football Researchers Association, n.d.

Cusack, Jack. *Pioneer in Pro Football: Jack Cusack's Own Story of the Period from 1912 to 1917, Inclusive, and the Year 1921.* Ft. Worth, TX: self-published, 1963.

Davis, Jeff. *Papa Bear: The Life and Legacy of George Halas.* New York: McGraw-Hill, 2005.

Felser, Larry. *The Birth of the New NFL: How the 1966 AFL/NFL Merger Transformed Pro Football.* Guilford, CT: The Lyons Press, 2008.

Freedman, Samuel G. *Breaking the Line: The Season in Black College Football That Transformed the Sport and Changed the Course of Civil Rights.* New York: Simon & Schuster, 2013.

Griffith, Corrine. *My Life with the Redskins,* New York: A.S. Barnes, 1947.

Gruver, Ed. *The American Football League: A Year-by-Year History, 1960–1969.* Jefferson, NC: McFarland & Company, Inc., 1997.

Gunther, Marc, and Bill Carter. *Monday Night Mayhem: The Inside Story of ABC's Monday Night Football.* New York: Beech Tree Books, 1988.

Halas, George, with Gwen Morgan and Arthur Veysey. *Halas by Halas: The Autobiography of George Halas.* New York: McGraw-Hill, 1979.

Harris, David. *The League: The Rise and Decline of the NFL.* Toronto: Bantam Books, 1986.

Horrigan, Jack. *The Other League: The Fabulous Story of the American Football League.* Chicago: Follett Publishing Company, 1970.

Horrigan, Joe, and John Thorn, eds. *The Pro Football Hall of Fame 50th Anniversary Book: Where Greatness Lives.* New York: Grand Central Publishing, 2012.

Izenberg, Jerry. *Rozelle: A Biography.* Lincoln: University of Nebraska Press, 2014.

Klosinski, Emil. *Pro Football in the Days of Rockne.* New York: Carlton Press, 1970.

MacCambridge, Michael. *America's Game: The Epic Story of How Pro Football Captured a Nation.* New York: Random House, 2004.

———. *Lamar Hunt: A Life in Sports.* Kansas City, MO: Andrews McMeel Publishing, LLC, 2012.

March, Harry. *Pro Football: Its Ups and Downs.* Albany, NY: J. B. Lyon, 1934.

McDonough, Will, et al. *75 Seasons: The Complete Story of the National Football League, 1920–1975.* Atlanta: Turner Publishing, Inc., 1994.

Miller, Jeff. *Going Long: The Wild Ten-Year Saga of the Renegade American Football League in the Words of Those Who Lived It.* Chicago: Contemporary Books, 2003.

Myers, Gary. *The Catch: One Play, Two Dynasties, and the Game That Changed the NFL.* New York: Crown Publishers, 2009.

Patton, Phil. *Razzle Dazzle: The Curious Marriage of Television and Football.* Garden City, NY: The Dial Press, 1984.

Rathet, Mike, and Don R. Smith. *Their Deeds and Dogged Faith.* New York: Rutledge Books and Balsam Press, 1984.

Rhoden, William C. *Third and a Mile: The Trials and Triumphs of the Black Quarterback.* New York: ESPN Books, 2007.

Roberts, Howard. *The Chicago Bears.* New York: G. P. Putnam's Sons, 1947.

Rooney, Art, Jr., with Roy McHue. *Ruanaidh: The Story of Art Rooney and His Clan.* Pittsburgh: self-published, 2008.

Rooney, Dan, as told to Andrew E. Masich and David F. Halaas. *Dan Rooney: My 75 Years with the Pittsburgh Steelers and the NFL.* New York: Da Capo Press, 2007.

Ross, Charles, K. *Outside the Lines: African Americans and the Integration of the National Football League.* New York: New York University Press, 1999.

Sahadi, Lou. *Johnny Unitas: America's Quarterback.* Chicago: Triumph Books, 2004.

Sobel, Lionel S. *Professional Sports and the Law.* New York: Law-Arts Publishers, Inc. 1977.

Stram, Hank, with Lou Sahadi. *They're Playing My Game.* Chicago: Triumph Books, 1986.

Strother, Shelby. *NFL Top 40: The Greatest Pro Football Games of All Time.* New York: Penguin Group, 1988.

Thorn, John. *Pro Football's Ten Greatest Games.* New York: Four Winds Press, 1981.

Thorn, John, with David Reuther, eds. *The Armchair Quarterbacks.* New York: Charles Scribner's Sons, 1982.

Weiss, Don, with Chuck Day. *The Making of the Super Bowl: The Inside Story of the World's Greatest Sporting Event.* Chicago: Contemporary Books, 2002.

Whittingham, Richard. *The Chicago Bears: An Illustrated History.* New York: Rand McNally, 1982.

Willis, Chris. *Old Leather: An Oral History of Early Pro Football in Ohio, 1920–1935.* Lanham, MD: Scarecrow Press, 2005.

———. *The Columbus Panhandles: A Complete History of Pro Football's Toughest Team, 1900–1922.* Lanham, MD: Scarecrow Press, 2007.

———. *Joe Carr: The Man Who Built the National Football League.* Lanham, MD: Scarecrow Press, 2010.

AUTHOR INTERVIEWS:

Troy Aikman, Raymond Berry, Joe Browne, Len Dawson, Ed DeBartolo Jr., Joe Greene, James Harris, Michael Irvin, Pearce Johnson, Jerry Jones, Jerry Kramer, Willie Lanier, Bob Lilly, John Madden, Gino Marchetti, Virginia McCaskey, Jay Moyer, Joe Namath, Dave Robinson, Dan Rooney, Art Rooney Jr., Don Shula, Paul Tagliabue, Paul Warfield, Ralph Wilson Jr.

OTHER IMPORTANT SOURCES:

The author also accessed original papers, documents, financial records, correspondence, and league and team news releases housed in the Pro Football Hall of Fame's Ralph Wilson Jr. Research and Preservation Center, including materials from the Edward "Dutch" Sternaman Collection, the NFL league meeting minutes dating back to 1920, and the meeting minutes from the American Football League, 1959–1969.

Index